Baylor at Independence

R.E.B. Baylor

Tom Lea

Baylor
at
Independence

by
Lois Smith Murray

Baylor University Press • 1972 • Waco, Texas

To

Lily McIlroy Russell

and

Guy Bryan Harrison

"The preservers of history are as heroic as its makers."

—President Pat M. Neff

vii

Contents

List of Illustrations

xi

Acknowledgments

The founding of Baylor University is traceable to many individuals in early Texas history who dreamed of a Christian school for their descendants. Through their zeal Baylor University was chartered, and under their watchcare it became a respectable university, serving the needs of the young State of Texas. Hence, this research has become a social history of these farsighted, dedicated individuals, as well as a study of the university from its founding under the Republic of Texas in 1845 to the time of its removal from Independence in 1886. Because of the many inquiries made at the Office of Historical Research concerning people and places associated with Baylor at Independence, an effort has been made to answer many of the questions. We are hopeful that readers will supply additional information about Baylor's cradle period.

Enumeration of all the persons who have aided in this project is impossible. The abundant files of Mrs. Lily M. Russell became the incentive for continued research. Her indefatigable pursuit of information concerning people and places in Baylor's early history resulted in an invaluable storehouse of knowledge. Miss Sue Moore proved a competent archivist in filing and extending many of the accumulated facts.

I am particularly indebted to Professor and Mrs. Guy B. Harrison for their continual support, guidance, and assistance in my research in the Texas Collection of Baylor University. The resources and the excellent staff were ever available, a service for which I am deeply grateful. Equally cooperative has been the present Curator of the Texas Collection, Mr. Dayton Kelley and his staff of Miss Laura Simmons, Archivist; Mr. William Ming, Mrs. Virginia Ming, and their able student assistants.

For extensive research assistance I am grateful to the staffs of the Library of Congress, the University of Texas Library and Archives Collection, the Archives of the Texas State Library, and many public libraries, including those at Houston, San Antonio, El Paso, Dallas, Fort Worth, and Waco. Appreciation is expressed to the Gloucester Bureau of Vital Statistics for information on the Trask family; to

Mr. Coe Haynes of the American Baptist Home Mission Society of New York as well as to Margaret Wenger, Archivist, for reports and correspondence; to the Grand Secretary of the Grand Lodge of Alabama Masons of Montgomery, Alabama, and to Mr. Harvey C. Byrd, Grand Secretary of the Grand Lodge of Texas, A.F. and A.M.; to the Registrar of Brown University for information and photostats; to Mr. Rollin M. Rolfe, Dean of Students at Austin College, Sherman, Texas; to Mr. Edwin K. Tolan, Reference Librarian of Hamilton College; to Miss Lauren Foreman, Archivist of Sigma Alpha Epsilon; to the Department of Records, United States Army, Washington, D.C.; to Dean Alton Lee and his staff of the Records Office of Baylor University; to Dean Angus McSwain of the Baylor University Law School and Miss Della M. Geyer, Law School Librarian; to Mr. James M. Rogers, Baylor University Librarian, Miss Estaline Cox, Reference Librarian, and to Mrs. Jean Tolbert and Mrs. Lucy Sue Williams of the Moody Library Staff at Baylor University.

Students who have done yeoman service in detailed research, compilations, and other services in the accumulation of data are Misses Carol Toland, Cheryl Anderson, Katie Smith, Deborah Smith, Brenda Allen, Terri Combs, Pamela Beverly, Richard Taylor, Ron Murray, and Don Hollon. To these and to Mary Alice Brown, Nancy Williamson, and Cathy Groover for their typing skills I am deeply grateful.

For invaluable consultation in the preparation of the manuscript I appreciate the assistance of Professor P. D. Browne, Mr. Robert Bright, Dr. J. M. Dawson, Dr. W. J. Wimpee, Dr. H. Frank Connally, Jr., and President Abner V. McCall of Baylor University.

My deep gratitude goes to Mr. Marvin Goebel, Director of the Baylor Press; to Mrs. Betty Stuart, who painstakingly edited the manuscript; to Mr. José Ortiz, Mr. Joe Clark, Mr. Rudy Saenz, and Mr. Mario Saenz, of the Baylor Press; to Mr. Tom Nance, Mr. Holly Stewart, and Mr. Chris Hansen for photographic work; and to Mr. Lowell Browne for his skillful handling of photographs, many dim with age. I am indebted also to Mr. Erwin M. Hearne for permission to reproduce his paintings dealing with Baptist-Baylor history and to Senator William A. Blakley for his generosity in commissioning them. Thanks also go to Mr. and Mrs. Edward Burleson for permission to photograph their oil painting of the handsome young President Rufus C. Burleson, and to artist E. M. Schiwetz for permission to use his sketches.

I am deeply grateful to the following friends who have read all or part of the manuscript: Dr. Jefferson Davis Bragg, Dr. W. R. White, Professor Guy B. Harrison, Judge Frank M. Wilson, Mr. Robert E. Davis, Mr. Arthur Strain, Mr. Raymond Dillard, Mrs. Clyde B. King (Belle Hurst), and Miss Edna Haney. Also I extend my appreciation to Dr. Robert C. Cotner of the Department of History of the University of Texas for his careful perusal of the work and writing of the introduction.

The frontispiece—of Founding Father Judge R. E. B. Baylor—was executed particularly for this work by artist Tom Lea, who interrupted the writing of a novel to make the drawing, the original of which he graciously presented to Baylor University. To him and his artist-wife Sara Lea I express deep gratitude.

To Carl Hertzog, craftsman-artisan, go a multitude of thanks for his expertise in handling the manuscript and for consultations in its printing. I am grateful also to Vivian Hertzog for her specific aid.

Permission to use quoted material as indicated in the footnotes has been granted by these individuals. Lester H. Zapalac, owner and publisher of *The LaGrange Journal* for *Early History of Fayette County* by Leonie Weyland and Houston Wade, copyright 1936, and "Fayette County Heroes of San Jacinto"; Pat Ireland Nixon for *A History of the Texas Medical Association 1853-1934,* copyright 1953, the University of Texas Press; Joel L. Pyland, Managing Editor for Steck-Vaughn for William Stuart Red's *History of the Presbyterian Church in Texas,* The Steck Company copyright 1936; Llerena B. Friend for *Sam Houston, The Great Designer,* the University of Texas Press, 1954; Merle Mears Duncan for "David Richard Wallace, Pioneer in Psychiatry" *Texana* I ,1963; Doris Dowdell Moore for *Biography of Doctor D. W. Wallace,* Timberlawn Foundation,

1966; Jane Carson for *James Innes and His Brothers of the F.H.C.* of the Williamsburg Research Studies, the University Press of Virginia; C. E. Bryant for "A Brief Biographical Sketch of Judge R. E. B. Baylor"; Mrs. Joseph W. Hale for Judge Joseph W. Hale's "Judge Baylor in Perspective"; L. Tuffly Ellis for use of *The Handbook of Texas,* eds. Walter Prescott Webb and H. Bailey Carroll, copyright 1952, The Texas State Historical Association; Herbert P. Gambrell for "The Early Baylor University 1841-1861," M.A. Thesis, S.M.U. 1924 and *Anson Jones, The Last President of Texas,* Doubleday and Company, 1948; Helen Eby Craig for Frederick Eby's *The Development of Education in Texas,* copyright 1925, the MacMillan Company; Joe B. Frantz for *Gail Borden,* University of Oklahoma Press, copyright 1951; A. A. Grusendorf for "A Century of Education in Washington County," and "Henry Flavel Gillette," both MS in Baylor's Texas Collection; Martha G. Fornell for Earl W. Fornell's *The Galveston Era,* The University of Texas Press, 1961; J. M. Dawson for use of his sections in *The Centennial Story of Texas Baptists,* copyright 1936, Baptist General Convention of Texas; Wilfred O. Dietrich, *The Blazing Story of Washington County,* copyright 1950 by the Banner Press of Brenham; R. Henderson Shuffler for *The Houstons at Independence,* Texian Press, copyright 1966 and "The Signing of Texas' Declaration of Independence: Myth and Record," in *The Southwestern Historical Quarterly,* January 1962; Ellen Garwood for "Early Texas Inns," in the October 1956 *Southwestern Historical Quarterly;* Walter P. Freytag for "Soldier, Statesman, Patriot," *The Fayette County Record,* March 1962; Michael Allen White for *History of Baylor University, 1845-1861,* Texian Press, copyright 1968; J. D. Bragg for "Baylor University 1851-1861" in *The Southwestern Historical Quarterly,* July 1945; E. Bruce Thompson for "William Carey Crane and Texas Education," *The Southwestern Historical Quarterly,* January 1955; Dayton Kelley for "H. A. McArdle," in *Southwestern Art,* 1967; Laura Simmons for *Out of Our Past,* Texian Press copyright 1967; W. H. Jenkins, Jr. and Judge James R. Jenkins, executor, for Annie Jenkins Sallee's *Friend of God,* The Naylor Company, copyright 1952; Herbert R. Edwards for use of Margaret Royalty Edwards' "A Sketch of Baylor University," 1920; and Marjorie Mitchell of McGraw-Hill Book Company for R. S. Johnson's *A Family Album*, McGraw-Hill, 1965. Appreciation also goes to Miss Pauline Breustedt and Mrs. James H. Riley for consultations concerning their kinsman, David R. Wallace, as well as to many individuals who have contributed items of interest concerning Baylor's early history which could not be included in the already lengthy story.

A word must be said about names. In many instances two or more spellings have been discovered in records; for the sake of consistency we have used the spelling most frequently appearing.

Introduction

Since Samuel Eliot Morison wrote a history of Harvard University for the tercentenary of our oldest university, many of the distinguished and large universities have published their histories, including Yale, Pennsylvania, and Wisconsin. Baylor graduates, and all persons interested in the development of higher education as it spread westward, will rejoice that Baylor University now has an official history dating from its foundation at Independence to removal to Waco. Students who have been at Baylor since 1925 will know the diligent and able author, Dr. Lois H. Smith Murray. She has researched long and thoughtfully the minutes of the Baptist Associations involved, the records of the Baptist State Conventions, the minutes of the Boards of Trustees, presidential papers, faculty records, the personal letters and reminiscences of the Baptist leaders—laymen and clergymen.

This carefully documented volume will become the Baylor "source book." The extensive bibliography attests to years of research. Credit is given to over twenty-five M.A. and Ph.D. studies on varied aspects of Baylor's history. Probably, no one will ever again take the time to read the hundreds of books and articles and newspapers consulted to find that obscure bit of information which cast new light on a complex situation or explained a trait of character. This work should stir every son and daughter of Baylor to check files for letters, clippings, and autobiographical sketches which should be sent to the Baylor Collection so carefully nurtured by Pat Neff and the Guy B. Harrisons.

An Appendix includes a list of Baylor men who served during the Civil War, members of the Tryon Chapter of Phi Gamma Delta and the Theta Chapter of Sigma Alpha Epsilon, members of the Independence Baptist Church, faculty, trustees, and the law classes for 1857-1880. Here is reproduced the famous Charter for Baylor University approved by the Congress of the Republic of Texas in 1845. Surveying the names of the "duly chosen Trustees," you may read the names of R. E. B. Baylor, James Huckins, Eli Mercer, W. Tryon. It should not be forgotten that Baylor was co-educational from the start, and the "Female Department" under the leadership of Horace Clark was very successful even before it became popular to create colleges for women in the Northeast.

Unfortunately, it must be recorded that President Rufus C. Burleson, who also headed the Male Department, seemed to become jealous of Clark's success. While there was a public reconciliation, faculty relationships were strained. In the spring of the fateful year 1861, Burleson accepted the presidency of Waco University and took most of the faculty with him. To what extent his support for Sam Houston's efforts to keep Texas in the Union speeded up Burleson's departure is not clear. Thousands of Baylor students have studied the austere countenance on the statue of Burleson and tried to imagine the real man, knowing little of his constructive career at Independence during the prosperous 1850s. They have learned from Brooks, Neff, White, and McCall that he grew in character, developing a forgiving spirit, and inspiring a Samuel Palmer Brooks, Tom Connally, George W. Truett, Joseph M. Dawson and many others.

Dr. Murray has persevered to tell the whole story, emphasizing the importance of leadership and relating how the trustees, presidents and faculty met the problems and challenges of their times. Literally hundreds of questions are answered by the author. Just a few examples are given with the expectation that the readers will tell friends to read the heroic story.

Why was Washington County an ideal place to locate a university in 1845? Why had Independence ceased to be a first-class location by 1885? How did New Englanders, Virginians and Georgians assist in the formation and growth of Baylor? How did Henry Gillette, an Episcopalian, strengthen teaching at Independence? Did Baylor enroll over 400 students before 1861? What were the connections with Mercer and Brown universities? Did Baylor faculty and presidents board students to supplement their salaries? Were lawyers trained at Baylor at Independence? Did a future president of the United States have a relative who served as president of Baylor? Did President William Carey Crane write a biography of Sam Houston as requested by his widow? Did the Trustees ever seek assistance from the

Texas Legislature? If so, were they successful? Why did Baylor Female College separate from Baylor University in 1866? Did she remain at Independence until 1886? Did Burleson's transfer to Waco in 1861 hurt the enrollment? How did Baylor survive the financial and personal disasters associated with the Mexican War, the Civil War, the poverty and uncertainties of Reconstruction, the economic depression of the 1870s, and the recession of the mid-1880s? Did a Baylor president champion the creation of The University of Texas? How well did Baylor meet the pledge to train men and women to serve church and state?

Dr. Murray has answered these and many more questions, while vividly recreating the cultural and religious climate at Independence. The almost mythical characters of 1845-1886 have been recreated for us with their strengths and weaknesses. She has traced the valiant efforts of presidents, faculty, students and supporters of Christian education to keep the two Baylors alive at a time when many educational ventures were started and failed. The buildings at Independence have decayed, but the real Baylor lived on in the work of her students. Actually, the Convention and Trustees acted wisely in urging removal to Waco and Belton, recognizing the problems resulting from flooding and poor roads, no railway connection, a decline in local support, and the difficulty of finding a president able to build upon the work of Crane, following his death in 1885. A united Baptist effort at Waco gave promise of a larger student body and a wider choice of fields of study—a stronger university would be the result. Praise to the founders and the leaders they have inspired by their examples.

Robert Crawford Cotner

Baylor at Independence

CHAPTER I

Pioneer Texas: School and Church

TEXAS, TEXAS BAPTISTS, AND BAYLOR UNIVERSITY actually grew up together. Baylor University, now the largest Baptist university, was chartered in 1845 by the Congress of the Republic of Texas. Background events which led to the founding of the school are closely linked with the heroic pioneer spirit characterizing the early Texans who came to this new land carved out of Mexican territory. They were essentially "homeseekers" willing to face the difficulties of a new language and a state church along with the hazards of the usual American pioneer effort—cultivating the wilderness and withstanding Indian attack. Yet these stalwart pioneers did venture forth and build for themselves homes on Texas soil, homes which some were to defend with their lives. The new home meant for them a new life filled with opportunity and dreams for themselves and their children.

Despite the fact that the early Mexican colonial contracts demanded adherence to the Roman Catholic Church, a large percentage of the early settlers maintained a steadfast devotion to their Protestant faith.[1] Closely allied with their efforts toward economic and political security were religious and educational aspirations.

Among Austin's "Old Three Hundred" were at least eleven staunch Baptist families, and in "the first forty" was the John P. Coles family.[2] On August 19, 1824, Coles was granted eight and one-half leagues of the choicest Texas

[1] In 1826 Austin had characterized the requirement that colonists accept Catholicism as a "formal and unessential requisition." Colonists of 1831 listed 27 religious affiliations among the 72 newcomers to Nacogdoches. Pioneer historian, Henderson Yoakum, estimated that "nineteen-twentieths of the colonists of Texas neither observed nor believed in the religion prescribed by the Mexican constitution." Henderson Yoakum, *History of Texas*. (New York: Redfield, 1855), I, 233.

[2] J. M. Carroll identified these Baptists as Elijah Allcorn, Mrs. J. P. Coles, Thomas David, David Fitzgerald, Chester S. Corbet, William Kencheloe, Abner Kuykendall, John McNeill, John W. Moore, and John Smith. *The History of Texas Baptists* (Dallas: Baptist Standard Publishing Company, 1923), p. 29.
Coles, a native of Rowan County, North Carolina, was born in 1793, married Mary Eleanor Owen in Georgia in 1821, and came to the Brazos area in 1822.

{1}

land in what is now adjoining corners of Washington, Burleson, and Brazos Counties. For Texas, Coles became a man of destiny. The Texas Census of 1826 reported that he had a wife, a son, two daughters, five servants, and four slaves, and that he was building a mill on Yegua Creek.[3] He built a "public house" around which grew the community called Coles' Settlement. Known as a friend of Stephen F. Austin, he became a leader in the area and was made Alcalde of the Municipality of Washington in 1828. Early Texas history records the name of John P. Coles repeatedly in the affairs of government, and it is not surprising that he should show an active interest in the cause of education.

Dr. Frederick Eby, in the *Centennial Story of Texas Baptists*, suggested that "the enthusiasm for the education of girls that centered at Independence might have found its origin in the concern of a Baptist mother, Mrs. J. P. Coles." She had come from Georgia, where the crusading Baptist missionary, Luther Rice, had extolled the benefits of religious instruction as well as secular education. The Coles family soon increased to one son and five daughters, and there was good reason for interest in educational provisions.

General concern over education among the Anglo-Americans in Texas is indicated by a petition to the Mexican government to set up a system of schools. Provisions for elementary education were incorporated in subsequent laws. A few schools were established by the colonists in the larger communities of Coahuila and Texas, but on the whole little use was made of the provision in Texas.[4]

[3] Marion Day Mullins (Compiler), *The First Census of Texas* (Washington, D. C.: Reprinted from the *National Genealogical Society Quarterly,* 1959), p. 43.
John P. Coles, the first alcalde of the municipality and the first regidor of the jurisdiction, was a delegate to the San Felipe Convention of 1822, fought in the Texas Revolution, was appointed by President Houston the first Chief Justice of Washington County on December 20, 1836, and represented the county in the Senate of the Fifth Congress (1840-41). Several public welfare petitions carry his name, and he heads the list of citizens of the Municipality of Washington petitioning for a new jurisdiction on July 2, 1835. The organization was effected and the officers were elected and certified to by John P. Coles on July 18, 1835.
Wilfred O. Dietrich in *The Blazing Story of Washington County* (Brenham, Texas: Banner Press, 1950), p. 6, credits the Coles family with the first planting of corn in the county, Mr. Coles having made two trips to Mexico to procure seed. The first trip was unsuccessful because of a Brazos River overflow which resulted in his being stranded and eating the seed corn.
[4] During the Republic several Texas towns were allowed to incorporate and establish schools, using local funds: San Antonio, Victoria, Austin, Corpus Christi, and Galveston, but only Galveston succeeded in establishing a public

An advertisement in the December 13, 1834, *Texas Republican* of Brazoria made announcement of the first boarding school in Texas. A Miss Trask respectfully announced her intention of opening a boarding school for young ladies and misses on the first of January in Coles' Settlement. Board was $2 per week and tuition $6 to $10 per course. Interested persons were referred to John P. Coles and Asa Hoxey of Coles' Settlement, Dr. J. B. Miller of San Felipe, James F. Perry of Brazoria, and E. C. White of Columbia.

The teacher of the school was Miss Frances Judith Soames Trask. She had received her education in Gloucester, Massachusetts, and at a girls' school in New York City and had come to Texas from Dixboro, Michigan, with the John Dix family whom she was visiting. They arrived in Matagorda in February 1834 and removed to Coles' Settlement (later to be called Independence) by the following December.[5] No record of a land grant or purchase of ground for Miss Trask's school has been found; hence it is concluded that the school property belonged to John P. Coles.

In a letter to her father, Israel Trask, on July 6, 1835, the young teacher described her school of "seven boarders at $2.00 weekly" and some of the conditions in Texas at the time. Help was scarce and expensive; the diet was chiefly cornbread and bacon; and the school was "one frame building, 15 by 20 feet in size with two glazed windows on one side and folding doors at each end. This was the school room, parlor, bed chamber, and hall." Another building was a "rugged black log house, with a very forbidding exterior, but the interior very decent." This building was the

school financed by local taxation. Many people displayed great indifference to the establishment of county schools because they believed in private and religious schools. Children of the wealthier class were sent to the States or abroad, and itinerant teachers opened private schools. Likewise, "the Republic of Texas," states Grusendorf in *A Century of Education in Washington County, Texas*, "never put its legal provisions for a school system into effect," many of the counties not even having their school lands located and surveyed.

[5] A letter from J. B. Miller to James F. Perry on December 10, 1834, carries this statement: "I have taken the liberty to refer you to a school Miss Trask has just opened in Coles' Settlement." E. C. Barker, *The Austin Papers*, III, October 1834—January 1837 (Washington: Government Printing Office, 1924), p. 35.

Asa Hoxey described Coles' Settlement in a letter to E. G. Hanrick on May 24, 1834, stating that "We have . . . two schools." Hanrick Papers, University of Texas Library. Research has failed to establish the identity of these two schools at Coles' Settlement, and it is most likely that Miss Trask's school did not open until January 1835. (Miss Trask was born on July 20, 1806. *Gloucester Vital Report*, II, 1806).

TABLE 1 — *Institutions Chartered by the Republic of Texas*

Name	Male/Female	Location	Sponsor	Date of Charter	Terminated
FIRST CONGRESS					
Independence	F	Independence	Independent Board	June 5, 1837	Declined before 1845
Univ. of San Augustine	M/F	San Augustine	Independent Board	June 5, 1837	Closed 1847
Washington College		Washington-on-the-Brazos	Stock Company	June 5, 1837	
SECOND CONGRESS					
Manhattan College		Manhattan		1838	
Matagorda Seminary		Matagorda		1838	
THIRD CONGRESS					
De Kalb		Red River County	Independent Board	June 26, 1839	
FOURTH CONGRESS					
Union Academy		Washington County	Stock Company	Feb. 4, 1840	1843
Rutersville*	M/F	Rutersville	Methodist	Feb. 5, 1840	1859
FIFTH CONGRESS					
Galveston University	M/F	Galveston	Independent Board	Jan. 30, 1841	1844
McKenzie Institute†	M/F	Clarksville	Private	Feb. 10, 1848	June 25, 1868
Guadalupe College	M/F	Gonzales	Independent Board	Jan. 30, 1841	Never Est.
Trinity College	M/F	Alabama, Houston County	Independent Board	Jan. 30, 1841	Never Est.
SIXTH CONGRESS					
Marshall University§	M	Marshall	Independent Board	Jan. 18, 1842	Declined during C
EIGHTH CONGRESS					
Wesleyan College	M/F	San Augustine	Methodist	Jan. 16, 1844	Declined during C
Hermann's University		Frelsburg Colorado Co.	Independent Board	Jan. 27, 1844	Never Est.
NINTH CONGRESS					
Baylor University‡	M/F	Independence	Union Baptist Assoc. 1845-49	Feb. 1, 1845	Continual Existence
Rusk County Academy	M/F	Henderson	Independent Board	Feb. 1, 1845	
Matagorda University	M/F	Matagorda	Independent Board	Feb. 3, 1845	
Nacogdoches University¶	M/F	Nacogdoches	Independent Board	Feb. 8, 1845	1895

* By petition of the Board of Trustees, the Legislature separated Rutersville College from the Methodist Conference and consolidated it with the Texas Military Institute of Galveston to form the Monumental and Military Institute at Rutersville. The Institute ceased to exist in 1867.

† McKenzie Institute began in a log cabin with 20 pupils in 1841 and came under the Methodist Conference in 1860 for one year. Minutes of Rutersville Board of Trustees, Archives, University of Texas.

§ Marshall University was absorbed by the public school system in 1884.

‡ Baylor University opened in the two-story Independence Academy Building on May 18, 1846. The Female Department became Baylor Female College under charter in 1866. Baylor University, as a male school, remained at Independence until its consolidation with Waco University as Baylor University at Waco in 1886.

¶ Nacogdoches University was deeded to the Nacogdoches Independent School District in 1904.

kitchen. Miss Trask stated that the dining room was "of magnificent dimensions, extending all over creation."[6]

It is supposed that Miss Trask's school had to close during the Revolution. Letters reveal that her father sent her brother Olwyn to take her to New Orleans, but Olwyn joined the Texas Army and died at San Jacinto.[7]

With the difficulties of the Revolution behind them, the citizens of Independence concerned themselves again with community improvement. Stephen F. Austin had required his colonists to produce evidence of good character, and later arrivals were held to the same conditions. In a letter to Mr. Thomas White, Austin had written: "The settlers of this colony taken *en masse* are greatly superior to any new country or frontier I have ever seen, and would loose [*sic*] nothing by a comparison with some of the oldest counties of many of the southern and western states." Such people might have been expected to manifest an interest in education. They presented to the First Congress of the Republic of Texas the following petition on May 23, 1837:

Your petitioners being desirous to establish for the education of youth in Coles' Settlement a Seminary of the highest order, and being aware of the difficulty attending such objects and of their bad success, unless established by law:

Therefore your petitioners pray that the honorable Congress at its present session pass an act incorporating an academy in Coles' Settlement with such rights and privileges as they in their judgment may think best calculated to promote its success and prosperity.

We flatter ourselves that it will be seen that this point for the educating [*sic*] of such an institution is the most eligible one in Texas from the fact of its being healthy and surrounded with a flourishing and prosperous country and is very near the center of the Republic. We leave to Congress the naming of the institute and pledge ourselves

[6] This lengthy letter from Miss Trask also contains the statement: " . . . I think that it would be weak, and foolish, in me, after having come to Texas for the express purpose of endeavoring to obtain some little property for myself, to leave it [Texas] without having made all the exertions in my power to accomplish what I have undertaken. I have never applied for land, though entitled (by the courtesy of Col. Austin to single ladies) to a quarter league, for my friends here, advise my waiting the return of Col. Austin, thinking he will feel disposed to be liberal in consideration of my school, it being the first female school ever established in Texas." University of Texas Archives, Austin, Texas.

[7] A bill to grant Miss Trask 640 acres of land for teaching services 1834-36 passed the House in December 1838 but was indefinitely postponed by the Senate. *Telegraph and Texas Register*, December 22, 1838. See also "Foundation for Baylor University Created by Frontier Amazon," *Waco Tribune-Herald*, Sunday, October 30, 1949, p. 17.

to carry into effect its establishment as nearly as practicable by the creation of suitable buildings, etc.

Your petitioners in duty bound will ever pray

Jno. P. Coles	Asa Hoxey [later Hoxie]
Edwd. Nullally	M. Cummins
Ro. Stevenson	Jno. Dix

The charter for Independence Academy as a "non-sectarian, non-political institution" was granted on June 5, 1837, and signed by Sam Houston. It was the first school chartered by the Texas Republic.[8] Several early residents of the area stated that Colonel J. C. Giddings was the first teacher at Independence Academy, in 1837.[9] Some authorities contend that Henry F. Gillette opened the Independence Academy, but irrefutable facts indicate that he left school in Hartford, Connecticut, because of ill health in 1839 and came to Texas to join his cousin Ashbel Smith and taught in Houston in 1840; then in the summer of 1841 he came to Washington County to take charge of Union Academy until 1843.

News stories give us some information on Independence Academy. The *Telegraph and Texas Register* of May 29, 1839, states that the Independence Academy was in successful operation, "having already over fifty students" evidently both boys and girls.[10] *The Richmond Telescope* of June 15,

[8] Charter in Archives of Texas State Library. Other charters granted subsequently by the First Congress of the Republic were for Washington College and St. Augustine University.

Despite sparse information regarding Miss Trask's school at Coles' Settlement, several things may be inferred from this application. First, John P. Coles, Asa Hoxey, and John Dix, all affiliated with the Trask school, are signers of this petition and make no direct reference to the earlier school. Secondly, the statement that "the difficulty attending such objects and their bad success unless established by law" indicates a shortcoming of the earlier attempt which they intended to correct by founding a school "of the highest order" with legality resting in a charter. Thirdly, the Trask school did not meet the standards set up by the Mexican Republic in the laws governing primary schools in Coahuila and Texas, as announced from Saltillo on March 11, 1827. Fourthly, "the creation of suitable buildings" may have indicated the intent to found a school for girls at Independence and a school for boys at Washington, the charter for which was granted on the same date as that for Independence Academy. The institutions were intended to be complementary, not competitive.

[9] Dietrich, p. 33.

Toland listed the trustees of Independence Academy as Dr. Asa Hoxie, Shubal Marsh, Levi and John Pitts, Capt. John Dix, James Whitesides, Pincard Clay, Dr. James Miller and McCrocklin. Gracey Booker Toland. *Austin Knew His Athens* (San Antonio: The Naylor Company, 1958), p. 19.

[10] The May 15, 1839, issue of the *Telegraph and Texas Register* listed the trustees as Lewis Bond, Shubal Marsh, M. Cummings, J. J. Davis, James Whitesides, Hugh Wilson, with Joseph Blatton as Secretary and J. P. Coles as

1839, states that Miss McGuffin was teacher "in the female department" of Independence Academy with the aid and direction of Reverend Hugh Wilson, referred to as "the Father of Texas Presbyterianism." Records indicate that Reverend Edward Fontaine, former secretary to President Lamar, had 75 students (boys and girls from 6 to 25, the majority in the primary studies) at Independence in 1841.[11] By 1842 a girls' school of considerable merit was established in the academy building by the Simms sisters of South Carolina. They taught the first courses in fine arts in Washington County. On July 28, 1845, the *Texas National Register* announced "the second session of Independence Academy with C. W. Thomas as principal and A. B. Kerr as assistant.

Consideration of the sparse facts about Independence Academy shows that Washington County people during the early days of the Republic of Texas were serious about making educational provisions for their children—even for girls. Dr. Francis Moore, Jr., attacked this policy, however, in a *Telegraph and Texas Register* editorial:

> The girls . . . will grow up like mere parrots, accomplished in nothing except the art of killing time and spending their days in alternately lolling on a rocking chair or pouring over useless insipid novels.

Nevertheless Independence citizens were intent on continuous operation of the school founded by Miss Trask as well as improving the opportunities offered.

Being a new land, Texas was dependent for the most part upon imports for her early educational efforts, and many of the men who came were church-affiliated. Baptist historians, in tracing the early interest of Protestants of the United States in Texas, state that they looked upon Texas as "the gateway to the evangelization of Latin America." Only a few months before his death at the Alamo in 1836, William B. Travis had sent a plea to Methodism through the New York *Christian Advocate* which resulted in the sending of Dr. Martin Ruter, President of Berea College, Kentucky, to begin mission work in Texas. Upon his recommendation,

President. "Uncle Willie" Whitesides and Marsh were members of Austin's "Three Hundred." Levi and John Pitts were Marsh's brothers-in-law.

[11] Walter Prescott Webb and H. Bailey Carroll (eds.), *The Handbook of Texas* (Austin, Texas State Historical Association, 1952), II, 920.

the first college in Texas was opened in 1840 near La Grange. The school was named *Rutersville* in honor of this dedicated pioneer educator, who died on his return journey from Texas.[12]

Religious impetus in education during Texas pioneer days was immeasurable. While the governments delayed the development of an educational system, numerous private and denominationally-controlled institutions were chartered. Church historians assert that ministerial education was the motivating force for the organization of thirty-one Baptist colleges in the United States between 1813 and 1835, although many of them no longer exist.

One of these early colleges, Mercer Institute in Georgia, founded in 1833, had a dramatic connection with Baylor University. Jesse Mercer, who had supported missionary Luther Rice in founding Columbian College, devoted his time and fortune to the founding of Mercer.[13] Jesse Mercer used his influence and money to aid the American Baptist Home Mission Society in sending its first missionary to Texas—Reverend James Huckins, who became "a founding father" of Baylor University.

The chain of circumstances which resulted in Huckins' assignment to Texas is curious. Between 1820 and 1836 some twenty Baptist preachers served in sparsely settled Texas.[14] Joseph Bays, Freeman Smalley, Thomas Pilgrim, Thomas Hanks, Daniel Parker, Abner Smith, Isaac Reed and Zacharias N. Morrell were among them. Morrell, termed "the First Missionary Father" in Texas, was in the vanguard of the migration to the west. A tubercular and a cripple, this "cane-brake" preacher came to the Falls of the Brazos in 1835. "A pious sister, living near Gonzales, named Echols, who was a devoted Baptist; the wife of Eli

[12] In 1859 the Texas legislature granted the request of the board of trustees to consolidate Rutersville College with the Texas Military Institution of Galveston, thus separating it from the Methodist Conference. The new charter was granted to the Monumental and Military Institute as a state institution with Colonel C. G. Forshey as its president. It occupied the Rutersville buildings. With the outbreak of the Civil War five years later, cadets and graduates went into the Confederate Army and the school never reopened.

[13] Address by S. V. Sanford at the Centennial Celebration of Mercer University in May 1933, Macon, Georgia. See also Charles Dutton Mallary, *Memoirs of Elder Jesse Mercer* (New York: American Baptist Publishing Society, 1844).

[14] Carroll, p. 17.

Mercer, living east of Colorado; and Dr. R. Marsh, a Baptist minister advanced in age—these, according to my recollection embrace all the Baptists in Texas up to 1837," wrote Morrell.[15]

This pioneer minister founded the first missionary Baptist church in Texas at Washington-on-the-Brazos, just a few miles across the prairie from Independence. An imposter "preaching under Baptist colors" had bilked the citizens out of money and was later "seen on the race track." For the protection of the people an interdenominational "Committee of Vigilance" was organized in Houston in May 1837 with Morrell representing the Baptists. Henceforth ministers were required to exhibit their credentials. Morrell returned to Washington-on-the-Brazos determined to organize a church. He states that "eight Baptists assembled on the appointed day in 1837. . . ."[16] Organic members of the church were persons whose names were soon to appear in Baylor history:

H. R. Cartmell came to Texas in 1835, having served as deacon in the Nashville, Tennessee, Baptist Church; he was at once recognized by the body.

Anderson Buffington and his wife also came from Tennessee in 1835. Buffington served in the Texas Army, notably in the Battle of San Jacinto. He became an ordained minister and one of the two Texas appointees as missionaries. He published the first newspaper, *The Tarantula*, in Washington County in 1839.[17]

James R. Jenkins was born in Green County, Georgia, in 1810. He was converted and baptized at nineteen by Elder J. M. Lumpkin and became an active member of the Baptist Church. As a student at Mercer University at Penfield, Georgia, during the presidency of Reverend Billington Sanders, he made friends of William M. Tryon and Noah Hill. Jenkins studied law under General Hugh Haroldson in 1836 and began practice in Washington-on-the-Brazos in 1837. A large land and slave owner, he was a member

[15] Z. N. Morrell, *Flowers and Fruits of the Wilderness* (3rd ed., St. Louis: Commercial Printing Company, 1882), p. 73.

[16] *Ibid,* p. 74-77.

[17] Carroll, pp. 256-57; *The Handbook of Texas,* I, 242; J. B. Link, *Texas Historical and Biographical Magazine,* II, pp. 297-98.

of the Third Congress of the Republic. His Texas home
was the frequent meeting place of Morrell, Baylor, Tryon,
Huckins, and Rufus C. Burleson, who became his son-in-
law.[18] A missionary descendant states that Jenkins' wife,
Harriet Ann, was a charter member.[19]

Noah T. Byars, the blacksmith-patriot, turned preacher
and became the first missionary Baptist ordained in Texas
(1841).

Z. N. Morrell, minister-merchant, led in the organization
of the church after fourteen years of preaching in Tennessee
and was named pastor.[20]

This infant church was interested in the evangelization
of Texas and immediately appointed a committee to correspond with the Board of the General (Triennial) Convention of the American Baptists, asking for missionaries for
Texas. Acutely anxious for the success of their endeavor,
the committee of Cartmell, Buffington, and Jenkins sent
out several copies of their plea for aid, dated November 7,
1837.[21] Jenkins sent one copy to his brother, Reverend S.
G. Jenkins of Mississippi, who sent it to Jesse Mercer,
then editor of *The Christian Index.*[22] Mercer had relatives
in Texas; so he was doubly interested in the plea. He sent

[18] Harry Haynes, *The Life and Writings of Dr. Rufus C. Burleson*
(compiled and published by Mrs. Georgia J. Burleson, 1901), pp. 667-69.
[19] Annie Jenkins Sallee, *Friend of God* (San Antonio: The Naylor Company,
1952), p. 3.
[20] Carroll believed that Morrell's wife and daughter were among the "eight
gathered." J. M. Dawson added Morrell's wife and Richard Ellis, mentioned as
active in the prayer meeting group responsible for the church organization.
Morrell soon sold his mercantile business at Washington-on-the-Brazos to Peter
J. Willis and resolved to devote himself solely to the ministry. He left Washington on March 1, 1838, and the little pastorless church declined but experienced a rebirth in March 1841 through the organizational efforts of Tryon and
Baylor. Morrell became a member of the Board of Managers of the Texas
Baptist Education Society and was instrumental in founding Baylor. He served
as a "voluntary agent to collect monies" in 1847 and frequently attended board
of trustee meetings, as late as May 15, 1868, opening the meeting with prayer.
Baptist benefactors and Baylor College trustee, Robert John Sledge, provided
a home for Morrell during his last years. Woodrow Sledge letter to President
Abner V. McCall, Austin, August 6, 1968. Morrell died on December 19, 1883,
at Brownwood. *Encyclopedia of Southern Baptists,* ed. Norman Wade Cox, II
(1958), 925.
[21] This letter is in the Archives of the American Baptist Home Mission
Board in New York and bears the signatures of Morrell and the committee.
Annie Jenkins Sallee states that Jenkins wrote the appeal, but Carroll felt that
Morrell was responsible for some of the phraseology. See Sallee, p. 4; also
Carroll, p. 139.
[22] Mercer found the same letter published in the *Southwestern Religious
Luminary.*

his letter to the Baptist Board of Foreign Missions, for Texas was "a foreign field."

The endorsement of the Texans' plea by Jesse Mercer in *The Christian Index* carried weight. He was a member of the Foreign Mission Board and in 1835 had been elected president of the Board of Managers of the Triennial convention. It was the Home Mission Board that accepted the challenge, however, and tendered an appointment to Z. N. Morrell, whose name led the signatures in the letters of appeal. Morrell declined: "Good reasons, at the time, were between me and the acceptance of his proposition."[23] No further action was taken concerning the sending of missionaries to Texas, but correspondence continued and the subject was kept alive by the Baptist press.[24]

The first reference to James Huckins, who became one of the three "founding fathers" of Baylor University, is in The Annual Report for 1839 of the American Baptist Home Mission Society under a November 18 dateline.

Brother James Huckins made to the Committee a statement on the subject of his visiting Texas in connection with his agency in the South. Resolved that Brother Huckins be requested to visit Texas as our missionary.

A subsequent report under the caption of *Texas* in the 1840 Annual Report concerns Huckins:

To this interesting portion of the American continent, the eyes of all the world are now turned with deep solicitude. . . . In this as in all similar enterprises an establishment of religious institutions has received the latest and feeblest attention. But your committee rejoices to learn that, with a veneration for those institutions characteristic of the sons of puritans, they are beginning to feel their importance and desire their existence among them. A considerable number of the residents of Texas are sentimentally Baptists, and desirous of the establishment of Baptist churches there. . . . There is now a missionary of the Society on the shores of Texas; and his success, and the results of his observation thus far, furnish assurance that the people are prepared for any effort our denomination can make in their favor.[25]

A family history reveals that the missionary, James Huckins, was born on April 8, 1807, at Dorchester, New Hampshire, the seventh generation of a Puritan family in

[23] Morrell, p. 77.
[24] Reference to Texas as a mission field appeared in the July 6, 1839, and December 7, 1839, *Baptist Advocate*.
[25] Report supplied by Coe Haynes of the American Baptist Home Mission Society, 23 East 26th Street, New York, N.Y.

America.[26] Both parents died in a yellow-fever epidemic when the lad was six. Upon his conversion at fourteen he "promised the Lord that if a way could be opened for him to receive an education he would devote his life to the ministry." Through the assistance of the New England Education Society the earnest young man prepared for college,[27] under the watchcare of Governor Forbes of Vermont.[28] He took his A.B. degree from Brown University in 1832 and was ordained to the ministry in September of that year[29] and married Rhoda Carver Barton, granddaughter of General William Barton of Revolutionary War fame.

For a year Huckins was pastor of a Baptist church at South Reading, Massachusetts. He then removed to Andover, where he came under the influence of Dr. Francis Wayland.[30] From 1835 to 1837 he served the church at Calais, Maine, but impaired health led him to seek a home in the South. Then came his appointment by the American Baptist Home Mission Society, of which he became a Director for Life through a payment of $100.00 by the Western Association, Providence, Rhode Island, on November 16, 1839.[31] Historians feel that it was through the influence of James Huckins that Jesse Mercer became an ardent devotee of missions in Texas. The two men met on the first of Huckins' southern missionary journeys.

Since Morrell was not able to accept the appointment as missionary to Texas, Huckins came and "traveled extensively in the Republic in 1839-40."[32] On January 25, 1840, the Huckins family arrived in Galveston. In a letter to "My dear Father Mercer" he told of the baptism of Gail Borden, his wife, and her sister—"granddaughters of the late Rev. Thomas Mercer"—in the Gulf of Mexico on Tuesday, February 4. Jesse Mercer's interest in Texas had reaped a dividend, for Divine Providence had brought together the

[26] Photostatic copies of information supplied by descendant, Sara H. Creson of Galveston.
[27] J. B. Link, *Texas Historical and Biographical Magazine*, I, pp. 183-189.
[28] Huckins Family Records. Texas Collection, Baylor University.
[29] *Brown University Catalogue*, p. 161.
[30] Haynes, p. 676.
[31] Photostatic copy of Certificate, Huckins Papers. Texas Collection, Baylor University.
[32] Information supplied by Margaret Wenger from Archives of American Baptist Home Mission Society.

ardent Yankee missionary and Jesse Mercer's own kinsmen in a frontier land starved for the gospel.

Huckins remained in Galveston, then a town of some 3,000 people, long enough to organize the First Baptist Church at the home of Thomas H. Borden; then he entered immediately into his missionary work, traveling great distances on horseback. On December 7, 1841, he was appointed by the Home Mission Board to service at Galveston and Houston, where he had organized a church on April 10, 1841. So meagre was his salary that he supplemented it by teaching school. The invasion of a Mexican army interrupted his missionary activities.

In 1843 Huckins visited New York's Hamilton Literary and Theological Institution (later Madison University) and addressed the students on Texas as a field of religious enterprise. As a result Henry L. Graves (who became Baylor's first president), Jacob B. Stiteler (who became Baylor's professor of natural science), and Leonard Ilsley pledged to come to Texas.[33] On his missionary journeys in Alabama Huckins also interested Tryon (who became a Baylor founding father) and William Carey Crane (who became a Baylor president) in Texas.

Gail Borden, Jr., wrote to the Mission Society on April 3, 1843, requesting that James Huckins be authorized to extend his field to Texas. But by the end of the year Huckins experienced disagreement with the board's anti-slavery resolution and withdrew his connection with the American Home Mission Society.[34]

Huckins was to serve on the Board of Managers of the Texas Baptist Education Society from its inception and was termed its "master mind,"[35] for he was well acquainted with such organizations through his own school experience.

Jesse Mercer, influenced by his friendship with James Huckins, used his voice and pen for the cause of missions in

[33] Link, I, 400.

[34] Baker declared that "the entire agitation of 1844 in the Home Mission Society of the American Baptists was occasioned by the discovery that two of the Society's Texas Missionaries were slave-holders." Robert Andrew Baker, *Relations between Northern and Southern Baptists*, 1948 (N. P.), p. 66 f.

William Tryon, through his marriage to Mrs. Louise Higgins, acquired numerous slaves, and Huckins is known to have had household slaves.

[35] Letter from Frederick Eby to Lily M. Russell, March 7, 1944. Texas Collection, Baylor University.

Texas. In his will he made definite provisions for Texas missions after his death, which occurred September 6, 1841.[36]

Examination of the circumstances which brought Baptist leaders to pioneer Texas reveals the close ties of brotherhood between these men of like faith. Jesse Mercer, friend of Luther Rice and Columbian College, founded Mercer College in Georgia. James Jenkins, former student at Mercer, helped Z. N. Morrell, friend of the Eli Mercers, to organize the Baptist church at Washington-on-the-Brazos. The Washington church plead for a missionary, who fortunately was James Huckins—Jesse Mercer's friend. Soon William Tryon, also of Mercer Institute, was to join Morrell, Huckins, R. E. B. Baylor, and others in organizing the first Baptist association in Texas, out of which was to come the Texas Baptist Education Society. Step by step the plan for a school was evolving.

[36] The Home Mission Society in its Annual Report of 1842 under *Legacies* reported that "the Society has been encouraged in the past year by a bequest from the late Elder Jesse Mercer, of Georgia, of $25,000 [later corrected to $2,500] not yet received." Undoubtedly this was an estimated value of the bank stock. Litigation followed the probating of the will, and collection of the gift to the Mission Board was placed in the hands of Brother Thomas Stocks (President of the Georgia Baptist Convention in 1844 and several times delegate to the Triennial Convention) with authority "to make such compromise of the claims of the Board as will best promote the interests of the Society." In the 15th Annual Report (April 1, 1847) is a record of "the receipt of $1,331.76 from Reverend Billington M. Sanders, executor of the estate and later President of Mercer from Pennville, [*sic*] Georgia, a legacy from Rev. Jesse W. Mercer."

CHAPTER II

The Founding of Baylor University

THE INITIAL STEP IN A SEQUENCE leading to the founding of Baylor University was taken by the first organized body of Baptists ever assembled on Texas soil—the Union Baptist Association, which held its organizational meeting on October 8, 1840, at Travis with messengers from the churches at Independence, La Grange (then Clear Creek), and Austin (Travis County), representing a total church membership of approximately forty-four.[1]

ROBERT EMMETT BLEDSOE BAYLOR was one of the prominent men in this group. His first Texas residence was at La Grange in Fayette County. His illustrious ancestors claimed a Devonshire, English background.[2] One forefather, John de Balliol, was the founder of Balliol College, Oxford. His Virginia ancestors were strong in the Baptist faith, and grandfather Joseph Bledsoe was carried to prison for preaching the Baptist doctrines.[3]

The family moved into the region which became Kentucky and built a brick residence and a large mill near Dick's River. The settlement became known as Baylor's Mill. Here Robert Emmett Bledsoe Baylor was born on May 10, 1793.[4] In 1795 the Baylors moved to Lexington and hence to Bourbon County in 1804, where "Woodlawn" was built on Stoner Creek. Robert's schooling was interrupted by the War of 1812, for he, at nineteen, and his elder brother, Cyrus, enlisted.

After the war Baylor took up the study of law in the office of his uncle, Jesse Bledsoe, United States Senator from Ken-

[1] Hand-written record, Minutes of Union Baptist Association. Texas Collection, Baylor University.

By 1845, when Baylor was granted a charter, Union Association had grown to nineteen churches with ten ministers and 600 members. David Benedict, *A General History of the Baptist Denomination in America* (New York: Lewis Colley & Company, 1848), p. 786.

[2] Mary Seldon Kennedy, *Seldons of Virginia and Allied Families* (Privately printed, n. d.)

[3] Judge Baylor of "Holly Oak," Gay Hill, to J. R. Graves, March 25, 1869.

[4] Orval Walker Baylor, *Baylor's History of the Baylors* (Atlanta, Georgia: Le Roy Journal Printing Company, 1914), n. p.

tucky in 1814.[5] When Robert was admitted to the bar, he joined his brothers, George Wythe Baylor and Walker Keith Baylor, in law practice for a number of years. In 1819 he succeeded his brother George in representing Bourbon County in the legislature. Shrouded in mystery is the reason for Baylor's resignation from the Kentucky House of Representatives in 1820 and moving to Alabama. He practiced law, first at Cahaba in 1821, then at Tuscaloosa, and finally at Mobile. In 1824 he was elected to the House of Representatives of Alabama and was initiated into the Masonic order at Tuscaloosa in 1825[6] As a member of the legislature, he introduced a bill to reform the judicial proceedings of the courts. Although the bill was defeated, many states adopted the reforms suggested by Baylor.[7]

In 1829 Baylor was elected to the Twenty-first United States Congress and his service extended from March 4, 1829, when Andrew Jackson was sworn in as seventh President of the United States, to March 3, 1831. In Washington at the time was his kinsman, Robert Baylor Semple, President of Columbian College from 1827-1832 and co-worker with Luther Rice. Records also reveal his associations with Clay, Webster, and Calhoun. Because of his ardent support of Andrew Jackson, Baylor was defeated in his campaign for re-election, and he returned to Alabama law practice.[8] Military service claimed Baylor in 1836 when he commanded an Alabama regiment fighting against the Creek Indians. After the war he returned to Mobile.[9]

A highly significant fact in the life of Baylor was his conversion to the Christian faith, after years of avowed atheism, on the fourth Sunday of July 1839 under the preaching of his cousin, Thomas Chilton (later pastor of the First Baptist Church of Houston), at the Baptist Church of Talladega.[10] So strong was his experience that shortly thereafter he was licensed as a Baptist minister.

[5] *Biographical Directory of the United States Congress 1774-1961.*
[6] Records of Grand Secretary of Grand Lodge of Alabama Masons, Montgomery, Alabama.
[7] C. E. Bryant, Jr., " A Brief Biographical Sketch of Judge R. E. B. Baylor." MS, Texas Collection, Baylor University.
[8] Joseph W. Hale, "Judge Baylor in Perspective," MS, p. 16. Texas Collection, Baylor University.
[9] Service Record of Captain R. E. B. Baylor. Texas Collection, Baylor University.
[10] John Wellington Vandever, *Talladega County History*, p. 136.

Again Baylor sought a new land—this time Texas.[11] At La Grange the forty-five-year-old lawyer-minister established a small school, free to those unable to pay tuition. To this log school came James Huckins to visit Baylor, and Z. N. Morrell collaborated with him at a La Grange church service.[12] On record is a letter of April 1, 1840, which Baylor wrote to the *Christian Index* of Georgia, expressing appreciation for sending James Huckins to Texas.

Judge Baylor assisted in the organization of the Baptist Church at La Grange and subsequently in the organization of the Union Baptist Association—the forerunner of the Baptist General Convention of Texas. Although a minister, Judge Baylor was elected Judge of the Third Judicial District by joint ballot of the Congress of the Republic of Texas on January 7, 1841.[13] For a quarter of a century, with the Constitution, Statutes and Laws of Texas in one saddle bag and the Holy Bible, square, compasses and Baptist Covenant of Faith in the other, "this towering giant . . . traveled on horseback over this country . . . establishing courts, churches, and schools, holding court, preaching, teaching. . . ."[14]

WILLIAM MILTON TRYON was another man of destiny at the organizational meeting of the Union Baptist Association. He was the second minister sent to Texas by the American Baptist Home Mission Society. He, also, came from a distinguished English background. His mother was a descendant of Reverend Peter Buckley, graduate of St. John's College, whose library became the nucleus of the library at Harvard. Another forebear, Charles Chauncey (1592-1672), graduate of Cambridge, became the second president of Harvard in 1654. Another, Hugh Bigod, was one of the barons who stood surety for the Magna Carta in 1215, and ancestor

[11] In a letter dated April 13 (no year, but estimated as 1864) and addressed to Brother Stribling, Judge Baylor recalls his trek overland to Texas with Tennessee General Smith and his family, who were going to Fort Houston on the Trinity River. Smith had been with General Sam Houston at the Battle of Horseshoe Bend where both were badly wounded.

[12] Z. N. Morrell, *Flowers and Fruits of the Wilderness* (3rd ed.; St. Louis: Commercial Printing Company, 1882), pp. 108-9.

[13] This service continued for approximately twenty-three years, Baylor having been appointed one of the first district judges by the first Texas governor, J. P. Henderson, in 1846. He also served as a member of the Supreme Court of the Republic of Texas for five years.

[14] Hale, p. 20.

Peter Trieon came to England from the Spanish Netherlands prior to 1586 because of religious persecution.[15]

William Milton Tryon was born in New York City on March 10, 1809. His father died in 1818, and the lad was sent to Connecticut to live with a wealthy uncle so that he might be educated. Illness caused his return, and he took a job as a tailor to help support his mother and three younger children.

Despite a Presbyterian background, Tryon at seventeen was baptized into the fellowship of the South Baptist Church by Reverend Charles J. Summers. Tryon's search for health carried him south, first to Savannah, then to Augusta, where he affiliated with the Baptist Church and was licensed to preach on the same day—December 30, 1832—at the age of twenty-two. On January 14 of the next year he enrolled in the newly opened Mercer Institute at Penfield, Georgia. He was one of four young ministers receiving aid from the Educational Fund of the Georgia Baptist State Convention.[16] He studied at Mercer, then a manual labor academy, for three years, serving one year as an instructor because of his marked ability and diligence. Here in 1837 Tryon was ordained to the ministry with Jesse Mercer as one of the presbytery.

After college, Tryon served as an agent in Georgia, Alabama, and Mississippi under the direction of Columbian College of Washington, D. C., and the Georgia Baptist State Convention. When Adiel Sherwood resigned from the Mercer faculty "to give himself to the saving of Columbian College," he chose Tryon to aid him. The entire indebtedness of the college was paid and $100,000 was raised for buildings and endowment.[17]

Tryon ministered to churches at Washington, Lumpkin, and Columbus in Georgia and at Irvington (later Eufaula), Wetumka, and the Bethlehem Church in Barbour County, Alabama. Here on April 26, 1840, he was married to Mrs. Louise Jacqueline Higgins (nee Reynolds), daughter of a wealthy planter. Dr. William Carey Crane, pastor of the

[15] Mrs. S. S. Conway to Baylor President Samuel Palmer Brooks, November 8, 1929. Texas Collection, Baylor University.

[16] Bartow Davis Ragsdale, Story of Georgia Baptists (Atlanta: Foote and Davis Co., 1932), p. 16.

[17] Reverend Rufus W. Weaver address, "The Founders of Baylor University," June 13, 1920.

Montgomery, Alabama, Baptist Church, (and later president of Baylor) performed the ceremony.

As a result of Jesse Mercer's gift, the Home Mission Board of the American Baptists made an appeal to ministers: "Who among you will go to Texas?" Tryon answered at once: "Here am I; send me."[18] James Huckins wrote a letter from Galveston on March 28, 1841, telling of Tryon's arrival in Galveston. Colonel A. C. Horton (later a Baylor trustee and lieutenant governor of Texas) had requested that Tryon be sent to Matagorda; other requests came from Independence. Huckins, who was ill at the time, requested that he labor at Houston until the two men could confer. About ten days later, after consulting with friends, they decided that Independence was the more important location and Tryon left about February 12 for his station.[19]

Tryon found that the c h u r c h at Washington-on-the-Brazos, less than fifteen miles across the prairie from Independence, had been disbanded and the few members scattered and discouraged. Assisted by Judge R. E. B. Baylor, Tryon assembled them and reorganized the church (founded by Z. N. Morrell) with eleven members on March 14, 1841. Articles of faith were adopted, and Tryon was named joint pastor with Elder T. W. Cox.[20] One of the signers of the letter responsible for bringing missionary aid to Texas, A. Buffington, was named church clerk. In a revival meeting involving almost the entire population, Tryon received thirty new members into the church.

During his first year in Texas Tryon p a s t o r e d four churches: Independence, Washington, Providence (n e a r Chappell Hill), and Mount Gilead in Washington County. The Union Association report of October 7, 1841, showing nine months of his service, lists 174 received by baptism and 66 by letter. The other five associational churches reported a total of 27 by baptism and 35 by letter. He served the Independence Church almost five years, and it was regarded the strongest Baptist Church in the Republic of Texas.

[18] B. F. Fuller, *History of Texas Baptists* (Louisville, Kentucky: Baptist Book Concern, 1900), p. 111.

[19] J. M. Carroll, *A History of Texas Baptists* (Dallas: Baptist Standard Publishing Company, 1923), p. 134.

[20] J. B. Link, *Texas Historical and Biographical Magazine,* I, 193.

In a letter written from "Holly Oak" on March 1, 1859, Judge Baylor, then Chief Justice of Texas, gives a vivid description of the fervent missionary-pastor, whom he had heard once in Alabama before he came to Texas:

Holly Oak, March 1, 1859

My dear Sir:

The Reverend William M. Tryon, concerning whom you inquire, came to Texas a few years after I did, and we soon became intimate friends and fellow-labourers in our Master's vineyard. I had seen and heard him preach, once before that time, and was greatly impressed by his discourse as indicating a mind of very superior order. He came among us in the capacity of a missionary and ready to endure all the privations and sacrifices incident to missionary life. He came well dressed, and has the bearing and manners of a Christian gentleman,—presently, it must be acknowledged, rather strange appearance, to many who, at that early date, were seeking homes in our then untenanted solitude of nature. He, however, very soon became a real Texian, and I have often seen him going to church, mounted on an Old Spanish horse, with his black cloak fluttering around him, and torn by the bushes, so that his person was scarcely protected from the winds and storms he had to encounter. Immediately on his arrival, he entered on a course of vigorous ministerial labour which terminated only with his life. In organizing churches, establishing prayer-meetings, and giving directions to the religious state of things where all was new and unsettled, he exerted an influence the importance of which eternity alone can fully reveal.

As to his personal appearance—he was a little below the medium height, and his figure was symmetrical; his hair was dark flaxen or brown, hanging in profusion about his face; his eyes were grey and of mild expression; and his countenance, altogether intellectual, sedate, and sometimes tinged with sadness. At the greetings of friendship, however, his face easily lighted up with a pleasant smile which revealed to you a fountain of generous, glowing sensibility.

. . . .

As a Preacher, Mr. Tryon certainly had a rare combination of excellences. . . . His discourses were highly evangelical, and whatever his particular theme might be, he never strayed out of sight of the Cross. . . . His style was chaste, his gestures simple and natural, and his manner generally composed though I have sometimes seen him, in his addresses to impenitent sinners, affected to tears. . . . During his first two years' residence in this region, he baptised nearly two hundred individuals. . . . [21]

Tryon received a grant of 640 acres of land from the Republic of Texas on May 29, 1843, in Washington County,

[21] R. E. B. Baylor correspondence, addressee unknown. Texas Collection, Baylor University; also in William B. Sprague, *Annals of the American Pulpit,* VI, 812-14.

near Washington and Independence[22] and built a home on the Hidalgo Bluff four miles west of Washington. Burleson stated that Tryon lived chiefly from the support of his farm from 1841 to 1845.

The Reverend Tryon was named moderator of the infant Baptist association and Judge R. E. B. Baylor, corresponding secretary. Baylor was instructed to write a circular letter to reinforce the one written by a committee of the church at Washington-on-the-Brazos in November 1837 and published in the *Christian Index* of February 2, 1838, praying that faithful ministers be sent "to help us in our forlorn and destitute condition."

At the next meeting of the association, held at the Clear Creek meeting-house near Rutersville (La Grange Church) on October 7, 1841, Judge Baylor recommended "that steps should immediately be taken to provide a school for our people." The following resolution was adopted by the Association:

Resolved, that a select committee of three be appointed to take into consideration so much of the report of the corresponding secretary as related to education.[23]

Reverend William M. Tryon, Moderator of the Association, appointed to the committee William H. Ewing of the Washington church, Reverend James Huckins of the Galveston and Houston churches, and a Mr. Green, a visitor at the meeting. The committee met and reported at the same session:

Resolved, that this Association recommends the formation of an Education Society, and that the brethren generally unite with and endeavor to promote the objects of this Society.

The Education Society was organized immediately with R. E. B. Baylor as president; S. P. Andrews, recording secretary; William M. Tryon, corresponding secretary; and J. L. Farquhar, treasurer. On the board of managers were Stephen Williams, and Elders Hosea Garrett, N. T. Byars,

[22] Photostatic copy of grant in Texas Collection, Baylor University; original in State Archives, Austin, Texas.

[23] The new churches received into the Union Association were Galveston, Houston, Washington (just reorganized by Tryon), Providence (later Burleson), Mt. Gilead in Washington County, and Union (Macedonia) in Travis. Thus the association included nine churches representing 384 members.

Richard Ellis, and Z. N. Morrell.[24] The objectives of the society were (1) to found a school to help support young men studying for the ministry, and (2) to act as a statewide organization to place the entire body of Texas Baptists behind one institution for the education of a native ministry.[25]

A letter written by Reverend James Huckins from Houston, Texas, on November 14, 1841, confirms the date of the organization of the Education Society with the following statement:

> We then formed a Texas Baptist Education Society, with a view to establishing an academical and theological institution, and received very liberal subscriptions, also pledges of several very large tracts of land.

Formal implementation of the resolution was delayed by the Mexican invasion of 1842, but plans began to materialize in October 1843 when the Union Baptist Association met at the Providence Church (now Chappell Hill) in Washington County. Included were thirteen churches, Plum Grove and three new churches—Gonzales, Dove (now Caldwell in Burleson County), and Ebemeyer near Franklin in Robertson County—having been received.[26] In 1844 James Huckins announced that:

---

[24] Morrell, in *Flowers and Fruits*, written thirty years after the event, lists Brother W. T. Collins as treasurer of the Education Society and "Elder Jas. Huckins, Elder Z. N. Morrell, and brethren J. L. Farquhar, Gail Borden, Stephen Williams, Tom H. Ewing, and J. B. Lester on the board of managers." Huckins, Farquhar, Lester, and Garrett became Baylor trustees.

Richard Ellis, born of a family of ministers in Southampton County, Virginia, on June 22, 1813, came to Texas in September 1837. He was the first Missionary Baptist preacher ordained in Texas—in August 1842 at the Plum Grove Church of Hopewell in Fayette County, with Z. N. Morrell and R. E. B. Baylor composing the presbytery. Carroll, p. 128. He was later on the board of managers of the Education Society and voluntary unpaid agent and frequent proxy trustee for Baylor University (May 16, 1845 to February 4, 1847). He was the first moderator of the Colorado Association, organized in November 1847. He married Mary Munn, half-sister to Reddin Andrews, last president of Baylor at Independence. Link, I, 29-31.

[25] Frederick Eby, "Education and Educators," *Centennial Story of Texas Baptists* (Dallas: Baptist General Convention of Texas, 1936), p. 131.

[26] In Tryon's address at Dove Church on October 1, 1945, the Minutes of the Association yield this statement: "In 1841 during session of this association at Clear Creek in Fayette County, a Domestic Mission Society was formed. Z. N. Morrell and B. A. Buffington received commissions from the Society and labored under its patronage. In 1843 was organized the Texas Baptist Education Society, which in 1845 procured from the Congress of Texas the Charter for a Literary Institution. . . ."

Tryon was moderator at the 1841 meeting and attended subsequent meetings. It may be concluded that the early organization of the Education Society was

It was resolved to found a Baptist university in Texas upon a plan so broad that the requirements of existing conditions would be fully met, and that would be susceptible of enlargement and development to meet the needs of all the ages to come.

Early in 1845 the Society directed a committee to go before the Texas Congress, then sitting at Washington-on-the-Brazos, to request a charter for the proposed institution.[27] These pioneer Baptist leaders presented their request, and the Journals of the Ninth Congress of the Republic of Texas reveal the procedure. A called meeting of the Baptist Education Society, at which the honorable R. E. B. Baylor presided, convened at Independence, Washington County, on January 13. The committee consisting of Wm. M. Tryon and J. G. Thomas which had been appointed at a previous meeting to petition the Congress of Texas to charter a literary institute, reported, "which [report] with the charter was accepted and the Baylor University received under the patronage of the Society."[28] Corresponding-secretary Tryon and Thomas secured the assistance of the society president, Judge Baylor, in drafting the petition. His legal training and position as judge made him invaluable.

Judge Baylor gave Tryon credit for originating the project of establishing a Baptist university in Texas: "He first suggested the idea to me, and I immediately fell in with it." He also made the suggestion of applying to the Texas Congress for a charter, and "as I was most familiar with such things I dictated the memorial and he wrote it," declared Baylor.

The memorial of *R. E. B. Baylor et al* was presented on December 28, 1844, by Senator George A. Patillo of Jasper and Jefferson Counties. The bill was read the second time on December 30. John Alexander Greer, chairman of the

---

informal, but it is known that meetings under the board of managers were held with President R. E. B. Baylor. The minutes of the society appear for the first time in 1847 with those of the association. The 9th Annual Meeting at Independence, September 28-October 2, 1848, "gives permission to the Texas Baptist Education Society to append its minutes to those of this body by its paying the extra expense."

[27] The government of the Texas Republic had moved to Washington in September 1842 and remained until July 4, 1845.

[28] William M. Tryon, "Baptist Education Society," *Telegraph and Texas Register,* January 28, 1846.

Committee on the State of the Republic, on January 3, 1845, recommended the incorporation of *San Jacinto University*. Senator Patillo, on January 7, moved to change the name from *San Jacinto* to *Milam University* (undoubtedly in honor of the hero, Colonel Milam), but the next day he moved to strike out *Milam* and insert *Baylor*. The bill was read a third time, passed the Senate, and went to the House. The House Journals reflect that on January 9, 1845, the bill was taken up and read the first time. On motion of Robert McAlpin "Three-Legged-Willie" Williamson the bill to incorporate Baylor University was referred without further reading to a select committee consisting of Messrs. William Menefee (chairman), George Sutherland of Jackson County, Simeon Jones of San Patricio, and McLeod. On January 21, the committee referred the bill to the House and recommended its passage. On motion of Mr. Menefee, on January 25, the bill was read a third time and passed. It was then sent back to the Senate, where it was approved and signed on February 1, 1845, by Anson Jones, President of the Republic of Texas; by John M. Lewis, Speaker of the House; and by Kenneth L. Anderson, President of the Senate and a member of the Education Society.

Carroll states that at no time had the question of a name for the institution arisen until the charter brought the necessity.[29] The petitioners had no time to confer with the sponsoring Society, lest the charter-granting be deferred. Baylor is said to have suggested the name *Tryon*, because "the thought of establishing a Baptist University in this country originated with Tryon." Tryon, however, remonstrated, saying that he "had had so much to do with bringing the enterprise forward that he feared it might be thought that he was working for his own honor, and so it might injure the prospects of the school." Immediately he took the charter and wrote in the blank, *Baylor*, despite his co-worker's vigorous protest. Judge Baylor offered his objection because, "First, I do not think I am worthy of such a distinction; second, my humble donation [he had subscribed $1,000 to the proposed university] might be misunderstood and the motives prompting it misconstrued." Kenneth L. Anderson, Vice-president of the Texas Republic, joined Tryon in his

[29] Carroll, p. 229.

effort, and the name of the university became *Baylor*, although its heritage from Tryon was unquestionable.[30] "Of the fifteen institutions chartered by the Republic . . . only Baylor has survived."[31]

The charter of Baylor University was granted in the same town from which the Texas Declaration of Independence had been announced and in which the constitution of the Republic had been drafted—Old Washington-on-the-Brazos.* The building used by the Senate on these historic occasions was Mr. W. M. Massie's store; members of the House of Representatives climbed the weathered stairs outside Major Hatfield's saloon to their quarters. Texas population had increased from 50,000 in 1836 as indicated by the vote for the first President of the Republic, to 125,000 during the last year of the Republic in 1845, when Texas became the 28th state of the United States on December 29.[32]

The Texas National Register of Washington, Texas, on Saturday, March 22, 1845, printed the act creating Baylor University and listed fifteen original trustees. Founders Baylor, Huckins, and Tryon undoubtedly selected the most able men in the area to join them in planning the educational venture.

The same stormy circumstances that formed the backdrop of Texas history at this time affected the founding of churches and schools. The Texas-Mexican conflict of 1836 was still fresh in the minds of the people; conflicts with Indian tribes were still possibilities; and the Santa Fe Expedition, the Somerville Campaign, the Battle of Mier, and the Snively Expedition contributed their share of anxiety. Then came the tumultuous problem of annexation to the United States, followed by the war between the United States and Mexico. Unrest, confusion, and uncertainty characterized all phases of life in Texas. It was an ominous time to found a university.

[30] In a letter to James Huckins, now in the Baylor Archives of the Texas Collection at Baylor University, Judge Baylor relates the circumstances of his objections, adding that "Brother Tryon and Vice-President Anderson were inflexible. They were determined upon it. This may account for the name of Baylor University. How well or how wisely they acted it is not for me to say, but I leave others to judge."

[31] William Stuart Red, *A History of the Presbyterian Church in Texas* (San Antonio: The Steck Company, 1936), p. 224.

* See Appendix for charter.

[32] *Texas Almanac 1949-1950*, p. 91.

The Charter of Baylor University, granted by the Senate and House of Representatives of the Republic of Texas, provided in Section 3 for "the following persons . . . duly chosen Trustees of said University . . . to wit: R. E. B. Baylor, J. G. Thomas, Albert C. Horton, Edward Taylor, James S. Lester, R. B. Jarmon, James Huckins, Nelson Kavanaugh, O. Drake, Eli Mercer, Aaron Shannon, James Farquhar, Albert Haynes, Robert S. Armstead, and W. Tryon."

These men responsible for the destiny of the new school brought varied backgrounds to the board of trustees, for a native Texan was a rarity indeed in 1845. Baylor, Huckins, and Tryon, previously introduced, were recognized men of merit. Many of the remaining twelve had already proved their sterling qualities in the pioneer society, in the battle for freedom, and in their devotion to religious faith.

ROBERT STARK ARMISTEAD (frequently spelled Armstead) is listed with Austin's colonists as applying for land in 1835. An old family Bible reveals the birthdate of Armistead to be 1800.[33] He married Lou Brown, daughter of Rhoda Vickers Brown. The Vickers family was prominent in early Texas life. Robert Armistead's name appeared on a list of delinquent taxpayers from Gonzales County for 1840; the amount due was 84 cents![34] His name was listed in the Articles of Incorporation for Baylor University printed in the *Texas National Register* of February 15, 1845, and March 22, 1845. Another entry of the name was in the "Diary of Adolphus Sterne."[35] Armistead became the first trustee to resign from the board (April 24, 1847). He was termed an outstanding citizen, living at Gay Hill.[36]

ORIN DRAKE'S name also appeared on the list of applicants for the charter of Baylor University.[37] The 1850 Census of Fayette County listed O. Drake, age 38, birthplace New York, as a farmer with property evaluation of $1000. His wife, Luisa, born in Tennessee, and three children were listed. His name also appeared on the delinquent tax list in 1840, for the sum of $1.00. Drake served as secretary pro tempore

---

[33] Gus Newman, writing for Mrs. George Armistead of Houston, about her husband's uncle, January 1, 1939.
[34] *Texas Sentinel*, June 17, 1841, p. 3.
[35] *Southwestern Historical Quarterly*, XXX, 323.
[36] W. C. Crane, *History of Washington County* (Reprint, Brenham, Texas: Banner Press, 1939), p. 31.
[37] *Texas National Register*, March 22, 1845, p. 2.

for the Baylor Board of Trustees on December 22, 1847, but by August 21, 1849, fell into disfavor with the members, and the clerk was instructed to request his resignation. Nearly two years later the secretary was asked to report to Mr. Drake the following resolution:

Whereas, Mr. Orin Drake has for a long time neglected entirely the meetings of this Board and whereas he has for sufficient reasons been requested by the Board to resign his place as Trustee of Baylor University and having received satisfactory information that he has resigned, Resolved, therefore, that his place as Trustee is hereby declared vacant. And it be further resolved that the Sect. notify the Board of Managers of the B. S. Convention of this vacancy and request that it be filled.[38]

JAMES L. FARQUHAR's association with the Education Society began at its inception in 1841.[39] His continuous service with the group made it logical for him to be named an original trustee of Baylor University. Since Farquhar had five children, he induced Henry Flavel Gillette to open Union Academy in 1841 at Washington. A thrifty planter, working about twenty hands, "he boards me gratis," wrote Gillette.[40] Farquhar's term of service as a Baylor trustee was one of the longest—until his death in 1873.[41]

ALBERT GALLITAN HAYNES, original trustee, bears the distinction of making the first motion in a trustee meeting— the nomination of Judge R. E. B. Baylor as board president. Haynes was born in Green County, Georgia, on August 1, 1805, of English stock dating back to 1614. Ancestor Reverend John Haynes had come to America with the unfrocked

[38] Minutes of the Baylor Board of Trustees, June 14, 1851.
[39] Carroll, p. 229.
[40] Gillette to Ashbel Smith, September 1841. Ashbel Smith Papers, Archives University of Texas. Gillette became the first teacher at Baylor University.
[41] Farquhar and Haynes supplied a house for Principal Horace Clark when he joined the school in November 1851; and on June 15, 1851, the treasurer was authorized to pay them $600 with 10% interest. Farquhar served on various committees concerning property, notes, and the building program for the school. The Baptist State Convention of 1870 paid tribute to him, citing him as "one of the two organizers yet living." The Baylor Board on July 9, 1873, in resolutions presented by J. W. D. Creath, paid tribute to his "unflagging zeal in the discharge of his duties as trustee" and extolled his "liberal contributions of time, influence and money." When attendance at a trustee meeting was impossible, he designated his proxy to J.W.D. Creath, N. Kavanaugh, John H. Graves, or A. Shannon.
Farquhar children who attended Baylor were Celestra Ann (1851-52), Bud (no date), Felix H. (1856-58), Cornelius E. (1856-59), Alfred (1872-73), and Samuel (1872-73). Bud, Felix, and Cornelius left school to join the Confederate Army.

nonconformist minister John Hooker and 3,000 dissenters and located in Hartford, Connecticut. Along with Roger Williams, Haynes became a pioneer spokesman for civil and religious liberty.

Descendant of these early patriots, Albert G. Haynes was converted to the Baptist faith and baptized into the Concord Church in Green County in 1828.[42] Haynes married Matilda Freeman of Monticello, Jasper County, Georgia, in 1831. Then, after a residence of seven years in Noxubee County, Mississippi, he moved his family to Texas in the fall of 1841. When he reached a particular live oak grove in the little village of Independence, Washington County, Texas, "his entire fortune consisted of his wife, five children, several Negroes, a pair of jaded horses and a debt of $50." The weary traveler of 1200 miles in two months mounted the summit of the hill east of the village and said: "This land is lovely to behold—here we have rich soil, a pure atmosphere, a healthy location and some neighbors, and if it suits you, we will cease our journeyings and prospecting, locate here, and spend the remaining time allotted to us on earth."[43]

The thirty-six-year-old Haynes rented a little log cabin from Alcalde John P. Coles until he could build one of his own. With the help of his Negroes, he cut, split, and dressed the logs to erect a home on the sixteen-acre plot just west of the limits of Independence—where later he built a handsome residence. From Coles he rented fifty more acres and during the first year harvested seventy-five bales of cotton which he sold at the unprecedented price of seven cents a pound. His fortune mended year by year. "No worthy, charitable or benevolent enterprise ever appealed in vain for aid, and he has been heard to say, with a face radiant with gratitude, that he had invested more money in churches and schools than in Negroes and land, and he thanked God for the opportunity to do so."[44]

In 1842, the Haynes family affiliated by letter with the Baptist Church in Independence, and the Major served as pacificator during what Link termed one of the stormiest

[42] Link, II, 371.
[43] Link, II, 372.
[44] Ibid.

periods of the church's history. He was ordained a deacon in 1843 and served to the end of his life as one of the pioneer church's strongest servants. Famed for his rich baritone, Haynes sang at many revivals held by Tryon, Huckins, Baylor, and Morrell. Five years after the organization of the Union Association, a departure was made from the usual practice in the election of Albert G. Haynes, a layman and deacon, as moderator of the association. He had served as treasurer in 1843 and 1844 and again in 1846-48.[45] Haynes was a man who commanded respect and his service was broad.[46]

ALBERT CLINTON HORTON had garnered fame in the military and political arenas by the time Baylor was founded. He was born in Georgia on September 4, 1798. His father, a man of position and affluence, died when Albert was only a boy, and he was reared on a small farm by his widowed mother. In 1823 he moved to La Grange, Alabama, and married Eliza Holliday in 1829.[47] Burleson related a different story—one concerning Horton's addiction to gambling. He states that in 1823 he wandered into the Tennessee Valley of North Alabama where the reigning belle was a Miss Dent. She was infatuated with the young blades at the races and the accompanying balls. Her distraught father said, "I do believe my poor child is doomed to marry a gambler, and if I could find a decent gambler, she might marry him." Upon

[45] *The Union Baptist Association, Centennial History 1840-1940* (Brenham: Banner Press), p. 284.

[46] Haynes served as a Baylor trustee from 1845 until 1870. Trustee meetings were frequently held at his home, which he also opened sacrificially to students of limited means for "$5 per month for "lodging, food, lights, washing, and every item of expense." In June 1851 the Haynes family entertained sixty-three persons "in three large rooms and under four live oaks" at the meeting of the Texas Baptist State Convention at Independence.

In 1848 he was elected justice of the peace for the Independence precinct, and in 1856 Washington County elected him by a large majority to the State Legislature. His last civic service was a two-year term, beginning in 1869, on the Commissioners' Court of Washington County.

During the Civil War Haynes lost a fortune estimated at $85,000 in property and slaves, but his greatest loss was two sons—Tom (LLB. in 1858 from Baylor) in the battle at Perryville, Kentucky, and Dick at Seven Pines, Virginia. Son Harry survived his military service and later wrote the *Life of Dr. Rufus C. Burleson.* Haynes himself took a large force of his Negro men to Galveston to build fortifications.

[47] Walter Prescott Webb and H. Bailey Carroll (eds.), *The Handbook of Texas* (Austin: The Texas State Historical Association, 1952), I, 840. *The Record of Southwest Texas* (Chicago: Goodspeed Brothers, 1894), confirms the 1829 marriage to Eliza Holliday at the residence of her brother-in-law and guardian, W. J. Croom, father of Colonel John L. Croom of Matagorda.

hearing his declaration, young Horton presented himself to Deacon Dent and frankly admitted: "Sir, what you ask is not on this earth; they are a race of heartless demons. I am among them, but not one of them. If you will trust your beautiful, angel daughter to me, I will make her happy." Burleson states that the couple was married about 1828.[48] Horton and Eliza Holliday were the parents of six children, and no other evidence of the previous marriage has been found.

Horton became a Mason, with Reverend William Leigh (grandfather of Leigh and Rufus Burleson) and Mr. Segim B. Moore conferring the degree at La Grange, Alabama. Burleson relates that the impressive ceremony affected Horton deeply, and he declared: "This night I begin a new life. . . . I have bet my last dollar." Soon he was converted under the ministry of Daniel P. Baptis [sic], who had married a Miss Townes, close friend of Horton's young wife. Both couples soon moved to Green County, Alabama, where Horton was elected to the Alabama Senate from Greensboro in 1832.

Horton began his Texas career in late 1834 when he bought several leagues of land, opened a large plantation on Old Caney in Wharton County, and settled in Matagorda.[49] His military service began in 1835 when he went to Alabama to aid in the organization of the Mobile Grays, with whom he returned to Texas in late December. The following spring he recruited a cavalry company and went to the aid of James W. Fannin, Jr. One of Fannin's companies—that of Captain (Doctor) Shackleford—was composed of sons of Horton's Alabama friends. With the fall of the Alamo, General Houston ordered Colonel Fannin to demolish the fortification at Goliad and retreat to the Colorado. Horton, using oxen to transport the cannon, arrived at Goliad on March 16, 1836. He urged Fannin to comply speedily, but the gallant Fannin lingered and was captured on Coleto Creek seventeen miles from Goliad. Colonel Fannin had ordered Captain Horton and his cavalry to intercept spies from Santa Anna's army and to scour the country between Goliad and Victoria. Thus

[48] Harry Haynes (ed.), *The Life and Writings of Rufus C. Burleson* (compiled and published by Mrs. Georgia J. Burleson, 1901), pp. 707-708.
[49] Homer S. Thrall, *A Pictorial History of Texas* (St. Louis: N. D. Thompson and Company, 1879), p. 555.

Horton's cavalry was a portion of Fannin's men who escaped capture and death. On March 17 Horton's unit had a skirmish with the cavalry of General Jose Urrea. Shackleford, witness to the fight, reported: "Horton behaved with great gallantry, and made a furious charge upon the enemy; but, encountering a heavy force of infantry, he retreated in good order." On the 19th—the morning of the retreat from Goliad —Horton went in advance to examine the crossing at Coleto Creek, but Fannin's force had been surrounded. Horton then took his company to join General Houston in the East. The military service of Captain Horton covered the period from February 1 to May 1, 1836, for which he received a bounty certificate for 320 acres of land.[50] The *Virginia Herald,* May 25, 1836, cites an item from the *New Orleans Bulletin* of May 9:

Col. A. Horton of the Texas Army has arrived in the steamboat *Caspean* and confirms the news of the Glorious Victory of General Houston, and has favored us with the following list of the Mexican officers killed, wounded or prisoners.

Horton participated in the campaign against Raphael Vasquez in 1842 to conclude his military career.

Politically, Horton represented Matagorda, Jackson, and Victoria counties in the Senate of the First and Second Congresses of the Texas Republic, 1836-1838. As a senator, Horton opposed "a bill for the protection of the frontier." He said that it was injurious to the people of the frontier to place $20,000 of public money in the hands of a nameless quartermaster. In the September 3, 1838, election, M. B. Lamar became president, and Horton was defeated by David G. Burnet for the vice-presidency. On January 14 of the following year, President Lamar appointed a commission of five men, headed by A. C. Horton, to locate the capital of Texas, since there was opposition to its location in Houston. Horton cast the deciding vote by which Austin was chosen as the capital site.[51]

A strong advocate of annexation, Horton was a committeeman from Matagorda County to the Annexation Convention in 1845. After annexation, James Pinckney Henderson was

[50] *Texas Constitution*, Section 23, 1st article.

[51] Garland Adair, *Texas Pictorial Handbook* (Austin: Austin News Agency, January 15, 1957), p. 14.

elected the first governor of Texas, with Horton as lieutenant-governor.[52]

After the expiration of his term in the governor's office on December 21, 1847, Horton devoted himself to the management of his estate, variously estimated at $300,000 to $400,000. Large-scale cotton planting produced 650 to 700 bales per year, but sugar cane took most of his time. A fair yearly estimate of his crop was 450 to 500 hogsheads of sugar and 1,600 barrels of syrup.[53]

Rufus C. Burleson tells of his first meeting with Horton at the organization of the Texas Baptist State Convention at Anderson on September 8, 1848:

> I served with him on the committee to draft the constitution. My father knew him intimately in Alabama, and often spoke of him as a remarkable man, but his penetration and vast compass of mind far excelled all my expectations, for though Brother R. S. Blont and I had been at work on the constitution two months, and had collated and culled from the constitutions of Virginia, North Carolina, Tennessee and Georgia, and secretly written out the constitution before leaving Houston, we were both startled at the questions and wisdom of Gov. Horton, who probably never saw a constitution of a Baptist State Convention. I knew him intimately afterwards as deacon at Matagorda and trustee and patron of Baylor University. Nothing ever impressed me more than his tender and deep interest for the comfort and religious welfare of his slaves. He owned nearly 300—a large number of them members of the Baptist Church. He made a church house, built conveniently between his plantations, and employed a preacher to preach to them. . . . [54]

Physically, Horton presented a memorable appearance. He was six feet, seven inches tall. The lid of one eye sustained an injury "so that it did not keep up like the other and was almost always weeping a little. Gov. Horton wore his hair in a long que . . . not uncommon among old men."[55]

[52] Nicholas H. Darnell had been declared elected on December 15, 1845, but a recount and tabulation showed that Horton received more votes; hence Horton was inaugurated on May 1, 1846. *The Handbook of Texas*, I, 840. When Governor Henderson was granted leave by an act of the legislature on May 9, 1846, to take command of all Texas troops in the war with Mexico, Horton became acting-governor and served until July 1847, receiving the pay of the governor during the period. The Texas Legislature in 1936 declared Horton to have been governor, and his picture was placed in the capitol with those of other Texas governors. Horton's last political service was attendance as a delegate at the Democratic National Convention in Charleston, South Carolina, in 1860.

[53] *The Record of Southwest Texas* (Chicago: Goodspeed Brothers, 1894).

[54] Haynes, pp. 706-767.

[55] Judge R. E. B. Baylor, "Reminiscences." Texas Collection, Baylor University.

R. B. JARMON (sometimes spelled Jorman) was a rugged, determined, devoted Texan. Link records that financial embarrassment caused him to sell his Tennessee holdings in 1837 and come to Texas. When the outlook for Texas independence was rather gloomy, some of his wife's brothers visited him in Texas and offered to buy back his Tennessee place if he would return. "Colonel Jarmon thanked them, but told them he was so interested in Texas, that he would remain by her, and that his bones should bleach on her prairies or she would be freed from Mexican misrule."[56]

The first notice of the name of this pioneer appeared in the *Telegraph and Texas Register* of March 3, 1838, when he was listed as administrator for one William House, deceased. The next was an offer of "$200 for the return of a Negro boy, Joe (Yellow)" to his farm at Cummings' Creek, Fayette County.[57]

Morrell records that he visited him some seventeen miles southeast of La Grange in the company of Elder R. E. B. Baylor.[58] Jarmon lived eighteen miles from Columbus, almost entirely a Methodist town. The school was taught in the Methodist church, it and the court house being the only public buildings in the town by 1850. Jarmon and his family affiliated with a Baptist church some eighteen miles out of Columbus where Elder P. B. Chandler preached. Here also came Eli Mercer and his wife from Egypt, Texas.

The Census of 1850 lists R. B. Jarmon of Fayette County, age 35; birthplace, North Carolina; value of real estate $20,000; wife, 38, born in North Carolina; children: Richard, 9; Adele and Mary, 6; Robert, 1; and an infant. The children were all natives of Texas.

Jarmon was termed the most active layman in the Colorado Association in attending meetings of the association and the state convention. Later in good financial circumstances, he owned extensive lands in the neighborhood of Lockhart and opened a large plantation on the Colorado River, where he built a fine residence. Link also pays tribute to "Sister Jarmon . . . pious, quiet, moving on in her sphere, she exerted an influence for good on all about her."

When Jarmon found it impossible to attend trustee meet-

[56] Link, I, 562-563.
[57] *Telegraph and Texas Register,* May 6, 1840.
[58] Morrell p. 197.

ings, he designated proxies, among whom were M. D. Anderson, B. Blanton, and C. J. Humphreys.[59]

NELSON J. KAVANAUGH, original trustee, was also destined to serve until 1866 and was consistent in his attendance of trustee meetings. He and his wife, formerly Mary Eliza McKay, came to Texas from Clinton, Missouri, in 1840 and first settled at Houston. Soon Kavanaugh sold his Houston general merchandise store and moved to Gay Hill, where he had bought land and slaves. He brought along daughters Rebecca and Mary Gentry, who became Baylor's first woman graduate, and son Charles, who was also graduated from Baylor. Kavanaugh served Washington County as county commissioner as well as proving himself a worthy, generous Baylor trustee. After the Civil War Kavanaugh moved to Brenham and engaged in the cotton business and the sale of farm implements.

JAMES SEATON LESTER was born on April 21, 1799, to a well-established family that settled in Virginia before the Revolution. Several members of the family served in the Congress of the United States.[60]

Lester received his education in Virginia, studied to be a lawyer and was admitted to the bar in 1831.[61] In 1834 he emigrated to Texas in time to join Colonel John H. Moore in his campaign against the Indians. He settled at Mina (Bastrop) and represented the district at the Consultation of 1835. He was also a member of the committee appointed to plan the organization of the provisional government,

[59] The last meeting of the board which Jarmon attended was on February 8, 1866. He was named treasurer of the Colorado Association which convened at the Plum Grove Church, Fayette County, September 10-14, 1852. Carroll, p. 304. The association then numbered 896, with eighteen ministers in the group. In 1858 Jarmon was one of eight committeemen to present a special request to the Baptist State Convention on the subject of new and larger buildings for the Male Department of Baylor University. He continued his activity in denominational affairs. An excerpt from the report of the corresponding secretary of the Baptist State Convention for 1870 records ". . . of the lay brethren present, Bros. J. L. Farquhar and R. B. Jarmon are the only ones left with us today. [Reference to the organization of the convention twenty-one years previously at Anderson, Grimes County, with the church then called Antioch.] Death has made fearful havoc in that little band that organized the Baptist State Convention of Texas."

The last mention of Jarmon in the *Minutes of Trustees of Baylor University* is a record of his having paid the school $250 on July 1, 1866.

[60] Walter P. Freytag (Chairman of Fayette County Historical Survey Committee), "Soldier, Statesman, Patriot," *The Fayette County Record,* La Grange, Texas, March 2, 1962.

[61] *The Handbook of Texas,* II, 50.

which culminated in the selection of Governor Henry Smith. Lester was elected by the General Council, "a supernumerary member of this body, but if he ever sat in its councils it was for a brief period only."[62]

In January and February 1836 Lester was stationed at Bastrop as a recruiting agent for the garrison at Bexar. In this capacity he met David Crockett and his men on the edge of Hill's Prairie and sent them to reinforce Travis at the Alamo. His official record reveals that he served in the Army of Texas from April 1 to May 29, 1836.[63] Had he not been on detached service, he would have been at the Alamo "to die with Fayette's Samuel Brown Evans."[64] Hence it can be concluded that he joined the army at Groces' Retreat when Houston was endeavoring to reorganize his army. He fought at the Battle of San Jacinto, where he reported the loss of a large pistol valued at ten dollars. Lester reenlisted on May 29, 1836, in Captain James R. Cook's artillery company and was honorably discharged on June 4, 1836. Then on July 1 he entered Captain Miller's company to serve until August 11, 1836.

When the Second Congress was in session at Houston, December 14, 1837, it authorized the organization of Fayette County. The petition was presented by James S. Lester, Andrew Rabb, and John H. Moore. County dimensions were "about 10 miles on each side of the Old La Bahia Road . . . to be formed into a county—Fayette, in honor of Marquis de La Fayette, who so materially aided the American colonies." The proceedings are the first written records of James S. Lester as acting county clerk.[65]

After the town was surveyed by Charles Lockhart under the direction of Colonel John H. Moore, enterprising Lester bought up one-fourth of the lots on the first sale. He continued to add to his holdings until he owned thirteen-sixteenths of the township. In addition he had been granted a third league of land near Warda—most likely for military

[62] Houston Wade, "Fayette County Heroes of San Jacinto," *La Grange Journal*, No. 42 (Based on information supplied by the Hon. L. W. Kemp, Mrs. Leonie Weyland, and John Schroeder.)

[63] Service Records Nos. 1301, 1302, 1303, cited by Wade.

[64] Service Record No. 2298, indicating detached service at Bastrop. Freytag.

[65] *Ibid.*

service. Lester's name appears on the first list of "free-holders" of Fayette County, made in 1839.[66]

In April of 1838 Lester entered the mercantile business, establishing the firm Lester and Eastland in Fayette County.[67] The license was renewed in June of 1839, and the firm took out an additional permit to sell liquor.

Politically, Lester represented Fayette and Bastrop Counties in the House of Representatives of the Republic of Texas during the First, Second, and Third Congresses. He sponsored the bill to locate the capital of Texas in Fayette County; the bill passed both houses but was vetoed by Sam Houston. Lester was elected senator and served in the Fourth and Fifth Congresses.[68] His last civil service was as county judge in Fayette County from 1844 to 1848.[69] Records show that Lester was frequently called upon as an estate administrator or as a bondsman.[70] In 1840 when the militant preacher Thomas Washington Cox, veteran of San Jacinto, organized the First Baptist Church at Rutersville, Lester became the first clerk of the congregation.[71]

Judge Lester served as a Baylor trustee from the first board meeting at Brenham on May 15, 1845, until his resignation on December 6, 1866. He found it increasingly difficult to attend meetings and was represented by the following proxies: R. Ellis, Willet Holmes, and C. J. Humphreys. Rutersville College (incorporated on February 5, 1840) also claimed Judge Lester as an original trustee. The school closed in 1859. The judge, who never married, lived at Winchester until his death on December 8, 1879, and was

[66] Leonie Weyland and Houston Wade, *Early History of Fayette County* (La Grange: La Grange Journal Plant, 1936), p. 50.

[67] The partner is thought to have been either Nicholas Washington Eastland or William Mosby Eastland, but records fail to identify. The firm furnished material for the county's first courthouse, a small clapboard building. Freytag.

[68] *The Handbook of Texas* II, 50.

[69] *La Grange Journal,* Fayette County, March 1, 1962.

[70] On February 27, 1843, Lester and A. A. Gardiner went on the bond of Nicholas Washington Eastland as surety for $1,400 when Eastland had been appointed administrator of the estate of Nicholas Mosby Dawson, deceased. Lester and Grassmeyer were named administrators of the estate of Christian Gotthelf Wertzner, estimated at $1,600. *Ibid.*

[71] Judge R. E. B. Baylor wrote in 1840: "A Baptist Church was lately organized near La Grange at a village about five miles distant. The membership amounted to 13 in number. The church was constituted by the name of the United Baptist Church at Rutersville; Brothers James Stephens and Joseph Shaw were unanimously chosen deacons, and the Hon. J. S. Lester, Clerk." MS, Texas Collection, Baylor University.

buried at La Grange. A local hotel, through a series of proprietors, still bears his name—Lester Hotel—and is renowned among several generations of "drummers."[72]

ELI MERCER served as the direct connecting link between the newly founded university and Jesse Mercer whose interest in Texas was so keen that he did all possible to aid the struggling Texas pioneers. Eli Mercer was born on June 28, 1790, in Georgia. His father, Thomas Mercer, a Baptist minister in Wilkes and Hancock counties, was the brother of "the galvanic Jesse Mercer"; he had helped found the Mississippi Baptist Association, had served as its first moderator, and had compiled the state's first hymnal.[73]

Son Eli, in his very young manhood, moved to Amite County, Mississippi, and on December 24, 1810, married Ann Nancy Thompson, then fifteen. Their eldest daughter, Penelope, at sixteen married young school-teacher Gail Borden, Jr. Eli Mercer was a prominent farmer in the Old Spanish grants off Wagoner Creek and served as a juror in two significant trials as a commissioner of roads, several times as an inspector of electors, and as a surety on Gail Borden's bond as surveyor.

Intrigued with the glowing accounts of Texas prospects that came from Uncle Tom Borden, who went to Texas in 1829 as one of Austin's famous "Old Three Hundred," Gail resigned his post as surveyor, and with the Mercers set out for Texas on September 17, 1829. With Mercer were his wife and five children and their slaves—ten people in all. They traveled by boat to Natchitoches, Louisiana, and overland by wagon to the Colorado River. On November 29 they reached a place later called *Egypt* because of the high production of corn in the area, finally to be named Wharton County. Mercer and his son-in-law, Gail Borden, each received a *sitio*—4,428 acres of land from the Mexican government.

J. A. Kimball records interesting personal recollections of the early days of the Mercer family in Texas:

[72] Wade, "Fayette County Heroes."
Personal facts supplied to author by Talley Hamlett, Lester relative and Baylor ex-student, McGregor, Texas.
[73] Joe B. Frantz, *Gail Borden* (Norman: University of Oklahoma Press, 1951), p. 55.

So far as I now remember, in that wealthy section of country on Old Caney, there were but few places where there was regular preaching in all Wharton County. At Egypt, Captain Heard was a Methodist, as were several other families. Here lived Eli Mercer, who was a Baptist. . . .

A Methodist minister was always appointed in Egypt. . . .

The Baptist Church worshiped in the court house in Wharton. I do not think that there was a school house in the place. . . . It must be recollected that the white population was small, and on many plantations there resided only the overseer. . . .

Much of the sugar used in Texas was made on the farms by the farmers themselves; sometimes only one kettle being used. The sugar thus made was dark. . . . The sugar mills on the Colorado that were fartherest up, and therefore easiest of access were two at Egypt—Captain Heard's and Brother Eli Mercer's. . . .

Brother Eli Mercer, of Egypt, was a member of the church in Wharton. . . . He was always an active man in whatever he engaged in. He attended the general meetings of the denomination. . . . His wife frequently accompanied him to these meetings until the infirmities of age kept her nearer home. After her death, Brother Mercer traveled more than before, giving up in a degree the affairs at his home to his son, who lived on the home place. He was a very useful man . . . in the work of our denomination.[74]

In fact, Rufus Burleson wrote that he was "a prince among farmers." And he assumed the role of leadership in young Texas political life when he attended the first convention of some fifty delegates at San Felipe on October 1, 1832, representing Mina (Bastrop). Mercer made the trek for the second convention—attended by such notables as Stephen F. Austin, David G. Burnet, James Bowie, Nestor Clay, Jared Groce, "Three-Legged Willie" Williamson, Sam Houston, and son-in-law Gail Borden. This group framed the Constitution of the Republic of Texas.

At the Battle of San Jacinto Eli Mercer served alongside his seventeen-year-old son, Elijah G. Mercer, and the Borden brothers in Captain William Jones Elliott Heard's company.[75] In 1836 he was appointed one of the Commissioners for organization of the militia for the jurisdiction of Austin. "He supplied the Texas Army with beef and other provisions and hid corn in the cane brakes so that the community had

---

[74] J. A. Kimball, "Recollections of Early Days in Texas," *Historical and Biographical Magazine*, II, 163-165.

[75] Letter from J. F. Barnett of Palacios, Texas (n.d.). Texas Collection, Baylor University.

food and seed when peace came."[76] Mercer supplied the wagon and team to Gail Borden and Joseph Baker to haul their printing press to Harrisburg before the approach of Santa Anna.

In 1838 the name of Eli Mercer appears again in public service when he was appointed, along with Thomas J. Rabb and William J. E. Heard, to receive subscriptions for the Colorado Navigation Company to promote the use of the river for commerce.[77] In 1840 he began his service as postmaster at Egypt in Wharton County.

Eli Mercer, like his forebears, was a dedicated Christian and civic-spirited man. His name appears in the list of those attending the 1856 meeting of the Union Baptist Association.[78] Judge Baylor related the circumstances under which Mercer became a Christian. Engaged in digging a grave for a friend, "he began to think seriously of time, death, and eternity and was immediately struck under conviction of sin. . . . He was a cousin to the celebrated Jesse Mercer and had always been a Baptist in principles (though never affiliated with a church); so he mounted his horse, rode up the Colorado River until he found a Baptist Church," gave his confession, and was duly immersed.

The benevolent Judge Baylor related an amusing incident at the first Baptist State Convention. He had been engaged in a sixteen-day meeting with Brothers Stribling and Morrell and had ridden during the night after service to arrive at the distant convention site. Hence he tried to beg off when he was named as one of the speakers, stating that "I am so wearied and fatigued that it would almost kill me to preach today." Mercer's reply was—"You have to preach if it kills you—just what I want—to see one Baptist minister die in the pulpit preaching Jesus to a lost world. . . ."[79]

Although the service of Mercer as a Baylor trustee was not long, it was effective and influential. It was Mercer who presented the proposition for locating the university at Travis, Austin County. At the extended trustee meeting

---

[76] Vernon P. Crockett, "Eli Mercer," *The Handbook of Texas*, p. 175.

[77] In September 1850 Mercer was involved in organizing an effort to remove a great raft from the Colorado and allow navigation.

[78] Minutes of Union Association, II, 2.

[79] Judge R. E. B. Baylor, "Reminiscences." MS, Texas Collection, Baylor University.

in June 1848, when the school was without funds to pay the president and teachers, the trustees agreed to pay $20 each "with Eli Mercer to pay the residue, providing it did not exceed $150."[80]

COLONEL AARON SHANNON, plantation owner and devout Baptist, was an original trustee who served until 1863. Shannon was born in South Carolina in 1796 and moved to Alabama in 1820. Settling in Tuscaloosa County, he operated a large plantation on the Tombigbee River and became a large slave owner. His wife was the former Elizabeth Kilpatrick, a granddaughter of General Charles Brandon of Tennessee, who had come to America for political reasons. Shannon was commissioned a colonel in the U. S. Army by Andrew Jackson. He had served as a member of the Board of Regents of the University of Alabama before he settled in the area to be called Shannon's Prairie in Montgomery County.[81] He purchased the lands of Joseph Yeamans near Washington on August 27, 1841.[82]

It was Aaron Shannon who presented the proposal for the location of Baylor University at Shannon's Prairie. On the motion of Trustee R. G. Jarmon, Mr. Shannon was appointed chairman of a committee of five to examine the several proposals and report to the board. They "fixed the valuation of all uncultivated land (except town lots) at 75¢ per acre." After the decision was made in favor of Independence, Shannon was placed on the committee to make collections. All of this momentous business transpired at the Mt. Gilead church meeting of the board on October 13, 1845.

Colonel Shannon gave the young school its first bell—his old plantation bell used to call his hands together for their daily tasks.[83]

Mr. Shannon was not a regular attendant at board meetings, and these men served as his proxy at one time or

[80] The Minutes of the Baylor Board of Trustees do not record the name of Mercer in subsequent meetings.
[81] Carroll, p. 504. Based on information from Grandson Tom Shannon of Independence. Montgomery was created from Washington County in 1837; Grimes County was created from Montgomery County in 1846.
[82] Worth S. Ray, *Austin Colony Pioneers* (Austin: privately published, 1949), p. 204.
[83] Josephine Shannon of Independence confirmed the fact of the gift in a letter on August 15, 1945. Her father, Thomas Brandon Shannon, a Baylor student, recalled the story to her many times. The bell was used to call students

another: A. G. Haynes, G. W. Baines, and B. Blanton.[84]

EDWARD WILLYS TAYLOR, a non-church member, was an enterprising Independence business man. He was interested in establishing a reputable school in the area, and with his partner John Bancroft Root, pledged the Female Academy, formerly used by Miss Trask, for the immediate use of the proposed school. This offer had a decided effect upon the choice of location.[85]

Taylor served the board until his resignation on the second day of the three-day board meeting during the first week of June 1848. His co-workers passed this resolution: "Resolved that the thanks of this Board be extended to E. W. Taylor, Esq., for the efficient and elegant manner in which he has kept the records of this Body."

JESSE GILBERT THOMAS was a member of the committee that requested the government of the Texas Republic to grant a charter to Baylor University. He was named an original trustee and served for twenty years. As a member of the executive committee of the board, he helped select the location for the school.

Thomas was born on June 11, 1807, in Hickman County, Tennessee, the son of Ezekiel Thomas and Jane Mitchell Thomas. He married Eliza Daniel Micheaux of Cumberland County, Virginia, in Courtland, Alabama, in 1832. Thomas brought his wife and five children to Texas in 1841 and settled at Davidson's Creek two miles north of Caldwell.

"to books" and to meals. Some of the teachers would say to Josephine, a second-generation student at Baylor: "Listen, Joe, do you hear your grandfather's bell ringing?"

J. M. Carroll wrote that the bell was in use when he was a Baylor student. Carroll was graduated in 1877. The bell is now in the Texas Collection of Baylor University.

[84] Records show that Mr. Shannon appeared at the August 15, 1863, meeting of the Baylor board at Plantersville for the last time. He served as a trustee of Baylor for twenty years. He died on his Grimes County plantation in July 1865. Surviving descendants were son Aaron (born in 1858) and daughter Mary E. (born in 1860), who became Mrs. Andrew Roone Dillon; and grandson John (born in 1882), son of Thomas Brandon Shannon.

[85] Taylor's first service as trustee was to act as secretary pro tempore at the meeting on April 7, 1845, at Brenham and served until December 22, 1847, at which time Orin Drake recorded the minutes. Taylor helped secure the services of Baylor's first teacher and the first agent; served on committees to establish rules and regulations, rates and terms of tuition; and was the first trustee listed to supplement the salaries of the president and principal when funds were non-existent. The business acumen of Taylor was relied upon, for he was requested to serve as chairman of the committee to examine the books of agent James Huckins.

Thomas was educated to be a lawyer, but Morrell states that he had an early conviction to be a minister, despite great timidity that prevented even his praying in public.[86] Deacon Pruitt convinced him of his obligation, and he turned to the ministry.[87] *The Minutes of the Union Association* reveal that he served as clerk from 1844 to 1855.[88]

In a sketch written by R. E. B. Baylor, acknowledgement is made of the paucity of Thomas' "preaching talent," but the judge concludes that "no man was ever more watchful for the cause of the Master; and consequently, the churches under his care increased in numbers greatly beyond those that were blessed with more talented ministers."[89] Thomas was a man of deep convictions and served both church and state with unselfish devotion.[90]

Thus Baylor University owes her existence to courageous Texas Baptist pioneers. Judge R. E. B. Baylor, Reverend William M. Tryon, and Reverend James Huckins and other members of Texas Baptists' first organized body—the Union Baptist Association—knew that education was a necessary ingredient in their pioneer society. They adopted the familiar

[86] Morrell, pp. 232-233.

[87] A small Bible bears this handwritten record: Jesse G. Thomas was ordained to preach in July, 1851, in the town of Caldwell, Texas. "The first sermon preached from this volume was on the 4th Lord's Day in December, 1870 at Leona, Leon County, by the owner, J. G. Thomas. He had immersed in his ministrations, in all, up to the first of September 1874, twelve hundred and seventeen persons all in Texas in various counties."

[88] In 1863 the Baptist State Convention, meeting at Independence, sent him along with William T. Wright, J. S. Allen, and J. W. D. Creath, as a missionary to Confederate soldiers. Again in 1865 the State Convention sent him "to carry on evangelistic work." In 1871 Thomas was a delegate from the Trinity Church at Centerville, Leon County, to the Trinity River Association, where he served as chairman of the Committee on the Condition of Colored People and as missionary for the association. *Minutes of Trinity River Association*, pp. 4-5.

[89] Judge Baylor, "Reminiscences."

[90] Thomas was a delegate from Fannin County to the Congressional District meeting at Henderson, Rusk County, June 9, 1851. The purpose of the convention was to nominate a Democrat able to defeat a Whig candidate, states the August 14, 1852, *Texas State Gazette*. In 1852 Thomas was listed as secretary to a Democratic Ratification meeting held in Caldwell, Burleson County, on July 10. He was a candidate for "Floating Representative" of Fannin, Hopkins, and Red River Counties, states the July 9, 1853, *Northern Standard*.

J. G. Thomas died at Caldwell on September 18, 1875, and was buried beside his first wife who died in 1845 shortly after arrival in Texas. Two years later Thomas had married a widow, Mrs. Sara Ann Eldridge; after her death he married Amelia Dawson of Crockett in 1871. Two sons were born to this union: Jesse Gilbert Thomas, Jr., who died in 1904, never having married; and William Rufus Thomas (named for his father's close friend, President Rufus C. Burleson), who married Fannie B. Goree of Navasota.

pattern of a church-sponsored education society. Organized without delay, the Texas Baptist Education Society had as its immediate aim the establishing of an academic and theological institution. The need for an educated ministry was of prime significance, but the announcement of Huckins in 1844 evidenced both wisdom and foresight. The resolve was to found an institution to meet existing conditions and allow for enlargement and development to meet the needs of all ages to come. The fifteen original trustees faced a Gargantuan responsibility.

CHAPTER III

The Locale of Baylor University

BY MAY 15, 1845, the Baylor Board of Trustees was organized at Brenham with R. E. B. Baylor as president pro tempore. It was in session at Mt. Gilead Church on October 13, 1845, for the purpose of receiving bids for the location of Baylor University. The following propositions were considered:

Travis, in Austin County (south of Brenham)	$3,586.25	submitted by Eli Mercer
Huntsville, in Montgomery County (now Walker)	$5,417.75	submitted by Rev. Stovall
Shannon's Prairie, in Montgomery County (east of Navasota)	$4,725.00	submitted by Aaron Shannon
Independence, Washington County	$7,925.00	submitted by E. W. Taylor[1]

These bids did not represent cash but an evaluation of "75 cents per acre on all uncultivated land, and the price of town property at what such property might be sold for in cash." Other considerations complicated the estimates. The following list constituted the bid of one town:

One Section of Land
One Yoke of Oxen
Five Head of Cattle
One Cow and Calf
One Bay Mare
One Bale of Cotton
Twenty Days Hauling
Cash, $200.00[2]

The site was selected by ballot; Independence received ten votes and Huntsville one. "In 1845, Independence was an excellent choice for a university . . . [for] Washington

[1] Minutes of the Baylor Board of Trustees, May 16, 1845.
[2] Harry Haynes, Part I "Biography of Rufus C. Burleson," *The Life and Writings of Rufus C. Burleson* (compiled and published by Georgia J. Burleson, 1901), p. 106.

County led the state in wealth, population, and influence."[3]
And Washington County, with the two towns—Independence
and Washington-on-the-Brazos—would be the focal points
of support for the new educational venture.

Independence, formerly the village known as Coles' Settlement, dating back to 1824 on land patented by Mexico,
was described by the "thoroughgoing cane-brake Baptist
preacher," Z. N. Morrell, as "looking more like dependence
than independence" in 1837. He was directed there by
pioneer missionary N. T. Byars in search of ammunition
for the commander of the fort at the Falls on the Brazos.
Such was the appearance of all Texas towns, he recalled
forty years later, "—not a very interesting place, when the
stream is swollen . . . and the stream *was* swimming for
about thirty feet in the main channel—the whole bottom,
nearly three miles wide, was a sea of water—no bridge."[4]
Nevertheless Coles' Settlement became the home and the
gathering place of many Texas heroes and statesmen. It was
termed the "Cradle of Liberty" and the "Little Williamsburg of Texas," and, like Rome, set upon seven hills. It was
a spirited town. Here in 1836 when Texas became a republic,
many of the signers of the Texas Declaration of Independence came from Washington-on-the-Brazos to spend the
night and to place a Texas flag in the town square. Enthusiasm ran high, and Dr. Asa Hoxey initiated a movement to
name the town *Independence*, as it is known to this day.

Even before Independence became a town, the area
was of historical significance. During a bitter winter night
Stephen F. Austin had camped in the area with his group
of colonists—his first New Year's Day in Texas. A landmark
at the Settlement was the Toalson House, built by the
Mexican Government in 1835 and used as a jail. Its two-
foot-thick adobe walls of Spanish influence still stand.[5]

A two-story store building boasted a broad veranda with
four tall white columns. The two hotels, private homes of
their owners, were the Lydia Hood House and the Blanton

[3] Michael Allen White, "History of Baylor University, 1845-1861," (unpublished Master's thesis, Baylor University, 1962), p. 23.
[4] Z. N. Morrell, *Flowers ond Fruits in the Wilderness* (3rd. ed., St. Louis:
Commercial Printing Company, 1882), p. 57.
[5] The building is now owned by Mr. and Mrs. C. Fount Toalson and is used
as a residence. Mrs. Toalson and her sister, Mrs. Lucille Wasson, are great
granddaughters of Dr. Hoxey.

House. Both were filled with Victorian horsehair sofas, drop-leaf tables, and spool beds—later to become collectors' items. The dining rooms were spacious and often used for church affairs. The Lydia Hood House was the scene of quilting bees when the Baptist ladies made covers for orphans. The Methodist ladies favored the Blanton House for their church suppers. Upstairs at the Blanton House was the Masonic Hall—Masons did not meet on the ground floor because of the secrecy of their ritual. Milam Lodge Number 11 was founded on February 2, 1840; R. E. B. Baylor, James Huckins, William M. Tryon, and other Baptist leaders held membership. Here young Henry L. Graves was to be initiated on December 9, 1849, after he assumed his duties as the first president of Baylor University.

On the town square was a building of general interest and utility—the stone structure housing the John McKnight drug store. Two large bow windows displayed amber and blue bottles of medicines along with fine old apothecary jars. Largest sales were for quinine—the prescribed treatment for malaria; next came calomel and castor oil. Owner John McKnight "helped Judge Baylor found Baylor University," averred townsmen.

Center of interest in the infant township was the Baptist church, organized in September 1839 by Elders T. W. Cox and Thomas Spraggins with eleven members. Charter members were John, Jay, Mary, and Jeanette McNeese; J. J. and Biddy Davis; Thomas and Martha Tremmier, "with O. P. H. Garrett, J. L. Davis and wife, and J. D. Allcorn and wife joining soon after."[6] An adobe structure built in 1849 was destroyed by fire, but the church was rebuilt of native stone and floored in cedar in 1872.

The Reverend T. W. Cox was the first pastor of the church, as well as two other new churches—Travis and La Grange. Because of a charge of preaching the doctrines of Alexander Campbell and a dismissal from the Talladega church in Alabama, Cox was excluded from the church at Independence at a council meeting of Morrell, Byars, Buffington, and others. Judge R. E. B. Baylor, away performing his duties as district judge, missed the trial, but he requested

[6] J. M. Dawson, "Missions and Missionaries," *Centennial Story of Texas Baptists*, ed. Harlan J. Matthews and others (Dallas, Texas: Baptist General Convention of Texas, 1936), p. 27.

the church to deal charitably with the affair concerning a writ of attachment issued against the property of Cox in Alabama.[7]

Despite the unfortunate circumstances of the pastor's dismissal, the church rallied and became a vital force in the Union Association.[8] Independence was not alone in her church troubles. An examination of the Minutes of the Union Association from 1841 until 1857 reveals that some 307 individuals were "excluded from membership" in the various churches, whose total membership did not exceed 2,178 at any time during the period. Matters of doctrine and private lives were of utmost concern to these devout Baptists. But Judge Baylor voiced alarm over undue preoccupation with minor doctrinal matters in a "circular letter" from the association on October 8-9, 1840:

> Should our little churches therefore be tenacious about these non-essentials, they will remain disjoined, and thus broken in fragments they will perish away.

One church brought to the associational meeting this query: "What course shall be taken in receiving those persons in the church who are separate from their companions?" The resultant recommendation of the body was that "the churches act agreeable to the circumstances governing the case, always having an eye single to the glory of God and the true disciples of the Gospel."[9] At the 1844 meeting, the assembly decided to excommunicate members "convicted of heinous crimes"—such as murder, adultery, theft, swin-

---

[7] Letter from Baylor to Brother Stribling, "Holly Oak," April 13 (no year on MS). Texas Collection, Baylor University.

[8] Ten of 38 annual meetings of the Old Baptist State Convention and most of the meetings of the executive board were held at the Independence church. Baylor University was closely identified with the church: ministers and laymen active in the convention were Baylor trustees and members of the Independence church; four Baylor presidents also served as pastors—Graves, Baines, Burleson, and Crane. James H. Stribling and Principal Horace Clark were ordained there in 1849 and 1858 respectively. Pastors of Independence Baptist Church during the Baylor period were the following:

Thomas Spraggins	1839	Rufus C. Burleson	1854-1856
(temporarily)		H. C. Renfro	1857
T. W. Cox	1839-1841	Michael Ross	1858-1864
W. M. Tryon	1841-1846	William C. Crane	1864-1867
Henry L. Graves	1847-1850	Henry C. Buckner	1867-1869
George W. Baines	1850-1852	William C. Crane	1869-1884
S. G. O'Bryan	1852-1853	George W. Pickett	1884-1885

[9] Minutes of Union Association, November 22, 1842, Called Meeting, p. 34. Handwritten original in Texas Collection, Baylor University.

dling, and counterfeiting money. No confession was necessary, and individuals twice convicted of drunkenness in a short space of time were dealt with in the same manner.[10]

Doctrinal issues were a disruptive force among Texas Baptists in the early years. Union Association moved that William M. Tryon in delivering the associational sermon for 1846 be requested to set forth the principles of the Baptist denomination. Following that address Brother J. G. Thomas moved "That this association deems it a breach of good order and Baptist usage for the members of our churches to commune with Pedo Baptists."[11] In line with the rigidity of their beliefs, these devout pioneers had declared Christmas Day 1842 a day of fasting and praying. A few years later they went on record with the recommendation that heads of families conduct family prayer.[12]

Despite the hardships of their rugged existence, when even the ministers of the gospel carried guns on horseback over the unchartered prairies, these early Texans had visions of a better world and made practical plans for their attainment. First they realized the significance of religious leadership in a land where churches and schools were yet non-existent or in their infancy. Serious indeed was their commitment to their church. Independence Baptist Church was a focal point; it became the home of the Union Association out of which developed the Texas Baptist Convention. Today portraits of pioneer church members line the walls in tribute to dedicated service. (See Appendix)

In 1845 Independence boasted several pioneer homes destined to become landmarks. The John P. Coles home was the first of these. Intimate friend of Stephen F. Austin, John P. Coles, Alcalde of Washington Municipality and delegate to the Convention of 1833, built the public house which gave the community its first name, Coles' Settlement. Coles was a friend to government officials in the United States, Texas, and Mexico.[13] Even before the war for independence from Mexico, the Settlement was known afar.

---

[10] *Ibid.*, p. 66.
[11] *Ibid.*, p. 84. "Pedo Baptists" practiced infant baptism.
[12] *Ibid.*, October 2, 1848.
[13] Mrs. Gertrude McCrocklin of Independence, whose husband, John Coles McCrocklin, was a grandson of John P. Coles, held in her possession a letter dated July 15, 1833, from Coles to Anthony Butler, U. S. Ambassador to Mexico, regarding Stephen F. Austin.

Colonel Austin wrote Gail Borden: "You might get some men from Coles' Settlement to go for the cannon at Tenoxtitlan. . . ." Coles was also a friend to Borden and had asked him to come from the Galveston area to the Settlement to survey some land in 1834. Borden's reply had been: "Should come myself, but am unable." Hence he sent a substitute. Coles, a pioneer from North Carolina, initiated educational interest in Washington County; and his daughter, the first white child born in the county, was destined to become a student at Baylor University in 1851, along with her sisters and brother.[14] John P. Coles died January 19, 1847, and was buried at Independence.

Jessie L. McCrocklin was the builder of another of these pioneer dwellings. McCrocklin and his wife, Isabella Harris, from Owensboro, Kentucky, settled his headright in territory near Independence soon after 1832. They built a cedar log house just outside of the village. It was later occupied by Judge Coles, a friend and relative by marriage to Isabella. The hospitable McCrocklins sometimes entertained as many as thirty-five at dinner. Just prior to the Revolution, Sam Houston, Dr. Asa Hoxie, Nestor Seward, and Jerome Robertson were guests. Jesse fought in the Battle of San Jacinto and was retained as a colonel of volunteers, returning home in the winter of 1836-37 with a bullet in his arm. With the improvement of his health he farmed and raised blooded horses. A man of impetuous spirit, he bet his farm on a horse race, lost, and moved his family to Blanco County in 1853.[15]

The Asa Hoxie home was the most renowned of the Washington County area. One of Austin's "Old Three Hundred," Dr. Asa Hoxie came to Coles' Settlement in 1826 and is said to have owned all the land on one side of the road from Independence to Brenham, a distance of over twelve miles. His two-story frame home, built in 1833, became headquarters for many famous people who made their way to Texas in the early days. A French cabinetmaker took a year

[14] Records show the following registrations at Baylor for the Coles family: Eliza and Victoria, 1851-52; Madora, 1857, 1859-60; William H., 1851-57. The diary of Bettie Graves Jones, daughter of President Graves, reveals that the girls were Baylor students also in 1858-59. Diary in possession of granddaughter, Mrs. J. L. Russell.
[15] Annie Doom Pickrell, *Pioneer Women in Texas* (Austin: E. L. Steck Company), p. 143.

to panel the walls and ceiling of "the parlors." Furnishings included Louis XV period pieces shipped from France to New York to New Orleans and brought to Independence by oxcart. Velvet carpets and handsome rugs—one representing Diana Vernon in the chase described by Sir Walter Scott in *Red Gauntlet*—candelabra, jardiniers, and large ornate mirrors added touches of luxury. Drapery cornices were washed with gold. Dr. Hoxie and his wife, Elizabeth Bennett, "subscribed to all the English magazines" and maintained an extensive library.[16] The Hoxie home was one of the showplaces of Texas. President of the Republic, General Mirabeau B. Lamar visited the home, became ill, and remained six months awaiting recovery. General Houston and his staff were entertained there on their way to San Jacinto. The story is told of Houston's taking in his arms the two-year-old Hoxie daughter and saying: "If this baby smiles, I shall win, but if she frowns, I shall lose the battle."[17] She smiled. When Dr. Henry L. Graves became president of Baylor University, he stayed at the Hoxie's until he could establish his own home.

Hoxie was an eminent physician, coming from Alabama in 1832 to buy land on the recommendation of Robert McAlpin "Three-Legged-Willie" Williamson, famous Texas barrister.[18] Dr. Hoxie became a prominent citizen: he signed the petition to organize the municipality of Washington on July 2, 1835; his name appeared in the announcement of Frances Trask's school in the *Texas Republican* in 1834; along with William Travis, James Bowie, Edward Burleson, R. M. Williamson, and Alexander Horton, he is listed by

[16] Mrs. S. L. Shipe, Sunday Magazine Supplement *Galveston News,* Horace Clark Scrapbook, Texas Collection, Baylor University.

[17] Houston had known Dr. Hoxie since 1835 as a member of the Consulation and the General Council of the provisional government. He had subsequently named him a medical censor of the Republic. Walter Prescott Webb and H. Bailey Carroll (eds.), *The Handbook of Texas* (Austin: Texas State Historical Association, 1952), I, 856.

[18] Asa Hoxie to R. M. Williamson, Dec. 2, 1832, Reprint, *Quarterly of the Texas State Historical Association,* IX, 285.

The Williamsons named their first son Hoxie Collingsworth (died in infancy) in honor of Dr. Hoxie and Chief Justice James Collingsworth. In 1847, at nearby Old Washington, the distinguished James R. Jenkins, member of the Congress of the Republic, named his son Warwick Hoxie, for their much beloved family physician. Asa Williams, who occupied the Nancy Lea home after her death, was also named for his illustrious grandfather. As late as 1882 records show that a sub-junior student, Hoxie Williams, won a silver medal as the "2nd best speller."

historians as a member of the *War Party*. He is named among
the petitioners for a charter for the academy at Independence, on May 23, 1837, as well as that for Washington College, and served on the board of each institution. Dr. Hoxie
was interested in providing the opportunity for education
for his own two children and those of his neighbors. [19]

Jerome Bonaparte Robertson was another Texan who
began medical practice at Washington-on-the-Brazos and
came to Independence for educational advantages for his
family. Born in 1815 in the same Kentucky county as
R. E. B. Baylor, he studied medicine in Owensboro and was
graduated from Transylvania in 1835. As captain of a company of eighty-six volunteers, he came to Texas to aid Sam
Houston. He was too late for San Jacinto but remained as
a captain in the Army of the Republic. Robertson was an
Indian fighter in the campaign against Woll in 1842 and
became a brigadier general of Hood's Brigade. He married
Mary Cummins, whose sister married Willet Holmes. Both
families were closely identified with the founding of Baylor
University.

Almost aloof from the rest of the village one mile south,
the Robertson house was built in 1845 and is still standing.
A memorial marker on the spot pays tribute to Dr. Robertson
who is said to have possessed "all the noblest qualities that
adorn humanity." The pioneer doctor, close friend of Judge
Baylor, took a lively interest in Texas politics as a delegate
to the Secession Convention and subsequently as a member
of each house of the Legislature. Julia and Felix Robertson
(the latter born in Washington County in 1832 and later
a graduate of West Point and a Civil War general) were to
be among the earliest students at Baylor, the struggling
university which received Dr. Robertson's benefactions.

Albert G. Haynes selected a beautiful live-oak grove as
the locale for the home he built for his wife Matilda. He
had come to Texas from Georgia, spending two years in
Alabama and eight in Mississippi. At once he became a
civic leader in Independence. He was induced by the citizens

[19] Dr. Hoxie's will revealed a substantial pledge for the endowment fund
of the Chair of Natural Science. Sally and Tom, his children, were enrolled
at Baylor from 1848-49. Thomas Hoxie, "as handsome as Apollo," was a
Civil War casualty.

to serve as justice of the peace, an office he held for two years without fee.

In 1843 he was ordained a deacon of the Independence Baptist Church and served as treasurer and moderator of the Union Association. About him Judge R. E. B. Baylor said, "Any man can preach far better after hearing Brother Haynes sing one of those good old songs with his heart overflowing with love and his eyes full of tears." Albert Haynes, as a trustee, was destined to become a guiding force and benefactor of the infant Baylor University.

E. W. Taylor and John Bancroft Root headed two prominent families living at Independence prior to mid-century. The two men were brothers-in-law. Root and Taylor joined in pledging the Independence Female Academy building (which they had bought at a sheriff's sale) to cinch the location of Baylor University at Independence instead of Huntsville. Root built for his wife Mary Porter a handsome two-story porticoed home of cedar with some yellow pine brought by oxcart from a little sawmill at Ticklefoot, between Anderson and Huntsville. The cedar was of local origin, cut and ferried across the Brazos.[20]

Taylor was to serve as the first recording-secretary of the Baylor Board of Trustees. Cora and Rose Taylor and cousin Sandy Root (later a Yale graduate) were to represent their families at Baylor during the school's first years.[21]

Nancy Lea, mother of Mrs. Sam Houston, owned a home diagonally across from the Root Home which Margaret Lea Houston purchased when she returned to Independence after

[20] The home was purchased by Mrs. Houston not long after the death of Sam Houston at Huntsville on July 26, 1863. This was the house where former slave Joshua brought $2,000 in gold and silver—his savings from blacksmithing—and placed it at widowed Margaret Houston's feet when the Confederacy crumbled and her needs were many. She declined his gift and asked him to use it for the education of his children. He did, and one son, Sam Houston, became president of Sam Houston Normal Training School for Colored at Huntsville. R. Henderson Shuffler, *The Houstons at Independence* (Waco, Texas: Texian Press, 1966), p. 34. The Root house was later bought by W. L. Williams, a Baylor trustee.

Margaret Lea, born in Perry County, Alabama, on April 11, 1819, was married to General Sam Houston in the Lea home in Marion on May 9, 1840. They occupied a series of homes: Cedar Point, Chambers County, Texas, and Galveston in 1840-41; Old Washington-on-the-Brazos in 1842; Grand Cane, about 20 miles north of Liberty in 1843-44; Raven Hill Plantation, about 14 miles east of Huntsville in 1847-53; Independence in 1853-56; Huntsville in 1856-59; Austin in 1860-61; Cedar Point in 1861-62; Huntsville in 1862-63, where Houston died.

[21] Information supplied by Mrs. E. A. Peden.

her husband's death. The front portion of the Lea home was one large room below with a half-story above. For a period in the 1840's the house was headquarters for a representative of the Queen of England. The Lea House became a social center for Baylor students and gave shelter to ministerial students who were in financial need. In the corner of the drawing room was a small stairway. On the stair-landing was an opening into the attic of the one-story addition. Here Mrs. Lea kept her metallic coffin, which served as her store-house for tea, sugar, and spices—unharmed by the "colored help," declared descendant Temple Houston Morrow. The big rambling L-shaped house later became the home of Mrs. Gertie McCrocklin, who recalled the nearby springhouse and the remark of Sam Houston: "The water's free as long as it lasts." Even today the Houston spring furnishes water for Independence families. When Sam Houston and wife Margaret Lea first came to Independence in 1853, they occupied the Thomas Barron home, built in 1837. A stone marks the site of this old home.

The Clay home interested chroniclers of pioneer Texas.[22] Son Tacitus was highly educated in Latin and Greek and conferred on his children such names as Atreus, Thetis, Tula, and Leila, who married the only son of Dr. Asa Hoxie. Descendants referred to him as an eccentric Tolstoy in that he dined and dressed simply, frequently without shoes. He was a large landowner and supplied the country-side with fruits from his orchards just for the gathering. Independence historian Madge Hearne declared that the four-story stone Clay home was "almost a castle." It was well known for its two great halls, each ninety feet in length, and a large third floor glassed-in ballroom for the gay dances frequently held there. Eldest son, Captain Thomas C. Clay, and wife Elizabeth Robertson reared their family of seven children in "The Castle." When Independence was incorporated in 1859, Tacitus Clay became mayor.

[22] Nestor Clay's name appears on the first tax roll of Washington County. A distant relative of Henry Clay, he had come to Texas from Kentucky with Austin's Colony in 1834 as a surveyor, receiving a league of land for each league he surveyed. Gracey Booker Toland, *Austin Knew His Athens* (San Antonio, Texas: The Naylor Company, 1958), p. 10. His mastery of the English language earned him the title of "the inimitable." A stone in the Texas State Cemetery at Austin marks his grave: Nestor Clay, 1799-1833, "Master Spirit of the Convention 1832."

Major Moses Austin Bryan, nephew of Stephen F. Austin, built a large two-story residence on the outskirts of Independence. Bryan was born at Sainte Genevieve, Missouri; he came to Texas in 1831 and became secretary to Austin in 1835 and later to General Edward Burleson. As a boy of eighteen he fought in the Battle of San Jacinto and, because of his fluent Spanish, served as interpreter for Santa Anna at his surrender to General Houston. The stately home was approached through a long avenue of trees. Nearby was the home of Colonel Thomas Power, whose wife was Mrs. Sam Houston's sister.

The Blue home, not far from the Old Plaza and north of the Female Academy, was built by early settlers in 1843. The eighteen-inch walls of the lower story were made of rock acquired from a hill a few yards west. The rooms were twenty by twenty and the interior was finished with mud mortar said to be as smooth as marble. The second story was frame. Long porches extended the length of both the first and second floors. James Harvey Blue was to live in the home sixty-eight years.

Samuel Seward and his wife Anna Stewart—relative of J. E. B. Stewart—were "rebels," although they belonged to the same family as William M. Seward, Secretary of State in Abraham Lincoln's administration. They came to Texas in an 1828 wagon train and to Coles' Settlement on Christmas Eve of 1833. The Samuel Seward home, begun around 1834 by Negro labor, has been termed "the first two-story house in South Texas." From its cupola old-timers aver "you could see forty miles." Broad verandas completely crossed the front of the house. Students of early Texas architecture have studied the width of its windows, the height of its doors and the fan lights that crown them, for the house-plans and specifications are recorded in the Congressional Library in Washington as typifying design and construction of Texas Colonial architecture.[23] A huge single rock formed the hearth before a fireplace, and it was kept burnished by little Negro children who rubbed the surface with a smaller stone.

Originally located about a mile from its present site, the home was moved on cedar logs to its present location on a

[23] Gertrude S. Wilson, "Trip to Independence," *Waco Tribune-Herald,* Sunday, May 28, 1950.

"rock bed." No sawmill existed in the area at the time of construction; so the pine floors upstairs were "brought in." The Sewards came from Illinois, bringing most of their furniture by oxcart. Secured later was a rare single-canopy bed and a dresser with a five-foot mirror that once belonged to Carrie Nation, declared descendant Colonel Oscar A. Seward, Jr., of Brenham. A plaque marks the location as the home of John Goblett Seward (1822-1892) and Laura Jane Roberts Seward (1839-19—).

Judge Abner S. Lipscomb was another pioneer with a Baylor-related history who settled at Independence in 1839. His plantation home was a "visiting stop" on the stage road between Washington and Independence.

Other families identified with Independence life and directly or indirectly with early Baylor were those of Amos Gates; James, Henry, and Boulin Whitesides; Shubal Marsh; John and Levi Pitts; Captain Lewis Kraatz, a soldier in Napoleon's army; James and Asa Willis, nephews of Dr. Hoxie; Jonas Rivers, lawyer; Mrs. Nancy Payne Edney of Tennessee, who sent her three children to Baylor; George B. Hice, one of Austin's "Three Hundred," who married Maria Coles; Moses Cummins, surveyor and original trustee of Independence Academy; Charles Carter Hairston of Georgia, whose wife Caroline, after his death in 1851, married John McKnight; the Breedloves and the Davises, both merchant families.

Independence was a tight little community by the 1840's, united by common needs and intermarriages. A study of the early tax rolls shows the relationship of names and the custom of naming children for relatives and friends. Slaves also received meaningful names. One is said to have rattled off her name so fast that "it ran together"—Caroline—Victoria—Roxianna—Hielow—Jenny Lind—Patty Patterson! A stable boy was named Albert Edward Prince of Wales because he was born when the Prince of Wales visited America.[24]

Such was the picture of Independence in 1845. Sturdy pioneer families had braved the hardships of the new land, and they were there to stay. The township seemed the logical place to locate a university.

[24] Toland, p. 13.

Independence may have been the "Athens of Texas," but about twelve miles across the prairie was its rival Washington, on the south bank of the Brazos just below its confluence with the Navasota. The bustling river-town was laid out by owner Captain John W. Hall, whose father-in-law, Andrew Robinson, had operated a ferry there since 1822. Located at a vital point, the ferry served the traffic on the old Bahia Road. During the winter of 1833 John W. Kennedy built the first home in the area, which was to be the population center of the country for fifty years. Hall conducted the first auction of town lots on January 8, 1836.[25]

Hardy pioneers had followed many of Austin's "Old Three Hundred" into the area, traveling overland by ox-wagon or by steamboat up the Brazos. Regular runs were made between Washington and Velasco and Quintana by the *Mustang*, the *Lady Byron*, and the *Washington*. Two boats weekly arrived at the wharves of Washington, the point of distribution of merchandise for central Texas. Imports were limited to basic necessities. One contemporary bewailed the breaking of all her household china on the rough overland route to Washington and the absence of any crockery in the town of some twenty buildings. Tinware with red-lettered aphorisms from Franklin's *Poor Richard's Almanac* became the substitute.

Washington-on-the-Brazos gained its first political fame by becoming the cradle of Texas liberty when the hastily formed Texas government called a convention at the tiny settlement of a hundred or so inhabitants on March 1, 1836. Virginia Colonel William Fairfax Gray, a visitor with hopes of becoming secretary of the convention,[26] described Washington as "a rare place to hold a national convention in. It is laid out in the woods; about a dozen wretched cabins and shanties constitute the city; not one decent house in it, and only one well-defined street, which consists of an opening cut out of the woods, the stumps still standing."[27] Many of the cabins were dirt-floored and contained hand-hewn furniture.

[25] *Telegraph and Texas Register,* December 26, 1835, an advertisement.

[26] R. Henderson Shuffler, "The Signing of Texas' Declaration of Independence: Myth and Record," *The Southwestern Historical Quarterly,* LXV (January 1962), 326.

[27] Lewis W. Newton and Herbert P. Gambrell, *A Social and Political History of Texas* (Dallas: Southwest Press, 1932), p. 174.

Gray stayed first at the John Lott Tavern near the river, one of the oldest establishments in the town—"the only place where fodder for horses was available." Gray reported that the frame structure with a fireplace at each end and a shed at the back, which served as a dining room, housed about thirty lodgers with the host, his wife, and children— "all in the same apartment, some on the beds, some on cots, but the greater part on the floor." The price of such accommodations during the time of the Republic was one dollar to one dollar and twenty-five cents per night—often in merchandise.[28] The combination of quarters and coarse food caused Gray to move to the Widow Mann's boarding house, where General Houston boarded.[29]

Such was the condition of the town where the Texas Declaration of Independence was signed. Romantic tradition declares that this document was signed on March 2, 1836, in the blacksmith shop of Noah Turner Byars. Louis Wiltz Kemp[30] and Shuffler[31] conclude that the date was March 3 and the place was a newly constructed building on Main Street just off Ferry Street.[32] Cotton cloth partially held back the "norther" from the windowless, doorless, unfinished wooden structure in thirty-three degree weather. On a long, rough table the fifty-nine delegates signed the documents and the papers of the convention under the direction of its president, Judge Richard Ellis, and secretary, H. S. Kimble.[33]

[28] Ellen Garwood, "Early Texas Inns: A Study in Social Relationships," *The Southwestern Historical Quarterly*, LX (October 1956), 224.

[29] Mrs. Mann later operated a hotel in Houston that rivalled the famed Fanthrop Inn at Anderson in Grimes County, the Whiteside Hotel at San Felipe, or the Berry Hotel at San Augustine. Mody C. Boatright (ed.), *Mexican Border Ballads and Other Lore* (Austin: 1946), p. 115.

[30] Louis Wiltz Kemp, *The Signers of the Texas Declaration of Independence* (Salado: Anson Jones Press, 1959), p. xviii.

[31] Shuffler, pp. 310-332.

[32] A plat of the town of "Washington City," preserved by freedman Jim Johnson and owned by A. W. Hartstock of Washington County, shows the roads from two ferries converging at the top of the bluff where the town is located. These two "streets" were Ferry and Main, with the City Market in the center of the latter.

Byars and Peter M. Mercer, owners of the building used as convention hall, expected the convention to last for three months, but rumors of the approach of the Mexican Army caused adjournment on March 17, with most of the citizens joining the "Runaway Scrape." The building owners were unpaid by the eleven men who signed the rental agreement; hence after an unsuccessful law suit Byars addressed two petitions to the Third Legislature on December 20, 1849, asking for the promised sum of $168.00.

[33] A list of 59 names appears on the memorial tablet erected by the State of Texas in 1936 at the site.

Spectators wandered in and out quietly to avoid disturbing the proceedings. Byars and Ellis were both Baptists, and the news of the convention reached the citizens of the new republic through the heroic efforts of Baptist-to-be Gail Borden and his *Telegraph* of San Felipe de Austin.[34]

A study of the members of this convention reveals many interesting things about the nature and background of the early Texans. In describing his entry into Texas, Morrell had written: "We now began to realize the truth of what we had so often heard, that Texas was a place of refuge for scoundrels." He rather expected the query from the ferryman: "And, gentleman, what have you done that you have come to Texas?"[35] Another writer refers to "G.T.T."—letters indicating "Gone to Texas" appearing on ledgers as bad accounts. Those who composed the convention were of other ilk, however. Despite the fact that they did not know at what moment they might be forced to flee or disband, they set about the business of declaring independence, framing a constitution, and providing for the defense of the infant republic. Forty of the delegates assembled were under forty years of age; nearly all came from the southern states —eleven came from the Carolinas, two were native Texans, and one came from England, one from Spain, one from Ireland, and one from Scotland. Richardson declared that "the body would not suffer in comparison with the constituent assemblies that formed the fundamental laws of other American states," and they completed their work in a shorter period than almost any other similar body in American history.[36]

To escape the panic-striking march of Santa Anna, the Texas government took flight to Harrisburg and thence to Galveston Island. After the Battle of San Jacinto, the treaty of peace was signed at Velasco; then Columbia became the capital of the first permanent government of the

[34] The *Telegraph and Texas Register,* the most influential of early Texas newspapers, was established on October 10, 1835. In May 1842 F. H. Harrison began publication of the *Texas and Brazos Farmer,* and in the fall "Ram Rod" Johnson established *The National Vindicator;* in December 1844 Miller and Cashney brought out the *National Register* at $5 a year; in 1845 Judge E. H. Erving started the *Lone Star and Southern Watchman;* in 1847 Captain Lancaster founded the *Texas Ranger,* then moved to Navasota and subsequently to Austin; in 1851 W. J. Pendleton of Virginia established the *Washington American.*

[35] Morrell, p. 30.

[36] Eugene C. Barker (ed.), *History of Texas* (Dallas: The Southwest Press, 1929), p. 250.

Republic of Texas. Houston was the seat of government from December 15, 1836, until the meeting of Congress in 1839 at Austin. The "Archive War" caused further complications, and Old Washington-on-the-Brazos again became the capital of the Republic in September 1842. Life there had changed after San Jacinto:

> . . . the glory of the town had departed with the government. Gunsmith Byars organized a Baptist Church, while his neighbor, Mr. John W. Hall, laid out a race track and began to breed quarter horses. A visiting clergyman in 1840 found there a "remarkable devotion" to the race course.
>
> . . . . .
>
> The faro banks along Main Street and the saloons of John Rumsy and B. M. Hatfield, "who sold only for cash, consequently did not commend the trade that was given to his rival." The highly respectful resident population of 250 watched with impotent disapproval the doings of the hundred or so gamblers, horse racers and sports, who had most of the money. The moral situation had been markedly, if temporarily, improved during the summer of 1841, when the Reverend W. M. Tryon and the Honorable and Reverend R. E. B. Baylor held a protracted meeting in Independence Hall. "Over half the town joined the church, which had a good effect on the inhabitants thereof."[37]

The *Christian Index,* November 19, 1841, carried Huckins' report of the revival in a letter to the Reverend Mr. Stow of New York: "This town has exceeded any town in the Republic for its wickedness," wrote Huckins. After the revival continued ten days and "100 came forward, a friend stated that grocery keepers had closed their shops, that every kind of business was laid aside, that vice had left the place and thirty had united with the church."

In many ways the town remained an isolated frontier community. Mail came by private messenger from Houston —a trip of three or four days, and Methodist minister John W. Kinney owned one of the two vehicles in the community. When the mobile, tired Texas Government returned to the little cluster of unpainted houses in the post-oak grove on the banks of the Brazos, every available space was used to house government officials. President Houston, "a little mud-spattered and bedraggled, entered his new capital astride a fine large pacing mule, which he called *Bruin.*"

[37] Herbert Gambrell, *Anson Jones* (Garden City, N.Y.: Doubleday, Inc., 1948), p. 263.

Texas experienced the third seat of government in ten months, and the tenth in the six years of its existence as the Republic. President Houston declared that it was unique in the history of nations, for it was "trying to exist without currency, without adequate revenue, without means of communication."[38] President and Mrs. Houston lived in Old Washington, and during his second term as president their first child was born on May 25, 1843, in a rude log home there. "Cousin Willie" (William P. Rogers), relative of Mrs. Houston, lived in Washington at the time, as did tavern owner S. R. "Esquire" Roberts, whose establishment Houston and convention delegates visited in 1836.

Senator Frosher, a minister, was employed as Chaplain of the Seventh Congress to replace Reverend W. M. Tryon, Chaplain of the Texas Congress held in Washington in 1843 and 1844. Senator Williamson, with great enthusiasm, had recommended Washington as the permanent home of the Supreme Court, declaring that town "a virtual repository of wisdom, asserting that the chief justice of the Republic had a library there of twenty-four hundred volumes."[39]

For some, Texas politics had a strong flavor before 1850. Williamson was such a thorough-going advocate of annexation that he named his son, born on January 13, 1845, *Annexus*! Few entertainments were as lively as election night frolics. Tables in the middle of Main Street held barbecued beef quarters and whiskey; and election winners rejoiced with lamp parades, music, and dancing.

Noah Smithwick recorded that Texas in these days was "a heaven for men and dogs, but a hell for women and oxen."[40] A feminine comment on the times at Washington-on-the-Brazos deserves notice, however, for it intones one distinct advantage:

. . . Texas is not the place for the old and decrepit but for the man fond of adventure. This he could always find; the man in search of fortune, if land would satisfy him, could secure it, or the man who loved life's shifting scenes spread out as it were upon a checker board, crowded with stirring events, which paled the cheeks and fired the hearts of those brave men, he could well feel that a single

[38] *Ibid.*, p. 267.
[39] Duncan W. Robinson, *Robert McAlpin Williamson* (Austin, Texas: Texas State Historical Association, 1948), p. 197.
[40] Noah Smithwick, *The Evolution of a State* (Austin, Texas: Gammel Book Company, 1900), p. 15.

hour here was worth an age of inglorious ease. Few women would scarcely have ventured down the street amid such crowds, and Fanny Fern's advantage of ugliness availed nothing, for woman's minority was so great that plainness of feature had lost its significance and all women were beautiful. . . .[41]

Texas' first missionary Baptist Church was established in 1837 at Washington-on-the-Brazos with Z. N. Morrell as pastor and H. R. Cartmell as deacon. From this church came the plea to the American Baptist Home Mission Society for missionaries to Texas which resulted in the coming of James Huckins and W. M. Tryon in 1840 and 1841. Because of removal of members from the area and numerous vicissitudes, the church was dissolved in 1838.

The summer "protracted meeting" held by Tryon and Baylor in Independence Hall was under the sponsorship of the Washington Church. Immediately after Elder William M. Tryon's location in the area in 1841, he and Elder R. E. B. Baylor reorganized the church at Washington on the second Sabbath in March. Organic members of the reorganized church were A. Buffington, N. Moore, J. L. Farquhar (later a Baylor trustee) and wife Huldah (and slaves John and Matilda), Ann Winfield, Eliza Crosby, Ann Moore, Rebecca Maxey, and Antoinette L. Bledsoe (sister of Mrs. Sam Houston). Tryon was named pastor, Farquhar deacon, and Buffington clerk. At the July 25 conference three persons were received by letter and twenty-nine by baptism. Messengers were elected to the Union Association to meet at La Grange in October and instructed to invite the association to hold its next meeting with the Washington church. Plans were made for a house of worship.

The church continued to receive new members, and Buffington was ordained to the ministry, with Elders Tryon, Huckins, and Baylor acting as the presbytery. W. H. Ewing was licensed to preach. Like other churches of the time, the Washington Church practiced watchcare over its members, as indicated by this entry in the Minutes:

. . . several were excluded, who had attended a ball, at the meeting in April. We deem it highly improper for members of the Baptist Church to send their children to dancing schools.

[41] Mrs. S. L. Shipe: "Old Washington in 1842," *Galveston News* (Magazine Section), July 23, 1905, p. 4.

The chief concern of the church became a suitable place of meeting, but no building was constructed for some time.[42] Pastors in addition to Tryon were the following:

B. B. Baxter, elected in May 1846.
R. C. Burleson, supply pastor, March 1852 (Baylor President).
J. B. Stiteler, December 1852 to December 1855 (Baylor professor).
R. C. Burleson, supply in February 1856.
Noah Hill, elected in November 1856 but could not accept.
Hill and Baxter preached occasionally in 1857-58.
A. W. Elledge, elected in June 1858.
R. B. Burleson, elected in March 1859 (Baylor professor).
Michael Ross, elected in March 1860.
Solomon Friend, "preached for three months" in 1862.
Michael Ross, re-elected in April 1863 and resigned in December because of ill health.
J. E. Paxton, December 1863 to November 1871.[43]
G. W. Baines, Jr., elected in January 1874.
J. M. Carroll, elected in 1877.

Just as at Independence, many illustrious Texans made their homes at Washington-on-the-Brazos. Some came with Austin's "Three Hundred" to make his first settlement in Texas; others were political figures in early Texas government; still others came to acquire land and new homes in what promised to be a prosperous area in Washington County.

Dr. Anson Jones, the last president of the Republic, moved his family to Washington-on-the-Brazos in 1844. Previously he had boarded at the home of James L. Farquhar, who became a Baylor trustee. In March of 1845 he occupied his new home, "Barrington," named for his Massachusetts residence.

The pre-Texas career of Anson Jones was varied and colorful. He was born at Great Barrington, Massachusetts, on January 20, 1789. Dissuaded by his parents, Solomon and Sarah (Strong) Jones, from becoming a minister, their thirteenth child studied medicine. He was licensed by the

---

[42] In October of 1850 Brother Jenkins was instructed to get a deed for the church lot. In April 1855 the group adopted a plan "to tax each head of a family in proportion to property on the assessor's roll, less indebtedness, to liquidate the present indebtedness and to pay for work under contract on the house of worship. Before the committee charged with the responsibility could perform, it was discharged and the order rescinded." J. B. Link, *Texas Historical and Biographical Magazine* I, 170-174.
[43] In 1866, the 125 colored members of the church separated and went into a church of their own, leaving the white membership at 62.

Oneida, New York, Medical Society and began practice in Bainbridge, then opened a drug store in Norwich—both unsuccessful ventures. Legal intervention by creditors detained him in Philadelphia where he taught until 1824; then he went to Venezuela for a two-year sojourn. Upon his return to Philadelphia, he again pursued medical practice, took an M.D. degree at Jefferson Medical College in 1827, and affiliated with both Masons and Odd Fellows, in which he attained high honors.

Because of meager practice, Jones renounced medicine and became a merchant in New Orleans. The cholera and yellow fever epidemics plus other factors contributed to another failure. Then Jeremiah Brown and John A. Wharton urged him to try Texas, where he soon had a $5000-a-year practice in Brazoria. Active in politics, he presented resolutions at Columbia in December 1835 favoring a convention to declare independence. During the war he served as surgeon of the Second Regiment under Robert S. Calder, but insisted on holding the rank of private in the infantry; then came service as "apothecary general of the Army" just at the war's end and his return to Brazoria.

Jones served as a representative to the Second Congress and was appointed by President Houston as minister to the United States in June 1838. President Mirabeau B. Lamar recalled him to Texas in May 1839, and he filled William H. Wharton's unexpired term in the Senate.

On May 17, 1840, Jones married Mrs. Mary Smith McCrory and declined the candidacy for vice-president. President Houston then named him secretary of state. Jones was elected president of Texas in September 1844 and took the oath of office on December 9 at Washington-on-the-Brazos. President Jones incurred disfavor because of his seeming vacillation concerning the annexation of Texas. The convention of 1845 even considered removing him from office. On February 19, 1846, he presided at the ceremony marking the annexation of Texas and gained the title of "Architect of Annexation." As President Jones concluded his address with "The Republic of Texas is no more," the flagstaff bearing the Lone Star broke as if in dramatic symbolism of the demise of the Republic, recorded observers. Then Judge R. E. B. Baylor offered the final prayer.

Ex-President Jones retired to Barrington to his wife and sons, Samuel,[44] Charles (who attended St. Paul's College which Jones helped found at Anderson), Anson Cromwell (named in honor of ancestor Oliver Cromwell), and daughter Sarah. "Barrington," the story-and-a-half plantation home built of hand-hewn timbers became "the Last White House of the Republic." One room of the house became a schoolroom, presided over by Mary, sister of Anson Jones. The library contained many books of historical, medical, and philosophical significance, as well as reams of correspondence, memoranda, diaries, and geneological manuscripts. Gambrell states that the top of the humidor of Anson Jones bore the Cromwell crest, as did the silver of the dining room. His was a proud heritage, dating in America from 1660. "Barrington" was located on the road to Independence, about four miles from Washington. There "the Last President of the Republic" spent his last uneasy years, pacing the wide center hall and the covered porch that led to the separate kitchen on the northeast corner of "Barrington." The political star of Washington-on-the-Brazos had set.

Jones brooded over his political career and became more despondent after an incurable injury to his left arm in 1849, and his life ended on January 9, 1858, in the Old Capitol Hotel of Houston, where he began his public career in the senate.[45] Jones served Texas in many capacities. He obtained the charter for the first Masonic Lodge in Texas (Holland Lodge No. 1, Houston) and was the first Most Worshipful Grand Master of Texas. He drafted the Constitution of the Independent Order of Odd Fellows and became their Grand Warden. He also helped frame the Constitution of Texas in 1836. His wife became the first president of the Daughters of the Republic of Texas. Jones was a charter member and vice-president of the Philosophical Society of Texas in 1837 and founder of the Medical Association in Texas.[46]

[44] Because of a deep animosity and resentment in being called "Houston's Shadow," Jones changed this son's name to Samuel *Edward*. Gambrell, p. 423.

[45] Jones was buried in Glenwood Cemetery of Houston. At Anson, in Jones County—both named in his honor—the Texas Centennial Commission erected a statute of the Last President of the Republic—the grantor of Baylor University's charter—"Barrington" was moved to the State Park at Washington-on-the-Brazos. Garland Adair, *Texas Pictorial Handbook* (Austin: Austin News Agency, May 1957), p. 37.

[46] Walter Prescott Webb and H. Bailey Carroll (eds.), *The Handbook of Texas* (Austin: Texas State Historical Association, 1952), I, 923.

John Lockwood evidently had a commodious home, for Gambrell records that he "entertained the president, his family, his private secretary, and acting secretary of war" when President Houston declared Washington the constitutional capital in September 1844. Since Washington had only one hotel but several saloons, the second floor of one, Major Hatfield's, reached by outside unpainted stairs, served as the meeting place of the House of Representatives. The Senate assembled across the street at W. M. Massie's store building. Space was at a premium, although "the proprietors of Washington" had proposed to furnish offices for the administration and suitable buildings for the Congress if the capital were moved there.

Robert McAlpin Williamson, c a l l e d "Three-Legged-Willie," lived on his farm at "Swisher's Post Office" on the road to Independence. Williamson was the champion of democracy and the Homestead Law and was the first major of the Texas Rangers. Fiery orator and propagandist and cousin of Mirabeau B. Lamar, he is credited with stirring up "one of the damnedest fights you ever saw"—the Texas Revolution. Williamson served five terms in the National Congress of the Republic and represented Milam and Washington counties in the Senate of the First and Second Legislatures of Texas as a state. Generous to a fault, this famous barrister let slip from his hands the greater portion of the money he received from the sale of enormous land grants acquired by his wife, who was as big-hearted as Williamson. Judge Charles L. Cleveland records that "Williamson's law office was a school without pay for every aspiring youth who desired an education or a profession. His pocketbook was the treasury of the needy and helpless."[47] In his closing years (1849-1859), Williamson liked to sit on his front porch in the summer evenings and play his banjo and sing— not as formerly when he would "pat jube" on his wooden leg as Noah Smithwick danced jigs and hornpipes—but he would sing spirituals, and the Negroes would join in the choruses. This is the same man who once prayed before a crowd of rustics in a drought-stricken area:

O Lord, Thou Divine Father, the supreme ruler of the Universe, Who holdest the Universe, Who holdest the thunder and the lighten-

⁴⁷ Robinson, p. 211.

ing in Thy hand, and from the clouds givest rain to make crops for
Thy children, who now face ruin for the lack of rain upon their
crops; and O Lord, send a bounteous rain that will cause the crops
to fruit in all their glory and the earth to turn again to that beauteous
green that comes from abundant showers. Lord, send us a bounteous
one that will make corn ears shake hands across the row and not
one of these little rizzy-dizzy rains that will make nubbins that all
hell can't shuck. [48]

At the Sixth Congress, Williamson indicated his interest
in the cause of education when he presented the petition of
the trustees of Washington College for a grant of land from
the Republic. [49] The colorful judge enrolled his second child,
Julia Rebecca, in Baylor. James and Asa Willie studied law
there. Asa Willie began practice at eighteen and became
attorney general during the administration of Governor
Pease.

Three other stalwart figures of Washington County just
prior to the founding of Baylor University were James
Huckins, William Milton Tryon on Hidalgo Bluff, and
Judge R. E. B. Baylor at "Holly Oak," Gay Hill. Machina-
tions of destiny brought them to this new land.

Now that Independence had won the bid for the proposed
Baylor University, the trustees were faced with the necessity
of organizing their body according to the charter granted
under the Republic of Texas and taking care of the business
at hand. The corporation was limited to "One Hundred
Thousand Dollars, over and above the buildings, library and
apparatus necessary to the Institution," a sum which proved
sufficient indeed for many years. The trustees were ordered
to have a "common seal for the business of themselves and
their successors, with liberty to change and alter the same
from time to time as they shall think proper." The trustees
were to meet annually, "at the time of conferring degrees,"
but the president might call other meetings when necessary.
The board of trustees was given the "power of prescribing
the course of studies to be pursued by the students and of
framing and enacting all such ordinances and by-laws as
shall appear to them necessary for the good government of
said university, and of their own proceedings: "Provided,

[48] Copy of prayer supplied by the late Waco Judge James D. Williamson,
grandson of petitioner.
[49] Harriet Smither (ed.), *Journals of the Sixth Congress of the Republic
of Texas*, 1841-1842, II, 185.

the same be not repugnant to the Constitution and laws of this Republic."

The head of the university was to be called the president, the male instructors thereof, professors; and the head of the Female Department, principal of said department. The trustees, "through the President or Professors," were given "the power to grant or confer such degree or degrees in the arts and sciences, to any of the students of the said University, or persons by them thought worthy, as are usually granted or conferred in other Universities, and to give diplomas or certificates thereof. . . ." Any vacancy to occur on the board of trustees was to be filled by the Executive Committee of the Texas Baptist Education Society. All salaries of the officers of the university were to be fixed by the trustees, and "the Professors of said University shall not be eligible to act as Trustee or Trustees for the same." The institution was declared to be free from any kind of public tax, and the Act was deemed a public one to remain in force fifty years, subject to renewal by Congress.

At the meeting of the trustees on December 7, 1845, the exact site of the university was determined. Under consideration were Independence Public Square, Allen Hill (a plot of 6.3 acres formerly called Wind Mill Hill donated by W. W. Allen), and the Academy Hill. Allen Hill received seven of the eight votes cast because of its proximity to a stone quarry. However, the building committee, after careful investigation, reported that they,

. . . feeling a deep solicitude in the premises devolving upon them, would not under the present situation of the pecuniary affairs of the Board, feel warranted in proceeding with such a building as the merits of your institution will soon require. . . . It is the desire of many of the patrons of the institution that a preparatory or primary school should be commenced as soon as practicable, and to expedite the matter we would suggest the propriety of repairing the building belonging to your Body, known as the Female Academy, by ceiling or plastering, building a chimney in the east end and constructing seats and benches. It cannot only be made comfortable and convenient, but will be commodious, capable of accommodating from 50 to 75 scholars. . . .

Hence the old Academy Building, used by Miss Trask, became the first building used by Baylor University at Independence.

At the January 12, 1846, trustee meeting at Independence, Reverend Henry L. Graves of Georgia was elected president of the institution. Judge Baylor made the motion and Secretary E. W. Taylor was directed to notify him. The following letter was sent to the Reverend Graves:

Independence Jany 20 1846

Rev. Henry L. Graves
    Dear Sir:
    I have the honor of informing you that at a meeting of the Board of Trustees of the Baylor University convened at this place on, the 12 Inst. you were unanimously elected President of the Institution.
    I would be extremely gratified in hearing from you.

Respectfully
Yr ob'dt Svt.
E. W. Taylor[50]

Pressure for immediate opening of a preparatory department in connection with Baylor University was strong in Washington County. Hence at the January 1846 meeting of the board, upon the motion of Trustee Farquhar, Henry Flavel Gillette was named teacher of the preparatory school "to commence as soon as the Academy Building can be fitted up." Trustees Baylor, Tryon, and Taylor were designated to confer with Mr. Gillette and offer him a salary of not more than $800. Gillette was well known by many of the trustees, for he had taught at Union Academy between Washington and Independence from the summer of 1841 until early 1843. Then he had served as superintendent of the Male Department at Houston Academy, said to be the first school opened in Houston. Advertisements stated that the teachers there had taught "in some of the best institutions of the North and supplied textbooks used in Northern schools."

Baylor University's first teacher, Henry Flavel Gillette, was born in Granby County, Connecticut, on July 16, 1816.[51] Records show that he was a member of the class of 1838 at Trinity College but left in 1839 because of a lung infection.[52]

[50] Gambrell, "The Early History of Baylor University, 1841-1861." (unpublished Master's thesis, Southern Methodist University), Appendix, p. iv½.

[51] P. S. Cossitt, *The Cossitt Family,* (Pasadena, California: F. H. White, Publisher, 1925), p. 55.

[52] Grusendorf quotes correspondence with Registrar Arthur Adams of Trinity College (February 16, 1937) to establish Gillette's college record. A letter from the Alumni Registry at Yale, Marion L. Phillips, (February 19,

He came to Houston, Texas, to regain his health under the care of his cousin, Dr. Ashbel Smith.

On March 16, 1839, Gillette and thirty-eight others united "as a Christian congregation in the city of Houston to observe the forms of worship . . . of the Protestant Episcopal Church in the United States of North America."[53] Gillette taught school in Houston—probably privately—and lived at the Winfields.[54] In the summer of 1841 Gillette moved to Washington County to continue his teaching career. He opened an academy—Union—about three miles from Washington, and thought the prospects flattering. As an inducement to open the school, Mr. Farquhar gave Gillette free board.[55]

Mr. Gillette was known also to the president of the board of trustees, William M. Tryon; at his marriage to Miss Lucinda Maxcy, Tryon was the officiating minister.[56] On January 10, 1843, Gillette wrote his cousin that he had closed his school and was "going to farm on the Trinity about ten miles from Swarthout." A letter on February 21, 1844, to Smith as Ministre du Texas, when he represented the Republic of Texas in France, tells of his success in farming. In 1844 Gillette returned to Houston, joining his Uncle Charles Gillette, who headed the Houston Academy.[57]

Gillette's abilities were known by Judge R. E. B. Baylor, whose name appears with Gillette's in a statement of educational needs in Texas printed in the *Telegraph and Texas Register* on November 19, 1845. This convention "of teachers and others [issuing the statement] interested in primary education" was possibly the earliest movement for the establishment of a college for teachers in the state.

1937) indicates that he did not attend Yale, as stated by some historians. A. A. Grusendorf, "Biography of Henry Flavel Gillette," (manuscript given to Professor E. H. Sparkman, November 21, 1939).

[53] Records of Christ Church, Houston, Texas.

[54] Gillette to Ashbel Smith, October 17, 1840. Ashbel Smith Papers, Archives, University of Texas.

[55] *Ibid.*, September 17, 1841.

[56] Gillette to Ashbel Smith, March 21, 1842. Ashbel Smith Papers, Archives, University of Texas.

Marriage Notice, *Telegraph and Texas Register*, March 9, 1842. Miss Maxcy, daughter of Mr. and Mrs. William Maxcy, was born in Alabama, April 23, 1826, and came to Texas during the days of the Republic. The first of the Gillette's thirteen children was born on March 10, 1843.

[57] B. H. Carroll, *History of Houston* (Knoxville: H. W. Crew and Co., 1912), p. 167. The school opened in the Telegraph Building at Main and Preston Streets as a preparatory school.

The preparatory department of Baylor University was opened by Professor Henry F. Gillette on May 18, 1846, in the two-story thirty-three by thirty-five foot frame building formerly used by Independence Academy. Twenty-four students responded to the first bell, brought by Trustee Aaron Shannon from his plantation.[58] Students numbered 70 by the end of the year. A trustee motion of May 19, 1846, which provided "that the said building committee are not authorized under any circumstances whatever to make any contract by which a debt will be incurred against said B. U." resulted in the rescinding of a motion to build a stone structure upon University Hill. Of happier moment was the announcement at this meeting of the acceptance of the presidency of the school by the Reverend Graves.

Expenses of the infant school reflected the economic picture in pioneer Texas. The terms of tuition, payable in advance, were as follows:

For Reading, Writing and Spelling, per Term	$8.00
For Geog., Arith., and Grammar with the above	10.00
For Philosophy, Rhetoric, Chemistry with the higher branches of Mathematics	13.00
For Latin, Greek, etc.	15.00

Odd to the twentieth-century students enjoying "cuts" was the announcement from the board that no pupil would be received for a less time than half a session and could be charged in proportion to the above rates. No deduction could be made for absence, except in the case of sickness, "when due notice must be given to the Faculty or any member thereof." The school year began with the first Monday in June, continuing for five months. The installation of fourteen desks and a stage in the Academy Building caused a delay in opening. Classes were held on the first floor because as yet no floor existed in the second story. Vacation was to be the month of November, after which the second term was to continue to June 1. The committee appointed to make inquiry about rates of board available to students reported that "board can be obtained in private families at $8.00 per month, including lodging and washing." As a further inducement to students, an announcement in the *Telegraph and Texas Register* of January 28, 1846, stated

---

[58] The bell is now in the Texas Collection.

that Washington County was well known as "one of the most healthy situations in Central Texas."

First-term tuition charges amounted to $468, of which only $347 was collected despite the "payable in advance" advertisement. Payment was even less for the second term when only $78 of the $512 due was received.[59] At the January 1846 meeting of the trustees the policy of naming agents to collect funds for the school was begun. Richard Ellis was appointed domestic agent, with R. E. B. Baylor and William M. Tryon "Domestic and Foreign Agents to solicit subscriptions for the University." Added to the list during the ensuing year were Stephen F. Williams of Mississippi and the following Baptist ministers

to act as voluntary agents in behalf of the B. U., in procuring monies, lands, books, etc., viz., R. E. B. Baylor, Jas. Huckins, W. M. Tryon, J. W. D. Creath, H. Garrett, and Z. N. Morrell, J. H. Stribling, Noah Hill, P. B. Chandler,—Rogers and H. L. Graves [the president not yet on duty] be requested to act as general agent.[60]

Interesting indeed are the sixteen Articles presented by the Committee on By-Laws for the management of the embryonic institution:

Article I. All the meetings of the Board shall be opened by prayer.

II. All officers of the Board shall be elected annually.

III. It shall be the duty of the President to preside at all meetings of the Board, to keep order at the same . . . to call meetings of the Board, whenever he may deem the good of the University requires it, and appoint all committees, with the concurrence of the Board.

IV. It shall be the duty of the Secretary to call the roll of members at the opening of each meeting, to make a minute of the proceedings, and record the same in a well bound book.

V. The Treasurer shall give bond with good security to the President and Trustees for the faithful performance of his duty.

VI. It shall be the duty of the Treasurer to keep a correct account of all receipts and expenditures, and report, annually or oftener, if required.

VII. No professor or teacher shall be elected unless by a majority of two-thirds. The same majority shall also be required in the election of President for the University, also for agents and Stewards.

[59] Minutes of Baylor Board of Trustees, April 27, 1847, p. 27.
[60] Minutes of the Baylor Board of Trustees, Independence, February 4, 1847, p. 25.

VIII.	Standing committees shall report at every meeting.
IX.	All motions and resolutions shall be submitted in writing, and every motion presented shall be acted upon before any other business shall be attended to.
X.	The presiding officers of the Board shall be addressed as President and members . . . by their respective names.
XI.	No member shall be allowed to speak upon one subject more than twice without permission of the Board.
XII.	Committees shall be appointed from time to time, who with the assistance of the Faculty shall prepare rules for the governing and conducting of the University, and report the same for the final action of the Board.
XIII.	No money shall be drawn from the Treasurer without a vote of two-thirds.
XIV.	The above ordinances may be altered or amended by a majority of two-thirds.
XV.	Agents shall report annually or oftener if required.
XVI.	Any member . . . who cannot be present in person may act by proxy. [61]

It can be readily seen that the original trustees of Baylor University took an active hand in the management, both financial and educational, of the young school. Selected quotations from the hand-written minutes reveal some of the problems of that first year of operation.

Trustee-ordered repairs on the Academy Building were slow in being effected, as shown by these excerpts from the October 9, 1846, minutes. School had started on May 18.

Resolved, That the Female Academy be put in good state of repair, to-wit; the upper room be finished and fitted up in the same manner as the lower room, the house weatherboarded, sash and window lights put in the windows, chimney with fireplaces, and the house painted.

. . . . .

Owing to high water, your committee have not been able to procure lumber to complete the work [on the Academy Building], the ceiling has been finished and an amount of ceiling material is now on hand nearly dressed, sufficient to ceil $\frac{1}{3}$ of the room overhead. Your com't would therefore recommend that the room be ceiled throughout.

. . . . .

. . . A. G. Haynes . . . had caused to be built a substantial stone chimney in the East End of the Academy . . .

. . . . .

. . . A. G. Haynes was authorized to employ hands to assist in surveying any tracts of land that they have or may be donated to the Institution.

[61] Minutes of the Baylor Board of Trustees, Independence, January 13, 1846.

. . . . .

Resolved, That a committee of two be appointed to select books for the Baylor University. [Huckins and Tryon were named.]

. . . . .

Resolved: That a com't of three be appointed to make arrangements for and supervise the next examination of the Baylor University, to arrange accounts for tuition, collect the same, and settle with the teachers. [Haynes, Farquhar, and Taylor were appointed.]

Elder Tryon had been asked to deliver the associational sermon at the Seventh Annual Union Association meeting in October 1846 in which he would give a history of Baptists. Concerning the young Baylor University he said that "it presents at present flattering prospects of ultimate success." [62]

Despite the problems of the initial year, Mr. Gillette was pleased with the progress. In a mid-August letter to Cousin Ashbel Smith he stated his satisfaction and intention of buying a few acres to work and on which to build a house. "If they will make my salary $1,000 I will stay a long time with them," he wrote. [63] Undoubtedly Mr. Gillette brought prestige and ability to the young school, for he was recognized in the Republic as an able educator and a religious leader. He was a friend of General Houston and President Anson Jones, through his kinship to Ashbel Smith. The fact that Gillette was an active Episcopalian indicates the tolerance of the Baptist founding fathers. Tolerance, as well as necessity, also dictated the use of the school building for church services of various faiths: Baptists on the first Sunday of the month, Methodists on the second, any Christian group requesting space on the third, and Presbyterians on the fourth. [64]

Thus began Baylor University in a pioneer area sometimes crossed by maurading Tehuacanies and Karankahwas, accessible by roads resembling cow trails. Only 1400 scattered Baptists lived in Texas. The dream of a Baptist university, even in this "Athens of Texas," seemed grandiose. Yet the determined Baylor Board of Trustees carried on.

[62] Union Baptist Association Minutes, Dove Church, Caldwell, Burleson County, October 1, 1846.

[63] Ashbel Smith Letters, Archives, Texas University, Austin, Texas. Smith, (1805-1886) a Phi Beta Kappa from Yale, was Ambassador to France during President Sam Houston's second term. He came to Texas in 1837 and was termed "the most intellectual physician of all Texas." Early Baylor catalogues show that Smith served on Baylor Boards of Examiners in June 1867 and 1870. He held the A.B., A.M. and M.D. degrees from Yale. Pat Ireland Nixon, *A History of the Texas Medical Association 1853-1934* (Austin: University of Texas Press, 1953), p. 10.

[64] Minutes of the Baylor Board of Trustees, January 12, 1846, pp. 23-24.

CHAPTER IV

The Administration of Henry Lee Graves
1847 - 1851

PRESIDENT HENRY LEE GRAVES began his duties at Baylor University in February, 1847, with the collegiate term starting the following June. During the first year of the Graves administration Mr. Gillette evidently assumed most of the teaching responsibility, for no reports indicate the success of a trustee committee in finding an assistant. The arrival of the new president was a welcome event. At the request of the board when he was tendered the presidency, Graves served as agent for the State of Georgia to collect subscriptions for the young institution; hence, he knew something of its financial status.

President Graves was not unknown to the Independence people. Eli Mercer was on the trustee committee to name the president, and he "had marked Dr. Graves' qualifications and standards" and recommended him to the committee.[1]

The heritage of Baylor's first president, Henry Lee Graves, was rich in pioneer tradition. He was a descendant of Captain Thomas Graves "who brought a ship to Jamestown in 1608 and became a member of the House of Burgesses of America's first English colony at the capitol in Williamsburg."[2] A namesake of the adventurous Thomas Graves moved on to North Carolina, where his son, Henry Lee Graves, was born on February 22, 1813, at Yancyville in Caswell County. By 1833 young Graves was graduated with hon-

[1] Interview with Mrs. Bettie Graves Jones by Laura Aline Hobby, April 16, 1931. Mrs. Jones was the daughter of the Graves and had come to Texas with them when she was seven years old. She attended Baylor from 1846 to 1853 and lived to be her oldest student. She died at 95 on July 8, 1935, at the home of her daughter, Mrs. J. Lewis Russell, of Dallas, Texas. The great-grandson of President Graves, Lewis Russell, is now Judge of Dallas County Domestic Relations Court.

[2] Joseph Martin Dawson, "Henry Lee Graves: A Major First," *The Baptist Standard,* February 28, 1962, p. 6; See also Mrs. H. P. Hiden, "The Graves Family of Spotsylvania County," *Tyler's Quarterly Historical and Genealogical Magazine,* ed. Mrs. Lyon G. Tyler (Holdcroft P. O., Charles City Co., Virginia), XVIII, 175-185; John Bennett Boddie, *Southside Virginia Families* (Redwood City, California: Pacific Coast Publishers); John Camden Hotten, ed., *The Original List of Persons of Quality 1600-1700* (New York: G. A. Baker & Company, Inc., 1913). Other data supplied by Louise Graves, Dallas, Texas, August 25, 1960.

ors from the University of North Carolina. While a student there in 1831, he was converted and baptized by the Reverend Dr. Hooper. In 1835 he went to Wake Forest, the North Carolina Baptist college, to teach mathematics.[3] Graves was first employed by the faculty in July 1835. In the report on the institution made to the Baptist State Convention of that year, Graves is referred to as a tutor. A year later his salary was increased to $600.00, and he was given in addition the rent of a house.[4] Of great concern at this institution was the manual labor feature, which was discussed at practically every board meeting. A writer, signing himself *Carolinus* and thought to be H. L. Graves, tutor in the Classical Languages for 1836 and 1837, had three letters published in the *Biblical Recorder* of October 5, 12, and 19, 1836. He favored the one-hour-a-day labor system "for the purpose of guarding the health of the students and giving them correct habits of industry." This source credits Graves with establishing a manual labor school in Georgia after he left Wake Forest.[5]

In 1836 Graves was married to a distant cousin, Rebecca Williams Graves, daughter of General Azariah Graves, member of the North Carolina Senate. The family of Rebecca Graves dates back to John Lea of Lea Hall, Cheshire, England. This branch of the family came to America in 1740 to settle first in Virginia and then in North Carolina. General Graves brought his daughter's wedding dress from London or Paris, where he made semi-annual trips to buy merchandise.[6]

At the County Line Church of Caswell, Graves was ordained to the ministry in November 1837 by a presbytery composed of Elder Stephen Pleasants of North Carolina and Elder John Kerr, reputedly the most eloquent preacher of his day in Virginia. Soon thereafter, the couple moved to Georgia, where Graves headed a Baptist high school at Cave

---

[3] Paschal's *History of Wake Forest College* (Wake Forest College, North Carolina, 1935, I, 1834-1846) reveals data concerning Graves' tenure there.

[4] *Proceedings of the Baptist State Convention*, pp. 17, 21, 25.

[5] *Ibid.*, p. 129.

[6] The exquisite satin and fine net dress was acquired by Lily M. Russell for Baylor's Collection of First Ladies' Dresses from granddaughter, Mrs. C. M. Ballenger of Coleman, Texas. Miss Louise Graves of Dallas was one of the six young women who supplied hair for the mannequin wearing her great-grandmother's dress. William C. Bernard, "Baylor Mannequin," *The Daily Times-Herald*, March 18, 1950, p. 11.

Spring. Then for two years he was a theological student in the Hamilton Literary and Theological Institute at Hamilton, New York, where Thomas J. Pilgrim and William Carey Crane (later to become president of Baylor) had been students.[7] When he entered on October 29, 1840, only twelve matriculated in the seminary, and he was one of fifteen in the 1842 graduating class. In 1843, he returned to Georgia and was teaching at Covington when the invitation to come to Baylor arrived.

The Graves family, then consisting of the couple and three small children, came to Texas by sea. "No ship that ever ploughed the waves between New Orleans and Galveston, I suppose, ever brought at one time, a more valuable cargo for Texas, than the one that landed Elders J. W. D. Creath, P. B. Chandler, Henry L. Graves, and Noah Hill."[8] Daughter Bettie recalled that the Graves family went from Galveston to Velasco, then proceeded to Old Caney (later Sugarland) to seek out Eli Mercer and Gail Borden. Burleson related the story with a touch of local color:

> Dr. Graves, with his family, servants, teams, wagons, and household furniture, landed at Galveston on December 4, 1846. Before proceeding to Independence, the family visited in the home of Mrs. Gail Borden, a devout Baptist. Mr. Borden was the inventor of the plan for condensed milk, which later made him famous and wealthy. While the Graves were his guests in Galveston, he took them up to the island to see his new plant, and a gift from Mr. Borden upon their parting was a barrel of molasses.[9]

Hopefully President Graves with his wife and children began the trip to the "Athens of Texas." Most overland travel was by stagecoach at ten cents a mile as "the dry weather rate" but doubled to the "flood rate" during rain. The members of the Graves group, however, traveled in their own conveyances and set their teeth against the rough trail, averaging eight or ten miles a day, depending on weather conditions. "Most likely they stopped at Houston, then a

[7] The institution, chartered March 5, 1819, bore the designation of Hamilton from 1833 to 1846, Madison University from 1846 to 1890, and Colgate University thereafter. The founding of Baylor closely parallels that of Colgate; both were sponsored by Baptist Education Societies "for the purpose of educating pious young men to the gospel ministry" as one of their aims. Colgate University, General Catalogue Number (Hamilton, New York: April, 1937).

[8] Z. N. Morrell, *Flowers and Fruits of the Wilderness* (St. Louis: Commercial Printing Company, 1882), p. 238.

[9] Burleson Papers, Texas Collection, Baylor University.

town of 4,737 people—607 qualified voters and 622 slaves," wrote Paul Haralson, a descendant of Parson Graves. They sought respite at inns, where every room boasted a water pitcher and wash basin—real luxuries in that day. The kitchens offered pioneer fare—wild turkey, venison roasts, crisp bacon, greens flavored with "side meat," and golden corn pone. The Graves entourage reached Independence on February 4, 1847. The village was then thirteen years old. The public house built by John P. Coles still served as the hotel. The focal point of interest was the adobe Baptist church, where the family immediately placed membership.

The Reverend and Mrs. Graves with children Mary Ann, Bettie, Charles, and Ophelia Florine (the last of whom was born at Independence) lived in a stately two-story, balconied home on College Hill. Built during the 1830's under magnificent live-oak trees, the place was known as the Mose Hairston House. General Sam Houston and wife Margaret Lea, a cousin to Mrs. Graves, lived across the street when the Houstons moved to Independence in 1854.

Graves served as president of Baylor University from February 4, 1847, to June 16, 1851. Concurrently he served as pastor of the Independence Baptist Church from 1847 to 1850. A recognized leader in Baptist affairs, he had been a Georgia delegate to the organizational meeting of the Southern Baptist Convention at Augusta on May 8, 1845. Daughter Bettie Graves Jones related an incident characteristic of Graves' vigorous methods and handling of emergencies. One Sunday afternoon the entire community had gathered on Rocky Creek near Independence for a baptismal service, with the Reverend Graves the officiating minister. As Rosanna Terrell, a pretty, rosy-cheeked girl of about eighteen, stood in her white baptismal robe, a huge water moccasin glided from the back waters. "My father saw it instantly, and in a flash, seized the serpent and flung it with all his might to the opposite bank. I well remember the scampering of the children and Negroes." Judge Baylor witnessed the act and turned to Elder Z. N. Morrell, saying, "Why, sir, the Apostle Paul could have done no more."[10]

Termed by Carroll "a princely gentleman, a ripe scholar,

[10] Bettie Graves Jones, MS, Texas Collection. Morrell also relates the story in *Flowers and Fruits,* pp. 295-296.

a strong and dignified convention presiding officer, and a splendid school man," Graves assumed almost insurmountable responsibilities, for the school was struggling to begin its existence.[11] Classes were held in the Academy Building for both the Preparatory and College Departments under the tutelage of Mr. Gillette and President Graves.

Despite the precarious financial situation of the young school, relations between the board and the administration were amicable. The president and the professor of the institution were "invited to be present at the meetings of the Board of Trustees and to bring before the Board any business pertaining to the prosperity of the Institution."[12] Begun at this meeting was the practice of appointing an Executive Committee of five to supervise the disciplinary management of the institution, attend to whatever business the board entrusted to them, and handle all problems that might arise during the interval between board meetings, subject to approval at the annual meetings. Baylor, Garrett, Haynes, Farquhar, and Taylor composed the first Executive Committee.

Upon the motion of Trustee Farquhar at the meeting on May 1, 1847, the board tendered to Dr. Graves and Mr. Gillette as compensation for their services the profits of the school for the next five years, to be divided in the ratio of twelve to Graves and eight to Gillette. The tuition for the collegiate department was set at $25 per session, payable in advance.

The college year for 1847 was to begin on the first day of June with one term of six months and the other of five. Vacations were scheduled for the months of December and June, with annual board meetings on the first day of June. An increase in enrollment was expected, for provision was made to equip the upper story of the Academy Building.[13]

[11] J. M. Carroll, *A History of Texas Baptists* (Dallas: Baptist Standard Publishing Company, 1922), p. 233.

[12] Minutes of the Baylor Board of Trustees, April 7, 1847, p. 26.

[13] The handwritten contract between the committee composed of R. E. B. Baylor, Hosea Garrett, and A. G. Haynes and the contractor, Mr. Hattox, reads: "the latter agrees to cut the upper room of the building now occupied by the faculty of the Preparatory Department at $3.00 per square and make desks and seats similar to those in the lower room but flat on top at $3.00 per desk and seat, to run a flight of stairs commencing at the outside of the building and running round the corner and up the side to the upper room at $30.00 to be sealed from the stairs to the hand rails, to case the windows and build on

In a hopeful article released at the end of 1847, Graves stated that there were approximately one hundred students in the two departments for the first term, that prospects were bright, but more laborers were needed.[14]

The year 1847 brought the loss by death of Baylor trustee, William M. Tryon. He died of yellow fever on November 16. When the yellow fever epidemic raged in Houston in the fall of 1847, Tryon and young Dr. S. O. Young attended a beloved friend, statesman Isaac Van Zandt, one of the first victims of the disease. Tryon held the funeral, despite friends' advice to retire to his former home in Washington County. On Sunday, November 6, 1847, after his morning service, Tryon walked a mile or two out of the city to visit a needy family. Upon his return, he, too, succumbed to yellow fever and ten days later died at thirty-nine years of age. Fallen to the dread disease also was Dr. Young. Tryon's funeral was held by the Reverend Charles Gillette, (uncle of Henry F. Gillette) Episcopal minister, with burial near the church that he helped erect.[15]

Impossible as it is to estimate the contribution of Tryon's seven short years in Texas, his contemporaries tried. Judge Baylor said, "I despair of doing justice to his pulpit talents" and credited him with suggesting the idea of establishing a Baptist university. "We soon after prepared a memorial to the then Congress of the Republic of Texas. As I was most familiar with such things, I dictated . . . and he wrote as I suggested."[16] Z. N. Morrell wrote that as "an orator my profound conviction is that no preacher has ever lived in Texas who was his equal." In the field of education he also paid Tryon a high tribute in stating that when he espoused the causes of education, he was master of the field and "moved the great Baptist heart to rally around the infant institution at Independence." He labored industriously to

the sash at $1.50 per window, to make panel door frames and casings at $2.50 per square . . . and said committee agrees to furnish all the materials. Signed and sealed this 15th of June A.D. 1847." Archives, Texas Collection, Baylor University.

[14] *South-Western Baptist Chronicle* (New Orleans, Louisiana), January 8, 1848.

[15] The church property, later the site of the old Milby Hotel, was sold between 1877 and 1883, and Tryon's remains were removed to the Glenwood Cemetery, Houston. Reverend J. Herbert Brown, Correspondence, Texas Collection, Baylor University.

[16] Carroll, p. 230.

provide means for the education of the rising ministry of Texas.[17] Link averred that Tryon "originated and laid the foundation of our educational interests in Texas. He was foremost in the organization of both the Education Society and Baylor University.[18] Dr. Carroll declared that [Tryon] was unquestionably "the prince among Texas Baptist preachers . . . and when he died the Texas pioneer Baptists went into mourning."[19]

Tryon's influence in denominational affairs is evidenced by his election less than a year after his arrival in Texas as Moderator of Union Association at its second meeting on October 7, 1841, at the Clear Creek Meeting House (now La Grange Baptist Church). He was moderator again from 1842-1844 and in 1847 and corresponding secretary in 1846. Tryon was elected by ballot five times to preach the missionary sermon for Union Association: 1841, 1842, 1844, 1846, and 1847. At the Clear Creek meeting in 1841, Tryon urged the adoption of the resolution "That the association recommend the formation of an education society. . . ."

By the next year the country was distracted by the Mexican Army and the association did not meet in regular session but in a called session beginning on November 26, 1842, at Mt. Gilead in Washington County.[20] At the Fourth Session in 1843 at Providence Church (Chappell Hill) Tryon was named agent to manage a book depository at Washington. Then at the Fifth Session in 1844 at Plum Grove in Fayette County Tryon wrote the circular letter on church membership, stating that "no candidate can be received against whom an objection or objections are urged by one or more members. . . ." The church, however, was to pass on the merit of the objection.[21] At the Seventh Session in 1846 Tryon reported on the Education Society, telling of its organization and subsequent chartering of Baylor University. To the credit of Tryon, too, belongs the introduction of the resolution at the 1847 Union Association meeting which led to the formation of the Baptist State Convention of Texas on October 21, 1848, at Anderson.

[17] Morrell, p. 134.

[18] J. B. Link, *Texas Historical and Biographical Magazine*, I, 192.

[19] Carroll, p. 231.

[20] *The Union Baptist Association, Centennial History 1840-1940* (Brenham: Banner Press (n.d.) p. 13.

[21] *Ibid.*, p. 15.

Through the influence of Tryon, Independence Academy building was included by Root and Taylor in the bid to locate the new school at Independence, suggests Link.[22] The minutes of the Baylor Board of Trustees show the great confidence the body had in the leadership of Tryon, credited with helping to found and to name the university. Tryon unanimously was elected first president of the board on October 13, 1845. His proxy, Hosea Garrett, later a beloved board member and long-term board president, had been named president pro tempore at the May 16th meeting. Tryon was named to the building committee on October 13 but resigned December 7 because of his removal from the locale. He was on the committee to inform Henry F. Gillette, Baylor's first teacher, of his appointment. Tryon, with Judge Baylor, served as "domestic and foreign agent to solicit subscriptions for the University in Texas and the States" after December 8, 1845. He was appointed to select books for the school on October 8, 1846, and again named president of the board on April 24, 1847.

Tryon was interested not only in Christian education but also in public education. At a meeting in Houston on January 9, 1846, a group termed "Convention of the Friends of Education" organized "The Texas Literary Institute," with Tryon being named treasurer. The proceedings of the Institute show that the Reverend Tryon opened the second annual meeting with prayer, in the Methodist Church, Houston, on Monday, November 3, 1847, at 10:30.[23]

Tryon also served the Texas government. The Journals of the Senate of the Seventh Congress of the Republic of Texas at Washington state that on Friday, December 2, 1842, at 9 o'clock a.m. Mr. Muse offered the resolution that a committee of two be appointed to wait upon the Reverend Mr. Tryon and request him to meet with the Senate in the Hall when convenient and give the opening prayer. For this service, performed thirteen times, Tryon received no remuneration. The Journals of the Eighth Congress of the Republic of Texas show that on Wednesday, December 13, 1843, on the motion of Mr. Webb, the Senate proceeded to the election of the Reverend Tryon as chaplain. "There

---

[22] Link, I, 151-152.
[23] *Democratic Telegraph and Texas Register*, Austin, November 18, 1847.

being no other nomination, Mr. Tryon was declared duly and constitutionally elected chaplain of the Senate."[24]

Soon after assuming his duties as missionary to Houston, Tryon had visited the older states and raised $3,000 for the erection of a church building, which became the third brick structure in the city of Houston. He also influenced seventeen missionaries to come to Texas, stated Rufus C. Burleson, as he recalled "the powerful appeal he wrote to me at the Theological Seminary in Covington, Kentucky."[25] Tryon's Houston work was marked by great success, with some sixty-seven additions to the church.[26]

Various tributes have been made to the memory of the beloved Tryon. Tryon Hall at Baylor, Independence, stood as a memorial to him. Denominational leaders formed a new association on February 14, 1858, at Laurel Hill (now Cold Springs) and named it Tryon Association. In 1901 it was combined with the Evergreen Association to become the Tryon-Evergreen Association.[27] The Tryon and Huckins pillars on either side of the Judge Baylor statue on the Baylor-Waco campus, pay tribute to the founding fathers, and a Tryon Chapter of the Daughters of the Republic of Texas perpetuates the illustrious name.[28]

Tryon was survived by his wife and four children: William Armistead, Ella Louise, Ann Baylor (who died soon

[24] Various historians have written that Tryon was unpaid for this civil service. In the first instance, since the service was rendered "when convenient," Tryon received no fee. When he was elected chaplain, however, records show that he received pay. The Senate Chamber Record of February 5, 1855, above the signature of Thomas Green, Secretary of the Senate, reads that "William M. Tryon has served as chaplain of the Senate from the 24th of December 1843 to the present date inclusive and is entitled to pay as fixed by law." Then follows the record of payment on February 6, 1844 of $132.00 for officiating 41 times. The order was signed by Charles Mason, Auditor, and approved on February 5, 1844, by Samuel L. Shank.

[25] Harry Haynes, *Life and Writings of Dr. Rufus C. Burleson* (compiled and published by Mrs. Georgia J. Burleson, 1901), p. 673.

Tryon was unable to reconcile views held by the American Baptists and the Texas Baptists and he disassociated himself from the sponsorship of the American Baptist Home Mission Society. Robert Andrew Baker declared that "the entire agitation of 1844 in the Home Mission Society of the American Baptists was occasioned by the discovery that two of the Society's Texas missionaries were slave-holders." Robert Andrew Baker, *Relations between Northern and Southern Baptists* (privately published, 1949), p. 66f.

[26] Carroll, p. 231.

[27] *Baptist Annual.*

[28] Through the indefatigable efforts of Lily M. Russell the Texas Collection of Baylor University has numerous articles and possessions of Tryon, secured from his descendants. In so far as known, no picture of him exists.

after the death of her father), and Joseph Milton (born after his father's death). Joseph Tryon, of New York, helped the widowed Mrs. Tryon educate the two older children, sending William to study abroad with his own son and sending Louise to school in Tennessee. Joseph attended Baylor at Independence. Many Tryon descendants live in the Houston-Beaumont area of Texas.

The Baylor Board of Trustees passed the following resolution after the death of William M. Tryon:

Whereas, in the Providence of Almighty God, our brother, William M. Tryon, the former President of this Board, has been removed by death from the duties of his office and from our society;

Resolved, That as friends of morality and religion and of the great cause of Education in Texas we have lost one of its best supporters and that Baylor University, especially, has sustained a very great loss in being deprived of the labors of one who aided in bringing the Institution into being and who ever felt the liveliest in its welfare;

Resolved, That we will ever hold in grateful remembrance the efforts of our deceased brother and that as a Board we will endeavor to imitate this noble example and faithfully carry out his plan for the promotion of the cause of Education. [29]

Baylor University carried on. T. J. Jackson was named by the Baptist Education Society to fill the Tryon vacancy on the Baylor Board of Trustees. President Graves concentrated on maintaining a high instructional level at the institution and secured Daniel Witt, Jr., as assistant teacher. Tuition collection was slow. At the December 22, 1847, meeting of the board in conjunction with the Baptist Education Society, a Mr. Reynolds was appointed to collect tuition fees, and a committee was designated to negotiate for a loan "not to exceed six hundred dollars for the Baylor University." Mr. Reynolds was also authorized to call on J. M. Norris for notes and subscriptions belonging to the university and to collect the same. The trustees ordered the liquidation of subscriptions already on hand. Thus the hard-pressed board took every expedient step possible to make the young school solvent.

Reverend James Huckins was appointed for the year 1848 as "agent for Baylor University to collect monies, lands, books, apparatus, or whatever may be donated for the In-

[29] Minutes of the Baylor Board of Trustees, June 2, 1848, p. 36.

stitution." His salary was fixed at $1,000 plus traveling expenses. President Graves was instructed to inform the Reverend Huckins of his appointment and that he be furnished a certificate of such authority, signed by the president and secretary of the Board of Trustees.[30] This devoted minister served in the capacity for approximately five years, frequently donating his expenses and even part of his salary to the support of the young school. Dr. Carroll estimated that he garnered between thirty and forty thousand dollars for equipment and endowment as he went on horseback to all parts of the North, East, and South, pleading Baylor's cause.

Maintaining a college was a herculean task in this pioneer area. Agencies of various kinds attempted the task, the most active being the Masonic Order. Among the religious groups, the Methodists, both through the conferences and private support, led in school support prior to the Civil War. Next came the Baptists and the Presbyterians. Schools were desperately needed. No sooner did a denominational group get a foothold in Texas than they concentrated their efforts on founding a school where "the morals as well as the manners" of their children would receive attention. Such was the case over the United States as the population moved westward. Of Baptist institutions in the States founded before 1900, nine were founded before 1825, twenty-five between 1826 and 1850, thirty-nine between 1851 and 1875, and seventy between 1876 and 1900. (See Appendix)

All of Texas in 1847 boasted a population of 135,000, of whom 39,000 were slaves.[31] By 1850 there were 212,592, of whom 58,000 were slaves and almost 400 free Negroes. Baylor University was not the only school purporting to serve these early Texans. On Galveston Island the Catholics established two schools in 1847: the Ursuline Sisters and Louis Chambodut's school for boys at St. Joseph's Hall. John McCullough organized the Galveston Female Collegiate In-

---

[30] Burleson stated that Huckins had accepted an appointment as missionary to Galveston from the newly organized Southern Baptist Convention in 1845. With help from friends in Georgia, South Carolina, and Virginia, a new $4,000 church was erected and dedicated in 1847, with Tryon preaching the dedicatory sermon. Burleson attributed Huckins' resignation to the desire of church members "to have a new preacher to go into the new church," and hence, the pastor was able to enter upon a wider field of usefulness as agent for Baylor. Haynes, p. 678.

[31] Partial enumeration of 1847. *Texas Almanac 1949-1950*, p. 91.

stitute under Methodist sponsorship in 1847, but it did not survive the fever epidemic of 1854.[32]

The modern educator may view with derision the early educational efforts of our pioneer states, but it seems remarkable that schools were maintained at all under such circumstances. A contemporary, E. H. Cushing, wrote caustically of Texas schools, asserting that it was time the legislature stopped giving college charters to common schools. He was a Dartmouth graduate who became a Galveston editor and felt justified in debunking the pretentious school men with questionable degrees and training.[33] Common to most Texas schools were these significant facts: a zeal for knowledge coupled with a rare religious spirit; the administration and financial management of the school by a designated president or principal; a universal prejudice against co-education above the primary grades; the maintenance by almost every presumptive college or university of a "preparatory department"; a non-denominational policy, despite the fact that practically all of the leaders of the schools were ministers; and, finally, the support of the state, which in many cases made existence possible.[34]

Chiefly because of the interest of President Mirabeau B. Lamar in public education, Congress passed an act on January 26, 1839, providing three leagues of land for each county's school fund in addition to a grant of fifty leagues for two universities for the Republic. The following year an additional league for each county's school fund was awarded. Lamar's key phrase in his first message to Congress in 1838 —"The cultivated mind is the guardian genius of democracy"—won him the title of *The Father of Education in Texas*. Baylor made application for state aid in the form of Bill No. 146 to the Second Legislature, which met in December 1847.

A BILL

To be entitled an act granting to the Baylor University two leagues of land.

Section 1. Be it enacted by the Legislature of the State of Texas: That the Chief Justice of Washington County be and he is hereby

[32] Earl Wesley Fornell, *The Galveston Era* (Austin: University of Texas Press, 1961), p. 79.

[33] *Ibid.*, p. 74.

[34] Frederick Eby, "Education and Educators," *Centennial Story of Texas Baptists*, ed. Harlan J. Matthews (Baptist General Convention of Texas, Burt Building, 1936), pp. 138-139.

required to issue to the President and Trustees of Baylor University
in Washington County two certificates for one league of land each,
which certificates shall be locatable in any of the public lands in
the state in accordance with existing laws regulating the location
of lands.

Section 2. Be it further enacted that the Commissioner of the
General Land Office shall issue patents on the same in accordance
with existing laws and that this act take effect from and after its
passage.

The Education Committee reported the decision to the
Speaker of the House:

Committee Room
Feb. 19, 1848

Hon. J. W. Henderson
   Speaker House of Rep.

The Committee on Education to whom was referred the Memorial
of the Trustees of Baylor University asking a donation of Land to
said University have considered the same and doubt the policy of
giving lands to particular institutions or corporations unless the same
could be extended to all others of a similar kind in the State. The
object is good and if the public domain can be appropriated otherwise
than in liquidation of the debt of the State, your committee would be
pleased to see it used for the promotion of education. Under the
circumstances however they are compelled to report the Memorial
back to the House without recommending any action but with the
request that they be released from the further consideration of it.

C. G. Keean
Chairman

By the end of the first term of 1848, conditions were still
precarious, with "the Institution justly indebted to H. L.
Graves in the sum of $1,200 and Gillette in the sum of
$800." The board made the following sacrificial arrange-
ment: E. W. Taylor, N. Kavanaugh, James Huckins, James
L. Farquhar, R. B. Jarmon, A. G. Haynes, T. J. Jackson, H.
Garrett, R. E. B. Baylor, and J. G. Thomas each should pay
twenty dollars to Messrs. Graves and Gillette as part compensation for their services for last year, and Eli Mercer
would pay the residue of their salaries, provided the amount
does not exceed One Hundred and Fifty Dollars, and provided Messrs. Graves and Gillette will receive the tuition
list at par. The plan was accepted.

When his contract expired in 1848, Gillette resigned, stating that eight years of teaching the youth of Texas had
induced him to "let others endure the hardships that I have

Stephen F. Austin
Texas Colonizer

Elder Daniel Parker's
Immigrated Church

Thomas J. Pilgrim
Sunday School

The Arrest of
George W. Slaughter

Byars Blacksmith Shop

Reverend Noah T. Byars
Pioneer Texas Missionary

Zacharias N. Morrell
"First Missionary Father"

Anderson Baptist Church
(1848)

Chappell Hill (Providence)
(1842)

Judge R.E.B. Baylor
Founding Father

The Granting of Baylor's Charter

Reverend James Huckins
Founding Father

Judge James Seaton Lester
Original Trustee

Jesse Gilbert Thomas
Original Trustee

Colonel Aaron Shannon
Original Trustee

Nelson J. Kavanaugh
Original Trustee

Major A. G. Haynes
Original Trustee

Governor Albert C. Horton
Original Trustee

The Toalson House

McKnight Drug Store

The Lydia Hood Hotel

The Blanton Hotel

Independence Store Building

The Home of John P. Coles

The Root-Houston-Williams Home

The Hoxie House

The Taylor Home

The Blue Home

The John Seward Plantation Home

The Baylor Home Interior

Judge Baylor's Servant

The Baylor Home

Anson Jones
President of the Republic of Texas

"Barrington," Anson Jones House
Old Washington

Independence Academy

Henry F. Gillette
Baylor's First Teacher

endured."[35] Several factors induced his resignation: first was
the difficulty of collecting his salary and the absence of the
expected raise; second was the $800 destruction brought to
his new home by a hurricane; third was the recollection of
the 1844 experience when eighty bales of his cotton were
sunk on the *Lady Byron* on the Brazos; and finally came
the request of his father-in-law, Mr. Maxcy, that the Gillettes
come to live with him after the death of his wife early in
1848. A letter to his cousin in 1847 also revealed a dejection
readily understood:

. . . I can assure you that I deeply regret the fortune that has
placed us so widely apart, and it seems to grow on me daily, and at
times makes me sad and gloomy for I have but few friends whom
I care very much for in Texas and to be almost entirely deprived of
their society, and interchange of sentiment, it appears at times that
my lot was harder than that of any other person, and were it not for
that resignation of spirit which kind nature has implanted within
one, I should at times be nearly or quite crazy.[36]

As a tribute to Baylor's first teacher, the Baylor Board of
Trustees passed a resolution expressing their thanks "justly
due" to Professor Henry F. Gillette for his "wise and faithful service to our cherished institution during its infancy."
The measure of success attained by the school was credited
to his learning, judgment, and tact as a teacher.[37] Leader in
church and state, friend of Sam Houston, Anson Jones, and

[35] Copy of Letter from Henry Gillette to Ashbel Smith, August 15, 1848.
Texas Collection, Baylor University.

[36] Gillette to Ashbel Smith, January 16, 1847. Ashbel Smith Papers,
Archives, University of Texas.

[37] Minutes of Baylor Board of Trustees, June 2, 1848, p. 33.
Mr. Gillette moved his family to Fireman's Hill in Polk County, with the
intention of farming. He did not escape the schoolroom, however, for a letter
of September 25, 1849, indicates that he was conducting an academy in the
area. By 1854 the community took the name of "Cold Springs," and Gillette
was listed as one of the original trustees of the Cold Springs Female Academy.
His letters in 1854 and 1855 indicate that he was in charge of the school and
that he constructed a new building 30 x 40 feet. The following year he
assumed direction of the Male Department. During the years at Cold Springs
Gillette was extremely active in the Episcopal Church, serving as a delegate
to the State Convention from 1850 to 1860 and as secretary to the Convention
in 1854.
By 1860 Gillette moved his large family (thirteen children, five of whom
died in infancy) to "Bell Prairie" on Cedar Bayou. Age and family responsibilities prevented active military service in the Civil War, but he served as
"supply sergeant" to families whose men were in the army. Ever public-spirited,
he was instrumental in establishing Bayland Orphans' Home in early 1867
and served as secretary of the board and superintendent for fifteen years.
Minutes of the Board of Trustees of Bayland Orphans' Home. Gillette, an
active Mason, died on April 25, 1896. John P. Sjolander, *The Semi-Centennial
History of Cedar Bayou Lodge No. 321.*

other illustrious early Texans, Gillette exemplified the pioneer spirit of courage and sacrificial service.

Upon the departure of Gillette, President Graves assumed responsibility for the preparatory department, including the selection and payment of teachers. According to his agreement with the trustees, he received all tuition and paid teachers at his own expense. The optimistic board at this June 1848 meeting decided to construct a permanent stone building on Allen Hill. The handling of the project is a commentary on architecture of the period. Trustee Huckins and Mr. J. R. Hines were appointed building agents "for the purpose of contracting for and commencing work as soon as practicable," with authority to handle financing subject to examination of the executive committee and approval of the board. They were authorized "to procure a plan of the entire work of all the grounds, buildings and improvements contemplated," and Huckins was directed to carry the plan to the public.

President Graves and the Reverend Huckins proposed specifications for the building:

Resolved that we construct the building for the preparatory department of Baylor University of stone, and to be fifty-three feet long and thirty-five feet wide and two stories high. The first story 12 feet between joists; the 2nd story, 10 feet between joists with a projection of one and half feet.[38]

The board moved that Eli Mercer be "appointed a committee to particularize the building in contemplation; having in mind a plain substantial and neat one." To expedite construction, Huckins resigned from the board to assume his new duties, and James R. Hines was appointed trustee. He had met with the board on three previous occasions as proxy for N. Kavanaugh and Judge Baylor. John McKnight was invited to meet with the board and requested to give any information relative to the building that he deemed important. Plans for "a good and sufficient cistern" were included.

Physical growth was not the only concern for the university. At the Union Association assembly at Anderson in Grimes County on September 8, 1848, the Committee on Education (composed of the Reverend Huckins, Governor A. C. Horton, and the Honorable Richard Ellis) reported:

[38] Minutes of the Baylor Board of Trustees, p. 33.

Whereas, the tendency of sound learning is to increase moral power, and hence the future prosperity and influence of the Baptist denomination in Texas will greatly depend upon their efforts to advance the cause of education in their own families, and in the community generally, now therefore, be it

Resolved, By the Baptist State Convention, That we regard the efforts of the Board of Trustees of Baylor University to build up and endow and furnish that institution so that it shall be able to give a thorough and polished education, as a subject deeply interesting to every Baptist, and that we recommend the institution to their prayers, their affection, and to their liberal support.

Further evidence that Baylor was endeavoring to capture the interest of the Baptists is seen in the request that Baylor President Graves preach "the introductory sermon," with Elder Noah Hill as alternate. "We were anxious to hear him [Graves]," wrote Morrell, "but to our great astonishment he declined to do it; so did Hill and subsequently a number of talented brethren." The large audience waited for over half an hour; then, when approached, Morrell agreed to preach. "Z. N. Morrell," he wrote, "had no reputation to lose in speaking to this most learned body of men that had ever been assembled in Texas up to that time." At this meeting President Graves was chosen the first president of the newly organized Baptist State Convention of Texas.[39]

This was the first general Baptist meeting in which Elder R. C. Burleson appeared. When the tall, slender Burleson took the floor of the convention for the first time, "seeing everybody in sight at one glance with those black, piercing eyes . . . beneath a manly brow, and pointing with his long, bony fingers [and with the] parted lips of an orator . . . spoke sweetly and tenderly the name of Jesus, the 'stranger' involuntarily asked his neighbor, 'Who is that?' "[40]

The year 1849 proved brighter for Baylor University. At a called meeting of the board on April 3, 1849, James Huckins' report was accepted. Significant were the following entries:

Obtained Subscriptions	$9,345.62
In stock and labour	338.00
	$9,683.62

[39] Subsequently he served as president twelve more times and vice-president three times. He preached the convention sermons in 1856 and 1879. Union Association also claimed his leadership—as corresponding secretary in 1847 and 1848 and as moderator in 1849 and 1850.
[40] Morrell, p. 197.

Amount due April 1, 1849	$2,061.50
Amount due April 1, 1850	1,775.50
	$3,837.00

Cash Collections

Sundry Persons	$ 811.12
Morgan L. Smith	200.00
Doctor Hoxie	106.00
John McKnight	50.00
D. Madden	37.00
Root and Taylor	16.31
	$1,220.43

Amounts paid out by Huckins[41]

Traveling expenses in Nov. 1848	$ 48.80
Traveling expenses from Nov. 1848 to date	27.45
To Jabez Dean for lumber	50.00
To J. R. Hines for quarry rock	15.00
To J. Echols for Horse	50.00
Exchange saddle	11.00
To J. Covington on execution	77.71
To J. McKnight for sash lumber	11.28
To Root and Taylor (account)	216.31
To H. L. Graves	50.00
To Henry Gillette	37.00
To John McKnight for sash	106.00
	$700.55

Huckins generously tendered the board the $480.12 due him as the balance of his salary as agent, plus $225 in cash. The board accepted the loan of both sums and retained Huckins as agent until June 1850 "with the understanding if either party becomes dissatisfied three months notice must be given." A committee of Creath, Jackson, and Farquhar examined the bids for the construction of the new building and recommended closing a contract with Mr. McKnight. Huckins was excused from the building committee, which was increased by the addition of trustees Garrett, Jackson, Farquhar, and Haynes. The board authorized Huckins to employ an agent to collect and drive to market any cattle due upon subscription. The building committee also contracted with H. Garrett to weatherboard the academy.

The Baylor Board of Trustees in its annual meeting, June 13, 1849, established a professorship of law, decreeing, that for the present, the duties be discharged by the voluntary

---

[41] Minutes of Baylor Board of Trustees, April 3, 1849, p. 38.

services of Abner Smith Lipscomb and R. E. B. Baylor with such other professional assistance as they and President Graves may provide.

One of the chief problems in pioneer Texas was the administration of justice. Happily, a number of eminent jurists came to Texas along with emigrants from other states. Judge Baylor and A. C. Horton, both trustees, saw the need for men trained in the legal profession. Baylor's former Alabama friend, Abner Smith Lipscomb, with a lucrative practice in Brenham, also realized the need.[42] Hence Baylor University made her first use of her charter provision—"to meet the requirements of existing conditions . . . and be susceptible of enlargement and development to meet the demands of all ages to come."

Mr. Lipscomb had volunteered to deliver a series of lectures on law, and the board gratefully accepted his offer at their April 3, 1849, meeting. Subsequently he was named a trustee by the Education Society and took his seat at this meeting and served until the spring of 1856, when he resigned. Fortunate indeed was the young school to have the services of these two judges—Lipscomb and Baylor.

John Livingston states that "no one is better entitled to consideration and respect in an assemblage of American lawyers and jurists" than the Honorable Abner S. Lipscomb.[43] Lipscomb was born in South Carolina in 1789 of Virginia parents, Joel and Elizabeth (Chiles) Lipscomb. He studied law at Abbeville Courthouse, South Carolina, in association with John C. Calhoun, and in 1811 removed to St. Stephens (now in Alabama) for law practice and then military service. He was a member of the territorial legislature, and upon the organization of the state government in 1819 he was elected one of the judges on December 17. He became chief justice on December 27, 1825, and served until his resignation in January 1835. He was a member of the legislature in 1838 just before his coming to Texas. A member of the Convention of 1845, Lipscomb served on the select committee which drew up a report on the General Land Office.

[42] C. S. Potts, Dean of the School of Law of Southern Methodist University, "The Three Musketeers of the Old Court," *The Dallas Morning News,* Sunday, September 1, 1929, Feature Section, p. 3.

[43] John Livingston (of the New York Bar), ed., *Biographical Sketches of Eminent American Lawyers,* June 1852, p. 622-630.

In Texas Judge Lipscomb took an influential part in the annexation convention. President Lamar named him Secretary of State, and he served from January 31 to December 13, 1849. After the adoption of the constitution, he was appointed a judge of the Supreme Court by Governor Pinckney Henderson in 1846; and in 1851 under constitutional change he was elected to a six-year term, commencing March 1852.

Lipscomb was married to Elizabeth Gaines in 1813. After her death in 1841 he married Mary P. Bullock of Austin in 1843. The Lipscomb Texas residence was in Washington County between Houston and Austin, where Judge Lipscomb "led the quiet life of a farmer . . . surrounded by intelligent and appreciative neighbors."[44] He served as a Baylor Trustee from 1849 until 1856.

Judge Baylor, minister, judge, and trustee, taught a course in Constitutional Law from 1849 until his death in 1873. He and Lipscomb, being trustees, could not receive salaries, according to a specific statement in the charter of the university. Baylor law lectures were to be delivered once every two weeks from May 1 until December 1, inclusive.[45] Tickets were $20 per session for those not registered as students of the university and $5 for regular students, payable in advance. Money secured was to support a scholarship in the university.

President Graves' leadership evoked support among the Baptists.[46] A letter from the highly respected Reverend R. H. Taliaferro published in the *South-Western Baptist Chronicle* summarized succinctly the denominational feeling concerning the university. In stating the aims he listed first that of supplying an educated ministry. He believed that the institution would "elevate the standing of our denomination," and that Baptists must support literary institutions or "suffer the neglect, and even contempt, of this intellectual age."

[44] Lipscomb died on November 8, 1856. A memorial marker in the State Cemetery at Austin pays tribute to his memory, as does Lipscomb County, created in 1876. See *Biographical Directory of Texan Convention and Congresses*, 1941; *The Handbook of Texas* II, 62; Amelia H. Williams and E. C. Barker, eds. *Writings of Sam Houston* III, 1940.

[45] The first law school in the United States, founded in 1802 in Litchfield, Connecticut, met in a simple frame cottage as inconspicuously as did Baylor's first classes.

[46] Baptist State Convention of Texas, *Organization Proceedings* (Anderson County, Texas, 1848), p. 10.

A Baptist school was desirable to prevent Baptists from having to send their children to other denominational schools then being established or to out-of-state schools. Such a school would create an "attitude of religious fervor" to aid in the salvation of its students. Baylor University was in a particularly advantageous position, he declared, to prepare a united ministry trained in the Texas tradition as well as missionaries for Mexico.[47]

The Education Society had a committee on ministerial education. At Houston in 1847 President Graves reported $305.50 for the cause. The first ministerial beneficiary at Baylor was James H. Stribling in 1846, who was baptized by Tryon at Providence Church. He was ordained in 1849. D. B. Morrill, a Galveston stage-driver, came under the influence of Huckins. He was licensed to preach on February 5, 1848, and entered Baylor as a beneficiary the following July. "It would require a volume to record the benefits that have flowed from the Education Society."[48]

Baylor's first incident of a disciplinary nature occurred in 1849. In the beginning the board of trustees had considered discipline at the institution within the scope of its authority, and the executive committee was charged with the responsibility. At its June 1848 meeting the board abrogated its previous action and invested the president with the authority to handle discipline.

President Graves had suspended a student, and the matter came to the attention of the board. The action of the president was upheld as "entirely meeting the approbation of said Trustees." It was recommended, however, that "the said student, evincing a proper degree of regret for his past conduct and satisfying President Graves that he will conduct himself with propriety in the future . . . be restored to his standing in the institution."[49] Another matter of an unpleasant nature involved trustee Orin Drake. At this same meeting the clerk was directed to write Mr. Drake, asking for his resignation as a trustee because of reported imbibing of alcoholic beverages.

[47] *South-Western Baptist Chronicle* (New Orleans, Louisiana), Nov. 17, 1849.

[48] Morrell, pp. 217-225.

[49] Minutes of Baylor Board of Trustees, June 13, 1849, p. 42.

In order to assist James Huckins in his solicitations for Baylor, Judge Baylor moved at this meeting that President Graves write a letter of recommendation "for our Traveling Agent" and that the editors of the *South-Western Baptist Chronicle*, the *South Carolina Baptist*, *The Christian Index*, the *Tennessee Baptist*, *The Banner*, *The Biblical Recorder*, the *Religious Herald*, and the *New York Recorder* be requested to print it.

President Graves further identified himself with the community when he was initiated into the Masonic Lodge Milam No. 11, on December 9, 1849, at Independence and became a Master Mason in 1850. With Judge Baylor and others he is listed as a petitioner for a charter for the Gay Hill Lodge.

Since the young college published no catalogue, the method used to inform the public of its activities was the conventional one of the day—newspaper announcements. *The Texas Ranger and Lone Star* of February 7, 1850, carried the following concerning Baylor University:

The present Session of this Institution commenced on the 14th day of January, and will expire on the 14th day of June.

Faculty

Rev. Henry L. Graves, A. M., President
R. Daniel Witt, Professor
Warren Cowles, Professor
Thomas Stribling, Tutor
Augustus Buttlar, Professor of French, German and Painting
Mrs. Louisa Buttlar, Teacher of Music and Embroidery

Terms in Preparatory Department

Elementary Branches	$ 8.00
English, German, Geography, Arithmetic	13.00
Ancient Languages, Natural Science and Mathematical Science, and Moral and Intellectual Philosophy	15.00
French language	10.00
German language	10.00
Music on piano with use of instrument	25.00
Music on guitar with use of instrument	25.00
Painting	10.00
Embroidery	10.00
Fee in the Collegiate Department	25.00
Boarding including fuel, washing, lights and lodging per month	$7.00 to 8.00

Tuition payable in advance. No deductions, except in cases of protracted sickness.

Hosea Garrett
Pres., Board of Trustees.

The hope was that Baylor would draw students from the surrounding counties. Neighboring township, Washington, was quite a cross-roads in 1850, for J. A. Kimball wrote of seeing twelve steamboats lying at her wharves. The town was "filled with large brick buildings and doing an immense business." But the prairie between Washington and Houston was frequently almost impassable because of mud.

At the Independence Board of Trustees meeting on June 13, 1850, Rufus C. Burleson made his first appearance and opened the meeting with prayer.[50] He was seated as proxy for A. S. Lipscomb. At the 1849 Baptist State Convention a committee was appointed to secure by an act of the legislature a change in the charter, allowing all vacancies in the Baylor University Board to be filled by the convention rather than by the Education Society. By the next meeting the change had been effected, and since 1850 the Baylor Board of Trustees has enjoyed the patronage of the Baptist State Convention.[51] At this time, however, the practice of a proxy trustee was still allowed, and there was no lack of representation.

The June trustee meeting of 1850 concerned itself with the acquisition of deeds to property donated to the university by Mr. and Mrs. H. Koonts, Mr. and Mrs. W. W. Allen, and Mr. J. M. McKnight. The college building to be known as Graves Hall was nearing completion; hence, the trustees authorized the purchase and installation of window blinds. The treasurer was ordered "to draw on A. C. Horton, L. W. Gross, and Henry Gibson, each for $100 against their subscriptions to the university." Suitable chairs and writing desks were to be provided, after a consultation with the president. The treasurer's report revealed that $730 in cash had been acquired through subscriptions, $600 of

[50] In February 1847 the Board had designated the Reverend Burleson of Covington, Kentucky, to act as agent for the university "to collect money, books, philosophical apparatus, etc . . . in the states of Kentucky, Ohio, Mississippi, and Alabama." He was to receive a ten per cent commission on all collections.

[51] Report of House of Representatives Committee on Education, Guy Morrison Bryan, Chairman, 3rd Legislature No. 107, December 26-28, 1849, Texas State Library, Authors Division, Austin, Texas; *Gammel's Laws*, III, pp. 703-704.

A letter from President Graves to B. E. Tarver in Austin, Texas, on December 14, 1849, states "there has been no stretch of power on the part of the Convention, for that body has done nothing more than yield to the request of the Education Board in asking the convention to appoint trustees of Baylor."

which had been gleaned by agent Huckins. Disbursements, primarily to J. M. McKnight on the building, totaled $580, leaving a balance on hand of $150.

The trustees had reason to be hopeful. They appointed a committee to wait on President Graves "to ascertain if he will accept the appointment of the Trustees in tendering him the university on the same conditions as heretofore for the next two successive years." The committee of Creath, Baylor, and Burleson was also asked to confer with the president concerning the propriety of endowing a professorship and to report the following day.

Judge Baylor reported for the committee, and the following *Plan of Scholarships* was adopted:

1. Permanent Scholarships $500
2. Family Scholarships $100
   if five or more are taken
3. Church Scholarships $200
   designated by the church for one young man
4. Individual Scholarships $150
5. Charity Scholarships . . . . $ 50
   recipient exempt from tuition only

The board hoped to raise a minimum of $10,000 toward endowing the presidency of the university by the sale of scholarships. Six agents, all ministers, (Graves, Creath, Stribling, Burleson, Baines, and Taliaferro) were appointed to sell scholarships as well as "to collect all information in their power on the subject" of such a project.

Of note also at this meeting was an assessment of one dollar per year on each student entering the institution, both in the male and female departments "for the purpose of making repairs and keeping said building and furniture in order." The president or treasurer would receive payments.

Significant, too, was the purchase of two pieces of land near the college ground: one by J. G. Thomas from J. A. McMurray, and the other by President Graves, who was ordered to be reimbursed $40, which he had paid J. M. Norris. R. E. B. Baylor and N. Kavanaugh were appointed to procure "a seal for the use of the University."[52] Baylor was planning for the future.

[52] Minutes of the Baylor Board of Trustees, June 15, 1850, p. 51.

The annual trustee meeting of June 1851 convened for several days. The trustees asked for a report from President Graves concerning the condition of the institution, the number of scholars, and the effectiveness of the new building. Communications with agent Huckins had been difficult; so the board ordered the treasurer to request Huckins to return to Texas as soon as practicable so that "the building committee could settle with him and ascertain all the indebtedness of Baylor University, and what is due said institution."

James Huckins had bought a set of philosophical and chemical apparatus for Baylor University from the Chamberlin firm in Boston in 1851."[53] At the mid-June commencement of 1851, President Graves requested J. A. Kimball to inspect it and, if possible, to perform some experiments publicly. Students had unpacked the boxes, and the contents "lay scattered over the floor in one of the rooms of the college," wrote Kimball. Nevertheless, he put together the pieces and performed quite a number of experiments before a crowded house. Kimball declared: "I do not know of any [chemical] apparatus in Texas before these."

On June 14, 1851, President Graves appeared before the board, gave his report, and submitted his resignation for reasons of health. It was tabled until the following Monday, June 16. Then the trustees accepted with regret the resignation and passed a resolution tendering "their sincere thanks to President Graves for the able and efficient manner in which he has presided over the said institution during the period of his presidency." During the last year of Dr. Graves' administration the institution had acquired its first permanent building, costing $6,000. Enrollment had reached 70 students in the two departments.

Again the trustees of Baylor faced a crisis. A committee of five was appointed to ascertain on what terms it might enter a new arrangement either with the former president or some other suitable person to take charge of the Baylor University as president thereof, and also on what terms the necessary tutors or assistants might be employed. The committee of Lipscomb, Creath, Haynes, Jackson, and Baylor was not successful in urging President Graves to reconsider.

[53] J. A. Kimball, "Editor's Drawer," *Texas Historical and Biographical Magazine* II, 434.

Failing health, characterized by a serious bronchial trouble, influenced Graves in his decision to resign from the presidency of Baylor University.[54]

C. C. Chaplin wrote of Dr. Graves, "As a presiding officer he excelled. Calm and courteous he commanded the confidence of the body. . . . As a speaker he was graceful, eminently chaste in his diction, logical in his argument, and sometimes almost fervidly eloquent. He was not an orator but a finished educator, a well-equipped theologian."[55] Historian J. B. Link wrote that "Texas Baptists never numbered in their ranks a purer, a more humble and truer man than Henry Lee Graves."[56]

The 1945 Centennial *Round-Up* of Baylor University pays tribute to Henry L. Graves, the institution's first president and "one of the very best school men of his day." Quoted there is a precept which governed his belief in Christian education: "Christianity demands the ablest minds God has created and sanctified." Baylor's Moody Memorial Library, dedicated on October 26, 1968, contains the Graves Seminar Room, honoring the first president of Baylor University.[57] Each year the Independence Homecoming Association pays tribute to Henry L. Graves by laying a wreath at the Brenham Cemetery marker bearing his name.

By coincidence, the Baptist State Convention was then in session at Independence on June 17, 1851. The trustees

[54] Graves retired to his plantation near Independence to recuperate. He still maintained a keen interest in the institution and served as proxy trustee in 1853 and on the Examining Committee for the Male Department in 1854. His devotion to the cause of Baptist schools is also indicated by the fact that he served as president of the Baptist Education Society continuously from 1855 to 1858. Subsequently Graves was called to the presidency of Fairfield College in 1859. He led the school through the vicissitudes of the war years. The death of his wife in 1865 and a series of lawsuits (on unpaid promisory notes signed to maintain the college which he owned) darkened his days. In December of 1869, Graves and his children sold twenty acres of land and all the buildings of the college to Alice N. Adams. In 1870 Graves moved back to Independence and served for approximately two years (1871-1872) as president of Baylor Female College. After his resignation he was married to Mrs. Myra E. Crumpler on July 9, 1872. He was active in Baptist affairs until the time of his death on November 4, 1881, at Brenham.
[55] Reverend Charles Crawford Chaplin, undated, unidentified newsclipping, evidently appearing at the time of Graves' death.
[56] Link, I, 53. Baylor Professor P. D. Browne has done extensive research in the Fairfield area and is the authority on President Graves.
[57] The room was given by the great-grandson of President Graves, Mr. Henry L. Graves of Dallas.

arranged a candle-light meeting that very night so that Judge Lipscomb could present to the convention the plan for the endowment of the presidency of the university. So effective was the address of Judge Lipscomb and the pleas of Eli Mercer and Jesse Witt to the convention assembled in the college building that $5,355 was pledged and the subscription book was handed over to the treasurer of the Baylor Board of Trustees, A. G. Haynes. Thus came realistic backing from the Baptists of Texas. A report consisting of three resolutions was subsequently presented to the body. Churches were urged to seek out promising young men and help them financially to prepare for the ministry. Pastors were to present to their churches the need for the presidential endowment. Members of the convention were asked to pledge cooperation with the Baylor Board through prayers, sympathy, and money.[58]

Next day the trustees unanimously elected Rufus Columbus Burleson president, and a committee of Creath, Kavanaugh, and Farquhar was named to notify him. Significant also was the fact that a future Baylor president, George W. Baines, presented his certificate of election from the Baptist State Convention and took his seat as a trustee of the university.[59] On the following day, June 18, 1851, the Reverend Burleson came before the board and accepted the presidency of Baylor University.

---

[58] *Minutes of the Fifth Annual Session of the Baptist State Convention of Texas,* 1851 (Washington, Texas: Texas Ranger Office, 1851), p. 13.

[59] Minutes of the Trustees of June 15, 1850, show that Baines opened the meeting with prayer and was named to a committee consisting of Creath and Baylor for the purpose of setting forth in a circular information about the university. At this time, Baines was also designated one of six agents appointed to sell scholarships for the endowment of the presidency.

CHAPTER V

Young Burleson Comes to Baylor in 1851

HARRY HAYNES STATED that Baylor University was "born in a storm, and lived in a storm up to the time Dr. Burleson was placed at the helm in 1851."[1] Destiny still reserved storms for Baylor. Haynes credits Burleson's coming to Baylor to Judge Abner S. Lipscomb, who placed the name of Burleson in nomination for the presidency. The sponsorship of the illustrious judge gave the twenty-seven-year-old Houston minister added prestige and confidence in the minds of the people.[2]

Despite his full pastoral duties during the three and one-half years he served the Baptist Church of Houston, the Reverend Burleson always attended the annual commencement exercises of Baylor University. Having ridden horseback from Houston, he was present when Dr. Graves resigned the presidency on June 17, 1851. When Burleson was named president, arrangements were made for him to assume responsibilities as soon as possible.[3]

Rufus C. Burleson was born on August 7, 1823, near Decatur, in Morgan County, Alabama. He was the son of Jonathan and Elizabeth Byrd Burleson. She was a sister of Governor William Adair of Kentucky and a descendant of Sir William Byrd, founder of Richmond and Petersburg, Virginia. The Burleson family, in its American branch, dated back to Sir Edward Burleson, who came from England in 1716 to settle in Connecticut, and Aaron, who came in 1724 to settle in North Carolina. Descendant Jonathan married the sheltered Elizabeth Byrd on September 17, 1813, near

---

[1] Harry Haynes, *Life and Writings of Dr. Rufus C. Burleson* (compiled and published by Mrs. Georgia J. Burleson, 1901), p. 110.

[2] With R. T. Wheeler and John Hemphill, Lipscomb was elected an associate justice of the first Supreme Court of Texas. Judge Lipscomb was interested not only in the Law Department of Baylor, but he later served on the Board of Examiners for the Female Department on July 27, 1854, and worked with a committee to define the course of study for graduation in October 1854. Minutes of Baylor Board of Trustees, p. 83.

[3] The trustees appointed a committee to inform the Houston Church and request the release of the pastor from his contract. In a special conference on July 5, 1851, such action was taken. *Ibid.*, p. 97.

Lexington, Kentucky, and in 1814 they journeyed by horseback through unbroken wilderness to found a home on the east fork of the Flint River of Morgan County, in northern Alabama.

Rufus was the sixth child of the couple and early learned the spirit of usefulness both in the home and on the plantation. An active explorer, he was credited with finding a cave, overlooked by geologists, which his father used as a refrigerator. His early education was directed by his "grand father" and "angel mother"—terms he always used to refer to his parents. He was an apt student, interested primarily in languages, literature, and philosophy. Soon he was challenged by the classics. At the age of seven, Rufus attended one of the district schools on the Flint River and continued in attendance at the "old field schools" at intervals for seven years.

In 1837 young Burleson entered Summerville Academy, conducted by Professor A. B. Wattson, later on the Nashville University faculty. Here he remained for two years, then entered a Danville school taught by a Dr. Sims. Because of the death of his mother on July 12, 1839, his attendance was brief. In the following September he entered Professor J. S. Perkins' school at Decatur, six miles from his home. School was interrupted by frequent visits to his home to place fresh flowers on his mother's tomb. On one of these visits he attended a revival meeting conducted by W. H. Holcombe and Leonard H. Milliken. But a minister of the Cumberland Presbyterian Church, a Dr. Porter, delivered the sermon under which he was converted on April 21, 1839, in his sixteenth year. Shortly thereafter Burleson was baptized in the Flint River by Reverend Holcombe. So dynamic was his conversion that he renounced all previously cherished plans to be a lawyer and statesman and vowed to devote himself to the ministry.[4]

Having decided to preach, he entered Nashville University in 1840 to prepare himself for admission to a theological seminary. Ill health forced him to withdraw from the university after a year. For the next five years he taught in the schools of Mississippi and was ordained to the ministry at the Catalpa Baptist Church, Okibbeha County, Mississippi,

[4] Haynes, pp. 5-39.

on June 8, 1845. William Carey Crane, as church clerk, signed the ordination papers. In January 1846, he entered Western Baptist Theological Seminary and was graduated the next year. While attending the seminary, he had become interested in Texas. Upon receiving his diploma, "surrounded by preceptors and pupils, he straightened his tall form . . . and with closed eyes . . . he raised his boyish face toward heaven, stretched both his arms toward the West, and in a clear voice and eloquent tones he exclaimed: 'This day I consecrate my life to Texas.' "[5]

Burleson applied to the Southern Baptist Domestic Mission Board for missionary work in the frontier country. He was assigned to the Gonzales District, but upon his arrival in Texas on January 5, 1848, he was approved as pastor of the First Baptist Church of Houston and on January 7, 1848, entered upon his pastoral duties as successor to the beloved Tryon.[6] Burleson was a successful pastor and soon came to be much in demand as an evangelist. He interested himself in Baylor University and was a frequent visitor. He was attending the Baptist State Convention in Independence in June 1851 when it met with the Baylor Board of Trustees.

The following notation in the Minutes of the Board of Trustees of June 1851—just before President Graves resigned and Burleson became president—has long been shrouded in mystery:

> The communication from Austin College was taken up and rejected. Baylor and Lipscomb were appointed a committee to answer said communication, showing the reason fully why it was rejected.[7]

Abner Lipscomb (also a member of the Austin College Board) with Henderson Yoakum and Sam Houston formed the Trustee Committee on "College Lands" for Austin College at Huntsville. Mr. Lipscomb had made forceful efforts to have the state legislature endow all church colleges with large land grants.[8] Judge Baylor had a friendly association with Austin College also, for on June 24, 1851, "Reverend

[5] *Ibid.*, p. 57.

[6] Walter Prescott Webb and H. Bailey Carroll (eds.), *The Handbook of Texas* (Austin: Texas State Historical Association, 1952), I, 250.

[7] Minutes of the Baylor Board of Trustees, June 13, 1851, p. 65.

[8] Rollin M. Rolfe, Dean of Students, Austin College, Sherman, Texas, July 24, 1956.

Chaplain R. E. B. Baylor offered the opening prayer when the Masons laid the cornerstone" of the college's first building—a handsome $17,000 edifice.[9]

An article written by former President Baines for the *Texas Baptist* nearly thirty years later sheds some light on the question of state aid. The occasion for his publication was the fact that Baylor President W. C. Crane had stood for state aid to denominational schools at a teachers' meeting in Austin. He wrote:

> . . . not long after he was elected president of Baylor University [Burleson] came before the board of trustees with a proposition that they should unite with other denominations in a petition to the legislature of Texas for aid to endow Baylor University and other schools. . . . A member of the board opposed his proposition on this ground that it would be a departure from Baptist principle, and he was defeated.

Baines added that a plan was "ingeniously arranged for carrying the resolution through the State Convention." The resolution proposed to unite the Methodists, Presbyterians, and Episcopalians in a petition to the legislature for a grant of forty thousand acres of land to each denomination for school purposes. Dr. J. V. Wright introduced the resolution and advocated its adoption. Then followed in succession speeches from J. B. Stiteler, J. M. Maxey, R. B. Burleson, Horace Clark and R. C. Burleson—all in favor of the resolution. The man who opposed the proposition and defeated it in the Board of Trustees then arose, and under the pressure of strong emotion addressed the president and said to the convention that from the array of popular talent which had been brought to bear in favor of the resolution it seemed that it must pass almost as by acclamation. But he, as an old-fashioned Baptist, "presented the well-known Baptist platform of true religious liberty." He cited Luther Rice and Jesse Mercer as having declined state aid and declared "I shall wash my hands clean from every Baptist body and institution that favors such a principle." Maxey replied but made no attempt to answer the argument.

R. C. Burleson said Brother Rice and Brother Mercer were great and good men in their day, but this is an age of progress and that

[9] William Stuart Red, *A History of the Presbyterian Church in Texas* (San Antonio: The Steck Company, 1936), p. 240.

we have discovered that there need be no great evil arising from the receiving of State donations to help us in our time of great need to build up our male colleges and he wanted it distinctly understood that this donation was to be for the male department of Baylor University. Horace Clark, who had spoken in favor of the resolution, then gave notice that he would vote against its passage.

Nine stood to vote in favor and about ninety against the adoption.[10] Baines was the man who led the opposition.

Undoubtedly this action was the initial controversy between Burleson and Clark which reached a crescendo in 1860 and finally resulted in Burleson's removal to Waco with his faculty.

Young Burleson made certain stipulations before he accepted the Baylor presidency:

1. That all disciplinary and internal matters of the school be under the jurisdiction of the faculty, and that all external and financial matters be handled by the board of trustees.
2. That the university refrain from assuming debts, and that a building plan be adopted.
3. That an endowment of $10,000 be raised at once and placed at interest; that the fund be increased to $50,000 at the rate of $10,000 every five years, and that adequate buildings be provided.
4. That the male and female pupils be separated and the two departments be conducted separately.
5. That as president of the school he not be required to give up preaching the gospel.[11]

At the June 18, 1851, meeting of the trustees, several other significant actions were taken.

Elder Horace Clark and his Lady with Miss Harriet Davis [were] requested to take charge of the Female Department of Baylor University, and Elder Clark [was requested to] be the principal of said department on the condition that he be entitled to the tuition fees arising from the same.

[10] G. W. Baines, Belton, Texas, February 1879; *Texas Baptist,* March 6, 1879. Morrell reported the same incident "at the Baptist State Convention in session with the Baptist Church of Independence." He stated that this was the leading question—"asking aid from the State in lands or otherwise to sustain the University." Differences of opinion prevailed. "Heavy artillery of intellect let loose by the tongue of eloquence" became a trap for the union of church and state. Baines rose to reply: " . . . if the State made appropriations of lands or otherwise, the natural result must be that the State would look after her investment."

Baylor University operated under a charter issued by the Republic of Texas and subsequently under the State of Texas.

[11] Haynes, pp. 114-115.

Clark had ridden horseback from La Grange to Independence in order to confer with the Baylor Board of Trustees. He promised to accept the position if a new building could be provided. Arrangements were made, and he made plans for the first session to open on the first Monday of August, 1851. July was a busy month, for Clark found it necessary to go two hundred miles to Houston for the purchase of flour and other provisions for his boarding house.[12]

Clark, at thirty-two, had already experienced an eventful life. Son of John and Catherine Aldrich Clark, he was born in Charleston, Massachusetts, on July 7, 1819. Two years later his father died. His mother, an able writer of both prose and poetry, assumed the responsibility for her son. Because of the influence of an uncle in the Merchant Marine, young Clark spent four years at sea. He sailed to South America, the Cape Verde Islands, St. Helena, around the Cape of Good Hope, to Java, China, and the Philippines. At fourteen he was shanghaied in Rio de Janeiro and experienced a daring rescue by Captain Brown.[13]

In 1836 Clark and his mother moved to Upper Alton, Illinois, and the boy entered Shurtleff College. After graduation he accepted a position at Georgetown College in Kentucky in 1841. Clark married a graduate of Monticello Seminary, Martha Davis, daughter of Reverend G. B. Davis of Bunker Hill, Macoupin County, Illinois, in 1844.[14] In 1846 Clark became principal of Henry Academy at New Castle, Henry County, Kentucky, and served for four years.

In 1850 the Clarks came to Texas. For one year Clark was president of La Grange Collegiate Institute; then he removed to Independence to become principal of the Female Department of Baylor University.

The building committee, on which the Reverend G. W. Baines replaced J. R. Hines (resigned), was authorized to prepare the Female Academy for "more comfortable use" and to assist Mr. Clark in obtaining a suitable residence for his family "by purchase or otherwise" and to use any available university funds for the project. A. G. Haynes and J. L.

---

[12] Student League and Alumnae Association, Baylor College, Belton, Texas, *After Seventy-Five Years,* p. 120.

[13] Mary E. Bryan, *Houston Post,* February 24, 1908.

[14] The couple celebrated their golden wedding anniversary in Corpus Christi, Texas, on March 31, 1894.

Farquhar advanced money to buy a building from W. H. Cleveland, a Baptist deacon.[15] The treasurer was ordered to repay Dr. Graves and Nelson Kavanaugh for their expenditures on window blinds shipped from Houston. Intent on endowing the presidency, the board appointed Baines and Haynes to secure an agent to obtain the remainder of the subscription. The Reverend Baines and Judge Baylor were directed to prepare a circular for newspaper publication telling of the new administration at Baylor and the new term to open on the first Monday in August 1851.

Despite the renewed hope for the institution and "the fact that Dr. Burleson, the president-elect, brought with him much learning and enthusiasm . . ." the trustees and many friends, both local and over the state, were full of pessimism. "To prepare himself for every issue that might arise in his administration," President Burleson sent letters to President R. E. Pattison of the Seminary at Covington, Kentucky; President Francis Wayland of Brown University; and President Basil Manly of Alabama University, asking for advice and suggestions.[16]

These men made timely suggestions and supplied "valuable literature covering the field of practical learning." They agreed that in an effort to build up a school in a pioneer country with unsettled and conflicting interests, divergent opinions, and unorganized society, it would be necessary to remodel and modify the regulations and courses of study "in older and more thoroughly organized and completely equipped institutions." The young president then presented the following outline of policy, which was adopted by the trustees:

---

[15] J. M. Carroll, *The History of Texas Baptists* (Dallas: Baptist Standard Publishing Company, 1923), p. 401.

Cleveland did not serve as a trustee at Baylor at Independence, but he was a great friend of the institution, his name appearing sixteen times in the minutes in regard to loans or work for the school. Cleveland later served as manager of some of Sam Houston's property, and a letter to him from General Houston is in the Texas Collection. Cleveland's descendants were closely associated with Baylor throughout the years: Virginia Cleveland was graduated in 1862, and she and her husband, Latin Professor S. E. Thompson, were in charge of Georgia Burleson Hall on the Waco campus; great-granddaughter Elizabeth Rowe Kennon and husband L. H. Kennon of Houston have been liberal donors to Baylor; great-great-granddaughters "Kitty" Williard Kennon (B.S. 1946), Beverly Hugghins, and Nell Hugghins (B.A. 1953), great-great-grandson Thomas Hugghins, and three of their uncles—Ernest, John, and Billy Guy Hugghins—attended Baylor.

[16] Haynes, pp. 116-117.

First: The government of Baylor University shall be strictly parental to all her students, in sickness and in health, in or out of school, and ever an *alma mater*, and not *injusta noverca*.

Second: The president and faculty will seek by every possible means, to guard the health, and cultivate the morals, as well as, develop the intellect of the student, that they may become useful citizens in church and state.

Third: All hazing, acts of vandalism, disregard of property rights, shall be placed under an eternal ban, as crimes against the college government, and well-ordered society.

Fourth: The president and faculty will seek to impress upon every student, the fact that every rule is made for his good, and its rigid enforcement is to promote his welfare.

Fifth: Adopt such a curriculum, prescribe such a course of studies and such modes of teaching as are calculated to arouse thought, and develop the habit and faculty of thinking rapidly, profoundly, and correctly.

Sixth: In addition to the usual course of college studies, give special attention to English literature, and the history of our own great men, so as to fire the soul with love for God, home, and the native land.

Seventh: The president and faculty will treat all students exactly alike, regardless of their circumstances in life; and personal favoritism and partiality will be eliminated entirely from all regulations governing the school.

Eighth: The mottoes of Baylor University shall be, "Pro Ecclesia, Pro Texana"; "Dulce et Decorum, pro patria, Mori."[17]

With this plan, Burleson began his career at Baylor, following his personal dictum: "A resolute mind is omnipotent." He recalled "that in the halls of my *alma mater* I had written in my diary, 'A Great Texas Baptist University is a necessity for the complete success of the Baptist cause in Texas.' "[18] Thus Burleson proceeded with the plan which made him the leader of Texas Baptist educational affairs for approximately half a century.

With the resignation of Dr. Graves, the current opinion was that Baylor was dead. In fact, the day before he was named president, Burleson himself wrote:

. . . there was not a single painted or even whitewashed house in the village, and one fourth of the business houses were deserted. It seemed a valley of dry bones compared with my Houston home.

The first necessity of the president was to correct the public impression. The task was difficult in the absence of

[17] Haynes, pp. 117-118.
[18] Rufus C. Burleson, "The Lights and Shadows of Baylor University for Fifty Years," *The Guardian,* XI (March, 1892), 159.

railroads, telegraph and telephones, daily and even weekly papers. Burleson had circulars printed relating the state of affairs at Baylor—that the school would be open in September with a full corps of teachers and that "board could be secured at $8 per month, which included lodging and table accommodations, fuel, lights, laundry, medicines and nursing in case of sickness."[19] This provision resulted from the sacrificial spirit of local residents. A half dozen couriers on horseback carried these circulars to every part of the state. Burleson wrote personal letters to the few newspapers and to acquaintances and informed church audiences of Baylor affairs. The school opened as scheduled with 35 students in the Male Department in Graves Hall, the new stone building named in honor of Baylor's first president, and with 22 students in the Female Department using the Independence Academy. The president emphasized daily oral recitations, and compositions and declamations were semi-monthly requirements. Oratory was of great significance to young Burleson. Four years previously he had written his brother, Richard:

I also devote much time to Rhetorical exercises. An orator can shake the world. And why are we not orators? We can be if we will strive as Demosthenes did. If I am not an orator in ten years then do not call me Brother.[20]

This forceful, stern man demanded excellence of his pupils and saw nothing incongruous in praying over a young delinquent and then administering a sound flogging.[21] A student of the 1850's recorded this reaction to the young president:

. . . and while we were shrinking back from the piercing glance, the hand of cordial welcome was extended. He is courteous and polite, yet we stand in awe. We do not dread him, for we love him.[22]

Principal Horace Clark is reported to have been less stern than Burleson and was considered by one campus visitor "one of the most affable men I ever met, and his wife even surpassed him in graciousness and politeness."[23] In his memoirs Judge Baylor described Mr. Clark as a gentle man

[19] Haynes, p. 120.
[20] Rufus C. Burleson to Richard Burleson, September 26, 1847. Burleson Papers, Texas Collection, Baylor University.
[21] Frederick Eby, *The Development of Education in Texas* (New York: The Macmillan Co., 1925), pp. 139-140.
[22] *Texas Baptist Herald*, Houston, March 18, 1857.
[23] *Texas Baptist*, Anderson, Texas, September 9, 1858.

. . . of medium height with a figure not denoting great sinual or muscular strength; blue eyes, light hair and complection [*sic*], features regular and well formed of the Grecian mould; the base of his forhead [*sic*] strongly marked and projecting which showed at once he was no ordinary man; with manners uniformly kind and polite.[24]

At the August 2, 1851, meeting of the Baylor Board of Trustees, Baines (then pastor of the Independence Baptist Church), Baylor, and Lipscomb were designated as a committee to work with President Burleson, Principal Clark, and the faculty "to make out a regular course of study for the different classes of students in both Male and Female Departments of the college proper and the Preparatory Department, so that each student who may desire it may continue regularly on to graduation." No record of this committee's work is available; but President Burleson, according to Haynes, wrote: "It is the fixed determination of the President and Trustees, to fully meet the educational wants of Texas, and to qualify their students to become the brightest ornaments, and the firmest pillars of this great and growing commonwealth."[25] At this board meeting W. L. Foster was named professor of French, Spanish, and mathematics and Thomas G. Edwards professor of English and tutor in the Preparatory Department. Their tenure was short, however.

Baylor's first catalogue, termed by Haynes "the first issued by any school in the state," presented a classical curriculum. Upon entering, freshmen were given an examination on Latin and Greek grammar, Caesar, Virgil, Cicero's Orations, and algebra. Since the majority of the entrants were unable to pass the rigid entrance examinations, a two-year preparatory division was offered. The college curriculum provided for a three-year course of Greek and Latin; four years of mathematics; and other studies such as ancient history, philosophy, physics (natural philosophy), chemistry, geology, astronomy, logic, surveying and navigation, political economy, rhetoric and "Evidences of Christianity."[26] The

[24] Judge R. E. B. Baylor MS, Texas Collection, Baylor University.
[25] Haynes, pp. 142-143.
[26] *Catalogue of the Trustees, Officers, and Students of Baylor University,* 1851-1852, pp. 6-7.
    Students classified in the Male Department were sophomores Isaiah Harlan, T. S. Moore, D. B. Morrill (ministerial student), William Robertson, Thomas B. Shannon, and Stephen Decatur Rowe and eleven freshmen, one of whom was James L. Smith (later to be principal of the preparatory department from 1857 to 1860).

following table shows the enrollment of students during the 1851-1852 school year:

	Male Department	Female Department
Preparatory	77	71
College Freshmen	11	7
College Sophomores	6	7
College Juniors	--	2
Total	94	87
		Total 181

College students had four classes daily; preparatory students had even more. Semi-monthly compositions and declamations were required. Instructors kept daily records of attendance, conduct, and recitations for each student with a weekly report in a permanent file. Students were required to attend prayers in the chapel each morning and evening.

For the November 1851 board meeting a large committee had been appointed to consider the organization of a theological department. At the December 13th meeting the committee reported that "it is inexpedient at the present to organize such a department." It was recommended, however, that "the President arrange such young men in a Theological class and give them whatever instruction he may be able, also that Brother Baines be requested to deliver to said class lectures on Pastoral Theology." Also organized at this early time was the Philomathesian Society, which "held weekly meetings for debates, lectures, and other forms of mental culture."[27]

The November 4, 1851, meeting of the Baylor board passed resolutions on the first Baylor teacher to die in service:

---

[27] Haynes, p. 132; Baylor Catalogue, 1851, p. 7.
Organization date was February 26, 1851. President Burleson endeavored to move the charter of the fraternity to Waco in 1861 when he assumed the presidency of Waco University, but national headquarters would not permit the action. Later, after Baylor and Waco Universities were combined as Baylor University, the change concerning the Philomathesian Society was made. The Constitution and By-Laws of the Society were revised and adopted in January 1890.
First officers of the Philomathesians were Stephen D. Rowe, President (Baylor's first graduate, A.B. 1854); William Morgan (1851-4), Vice-President; James L. Lade, Recording Secretary (n.d.); Thomas B. Haynes, Treasurer (1851-4); James Steen, Supervisor (1851-2). *Baylor University Annual* 1896, p. 173.

Whereas, Mr. Daniel Witt, Jr., A. M., was for some years connected with the Baylor University as professor and tutor with honor to himself and credit to the institution and it hath pleased the all-wise Arbiter of the Universe to remove him from amongst us by death to his reward in Heaven.

Resolved, therefore, that we deeply sympathize with his aged parents and afflicted relatives, who are called upon to mourn his early death, and

Resolved that a copy of this resolution be forwarded to Elder Jesse Witt, father of the deceased.

The Baylor Catalogue for 1851-52 also recorded the first deaths in the student body: William Cleveland and Henry Holmes, both of prominent Independence families.

At the December 13, 1851, meeting of the board of trustees young President Burleson found it necessary to fill several vacancies in his faculty. He presented S. G. O'Bryan to fill the place of Mr. Foster, resigned professor of mathematics. B. S. Fitzgerald was named tutor in place of Mr. Edwards, resigned.[28]

The Baylor trustees at this meeting noted a significant oversight during the tempestuous days of the preceding June when President Graves resigned. The thirteenth item of business stated:

By order of the Board the Sect. is appointed to obtain if possible the report of the committee appointed to obtain information in relation to filling the presidency, etc., of Baylor University made June 17, 1851, as it does not appear on the records of the Board.

Baylor's Dean of the Graduate School, Jefferson Davis Bragg, stated that "the greatest achievement of Dr. Burleson's administration at Independence was the broadening and liberalizing of the curriculum."[29] As evidence of this fact, in 1852 the catalogue listed lectures on modern history, and sophomores took a *French History of the United States* by Barbaroux. Proximity to Mexico made Spanish a significant foreign language, and German found favor because of the large German population in that part of the state.

[28] Fitzgerald served on the Baylor faculty intermittently. (See appendix). Dr. J. A. Kimball states that he brought "the first set of philosophical apparatus" to Texas in 1850, disposed of it to B. S. Fitzgerald, who carried it to Baylor Female College. J. A. Kimball, "Editor's Drawer," *Texas Historical and Biographical Magazine* II, 434.

[29] J. D. Bragg, "Baylor University 1851-1861," *The Southwestern Historical Quarterly*, XLIX (July, 1945), 52-53.

Ministerial students substituted Hebrew for a modern foreign language.

At the insistence of President Burleson, negotiations were made with Reverend James Huckins, then in the States, again to assume the duties as agent for the university. J. W. D. Creath was designated agent in the *interim*, and letters addressed to *Southwest Baptist, The Christian Index*, and the *New York Recorder* requested Huckins' "forthwith return" to Texas if possible. Money matters were pressing, and at the December 14, 1851, trustee meeting President Burleson volunteered to raise $2,000, Creath, $2,000, and Garrett $500 on the endowment fund.

James Huckins received the urgent message from the trustees and appeared at a called meeting of the board on January 22, 1852. He had collected $1,300 above expenses. The sum was "to be loaned, the interest on which to be applied to the payment of the President's salary: conditioned further that one poor young man studying for the Gospel ministry may be educated free from tuition fees for six hundred dollars of said amount." Baylor then borrowed $1,325 at 8% interest. Various bills were paid, including the following:

J. W. D. Creath, agent	$ 13.56¼
F. W. Robertson	200.00
and a load of sugar and molasses if the sugar and molasses can be obtained from A. C. Horton on whom the Treasurer is hereby authorized to draw for the same.	
James L. Smith, repair of desks	$ 15.00
D. B. Madden, merchandise	15.00
W. H. Cleveland, part payment on note	250.00
N. Kavanaugh, on blinds	50.00
R. C. Burleson	114.00

Huckins received the thanks of the board in the form of a motion, and he was requested to serve as agent for the year 1852 through a committee appointed to confer with him. Huckins addressed a letter to the Trustee Committee of Baylor, Baines, Haynes, and Holmes in which he made five stipulations:

First: That you make no further appropriations until all the liabilities of the school are liquidated.

Second: That you make immediate efforts as soon as the debts of the institution are paid, to build suitable edifices, for rooms to accommodate the students of the college department, and also a boarding house.

Third: That at the close of the present session, or your contract, you either sell the property you have purchased for a boarding house or rent it, and apply the income to the payment of interest due from the Trustees to the endowment fund.

Fourth: That whatever is done in future by way of expenditure by the Trustees, so far as the funds department is concerned, shall be done by funds subscribed, and given expressly for the purpose, as no money as yet received was subscribed for this department.

Fifth: That a more judicious and economical system of expenditures be adopted, and that a statement, or memoranda of your past disbursements, be collected and arranged in a book by your Treasurer so as to show the plain standing of all your financial transactions. [30]

The board saw the realistic wisdom of Huckins' suggestions, and he was instructed to solicit subscriptions: (1) to pay debts that had been incurred; (2) to erect a dormitory for the Male Department; (3) for the endowment of the professorships now established or which may be hereafter established in the Male Department; (4) for funds for repairing the present house occupied by the Female Department; (5) to collect all debts now due the university or which may hereafter become due to said institution, to receive new subscriptions in money, personal property or real estate, and to perfect all titles to property which has been given to said university, and that the contributions of any kind and descriptions be sacredly applied to the purpose for which the donations were given; (6) that the said agent be required to report quarterly of his actions to the treasurer of said board of trustees, whose duty it shall be to lay said reports before the Board at their stated meetings. [31]

Captain W. P. Rogers delivered an "able and eloquent address on the important and interesting theme of Female Education" at the annual examination on June 10, 1852, and a committee of trustees—Farquhar and Shannon—was designated to request it for publication.

The trustees were concerned with the Female Department. Purchase had been made of a house and eight acres from

[30] Haynes, p. 125.

[31] Minutes of the Baylor Board of Trustees, June 10, 1852, pp. 65-68.

W. H. Cleveland for $1,230, and the deed was in the hands
of Brother Baines. Arrangements were made for Principal
Clark to occupy the house at $100 per year, with the rent to
be discharged in improvements, subject to the approval of
the building committee. At the July 20th board meeting,
Mr. Clark proposed to buy the property at the price paid by
the trustees with payment in three installments, and with the
institution holding an option to buy "at a fair valuation in
the event he becomes disconnected with the B. U." This was
the only dormitory for girls during the entire time Baylor
was at Independence.

By the last of July the building committee was authorized
to proceed with the plans for building the dormitories for the
Male Department. The minutes carry this directive:

> The size and location of the dormitories are to be determined by
> said committee. The plan of the buildings is one-story framed houses,
> neatly made, with two rooms and stack chimneys. [32]

Despite the fact that President Burleson received only
$336.00 in cash for his first year at Baylor, he worked
diligently and was optimistic, as indicated by an excerpt
from a letter to his brother:

> My present situation is easy and lucrative. My income is about
> $1,000 per annum. We have a glorious school here. We have 162
> scholars and our reputation is widening everyday. . . . No human
> knows what toil and labor I have expended on this university. [33]

At the last board meeting of the 1852 year on December
16th, the trustees resolved to raise an endowment of $10,000
for the support of a professorship of physical sciences. J. B.
Stiteler, who had heard Huckins' fervent plea for Texas at
Madison University, was elected to fill the chair, his duties
to begin at the next session. Stiteler was also delegated the
task of raising the sum for the endowment of the professorship. [34]

[32] Minutes of the Baylor Board of Trustees, July 30, 1852.
[33] Rufus C. Burleson to Richard B. Burleson in Moulton, Alabama, on
November 8, 1852. Burleson Papers, Texas Collection, Baylor University.
[34] Jacob Beverly Stiteler was born in Philadelphia, Pennsylvania, on February 4, 1823. At an early age he was baptized with his entire family and
became a devout church worker. By his own efforts he financed a collegiate
course at the University of Pennsylvania and was graduated with distinction
in 1846. Colgate University Catalogue I, 88. Subsequently he took a theological
course at Hamilton Theological Institute in New York and was graduated in

Minutes of the trustees reveal that Stiteler had attended the Baylor trustee meeting on January 18, 1851, when he was asked to serve with Judge Baylor to request the Houston Baptist Church to release Pastor Rufus Burleson so that he might assume the presidency of Baylor. At a subsequent meeting he was delegated to write a letter to Agent James Huckins who was "in the field" procuring funds for the university.

The board requested Baines and Baylor to serve with President Burleson in inviting a visiting committee to attend the examinations of the various classes to be held the second week in July. This committee was also charged with the responsibility of drawing up a code of laws for the university. The education committee's report to the Baptist Convention was indicative of a healthy condition: a new college building had been erected; enrollment had increased; the endowment for the presidency was almost $10,000; the faculty consisted of six instructors; the school had "good chemical and philosophical apparatus including a small but valuable library."[35] The promise of Baylor University at the time was so great that the convention rejected a proposal to establish a female institution near Tyler.

Undoubtedly one reason for the optimism and enthusiasm of the young president was his marriage on January 3, 1852, to Miss Georgia Jenkins. This charming young woman, daughter of the eminent Judge P. C. Jenkins, was born in Merriweather, Green County, Georgia, and came to Texas with her family in 1836. She was educated at Judson Female Institution in Marion, Alabama, where she was graduated with high honors in 1852. Burleson had met her on his frequent visits to Independence during his Houston residency; hence the romance developed. Back in 1849, it was

---

1848. The following year he served as pastor of the Baptist Church of Jackson, Mississippi. Impressed as a student by the needs of Texas, Stiteler removed to Galveston, Texas, on January 12, 1851, as the fourth pastor of the Baptist Church—Huckins, Hillyer and Talliaferro having served since its organization in 1847. Stiteler's "rare gifts . . . had attracted the regard of the prominent members of the denomination throughout the state, and he was deemed to require another and much more important field." J. P. Cole, *The First Baptist Church of Galveston* (Galveston: News Stream Job Press, 1871), p. 7. He therefore left to become professor of physical sciences at Baylor.

[35] *The Fifth Annual Session of the Baptist State Convention of Texas,* Marshall, Texas (Washington, Texas: Lone Star Office, 1852), pp. 10-11.

Miss Jenkins who presented the silk banner of the State Sons of Temperance to Mr. Burleson, who made the principal address at the meeting.

Haynes records that "the faculty of the University very generously made some financial concessions to Dr. Burleson, and excused him from active teaching duties, which enabled him to make a bridal tour." The events of the tour are of interest to social historians. Friends "drove the bridal pair to Chappell Hill," where they visited for two or three days before taking the stage to Houston, then the steamer to New Orleans. Mrs. Burleson spent five weeks there "in social recreation, and Dr. Burleson in perfecting himself in the Spanish language." The tour continued to Raymond, Mississippi, before the couple returned to their Independence cottage. Thus began a forty-eight year union in which the cultured, intelligent, Georgia Jenkins became the beloved partner and trusted counselor to this early educator.

One of Mrs. Burleson's first acts at Baylor as a bride was to arrange a social for the girls from Academy Hill. Principal Clark refused to allow the girls to attend because "boys and books don't go together," reported one student. President Burleson was offended and termed the refusal "dis-respect to Mrs. Burleson."

On May 16, 1853, the trustees had a called meeting at which time the subject of discussion was the housing of women students, a matter of high interest, since the completion of the dormitories for men. Principal Horace Clark was requested "to make known the wants of the Female Department of Baylor University at our annual meeting in June and also to present a plan of college building for the same." The annual meeting, however, was held on July 5 and 6, 1853. Dr. Horace Clark later recalled the circumstances which led to the construction of the new building. "The first recognition of the Female Department as being aught else than a quite dispensable attachment to Baylor University" came through the report of the Committee on Education to the Baptist State Convention in 1853.[36] Growth made "the crazy old building" inadequate. Conservatives

---

[36] Commencement Address, Baylor College, Reverend Horace Clark, June 3, 1884. Printed by George Dunlap, Bryan, Texas, pp. 4-5.

were in the majority on the board of trustees, but the minority were strong in their conviction that new quarters for women were a necessity. On the first day of the trustee meeting Principal Clark presented his plan for providing a new building for his department. It was "somewhat discussed and laid over" until the next morning at 8 o'clock.[37] Dr. Clark recalled a night session held in the little concrete office in the old boarding-house yard. "Upon the results of that meeting the fate of the institution was to all human appearances depending. The discussion was carried on until near midnight," declared Clark. General Sam Houston then slowly rose and "in his calm and collected way moved that the plans be adopted and that a contract be forthwith entered into for the erection of the new building." The motion was put to a vote by President Hosea Garrett, and it carried without a dissenting vote. "The Rubicon was passed," recalled Clark. General Houston attended as a guest, for he did not hold board membership. The minutes of the trustees carry no record of this night meeting; hence we may conclude that it was an unofficial meeting. Houston had come to Independence on the last of June to bring son Sam, Jr., to enter Baylor University.[38] Eldest daughter Nancy Elizabeth had enrolled in the Female Department earlier in 1853. Houston wrote to her there: "It is a rule of Mr. Clark's school that no scholar of his shall correspond with any gentleman unless he is a relative." Houston had personal reasons for being interested in the women's accommodations at Baylor. In the autumn he bought from John R. Hines the Thomas Barron house, built in 1837. The acreage joined the Baylor property. He paid $4,000 for the place with 200 enclosed acres and 165 acres of timberland.[39] Houston took an active part in community and school affairs and was a frequent chapel speaker.

During 1853 Sam Houston was deeply concerned with railroads for Texas, and he and General Rusk made speeches before the legislature. Houston called on President Burleson to solicit his support "to decide whether [Texas] is to be a

[37] Minutes of the Baylor Board of Trustees, July 5, 1853, p. 73.
[38] Llerena B. Friend, *Sam Houston, The Great Designer* (Austin: The University of Texas Press, 1954), p. 224.
[39] Deed Records of Washington County, Volume N, p. 175.

mere cow pen and sheep ranch, or a great Empire State." Burleson promised to enter the fight with "fervency and zeal," and he used his great influence in support of railroads, not only because of Baylor but for the benefit of the entire state.[40]

On the morning of July 6, 1853, the Baylor trustees passed the following resolutions:

1. That the present building of the Female Department is not adapted to its needs.
2. That the constantly increasing number of pupils, the rapid increase of the population of this State, the already great and constantly enlarging demands of the denomination and of the people at large upon this institution, the obligation to furnish within our borders any needful means for the thorough and finished education of our youth; in short, that both a new policy and an imperative necessity demand of us an effort to provide for the institution a large and commodious house, combining as much elegant taste in its construction as our means will permit.
3. That the sketch of the building submitted . . . is approved, subject to such modifications as may be deemed necessary to finish it with as much elegance as possible.
4. The material of said house shall be brick or stone.
5. Until an agent is employed, funds are to be solicited, payable in three annual installments, the first due on January 1, 1855.
6. That as a Board and as individuals, as friends of education devoted to the future power and influence of our denomination in this our most rapidly rising State, we will use our best endeavors to concentrate the energy and ability of the denomination upon this important measure till it shall be accomplished.
7. That the above resolutions be laid over for final action until December, 1853.
8. Resolved that H. Clark be requested to ascertain the size, the amount as nearly as possible of the entire cost of the building, and that he make an effort on a conditional subscription among the friends of the institution to ascertain what can be raised and report to the Board in December, 1853, at which time, the Board will consider the expediency or inexpediency of undertaking the above enterprise.

These resolutions are a realistic commentary on the condition of education in the entire state. Responsible people realized the necessity of meeting the need, but they were also conscious of financial responsibility. The cause of educa-

[40] Haynes, p. 543. Address on General Houston before the Texas Legislature, March 2, 1893.

tion for women was being heard. Enrollment figures were significant: the Male Department reached a total of 93 (16 collegiate and 77 preparatory), and the Female, a total of 69, with Baylor's total enrollment for July 1852 to December 1853 being 162 students.[41]

At the July 1853 meeting of the board of trustees, agent James Huckins made his final report. He was directed to be paid $803.20, including a balance for 1852, in this manner: $215 out of funds on hand, $437 by draft on R. E. B. Baylor, and $151 by note made by the trustees, payable the first of January next. Huckins was requested to serve until June 1854 without compensation, for the Galveston Baptist Church, organized by Huckins in 1846, had called him as pastor. Huckins raised approximately $30,000 during these arduous times for Baylor University, a small part of which was in cash, the gifts consisting mainly of "wild lands, cows, horses, mules, hides, wools, berries, and cotton." Of more significance than the financial support, believed Haynes, was the advertising which Huckins gave the school as he traversed the country on horseback.[42]

Burleson believed that Huckins was forced into the schoolroom at Galveston and "to trading in town lots to support his family," but paid tribute to his business acumen in calling him "a born financier [having] accumulated at least $40,000 worth of property by 1855." He is credited with a leading part in founding the Galveston Lyceum, which "eclipsed the silly parade show of the ballroom and theatre," wrote Burleson after holding a four weeks' protracted meeting there in 1848. With the organization of the Southern Baptist Convention in 1845, Huckins had accepted appointment as missionary to Galveston. He pastored the church there until February 1848, when he began his five years' active agency for Baylor. Burleson said that in all Texas there were but "four Baptist houses of worship and only 1,400 Baptists" at the time.[43]

[41] *Baylor Catalogue,* 1852-1853, p. 7.
Haynes reported 95 students in the Male department and "about 90 in the Female department," with a total enrollment of 185.
[42] Haynes, pp. 131-132.
[43] Huckins returned to pastoral work at the Galveston church, remaining until 1859, when he accepted the call of the Baptist Church of Charleston, Virginia. He had aided Dr. Richard Fuller in conducting a six weeks' protracted meeting

Similar to the financial arrangement with Huckins was the reimbursement of President Burleson whom the board paid $98.75, (for window sashes and freight on apparatus case $18.75; for printing Captain Rogers' speech $40.00; for printing the catalogue $40.00). He was also given an order on Principal Clark for $116.00 (that being the amount due from Clark as interest on the purchase money for the house and lot bought from the trustees) as partial payment of his salary as president. Such actions obviated the necessity of a treasurer! An evidence of further conservatism is seen in the board's ruling "not to pay for printing catalogues and speeches" in the future. Affecting the Female Department in particular was this board action: a committee of Baylor, Haynes, and Holmes was to consult with the president and principal "to make out a full uniform for the students of the institution, rejecting all jewelry during their connection with the institution." The uniform was to be enforced for the 1854 session.

The board met in a called meeting on the last day of October 1853 to appoint John Clabaugh as agent at a salary of $250 per annum. Extended discussion was held on financing the dormitories; Reverend J. B. Stiteler was requested to write Huckins for information about shingles and window sashes and to ascertain if any money had been received to pay for the same. In the meantime, the Baylor Catalogue of 1853-54 stated that "young men can procure board in good families for $10 per month" and that Mr. Robert S. Love had just opened "a very large commodious boarding house with every necessary comfort and convenience." Also included was the statement that the president had engaged board for at least 50 young men, but "no one unless of good moral character need apply."

---

there in 1850. Texas grieved in relinquishing Huckins. J. M. Carroll stated that he knew no creed nor race nor color. Carroll, p. 199. In a letter published in *The Index*, April 28, 1843, Huckins had written " . . . in Brazoria County . . . there are more than 500 blacks . . . and I will embrace that settlement in my field of labor. . . . On the evening of every Sabbath I adapt my sermon to the capacity of the Negroes [several native Africans at Fort Bent] and at the close give the opportunity of holding a prayer meeting. These I always attend. These meetings are considered a kind of jubilee with our colored brethren." Dr. Carroll termed Huckins "the balance wheel, the needed accompaniment for the hortatory, persuasive and emotional preaching of Morrell and Baylor, and the overwhelming eloquent, evangelistic preaching of Tryon."

As pastor and chaplain in his ministry to the soldiers, he fell prostrated on the street in Charleston and died August 14, 1863.

At the last meeting of the year on December 16, 1853, the charter of the institution was read, followed by the appointment of a committee to investigate the suspension of several students and to request of President Burleson a copy of the rules of discipline adopted by the faculty. On the following day, Dr. Burleson appeared before the board and presented the adopted rules and the charges against two young men. Over the signatures of Burleson, Stiteler, and O'Bryan, the president presented the following statement:

When a young man presents himself for admittance into our institution, he is brought before the whole faculty, and the following laws are laid down and explained by the President:

1. You are not to use profane or obscene language about the campus.

2. You are not to use ardent spirits to treat others or to visit dram shops or drinking houses.

3. You are not to carry about your person or to keep in your room pistols, dirks or any other such weapons; if you have brought such with you, you must surrender them to the faculty or send them home immediately.

4. You are not to play cards or any game of hazard.

5. You are not to be out of your room after 9 o'clock at night. You are not to engage in any nocturnal disorder or revelings.

6. You are not to interfere in any way with the discipline of the school—that being the exclusive business of the faculty.

7. You are not to leave the Institution without the permission of the faculty.

8. You are to pursue diligently the course of study prescribed by the faculty.

If the young man can pledge his honor to observe the above rules, he is received and his name registered. . . .

Finally the two young men appeared before the board. One was charged with "habitual neglect of studies; use of profane language, being in the company of midnight revellers, and intoxication." Because of his admittance of guilt and assurances of future good deportment the board recommended that the young man be allowed to apply for readmission at the next session. The other student was guilty of being in the company with disorderly persons at 3 o'clock in the morning; of improper behavior in leaving the college after the president had reprimanded him and for making disrespectful remarks concerning the president; of being in company during school hours with persons who were drinking intoxicating liquors; of neglect of studies and . . .

inciting fellow students . . . to insurrection and disorder. The board upheld his suspension until the next regular board meeting, when the case could be reopened.[44]

In addition to this tumultuous affair, another significant item came to the board's attention. Trustee Haynes presented a verbal request from Mr. Clark proposing to change the location of the female academy to a site on General Houston's land purchased from Mr. Hines. A committee of five was appointed to study the matter.

Controversy between the two departments had occurred as a result of student pranks. Boys "crossed the Jordan" to the girls' campus at night and made weird noises, rang the bell, and shot pistols. Principal Clark alleged that President Burleson dealt too lightly with the offenders on one occasion —if not actually condoning their conduct.

The resignation of Professor S. G. O'Bryan was accepted at this last board meeting of the year "with sincere thanks for the faithful and satisfactory manner in which he has discharged his duties. . . ."[45]

---

[44] Minutes of the Baylor Board of Trustees, December 17, 1853, pp. 78-82.

[45] Morrell records: "In the fall of 1853, I received information that O'Bryan was willing to resign his position as Professor of Mathematics at the school were he to receive a position as missionary or pastor, if one half of this amount could be secured for him. I had never seen him; but this made a deep impression on my mind . . . and I wrote him and urged him to visit us. He came, and in the spring of 1854, settled in Waco, and for six years served that church. . . . " Z. N. Morrell, *Flowers and Fruits of the Wilderness* (St. Louis: Commercial Printing Company, 1882), p. 283.

In 1856 O'Bryan became president of the Trinity River Associational Baptist Male High School, first conducted in the First Baptist Church, Waco. O'Bryan was a graduate of Wake Forest College. He married Sarah Anne Chandler in Independence. She was the daughter of Phyllis Brown Chandler, who sent all of his thirteen children to Baylor University. Pianist Van Cliburn, Baylor benefactor, and Robert L. Reid, named Outstanding Baylor Faculty Professor of 1968, are direct descendants of the S. G. O'Bryans. See J. B. Link, *Texas Historical and Biographical Magazine* I, 390.

CHAPTER VI

Baylor Attains Stature

THE BAYLOR BOARD OF TRUSTEES at a called meeting in March of 1845 named Mr. James A. Johnson professor of mathematics and directed Mr. Stiteler to serve as agent in "charge of window blinds and all lumber and other property subject to waste and dispose of same by sale for the benefit of the University." Other evidences of frugality were indicated in the effort to collect "all monies" pledged for lumber and the authorization of Trustee J. G. Thomas "to collect funds for the Female Department during his visit to Alabama and Mississippi during 1854." A. Daniels and the faculty were appointed "to have the college grass enclosed provided they can procure the means to have the work done without creating a debt against the U." Charles and George Breedlove had dropped out of Baylor in 1854 to work all year quarrying rock and hauling it by ox team for the erection of the new building.[1]

A letter from President Burleson to Judge Baylor is indicative of the scarcity of money at this particular time, yet of the eternal hope of Burleson.

. . . our Institution is going on more and more prosperously—180 students and never have I seen such order and attention to study. . . . I am owing our dear Bro. Wm. Norris $50 borrowed money which I must pay next week but I have not a dime in the world. I have therefore given him an order on you for the remainder of your subscription to the endowment.[2]

Records reveal that the balance of Judge Baylor's pledge was $33. He sent Burleson $20 on April 18, 1854.

The report of the president of the board of trustees to the Baptist State Convention assembled in Palestine, June 21, 1854, echoes a feeling of confidence:

---

[1] Captain Pleasant Ellis Breedlove had brought his family to a farm five miles east of Independence on Hidalgo Bluff in March of 1847. Son Charles received both the A. B. and the law degree in 1858 and became the first student to achieve such a distinction. He was admitted to the bar in 1859 and entered law practice with E. W. Ewing. Newsclipping in Crane Scrapbook, Texas Collection, Baylor University.

[2] R. C. Burleson to R. E. B. Baylor, April 7, 1854. Burleson Papers, Texas Collection, Baylor University.

Dear Brethren:
In compliance with the request of your body, I lay before you as
nearly as possible, the condition of Baylor University:
Baylor University was founded chiefly by the instrumentality of the
devoted and lamented Wm. M. Tryon, and was charted [*sic*] by the
Republic of Texas, in 1845. And, though it has had the many difficulties of a new and thinly settled country to contend with, yet the
progress of the institution has met the most sanguine expectations
of its friends. Our institution is almost the only one in the State that
has not been subject to great fluctuations and changes of prosperity
and adversity; its progress has been gradual, permanent, upward.
This fact has been owing, under God, to the harmonious feeling and
action of the Trustees, the liberality of the Texians, and the energy
and zeal of its teachers and professors.

Cultural aims were a part of the progress indicated by the
president of the board. Since the time of Miss Trask, who
listed as one of her accomplishments the teaching of music,
Independence people had been serious about the instruction
of their children in both instrumental and vocal music.
Lutheran pastor Adolf Fuchs, renowned for his musical ability in Mecklenberg, Germany, joined the Baylor faculty in
1855. He had brought his family to Texas in the group of
Prince Carl of Solms-Braunfels and settled in Austin County.
He first taught music in the homes of plantation owners on
the Brazos. Although his connection with the Baptist school
was limited to about two years, his legacy was great.[3] Another notable musician, Madame Rheinhardt, pupil of Men-
delssohn, gave numerous concerts in Texas in the 1860's
and from 1863 to 1866 taught at Baylor. Composer F. W.
Smith, author of "Holly Oak Grand Waltz"—one of the
first early compositions published by a reputable firm—was
a teacher at Baylor College. The title of the composition is
reminiscent of music-lover Judge Baylor's home, "Holly
Oak."

Concerning the academic, the school was also making progress. Separate trustee committees were appointed to con-

[3] The grandson of Adolf Fuchs, Oscar J. Fuchs, born in 1878, is termed
the first native composer to achieve fame through the use of the Texas back-
ground. See Lota M. Spell, *Music in Texas*, Austin, n.p., 1936, p., 137. A granite
memorial to him near Marble Falls pays tribute to his famous "The Hills of
Home." Descendants of Adolf Fuchs have long been connected with Baylor
University: M. R. Goebel, Manager of the Baylor Press (1910-1960); Marvin
Goebel, Manager of the Baylor Press (1960-   ) L. T. Goebel, Pressman and
Compositor (1934-   ); Mrs. Bernice W. Casey (1956-   ).

duct an annual examination at the close of the ten-month session in December for the Male and Female Departments. The suspended student was reinstated, and a special committee of T. J. Jackson, Dr. Robertson, and A. Daniel was named "for the specific purpose of raising funds to build a commodious stone building on the present Female Academy lot."

Minutes of a called board meeting in mid-October 1854 reveal the first mention of General Sam Houston: acknowledgement is made of several valuable public documents, and the offering of Houston's "large and well-selected library" for the use of the university students.[4] Baylor welcomed the support of Sam Houston. He had lived in Huntsville, where he was an original trustee for the Presbyterian Austin College.[5] Sam Houston had moved his family to Independence on October 25, 1853, with the intent of spending the rest of his days in the lovely little university town. Such he had written to Austin newsman Washington D. Miller.[6] Actually three factors motivated his action: the hope that a change in climate would help Mrs. Houston's asthmatic condition; his feeling that neither "Austin nor anywhere else presented the same educational advantages" as Independence; and the fact that Nancy Moffette Lea, Mrs. Houston's mother, lived there.

Sam Houston became a member of Independence Baptist Church in 1854, and today a Texas flag marks his pew. Houston had been a regular attendant at Washington, D. C., services conducted by Reverend G. W. Samson, "out of respect for his wife," during his twelve years as senator.

[4] *Baptist State Convention Minutes of 1854*, p. 13.
Burleson, friend to Houston, had asked Houston to speak on national politics at the Baptist Church in Brenham on the preceding April 15. Because of his stand on the Nebraska bill, Houston was not the success anticipated, and the *Brenham Inquirer* reported that the crowd was noisy. Llerena Friend, *Sam Houston, The Great Designer* (Austin: The University Press, 1954), p. 232. Houston's generosity to Baylor enhanced his local reputation.

[5] In June 1853 Houston was one of a committee of three designated to examine Austin College. A difference of opinion developed between Houston and President Samuel McKinney. The president resigned and returned to Mississippi, and two months later Houston moved to Independence. William Stuart Red, *A History of the Presbyterian Church in Texas* (San Antonio: The Steck Company, 1936), p. 425.

[6] R. Henderson Shuffler, *The Houstons at Independence* (Waco, Texas: Texian Press, 1966), p. 13.

During the session of 1854 he expressed the conviction that he should make a public confession in baptism—the question was *where*. Houston conversed later with Reverend George W. Baines, then pastor at Anderson and a visitor at Independence, about some doctrinal matters which had long disturbed him. The result was that Houston was satisfied and forthwith presented himself as a candidate for baptism at the Independence Church.[7] Dr. Rufus Burleson recalled that Houston was sitting in the sixth row on November 19, 1854:

> I took as my text the passage: "He that is slow to anger is better than the mighty; and he that ruleth his spirit than he that taketh a city." When I had finished my sermon, General Houston arose and came down and extended his hand to me and when I grasped it he said, "I give you my hand and with it I give my heart to the Lord." That afternoon I baptized General Houston in the icy waters of Rocky Creek.

Dr. Burleson had constructed a baptistry in the shape of a coffin in the rock bed of Kountz Creek north of Independence. When announcement was made that General Houston was to be baptized there, "some mischievous boys . . . filled the baptistry with mud and tree tops." Upon discovery of the mischief, Dr. Burleson calmly said, "Very well, I will out-general these mischievous boys from the country and baptize General Houston in Little Rocky."[8] A Texas State marker some mile and one-half away honors the spot.

Oft repeated is the remark attributed to Houston as he emerged from the baptismal pool. "Well, preacher, you've baptized my pocket book!" And the generosity of the General gave testimony to the accuracy of his statement in succeeding years. Burleson is also said to have remarked: "Now Sam, your sins are all washed away." Houston's salty reply was "God help the fishes!"[9] Houston's feelings concerning religion were deep. Even though the Reverend Baines had satisfied his questioning of theological matters and his conscience allowed him to join the Independence Church, he

---

[7] J. B. Link, *Texas Historical and Biographical Magazine,* I, 360.

[8] Harry Haynes, *Life and Writings of Dr. Rufus C. Burleson,* (compiled and published by Mrs. Georgia J. Burleson, 1901), p. 166. The coffin shape of the baptistry symbolized the burial of sin and resurrection to a new life.

[9] Pauline Crittenden, "Texas Tours: Caldwell Area," *The Dallas Morning News,* June 20, 1965.

still felt unworthy to partake of the Sacrament of the Lord's Supper.[10] Yet Houston paid half of his pastor's salary.[11]

Mrs. Nancy Moffette Lea, Houston's mother-in-law, was a devout member of the Independence Baptist Church. She and daughter Margaret were "vigorously active" in church and Baylor University affairs. Each summer they gathered and dried fruit to serve the school tables during the winter. In 1856 Mrs. Lea gave the church its melodic bell with the request that she be buried within its sound. Local stories aver that Mrs. Lea gave her family silver to be melted into the bell. Temple Houston Morrow, great-grandson of Mrs. Lea, questioned the story. Correspondence with Meneely and Company, Troy, New York, discloses the fact that no silver was used in casting the bell. "One Rufus Burleson sent the money to have the bell cast," the company official wrote. Family members believe that Mrs. Lea sold her family silver to obtain money for the cost of the bell—approximately $500. The time-worn inscription in the bell, now resting in the adjacent museum, reads:

Meneely's West Troy, N. Y., 1856

— — — — — — — —

Presented
First Baptist Church, Independence, Texas
By Mrs. Nancy Lea

A belfry made from the stones of Tryon Hall housed the beloved bell and marks the nearby resting place of Mrs. Lea and her daughter, Margaret Lea Houston.[12]

The last trustee meeting of the 1854 year produced a report from a committee on the granting of certificates or diplomas. Trustee Creath brought the recommendation that Baylor adopt the plan pursued in Brown University or the

[10] Sam Houston to Margaret Lea Houston, March 1856.
[11] Marquis James, *The Raven* (Indianapolis, Indiana: Blue Ribbon Books, 1929), p. 385.
[12] Tryon Hall, the main building on the boys' campus at Old Baylor, was torn down in 1934, and the stones for the belfry were secured from Mr. Fritz Leuckemeyer. He had received the stone in payment for demolishing the building when a highway took the property. Mrs. W. A. Wood, Mrs. F. O. Maxwell, Mrs. W. A. Morrow of Waco, and Mrs. T. C. Hairston of Independence were responsible for the preservation of this historic shrine, erected in 1934. A letter from Dr. Hairston states that the railing formerly enclosed the Independence grave of Judge Baylor. On March 5, 1969, the bell cracked as Pastor Earl Allen rang it for prayer meeting. It was removed from the tower and a new bell was placed in the tower in 1970.

University of Virginia—"to give certificates or diplomas to students, specifying the branches of which they have a full or correct knowledge." The plan was to embrace both departments of the school, and such certificates were to be signed by "the president in behalf of the Males and the principal of the Female Department in behalf of the young ladies."[13]

President Burleson then recommended that the A.B. degree be conferred on Stephen Decatur Rowe, who became Baylor University's first graduate, in December 1854. Rowe was listed as a sophomore from Galveston in Baylor's first catalogue in 1851-52 and is listed in succeeding catalogues. In 1855-56 he is termed assistant professor of ancient languages and resident graduate. On December 18, 1856, he signed a faculty recommendation to the trustees that the A. B. degree be conferred on Oscar Hopestell Leland.[14] In the old subscription book of Hosea Garrett, president of the board of trustees and one-time agent of Baylor, Rowe is listed as pledging $100 to the endowment of the presidency; the sum was marked "paid" by 1852.[15] A similar pledge appears in another list of subscribers in the trustee minutes of June 25, 1870. Young Rowe addressed a poem of three stilted quatrains "To Miss Sarah" in an autograph album, such as those kept by most coeds in the 1850's.[16] Rowe also served as the first president of the Philomathesian Literary Society, organized in 1851.[17] He took his first degree in Masonry in the Milam Lodge at Independence, Texas, on August 16, 1853.

[13] The authority to grant degrees in privately controlled institutions derives from their charters. Charters vary in their degree-granting powers, but as a rule give the institution the right to confer the "usual college degrees." Degrees have been in use for more than 800 years, the first known record being the doctorate conferred by the University of Bologna in Italy in the middle of the 12th century. The University of Paris and later the British universities introduced the preparatory degrees of licentiate and baccalaureate. The Bachelor of Arts was the only earned degree used in American colleges for some 125 years after Harvard first conferred it in 1642. *Academic Degrees,* U. S. Department of Health, Education and Welfare, Office of Education (Washington, D.C.: United States Printing Office, 1960), pp. 5-22.
[14] Minutes of the Baylor Board of Trustees, p. 108.
[15] Hosea Garrett Record Book. Texas Collection, Baylor University.
[16] Album of Miss Sarah Pier (Baylor student 1856-57). Texas Collection, Baylor University.
[17] *Baylor Literary Annual,* 1897, p. 93.

Gratitude was expressed by the trustees at this last meeting of the year to Professors Johnson and Fitzgerald "for their faithful and indefatigable efforts" during their connections with the institution, and they were recommended "to public patronage and confidence."[18] President Burleson recommended one of Baylor's own as teacher of the preparatory department—James L. Smith. Son of Mary Anne Ashmore Smith and William Berry Smith, James Lowery was born in North Carolina in 1827. The family came to Texas in 1834 and settled in Milam County about ten miles east of Cameron. Indian depredations were so severe that the Smiths moved to Washington County between Chappell Hill and Independence.[19] Because of humped shoulders, the elder Smith was called "Camelback" and later "Uncle Billy." He was an expert gunsmith, marksman, and fearless Indian fighter. He served in the Texas Revolution and was a close friend to Houston, Burnet, Lamar, Sterling Robertson, and "Deaf" Smith.[20] William Smith died in Bosque County June 11, 1877, and his wife died the following year, leaving the following children: James L., Alexander, Henry, Lula (Mrs. Pitts), Lizzie (Mrs. Russell of Iredell), and Sarah (Mrs. Tandy).

James L., the eldest child, attended Baylor at Independence from 1851 to 1855.[21] On December 15, 1851, the university treasurer was ordered to pay the young man fifteen dollars for repairing desks, and on December 21, 1854, he was named teacher of the preparatory department for the next year, a position he held until 1860. From 1856 to 1860 he was termed "Principal of the Preparatory Department," and on June 28, 1860, he was awarded the honorary degree A. M. "Secundum Gradum" as requested by

[18] Ben S. Fitzgerald later joined President Burleson's staff, for on March 21, 1861, he was the last of seven faculty members of the Male and Female Departments who signed a statement dispelling rumors about "relations of an unfriendly character." Minutes show that he remained at Baylor until his resignation on February 8, 1866. On July 8, 1865, Baylor conferred on him an honorary A. M. degree.

James A. Johnson had been employed as professor of mathematics "for the remainder of the year" on March 21, 1854.

[19] Anne Doom Pickrell, *Pioneer Women in Texas* (Austin: E. L. Steck Company, 1929), p. 323.

[20] J. M. Carroll, *The History of Texas Baptists* (Dallas: Baptist Standard Publishing Company, 1923), p. 73.

[21] *Baylor University Catalogues*, 1851 to 1855.

President Burleson.[22] A January 9, 1861, listing shows that he was paid $1,031.10 for his services during 1860. While at Baylor, Smith took a German lad, Frank Kiefer, from a marble game to Sunday School with him. Ultimately the lad was baptized by President R. C. Burleson and became the minister who had "more people converted under his ministry than any other man in Texas save Major W. E. Penn."[23]

Finances continued to be the prime concern of Baylor. Principal Horace Clark was requested "to pay Elder R. C. Burleson $162.00 on January 1, 1855, balance due the endowment as interest on note," and the treasurer was instructed to change the contract with Clark so that the interest would fall due at the same time the payment to Burleson became due. Again President Burleson had advanced money from his private funds and presented the accounts to the board through Trustee Barnes at the annual meeting, December 20, 1854:

To John McKnight for lumber for the middle dormitory,
    May 13, 1853 . . . . $118.

To Thomas McKnight for work on same,
    May 25, 1853 . . . . 25.

To Hubb & Wilson for stove for cottage,
    October 31, 1853 . . . . 14.

Desk . . . . 10.

To Newton Allen for hauling sash 4.65

                                                                             $171.65

[22] Minutes of the Baylor Board of Trustees, p. 140. The same degree was awarded to Elder James H. Stribling (former ministerial student), and to Professor O. H. Leland.

[23] Carroll, pp. 589-90.

Smith taught at Alma Male and Female Academy in Hallettsville in the session opening in January 1854 and for several years after leaving Baylor. C. Y. Early, *Walker-Smith Company—1894-1944* (Dallas: Harben-Spotts, Inc.), p. 17. In 1862 Smith served as the captain of Company H, First Regiment, 27th Brigade, T.S.T., Milam County. James L. Smith married Julia Catherine McDowell, and they were parents of seven children. For eleven years Smith was president of Salado College in Bell County, and after his death on January 10, 1883, this inscription was placed on his tombstone:

This monument is the offering of grateful and sorrowing students—a slight token of the memory of one who in all the relations of life whether as citizen, parent, teacher, or friend, beautifully illustrated in his unobtrusive career, all the traits of the Christian gentleman and scholar and whose individual annals were an epitome of those blessed humanities of life, virtue, honor, and truth.

He also submitted receipts for $396 for money received from the treasurer as reimbursement for bills he had previously paid. The resolution of the difficult financial state was that a committee of Dr. Graves and Trustee Haynes was requested to settle with President Burleson "and sell him in payment of his bill one of the dormitories at cost."

Mr. Blount wished to be paid for a lot adjacent to the campus. The treasurer was directed to tender him all unappropriated money. Burleson and Graves constituted a committee with the responsibility of raising the balance due on the lot, and the Reverend Creath was appointed to deliver an address appealing to the people for contributions. Disposition of this obligation was made the following April when $300 or $330 contributed for the education of ministers was borrowed at 10% interest and the debt retired. (Sam Houston contributed $300 to the fund on April 10, 1855.)

Further indicative of financial stress was the release of Professor Stiteler for one-half of each day to collect interest on the Natural Science Professorship Endowment for his own salary. He was also named to obtain subscriptions for the university "during his visit to the North to buy chemical apparatus and books." Creath, after first declining, accepted the agency for Baylor University "from January 1855 for five years at $600 per annum."

Despite money matters, President Burleson maintained his optimism for the school. In a letter to his brother he offered him a job as professor of mathematics at $1,000 at the end of 1854, with one-third to be paid in advance. He reminded Richard of "our Sainted Mother's ardent wish that we 'live, love, labor and die together,'" The young president stated that the prospects were for "not far from 250 students with 7 or 8 ministers." As further inducement he wrote:

You are so entirely misconcerned and are so profoundly ignorant of the real condition, and the future greatness of Texas that you will probably regard this offer as a small affair, but if we live 10 years you will see Texas the New York of the South and Baylor University the highest ornament of Texas. One of your letters spoke of Texas as a wild savage country. My dear Brother there are more learned men, classic scholars,—regular graduates in this Association [Union] than in all North Alabama. Huckins is a graduate of Brown, Baines,

Maxey, and Cleveland of Alabama, Creath of Richmond College, Stiteler of both Penn. and Hamilton Theological Sem. and Graves of Hamilton and North Carolina. You may ask how it is that I hold such a prominent position among such men. Well, I assure you it is not from superiority but from surplus vigilance and untiring energy. I have traversed the whole state and know every prominent person in our church.

I have a large house with seven rooms and would be glad for you to make your home with us till you can improve. . . .[24]

Brother Richard remained unconvinced, and records show that the board directed President Burleson to employ Gilbert L. Morgan of Tennessee as professor of mathematics "upon the best terms and conditions his services can be had for" at the April 10, 1855, meeting. However, a brief letter of May 14, 1855, from the president to Richard tells of his impatience to hear of his decision concerning the proffered position and asked if he could accept it either at the first of next August or at the first of March 1856. "I think we can build up a glorious Institution, one that will reflect immortal renown on us and contribute vastly to the cause of our dear Redeemer." A significant postscript carries a request that "you . . . aid my friend Sam Houston to the Presidency, he is a great and good man and a Baptist." A letter of October 7, 1855, to Richard notes Burleson's joy "to hear that you are on the wing for Texas" and urges him to take the post vacated by Professor Stiteler for a year at least so that "my sweet wife [will be] a mother to your children."

By the March meeting of the trustees, the designated committee had raised subscriptions of $3,785 for the proposed Female Academy building, and the plan submitted by Principal Clark was chosen for the structure. Various denominations given the privilege of worship in the new college building were now to pay $2.00 per month to the treasurer. The board also directed the building committee "to have built for the use of each the Male and Female Departments, a suitable privy for their accommodation." At the June meeting, Burleson and Clark were assigned this responsibility for their respective departments. Clark submitted a proposition from John P. Collins to erect the proposed

[24] R. C. Burleson to Richard Burleson, February 6, 1854. Burleson Papers, Texas Collection, Baylor University.

Female Department building for $8,000. At a meeting on July 11, 1855, the contract was closed with Collins, the building to be completed by January 1, 1857. A committee of Clark, Haynes, and Dr. Robertson was designated to work with him. Dr. Robertson was also appointed agent to collect funds for the building. With letting of the contract, female education won a victory in Texas. (See appendix) The building was not completed on time, however; for on March 3, 1857, the building committee requested the contractor to complete work on the basement as soon as possible so that classes could meet in the rooms.

Another matter of significance came to the attention of the board at the July meeting. Trustees Graves, Baylor, and Jenkins were appointed "to acknowledge in suitable terms the receipt of a copy of Jefferson's works from the Congress of the United States."

At the December 20, 1855, board meeting, a recommendation was made by Professor H. Clark that a diploma be given to Miss Mary Gentry Kavanaugh, who had completed the course of study prescribed in the Female Department, and also that certificates of scholarship be given to Misses Zilphia Fuller and Carrie Mooney.[25] The request was signed by the President of the Board of Trustees and H. Clark, Principal of the Female Department. The order was given for the honors to be conferred at the close of the examination. The topic of Mary Gentry's graduation essay was "Night Brings Out the Stars." Daughter of Trustee Nelson Kavanaugh, she began her Baylor attendance as a seven-year-old when the school opened in 1846.

Mary Gentry recalled many incidents of her school days. She had four roommates. Since their room was above the kitchen, the Negro cook frequently supplied them with "feasts" which she put in a basket lowered by cords from the window above. Another surreptitious activity occurred

[25] Granddaughter of Mary Gentry Kavanaugh, Mrs. J. E. Farrington, Port Arthur, Texas, states that Mary Gentry was the first woman graduated in Texas.

The Baylor Historical Society celebrated the centennial anniversary of Baylor's first woman graduate in 1955. Present were Mrs. J. E. Farrington, who brought the address, and Mrs. John R. Sadler, great-granddaughter.

Through the diligent efforts of Mrs. Lily M. Russell, Mary Gentry Kavanaugh's graduation dress was displayed in Baylor's Centennial Collection.

off-campus. Parents of students stabled horses near the school. The caretaker loaned the horses to young men students. Then by prior arrangement the girls would arrive at a designated spot where they would indulge in races against the boys. Girls dressed in riding habits with long skirts and rode sidesaddle. How they escaped from the dormitory unseen is still a mystery.

An amusing incident concerning "beauty aids" is a part of Mary Gentry's reminiscences. All cosmetics—powder, creme, and rouge—were "homemade." Someone told the girls that honey mixed with flour and applied to the cheeks overnight made an effective mask. It did—it hardened like plaster and had to be cracked off—but it *did* give the girls rosy cheeks.

The 1855 catalogue carried the announcement of the degree of Bachelor of Philosophy, "a scientific course for the benefit of students preparing for business pursuits, or those whose age or means do not allow them to complete the regular course." The course of study embraced "the entire course of sciences, mathematics, belles-lettres, and one of the modern languages."[26]

The trustees also discussed the subject of the education of Baptist preachers' children and placed the matter on the March 1856 agenda. Of prime significance was the request that "Brother Burleson raise by donation and subscription one thousand dollars to buy a Library for the University."

Money to pay the faculty still was a problem for the trustees. Burleson was "authorized to use $250 paid on endowment to the Presidency, by giving note with good security at 10% per annum interest in advance, note payable in twelve months." A committee was then appointed to take the notes of Wm. H. Cleveland and R. C. Burleson and have a settlement with H. Clark on his notes and renew the same at 10% per annum.

The cleavage between the departments grew, and at the December 22, 1855, meeting all catalogues thereafter pub-

---

[26] The degree of Bachelor of Philosophy was inaugurated by Brown University in 1850 and conferred on one graduate in 1851. In 1852 Yale University granted the degree to the newly established Sheffield Scientific School. The Commissioner of Education's *Annual Report, 1900-1901,* indicated a continuing disuse of the Ph.B. degree.

lished were ordered to be styled "Baylor University Male Department" and "Baylor University Female Department."[27]

Further separation is indicated in the directive that both Burleson and Clark present an annual report to the board stating the number of teachers employed, salaries, enrollment, and amount of tuition collected. Minutes of the 1855 Baptist State Convention reveal a knowledge of the state of affairs at Independence and indicated the hope that Clark "could soon be released from serving tables." Rivalry between Burleson and Clark in administering the two departments of Baylor was evident even at this period, and circumstances seemed to add fuel to the flames. Dissatisfaction and gossip directed against the school grew to such an extent that Baylor's first graduate, Stephen Decatur Rowe, wrote an article for the *Texas Baptist* defending the standards of the university. Charges had been made that graduates of the institution would not be accepted as sophomores in institutions of other states. Rowe was forthright in his defense of Baylor and urged denominational support.[28]

Nevertheless, a confident announcement in the *Washington American* on December 14, 1855, gave a generous estimate of enrollment as 230 with 40 in the "Male Collegiate branch" to mark the anniversary of Baylor University:

> The tenth anniversary of this flourishing Institution will commence on Monday the 17th of December and continue for four days. Each night will be occupied by speeches by young gentlemen or with compositions by the young ladies, all to be interspersed with music.
> On Friday, at 11 o'clock, Rufus Elder, Esquire, will deliver the literary address before the Philomathesian and Erosophian [*sic*] Societies. The friends of education are generally invited to attend.
> Rufus C. Burleson, President
> Washington, Texas, December 14, 1855.

At this time the trustees ruled that "no question involving politics shall be discussed by the students, either in original speeches or compositions in Baylor University" and the faculty was requested to have the above resolution enforced. Request was made that the directive be published in the

[27] The Baylor Catalogue of 1851 included information for both departments; the Male Department catalogues from 1852-1856 stated that the Female Department catalogues were in separate publications, but the first such catalogue of record was published in 1857.
[28] The *Texas Baptist* (Washington, Texas), December 14, 1855.

Texas Baptist until March 1856. This first instance of censorship at Baylor University was a result of the current discussions of the Kansas-Nebraska Bill and General Sam Houston's opposition to it. He had delivered an eloquent address in the Senate in vigorous opposition to the pending bill, which proposed the repeal of the Missouri Compromise. He predicted that passage of the bill would eventually mean war between the states. Student feeling ran high at Baylor.[29] Because Houston was an active member of the community, of the Baptist Church, and a great friend of the school, the administration was desirous of keeping the peace on the campus.[30]

Just after this ruling on politics, Sam Houston, Jr., was invited to make the official San Jacinto Day speech—on April 21, 1856. The young man had entered Baylor at the age of ten in 1853 and remained until 1859, when he entered Bastrop Military Institute.[31] His father is known to have held strong convictions concerning the schooling of young men. He wrote in his will in 1863: "I wish my sons to be taught an entire contempt for novels and light reading. . ."[32] preferring that they study geography, history, English, Latin, and the Holy Scriptures. He is also reported to have said: "If one of my sons should misspell a word, I would be humiliated; if a daughter of mine misspelled a word or made a mistake in grammar, I would be disgraced."[33]

Another subject of public discussion was that of college societies. At the opening of the 1855 session, President Burleson delivered a lecture on secret societies. Baylor at the time had three literary societies. The Philomathesian, listed in the first catalogue in 1851-52, and the Erisophian, listed first in the 1854 catalogue, were both debating societies

[29] Frank E. Burkhalter, *Waco Tribune-Herald,* August 4, 1957.

[30] J. D. Bragg, "Baylor University, 1851-1861," *Southwestern Historical Quarterly,* XLIL, 1949, 60.

[31] From the military school young Sam went to the Confederate Army. Despite his feelings about secession, Houston had written his son: "If Texas demands your services or your life, in her cause, stand by her." Llerena Friend, "Sam Houston," *Heroes of Texas* (Texian Press, 1964), p. 93. Sam Houston, Jr., was wounded at the Battle of Shiloh on April 7, 1862, then became a prisoner at Camp Douglas, Missouri. After the war he returned to Baylor and in 1867 entered Medical school at the University of Pennsylvania.

[32] Alfred M. Williams, *Sam Houston and the War of Independence in Texas* (Boston: Houghton Mifflin, 1898), p. 376.

[33] R. Henderson Shuffler, *The Houstons at Independence* (Waco, Texas: Texian Press, 1966), p. 25.

open to any student. The Erisophian Society, organized in 1853, boasted about twenty members.[34] There was also the Wheeler Law Club, named in honor of Judge Royal T. Wheeler of the Law Department. The Adelphian Society, mentioned first in the 1854 catalogue, was termed "an association . . . for the cultivation and preservation of the purest morality." This society, composed of ministers, was designed to be "truly a band of brothers, and the palladium of the Institution." Haynes avers that there were several secret societies. Reverend R. H. Taliaferro, an Austin pastor, had given an eloquent address at the 1854 commencement which added to the prestige of the societies.[35] President Burleson had encouraged the organization of the literary societies, but their attitudes toward student life gave him pause. Opposition to secret societies of any kind was widespread over the United States. College Greek letter societies, even the eminently proper Phi Beta Kappa, did not escape the ban at this time.[36] President Burleson declared, "there were more

[34] Charter members are listed as Charles T. Kavanaugh, Thomas J. Goree, W. H. Ledbetter, Y. R. Hoxey, J. G. Hairston, Dabney A. Burleson, Norvel G. Wilson, H. C. Renfro, and Bennett Wood.

[35] Robert H. Taliaferro, born in Kentucky on October 19, 1824, was educated at Granville College, Ohio, and the Western Baptist Theological Seminary of Kentucky. He was ordained to the ministry by Luburgrund Church of Montgomery County, Kentucky, on September 15, 1846, and came to Texas in 1847. His first service was at Austin and in the Colorado Valley, then at Galveston as the third pastor of that early church from March 1849 to July 1850. Feeling a sense of obligation, he was missionary to the Choctaw Indians for several years. After marriage to the only daughter of Washington Anderson of Round Rock in 1855 he preached at Webberville, Bastrop, and Austin, sometimes walking eighteen miles to fill an appointment. "His fluency and brilliance . . . created a wonderful sensation," declared his contemporaries. He could quote passage after passage from Milton, Young, and other poets, and his hearers were almost mesmerized. "No purer, abler, more devoted, self-sacrificing minister of the New Testament ever lived in Texas," wrote a peer. He organized the first church in Williamson County "when there was not a glass window or a plank floor in the county."
Taliaferro was elected Chaplain of the Senate of the 12th, 13th, and 14th Legislatures of Texas and served as one of the volunteer chaplains of the Constitutional Convention of 1875. He was associated with Reverend G. W. Baines as special correspondent to the *Texas Baptist Herald* from the first number in December 1865 until the end of February 1868. He died in Austin on November 19, 1875. *The Herald* of the First Baptist Church, Galveston, Texas, V (March 29, 1936), 1.

[36] Ralph Volney Harlow, *The Growth of the U. S.* (New York: Henry Holt & Company, 1923) p. 363.
The first college fraternity in British America was the F. H. C. Society of the College of William and Mary. Jane Carson, *James Innes and His Brothers of the F.H.C.*, Williamsburg Research Studies, The University Press of Virginia, The Rotunda, Charlottesville, Virginia.

heart-burnings, secret whisperings, and conflicts among our students than had ever been known in Baylor University."[37]

Despite the jealousies and dissatisfactions, student participation in school activities was high, as is indicated by the following program which closed the school term with appropriate fanfare:

SENIOR EXHIBITION
of
BAYLOR UNIVERSITY
December 20, 1855
Seven o'clock

Prayer
1. "Footprints of Man"—Charles Breedlove, Independence
2. "Destiny of Man"—Taylor M. Cox, Huntsville

Music
3. "A Resolute Mind is Omnipotent"—Blackston H. Davis, Austin
4. "Eulogy on Geo. Green"—H. C. Oliphant, Huntsville
5. "Stability of the Union"—Daniel Bradshaw, Preston
6. "Americans Kneel to None but God"—Thomas J. Goree, Madisonville
7. "The Indian Race"—William H. Jones, Bastrop
8. "The Chief Glory of the Nation"—Daniel E. Thomson, Nashville

Music
9. Chas. T. Kavanaugh, Chappell Hill, Debate on Utility of Studying the Ancient Languages
10. W. H. Parks, Anderson

Music
Valedictory—James P. Davis, Austin

The Independence paper of June 13, 1855, carried an announcement of the Baylor Law School. Just beneath it was the announcement of the opening of H. S. Whitehead's Dancing School, with a list of all the dances to be taught— Redowa, Cotillions, Spanish Dance, Five Step Waltz, Mazourka, Varsovia, Imperial, Highland Fling, Schottische, Esmeralda, Carmelia, Scotch Red. Mr. Whitehead's rooms were in A. W. Hood's Hotel.[38] Baylor's *By-Laws* handled such temptation in No. 9—"A student may not become connected with a dancing school, a society, or social club without the approval of the faculty."

[37] This speech was later expanded for delivery to the Texas State Teachers Association at El Paso in 1898.
[38] *Southern Star,* June 13, 1855.

The resignation of Professor J. B. Stiteler because of ill health early in 1856 occasioned this resolution in the minutes of the Baylor Board of Trustees on March 4:

. . . the Trustees of Baylor University extend to Professor Stiteler our sincere thanks for the marked ability and efficiency with which he has discharged the important duties of the Professorship of Natural Sciences.

Resolved, furthermore that we commend Prof. Stiteler to the affectionate regard of Brethren and friends, wherever he may travel, not only as a ripe scholar, but as a finished gentleman, and an able minister of the Gospel.

Resolved, That the foregoing be published in the *Texas Baptist* and *Christian Index*.[39]

Baylor students also adopted resolutions on the resignation of their beloved professor. They were signed by Charles R. Breedlove, Chairman, and William B. Denson, Secretary, and appeared in the March 22, 1856, *Texas Baptist*.

Although the minutes of the trustees reveal no record of appointment, Dr. David R. Wallace, eminent Independence physician, replaced Professor Stiteler as Professor of Natural Science. Dr. Wallace came to Independence in 1855 and began the practice of medicine with a Dr. Randall. Born on November 10, 1825, in Pitt County, North Carolina, he took an A.B. degree from Wake Forest College in 1850 and a Master's in 1852 and was graduated from the Medical Department of the University of New York in 1854. The first mention of Wallace's connection with Baylor in the minutes of the trustees was on December 17, 1856, when, as a staff member, he recommended a degree for O. H. Leland.

[39] Minutes of Baylor Board of Trustees, March 4, 1856, p. 102.
Travel brought sufficient restoration to his health for him to accept pastoral charge of the First Baptist Church of Savannah in February 1856. By October, however, he was forced to resign because of active tuberculosis, and he repaired to Orange Springs, Florida, where he died on December 25, 1856, at the age of thirty-four. He was survived by his wife, Frances M. Halbert Stiteler, and three children. The First Baptist Church of Galveston placed a bronze plaque in the auditorium in honor of Reverend and Mrs. Stiteler. Years later, the Jacob Beverly Stiteler Chair of Greek was endowed in honor of this early Baylor teacher. Daughter Kate Stiteler McKie became one of Baylor's greatest benefactors, matching every gift made by the W. M. U. for Woman's Memorial Dormitory on the Waco campus in 1928. Baylor awarded her an LL.D. in 1933. Stiteler descendants at Baylor include Dr. Rowland Stiteler and his wife Kathleen (former Baylor faculty member), Bill McKie, Ben McKie of Corsicana, Nancie Stiteler Felice (A. B. 1964), and Rowland Stiteler, III.

Dr. Wallace taught four hours a day at Baylor until he entered the Confederate Army as Surgeon of the 15th Texas Infantry in February 1862 and joined Colonel J. W. Speight's Battalion encamped at Galveston. On May 27, 1857, Wallace was married to Arabella Daniel, niece of Dr. Randall, at the Independence Baptist Church, with President Rufus C. Burleson performing the ceremony. The couple bought a home near the Sam Houstons. The two men became close friends, and Houston wanted Dr. Wallace to write his biography, but circumstances prevented Wallace's accomplishing the task although he wrote numerous articles for various journals.

During his Baylor service Dr. Wallace's name appeared several times in the minutes of the trustees: once to inform the board that the interest for the Chair of Natural Science had not been paid, and consequently his salary; on October 28, 1858, he and Dr. W. H. Gant sponsored the proposed medical school for Baylor; on February 1, 1859, Wallace bought for $1,000 (and signed a note at 10 percent) the land donated to Baylor by Moses Evans; on January 1, 1861, Wallace was paid $1,258.96 (in money, accounts, and endowment fees) for his services; and on May 15, 1861, he joined other members of the Male Faculty in signing an agreement signifying cooperation with the Female Department; and on June 28, 1861, he resigned from the Chair of Natural Science. The *Dallas Herald* of October 15, 1859, in an announcement of the Faculty of the Male Department of Baylor University at Independence, lists Dr. D. R. Wallace, A.M., Professor of Natural Science and French.

The removal of President Burleson to Waco probably induced Dr. Wallace to move his family there after the war in 1865. He supported Burleson in the controversy with Clark.[40]

Lost by resignation from the board of trustees on March 4, 1856, was the Honorable A. S. Lipscomb, who was replaced

[40] Dr. Wallace practiced medicine in Waco until 1874, when he was appointed Superintendent of the Hospital for the Insane at Austin by Governor Coke, then by Governor Hubbard, and served until 1880. Governor Ross appointed him Superintendent of the East Texas Insane Asylum in Terrell, where he served until 1891. He is said to have done "more to upgrade and redirect the treatment of the mentally ill in Texas than any other one person." Doris Dowdell Moore, *The Biography of Doctor D. W. Wallace* (Dallas: The

by G. W. Graves by action of the Baptist State Convention. The Reverend Creath requested release from his position as agent for the school and donated the $60 paid to him for his service. Reverend Hosea Garrett was tendered the difficult job. The trustees concerned themselves with getting titles to lands donated to the university and to collection of subscriptions. President Burleson bought six acres of the college ground, "three acres, fifty dollars per acre and the remainder at twenty-five dollars per acre."

The board took notice of some dissatisfaction concerning the music department and requested that Professor Clark confer with a committee about the employment of a new teacher.

The Burleson household was also subject to vicissitudes in early 1856. On May 10 the couple's little daughter died at birth.[41] Burleson was also concerned about his brother. Richard had come to Texas as pastor of the Baptist Church at Austin in 1855, where he conducted a female school in 1856. He was on the point of leaving when President Burleson wrote him:

. . . you erred greatly in not locating here as Prof. of Natural Science. We have now 146 students and will have 160 in 4 weeks from today. My income from tuition will be after paying my Professors $2,000, from preaching $600, from endowment $800, and my boarders will pay all my family expenses and store bills. . . . I am just commencing me a splendid house on the college lot.[42]

Timberlawn Foundation, Inc.), 1966. See also Merle Mears Duncan, "David Richard Wallace, Pioneer in Psychiatry," *Texana*, Fall 1963, I, No. 4, 341-362; Dietrich, *The Blazing Story of Washington County* (Privately printed), p. 73.

Arabella Daniel Wallace died in 1868, leaving three daughters: Sue, born at Independence and educated at Baylor (A.B. in 1877) and married to the Honorable George Tyler of Belton; Estelle, who married D. R. B. Dupree of Marlin; and Anna Belle, who married William Breustedt of Waco. Dr. Wallace married Mrs. Robert, his wife's sister, in 1871. Their son, Coke, died at thirteen.

In 1882 Baylor University conferred the LL.D. on Dr. Wallace. He was one of the organizers and one of the presidents of both the Waco and Texas Medical Associations. He was a frequent speaker at colleges: at Texas A&M in 1878 on "The Mission of Letters"; at Baylor in 1906 on "Sam Houston, by a Personal Friend"; at Wake Forest on the thirtieth anniversary of his graduation, and again when at 83 he was the school's oldest graduate.

Dr. Wallace died on Tuesday, November 21, 1911, and was buried in Oakwood Cemetery with Masonic rites. Granddaughters Mrs. James B. Hubbard of Temple, and Mrs. James H. Riley of Waco; Mrs. Joe Gilliam of Brownwood; and great-grandson R. B. Dupree of Fort Worth survived him.

[41] R. C. Burleson to Richard Burleson, May 11, 1856. Burleson Papers, Texas Collection, Baylor University.

[42] R. C. Burleson to Richard Burleson, September 16, 1856. Burleson Papers,

This was the famous octagonal house one hundred yards east of Graves Hall for which Burleson borrowed money from the board, using land inherited from his father as security. The house was of three-story construction "with three-story galleries running entirely around it . . . it contained twenty-five large rooms, each capable of accommodating four young men, and a six-room residence for the Burlesons. A large, stone stack chimney in the center gave a fireplace to each room." Haynes stated that Burleson built the house to end the dissatisfaction among boarding students over inadequate housing and boarding arrangements in Independence.[43] Burleson's expenditure for college improvements was about $16,000, almost his entire patrimony. The benefits to the university were incalculable, but Burleson never fully recovered from the investment.

On the first of the following month, the president wrote again to his brother assuring him that there were "no dismissals nor supplantings" in the proffered position. Burleson felt that Wallace "would prefer the chair of ancient languages and Bro. Rowe fully intends to vacate as he is prepared to attend the medical lectures." Burleson also declared his own intent to rest, to visit his father, and to attempt to raise some funds in the older states "for our new hall for young preachers and would like for you to come on forthwith, and aided by Professor Morgan and Wallace, fill my place for the rest of this year and I give you at the rate of $1200 a year." A postscript declares "there is a telegraphic wire from here to Austin."[44]

To encourage enrollment, President Burleson wrote the following circular letter, which was distributed in the early summer of 1856:

Independence
June 23, 1856

Mr. — — — :
    As I have not time to write answers to the numerous inquiries made of me in regard to this flourishing institution, I have concluded

---

Texas Collection, Baylor University.
    The Texas Baptist, March 5, 1856, related facts concerning the Austin venture.
    [43] Haynes, pp. 171-172.
    [44] R. C. Burleson to Richard Burleson, October 1, 1856. Burleson Papers, Texas Collection, Baylor University.

to publish this circular, setting forth the principal points of information desired.

Location—Baylor University is located at Independence, a beautiful and quiet village in Washington county, on the great stage roads from Houston and San Augustine to the city of Austin. The citizens of Independence and immediate vicinity are unsurpassed in the state for intelligence, moral and religious worth. The refined society, splendid landscapes and beautiful liveoak groves, all combine to make Independence an eligible point for a great literary institution.

Health—The statistics of Baylor University show that no institution in America has been healthier. During the past five years, the average number of students, in both departments has been 150; and in all this time there have been two deaths, and neither of these from any local cause. One was from measles, and other from extraordinary exposure while at home. It often occurs that students who come here in bad health soon become vigorous and strong.

Expenses and Boarding—Tuition in the preparatory department is $26; in scientific department $40; and in the collegiate $50 a year. Board can be had in excellent private families, near the College, for $10 to $12 a month.

Building, Library and Apparatus—The buildings occupied at present, are a commodious two-story rock building, and two smaller framed buildings, for study room. The library is small but select. The Apparatus is very excellent, and was selected in Boston, with special care, by the Rev. James Huckins.

Permanency— . . . [The University] is now worth about $50,000 in lands, buildings, endowments, etc., and has ten professors and teachers, and over two hundred students in both male and female departments.—The Trustees and professors are fully determined to spare neither time, toil, nor money, in making it an ornament to Texas, and a rich blessing to the present and future generations.

Rufus C. Burleson,
President[45]

Astute business methods were employed to collect subscriptions made to the institution and to procure title to lands pledged or to effect their sale. The following printed letter was used:

Independence, Texas
November 25, 1856

Dear Sir:

I am happy to inform you that our University, to which you have generously contributed, is in a flourishing condition; one hundred and fifty students have been matriculated during the year.

Our President and four Professors are all at the post of duty, and are toiling by day and by night to sustain this great enterprise.

[45] Reprinted in the *Texas Baptist,* July 15, 1856.
The Austin branch of the Houston and Texas Central Railway was started

The year however, draws to a close, when their salaries will be due.
I therefore, by appointment of the Trustees wish to inform you
that the sum of _____ now due, is greatly needed.

Will you, therefore, send the amount by mail at our risk, or retain
it till called on by an agent?

Yours truly,
G. W. Graves
Treasurer of Endowment Fund [46]

Along with the rigid rules of the institution also came a
privilege. Every student over fifteen years of age, in good
standing, was allowed to wear a "lone star," as a badge of
distinction, and on special occasions he might wear a plume,
in imitation of the "Texas plume." But rings or other
jewelry were not allowed.

An embryonic honor system was created. At the beginning
and middle of each term, the faculty appointed a "grand
jury" of twelve students over eighteen years of age, who
were honor bound to "report immediately every violation
of the laws of the university." [47]

Chapel was highly organized and conducted by the president. Junior and senior students were seated in front and al-
ternated in reading Scripture and leading prayers. President
Burleson spoke on such subjects as "Man's Homogeneity,"
"Reciprocal Relations," and "Altruism." When a visitor entered, every student rose and "bowed gracefully."

An unsigned letter appeared in the *Texas Baptist* on June
17, 1856, giving an outsider's comment on the condition of
Baylor. The writer stopped by Independence on Friday,
"the regular day for the exercise of declamation and composition," and experienced a "treat." He noticed "a voluntary
gentlemanly deportment among all students, among themselves as well as in their conduct toward their professors and
in the social circle." Regret was expressed over "the feeble
health" of President Burleson, who "yet attends to his
various duties with his usual assiduity. The school is constantly increasing and of course his cares and labors increase.
I am abundantly satisfied that we have the right man in the

---

in 1856, with two Baylor Trustees, H. Garrett and T. J. Jackson of Chappell
Hill, among the incorporators. Hence there was hope that Independence could
lessen her transportation problems.

The two student deaths referred to were listed in the catalogue: William
McKnight, Independence, 1852-53; Earl Chapman, Independence, 1854.

[46] Printed sheet, Independence Papers, Texas Collection, Baylor University.
[47] *Catalogue of Baylor University*, Male Department, 1856-57, p. 23.

right place. By nature, as well as mental training, he is eminently fitted for his high position."

At the close of the school year of 1856, Baylor awarded a degree to Oscar Hopestill Leland, the first transfer student to receive such an honor. In his letter to the board of trustees, President Burleson stated that Leland had attended the university for five months and had reviewed the full course of study "prescribed by your honorable board," and in the department of mathematics especially "he is unequalled by any one we have presented." He had been a teacher in the state of Georgia for several years and was fully qualified and evidently deserved the honor sought.[48]

Professor Clark presented the names of Miss Carrie Mooney and Miss Zelphia G. Fuller to whom diplomas were granted.[49] On the previous December these two young ladies had received certificates of scholarship.

In his address to the graduating class of 1856, Professor Clark gave a defense of the education of women, an excerpt of which claimed that

. . . the education of women is as much her birthright as is the air she breathes. . . . It is not necessary that you contend for the intellectual equality of your sex with man. . . . It is enough that woman is entitled, *equally with man*, to such mental culture as will discipline her mind, cultivate her taste, and elevate her character.[50]

Other actions of academic significance were the following recommendations: that funds be collected by Burleson and Clark to secure an engraved plate for printing diplomas with the college seal engraved on same; that the professor of natural science be required to lecture once a month to the young ladies of the Female Department; that after the year 1857, the academic year commence on the first Monday in February and continue until the first Tuesday in December, at which time the annual examination be held; that Richard B. Burleson be employed as professor of moral and mental philosophy and belles lettres, Oscar H. Leland as professor

---

[48] Minutes of the Baylor Board of Trustees, December 18, 1856, p. 137. Leland served as professor of mathematics and astronomy from December 18, 1856, until September 2, 1861.

[49] *Ibid.*, p. 138.

[50] *Catalogue of Baylor University, Female Department* (Galveston: New's Book and Job Establishment, 1857), p. 17.

of mathematics and astronomy, Frank Keifer as teacher of German, and Charles T. Kavanaugh as tutor; and "that the President of the Male Department be required to collect from each student over sixteen years of age, entering hereafter, the sum of five dollars to be expended in purchase of books for the *Library*." Because doubt had arisen concerning the policy of fee payment by children of Baptist ministers, the board entered this statement in the minutes of March 5, 1856:

> Be it resolved that the children of Baptist ministers in good standing and who give themselves wholly to the ministry, or have done, or may do so, may have the advantages of this Institution, Male and Female Departments free of any charge of tuition.

Resolutions of appreciation for services were passed upon the resignation of Gilbert L. Morgan from the Chair of Mathematics.

The senior class of the Male Department presented the following program at the July 25, 1856, commencement, with prayers and music interspersed:

1. H. C. Oliphant, Huntsville—"Duties of an American Citizen"
2. Thomas J. Goree, Madisonville—"Life is Real! Life is Earnest!"
3. C. T. Kavanaugh, Chappell Hill—"True Heroism"
4. William H. Parks, Anderson—"Hoc Iter ad Astra"
5. Milton M. Callaway, Wharton—"Academicorum Officiorum Finis"
Baccalaureate Address—President Burleson, Conferring of Degrees[51]

In spite of President Burleson's feelings concerning "secret societies," in addition to the "Volunteer Literary Societies," two national fraternities were founded at Baylor during these early years. The Kappa chapter of Phi Gamma Delta was organized on April 8, 1856, with the charter being sponsored by the chapter of Union University, Murfreesboro, Tennessee. Professor G. L. Morgan aided in the organization, which consisted of six charter members with three others admitted by May 18, 1856.[52] Haynes stated that almost every student in the university was a member of some one of the organizations—literary or debating or "secret" even in 1854.

---

[51] Printed program presented to Texas Collection, Baylor University, by Mrs. Sue Goree Thomason, daughter of Major Thomas J. Goree, Baylor A.B. 1856; died March 5, 1905.
[52] C. R. Breedlove and Thomas J. Goree, Letter in *Phi Gamma Delta,* April 1881.

The Baylor Phi Gamma Delta chapter was called *Tryon* in honor of the beloved William L. Tryon. The young men, described as having integrity of purpose, and being of the highest moral worth and intellectual attainments, believed the organization "just such a one as we have need at our college to bind together in a more lasting brotherhood those of like inclination who are striving for one common object, an undying reputation." The Tryon Chapter of Phi Gamma Delta was inactive during the Civil War, but it was rechartered in August 1881 and continued until 1886 when Baylor University moved to Waco. University records carry no mention of the fraternity. (See Appendix for membership list.)

The roll of the Baylor Theta Chapter of Sigma Alpha Epsilon, Baylor's second fraternity indicates a membership of nineteen. The archivist of the fraternity believes that the Baylor chapter was organized and affiliated by correspondence in 1858.[53] Francis Marion Dunklin, when a student at the University of Alabama, is thought to have had some connection with the Alabama Mu Chapter, although his name does not appear in the minutes of the chapter. The Alabama chapter is termed the mother chapter, and it is believed that Marion Dunklin and his brother Timothy Lincoln founded the Baylor chapter. (See Appendix for membership list.)

Of significance as Baylor's first publication other than the catalogue and addresses given by visitors was the proposed *Texas Literary Journal*, announced by one Texas paper on December 18, 1856, and the *Texas Baptist* in January 1857. The "prospectus bore the signatures of Rufus C. Burleson, David Wallace, Richard B. Burleson, and O. H. Leland." The monthly magazine of sixty pages would cost $2.50 if paid in advance. Its coverage was to be (1) education in Texas, (2) science, and (3) history. It proposed to be "purely literary—, entirely neutral, both on religion and politics."[54] The *Texas Baptist* announced the first issue to be published on February 1, 1857.

[53] Lauren Foreman, Archivist, *Sigma Alpha Epsilon*, June 10, 1954.
[54] Undated news clipping from unnamed paper. Independence Papers, Texas Collection, Baylor University.
No issue of the journal has been found, and Ernest W. Winkler in his *Check List of Texas Imprints, 1846-1860*, terms it "not seen."

CHAPTER VII

Growing Pains and Quarrels

A DEVASTATING DROUGHT ACCOUNTED for a crop failure in 1857, but enrollment at Baylor University was unexpectedly high: five young men presented themselves as candidates for graduation in December. The catalogue listed also 4 seniors, 14 juniors, 13 sophomores, and 16 freshmen, with 34 additional students enrolled in the scientific course of study and 121 in the preparatory school, making a total of 207 students in the Male Department.[1]

Likewise, the Female Department prospered in the new building with "a new set of pianos as well as philosophical and chemical apparatus."[2] Six professors and teachers conducted classes for about one hundred students, and by the close of the 1857 term in December, fourteen young women had been graduated. So popular had the school become that local patrons stated the need of a preparatory school in the area.

There never was a time we venture to assert, when Washington needed a good female school more than now; in fact, in this respect, with a large, growing and prosperous community we are absolutely compelled, though unwillingly to acknowledge the humiliating fact, that the girls of Washington are without an institution of learning to fit them in the elementary branches for admission into the female department of Baylor University. What is the reason?[3]

The first meeting of the Baylor Board of Trustees in 1857, on March 3, gave attention to the physical plant of the institution. A committee was instructed "to erect a suitable enclosure around the new Female Building." This task was shortly accomplished at a cost of $600. The building committee was requested to furnish the basement of the building for use as classrooms, and at the December meeting seats for the Audience Hall were ordered, the committee to report on the first Monday in February 1858. Principal Clark sold the house which he had purchased from the trustees to Mr. J. P. Collins, who assumed the note for $1,362.

[1] *Baylor Catalogue*, 1856-1857, pp. 5-12.
[2] *Baptist State Convention Minutes*, 1858, p. 18.
[3] "Female School," *Washington American*, March 19, 1857.

Of academic importance this year was the establishment of a Law Department with the Honorable R. T. Wheeler, the Honorable R. E. B. Baylor, and Captain W. P. Rogers designated as professors.[4] Wheeler had served as Professor of Law at Austin College, then located at Huntsville.[5] He was born in Vermont in 1810, grew up in Ohio, and began law practice with W. S. Oldham in Fayetteville, Arkansas. After his marriage to Emily Walker in 1839 he established a law firm with Kenneth L. Anderson, later Vice-President of the Republic of Texas, in Nacogdoches, Texas. In 1842 he was appointed district attorney for the Fifth Judicial District and in 1844 became district judge and a member of the Supreme Court of Texas. He succeeded Judge Hemphill as Chief Justice and served until his death in Washington County on April 9, 1864. Wheeler County, created in 1876, was named in honor of this early Texas jurist.[6] Wheeler showed his interest in education by being a member of the Education Society.[7]

William Peleg Rogers, also named professor of law, was born in Georgia on December 27, 1817, and spent his youth on his father's plantation near Aberdeen, Mississippi. Ancestor Peleg Rogers had come from Pennsylvania to North Carolina in 1736 and settled on Catfish Creek, much to the disgust of his aristocratic English wife, Mary. She always wore silk dresses and lace caps and clung to her Church of England Prayerbook. Captain William Rogers had been educated for a medical career but changed to law at twenty-one. In 1840 he married Martha Halbert of Tuscaloosa, Alabama. An advocate of education for women, he sent their three daughters as well as their three sons to Baylor.[8]

[4] The first law department in Texas was inaugurated on February 12, 1844, with lectures by the Honorable James M. Ardney at San Augustine University. William Stuart Red, *A History of the Presbyterian Church in Texas* (San Antonio: The Steck Co., 1936), p. 222.

[5] Rollin M. Rolfe letter, October 27, 1955.

[6] James D. Lynch, *The Bench and Bar in Texas*, 1885; *The Handbook of Texas*, II, 891; R. F. Miller, "Early Presbyterianism in Texas," *Southwestern Historical Quarterly*, XIX, 1915-1916; D. W. C. Baker, *A Texas Scrap Book*, 1875.

[7] Frank E. Burkhalter, "The Laymen and Their Work," *Centennial Story of Texas Baptists*, p. 250.

[8] Fannie Alabama Rogers (Mrs. George Harris) was graduated in 1858 as valedictorian and was Baylor's oldest graduate in 1928, when she officiated at ground-breaking ceremonies for Baylor's Memorial Dormitory on October 11—

Rogers served in Colonel Jefferson Davis's regiment of Mississippians in the Mexican War, his company being cited for gallantry at the Battle of Monterrey. He was named consul to Vera Cruz (1849-1851) by President Zachary Taylor. He came to Washington-on-the-Brazos in 1856.[9]

A diminutive buff-bound circular of eight pages was sent out over the signatures of Hosea Garrett, board president, and N. Kavanaugh, secretary, announcing the new law department. Prefatory remarks justified the step, "regarded by some as premature," and stated the object "to establish a method of instruction on correct principles, by which the young men of our state shall be enabled to enter upon the race for honorable distinction in the law, upon terms equal to those of other states."

In the description of the course of instruction, attention was given to standard textbooks, daily examinations, lectures, and moot courts. The department was to function as an integral part of the university. Students were not required to have previous professional reading or proficiency in classical literature. Tuition was $36 per session, one-half payable

---

she had watched the laying of the cornerstone for the Female Building at Independence. At Baylor's Diamond Jubilee in 1920 she received an A. B. degree. Mary Eliza Rogers, graduate of 1867, married Dr. J. T. Bolton. Margaret Houston Rogers, born June 14, 1855, and named for Mrs. Sam Houston, who was a cousin of Captain Rogers, was valedictorian of the class of 1873 and lived to be Baylor's oldest graduate at 100. She lived with older son Dr. Gordon Damon, professor at the University of Texas. Captain Rogers' sons also attended Baylor: J. Halbert, 1858-9; William Peleg, Jr., 1859; Timothy Lincoln, 1872-4. Mrs. Eleanor Damon Pace, *The Baylor Line*, 1953.

[9] Rogers settled in Houston in 1859 where he became a widely known criminal lawyer and public speaker. Offered command of a Virginia regiment, he took instead the position of lieutenant colonel of the Second Texas Infantry in the Civil War. At the Battle of Shiloh he was promoted to colonel in the field. At the Battle of Corinth he was killed as he led a charge inside enemy fortifications on October 4, 1862. General Rosecrans, Commander of Union forces, ordered that he be buried with full military honors because of his spectacular bravery. The U. D. C. placed a monument there in 1912:

Colonel William P. Rogers
Second Texas Infantry
Killed at Fort Robinette
October 4th 1862

As long as courage, manliness, patriotism exist, the name of Rogers will be honored among men. He fell in the front of battle, in the center of the enemy's stronghold. He sleeps and glory is his sentinel.

Written by General Earl Van Dorn

Great-grandchildren Bolton and Mabelle Outlar and John Austin Sanders participated in the ceremony. Great-great-grandson John Moncrief Sanders was graduated from Baylor in 1957—one hundred years after Colonel Rogers began his classes in the Baylor University Law Department.

in advance, plus the $5 library fee and $1 incidental fee required of all students. Board in private families was available at $12 per month.[10]

The Sixth Catalogue of Baylor University, 1856-57, published in December 1857, included a division on the law department and listed thirteen students. "The course of instruction . . . is designed to give a thorough and practical legal education, and especially to qualify the student for the practice of his profession in the Courts of this State." The course comprised two sessions, and the Bachelor of Laws degree was to be conferred upon qualified graduates.

At the 1857 commencement four young men—William Baldwin Denson, Cicero Jenkins, George Eaves Davis, and Joseph Peter Jackson—were awarded A. B. degrees. John Franklin Smith, "a student in the scientific department," was given the first B. P. degree—the precursor of the B. S. degree later instituted. Miss Ophelia V. Jenkins was awarded a diploma. This diploma now in Baylor's Texas Collection bears the engraved seal of the university, as directed by trustees in June 1856.

Another young lady, Mary J. Haynes, would have been a member of the graduating Class of 1857 along with Ophelia Jenkins had not she suffered illness. She did read the first valedictory at the college, however, and received the first medal for achievement—a silver medalion bearing a picture of the first academy.[11] She was the daughter of Trustee A. G. Haynes.

Matters of business included formal acceptance of the newly-constructed building for young women. The house formerly occupied by the Female Department was donated to Mr. J. P. Collins "for his faithfulness . . . in building the new college edifice, provided he remove the same in 12 months."

Of financial concern was Professor Wallace's statement before the board that the interest due the Presidency and Chair of Natural Science was unpaid. Burleson and Wallace

[10] *Circular of the Law Department.* Printed at the American Office, Washington, 1857. Texas Collection, Baylor University.
A little newspaper, the *Southern Star,* published by Jo Littlefield at Independence, carried the law department announcement in the June 13, 1857, issue.
[11] Laura Simmons, *Out of Our Past* (Waco, Texas: Texian Press, 1967), p. 33.

were directed to "collect all the notes so as to mature in one, two, or three years, or longer if the donor requires it." Then a committee was ordered to examine the notes to determine possible value and request the professor of each chair to raise the subscription to the original amount.

The December 1857 board of trustees meeting gave the first official recognition of the schism between President Burleson and Principal Clark. A committee of four was appointed "to wait on each of them, separate and apart and make known all the rumors afloat."

The conclusion of the deliberation was that "this Board believes that in the indications of Divine Providence, the time has now arrived when the two departments of Baylor University should be separated"—at least so far as holding President R. C. Burleson (or his successor in office) responsible for the manner of conducting the Female Department of the institution. Burleson was made responsible for the Male Department and Clark for the Female.

The board, in an attempt at arbitration, took notice of a circumstance regarding the attendance of young women at services or meetings held by Burleson and his successor, H. C. Renfro in 1857, as pastors of the Independence Baptist Church. The board stated that it reserved "the right to scrutinize and judge every law and regulation for the internal government of the schools." A further, pointed statement read:

... that while we claim no right to compel pupils to attend religious meetings of any kind, nor would we allow the professors to do so, or to teach any sectarian peculiarities in the Institution, yet we deem it imprudent and wrong to prevent those pupils from attending such meetings as they may desire to do, unless forbidden by their parents or guardians or rendered imprudent by a due regard for their health. We therefore deem it necessary for the best interests of the pupils and the promotion of the great ends for which our Institution is established that both the President of B. U. and the Principal of the Female Department shall as ministers, cooperate in a cordial, Christian and prudent manner with the pastor of the Independence Church in all *Revival Meetings* he may hold, and encourage the attendance of all the pupils, unless it shall be against the known will of their parents or the expressed desire of the pupils.[12]

[12] Minutes of the Baylor Board of Trustees, December 17, 1857, p. 148.

The board felt that a reconciliation had been effected, and Burleson and Clark came before the trustees to give "hands in a pledge of cordial cooperation."

Undoubtedly one stimulus for the differences between President Burleson and Principal Clark was the education and discipline of the young women. A statement by Principal Horace Clark in the 1857 catalogue for the feminine contingent of Baylor University sheds light on one point of disagreement—the feasibility of the education of women.

It is always better to let *facts* speak in such questions, than *theories*. It is enough to know that whenever woman has been called by the events of Providence from her own sphere to act in that which seems to be especially the sphere of manhood, she has proved herself equal to the emergency. . . .

It is enough, then, if it be conceded, that she is entitled, equally with man to such mental culture as will discipline her mind. . . .[13]

As a pioneer in coeducation, begun at Ohio's Oberlin College in 1833,[14] Baylor carefully preserved a pattern of discipline in accordance with strict Baptist precepts. During the Graves administration, actual coeducation was the policy; Burleson separated the departments scholastically. Physically, the buildings of the Male and Female Departments were approximately a mile apart. The small creek that split the campus became "the Jordan" that separated the men from "the promised land," declared a reminiscence of the Independence campus.[15]

Baylor's earliest catalogue, for the session of 1851-52, in the Female College division, stated that "a Boarding House, under the charge of Rev. G. W. Baines and his Lady, is attached to the Institution, where young ladies may enjoy . . . the comforts of home, and where their manners, intellectual habits and morals are the objects of constant attention."[16] The catalogue of 1852-53 refers interested persons to the catalogue of the Female Department (evidently not published); the catalogue of 1853-54 makes no mention of the Female Department, but the 1855 catalogue states that the

[13] *Baylor University Catalogue,* Female Department, 1857, p. 24.
[14] A. Godbold, *The Church College of the Old South,* (Durham: Duke University Press, 1944), p. 108.
[15] Fannie R. Harris, "Baylor at Old Independence," *The Baylor Monthly,* III (March, 1928), p. 6.
[16] *Catalogue of Baylor University, 1851-52,* "Lone Star" Office, p. 12.

Female Department "is located nearly one mile from the university, and communications in regard to it should be addressed to Prof. Clarke [sic]." A similar statement appears in the 1856 issue. Evidence of differing opinions concerning the operation of the two departments can be deduced in these statements concerning boarding arrangements:

[Men] students do not board in a common stewards' hall; but in families, where the restraining and refining influences of the family circle may always be felt. . . . The price of board, including fuel, washing, etc., will not exceed $12 per month. And will be as much lower as the prices of provisions will allow.[17]

The Female Department publication of the same year (which carried the first picture in a Baylor catalogue—a charming view of the new building as well as an engraving of the handsome school desks from Boston) states:

Stewards' Department

This department has been placed under separate management. The increased patronage of the School, and the numerous duties and responsibilities pressing upon the Principal, rendered this division of labor necessary. Mr. Collins, the present proprietor of the boarding-house, and his lady, will spare no pains to promote the comfort and convenience of those placed in the Institution. Several rooms have been already added to the premises, and a large dining hall has been erected. The Principal and his family, and the teachers, board with the pupils.

They are here under the immediate charge of the Faculty; have stated hours for study and recreation; are not permitted to attend parties, nor receive or pay visits, but at the discretion of the Principal; nor do they, under any circumstances, remain away from the Institution at night. The government is strictly paternal. . . .[18]

Haynes averred that some discussion was indulged in by the trustees and friends of the schools as to the propriety of making the Female Department a distinct school and placing Professor Clark at its head as president.[19] Yet Burleson maintained the position of president of the university and was justifiably nettled by the recent board action. Clark was ambitious for the success of the Female Department and

[17] *Fifth Annual Catalogue of Baylor University* (Galveston: The Civilian Book and Job Office, 1857), p. 22.
[18] *Catalogue of Baylor University*, Female Department (Galveston: New's Book and Job Establishment, 1857), pp. 17-18.
[19] Harry Haynes, *The Life and Writings of Rufus C. Burleson* (compiled and published by Mrs. Georgia J. Burleson, 1901), p. 214.

resented the secondary position to which it was relegated. Controversy was inevitable.

The 1857 catalogue of the Female Department praised the beauties of the locale with its refined and intelligent society and carried a glowing description of the new college edifice and its furnishings. It was termed an

. . . elegant building in stone, three stories in height, and contains, besides a spacious Audience Hall, a school room, library and apparatus room, and fine ample recreation rooms, each 13x28 feet. It is handsomely furnished throughout, can be thoroughly ventilated in summer and comfortably warmed in winter. The grounds are handsomely enclosed, and afford abundant space for sports and exercise. Ample accommodations are provided here for 250 or 300 pupils.

Other publications paid tribute to Principal Clark as "the designer, supervising architect, building contractor and solicitor of funds . . . for the magnificent conception so wisely planned, with its massive stone columns, easy stairways, convenient recitation rooms and beautifully arranged auditorium."[20]

Early catalogues for the Female Department noted the selection of Independence as the location of Baylor University "by the far-seeing and lamented Wm. M. Tryon, the projector and founder of the Institution." Government of the young ladies was benevolent with close attention to "the Divine authority of the Bible." The school day opened with the reading of the Scriptures, prayer, and sacred music, with preference shown none of the evangelical denominations. The curriculum consisted of courses in music, drawing and painting, German, French, and Latin, in addition to the usual offerings of the preparatory department. A statement concerning the annual examination appeared in the 1857 catalogue:

The practice of indulgent parents in removing pupils from the Institution before the close of the session to avoid these exercises cannot be too earnestly reprehended. . . . In future no young lady can thus leave without the consent of the Principal; nor can she resume the position in her class. . . .[21]

[20] *The Galveston News*, July 12, (n.d.) clipping in Clark Scrapbook, Texas Collection, Baylor University. This paper on June 18, 1857, had stated that the only respectable college building in the area was that of the Catholic college and convent in Galveston.

[21] *Catalogue of Female Department*, Baylor University, 1857. p. 15.

As with male students, supervision of finances was attempted. Accounts with merchants could be opened only "by direct expression of parents or guardians, and then purchases must be made under the direction of a teacher and confined to articles of utility or necessity." Letters to young women were addressed to the principal for delivery, and clandestine correspondence was sent unopened to the parents.

Following the dictates of the board of trustees, young women adopted modest dress during their period of residence. Dresses were plain, flounceless and untucked; bonnets were of white straw with plain ribbon trim—pink was allowed. A breast pin, "on account of its utility," was permitted. The intent of the regulations was to promote habits of neatness and economy.[22]

Social life for the Female Department of Baylor seemed not to exist prior to 1857. Men had literary societies, but girls had no type of organization. Church attendance seemed to be their chief contact with the outside world, and hence was a very important activity. Young women marched single file under faculty supervision to the Independence Baptist Church and sat in a group—across the aisle from the young men.

Life in the Female Department was made interesting, however, by the girls themselves, who delighted in "the new college edifice," and the close relationships with the faculty. Miss Mary R. Davis, who had come to Baylor as a teacher in 1857 after missionary work with the Indians,[23] was particularly acclaimed as "a preeminently superior young woman" possessing "a pretty wit." One day she rode horseback down the one street of Independence and encountered Judge Williamson. He asked, "Is that horse you are riding the one that has been behind my pasture with a bell on him?"

"Yes," Miss Davis countered, "and there's a belle on him now, too!"[24]

Records concerning the activities of men students outside of class hours are not so sparse. President Burleson's play

[22] *Ibid.*, p. 16.

[23] "According to His Purpose—Mary Hardin-Baylor College and Student Christian Life" (Pamphlet: Centennial Series, 1945), pp. 5-7.

[24] Mrs. S. L. Shipe, "Texas in the Sixties," *Galveston News,* (n.d.), Clark Scrapbook, Texas Collection, Baylor University.

at hide-and-seek with his students in their pranks provoked unintended entertainment, from which girls undoubtedly derived vicarious pleasure. Burleson averred that he had a "Detective Bird" that whispered in his ear when students slipped out a window or slid down a column to engage in some kind of fun. Several stories related by Haynes are typical of the activities.[25]

One night several young men improvised an elevator with rope and a sturdy blanket and lowered their companions from the third-floor gallery. The "look-out" was to watch for their reappearance and lift them up when they yanked the rope. Burleson's Detective Bird was working; he circled the house and slipped into the "elevator" and jerked on the rope. About half-way up the haul, the boys discovered the identity of their passenger. With great glee they secured the rope to the railing and waited. After feeling numerous jerks on the rope, they answered: "Doctor, we know who you are, and we do not intend to haul you up another inch until you promise not to give any of us demerit marks." Burleson agreed "to compromise our differences." The elevator was lowered upon the promise of no demerits, although the president admitted to being badly "done up."

On another night three roommates in the "Octagon" decided to go out to procure chicken for a late supper, leaving the fourth roommate to cover their absence with loud snores. Again the Detective Bird was alert. When the young man became impatient for the return of his cohorts and left his bed, President Burleson crept into the room, into the bed, and waited for the return. Consternation prevailed when the boys returned with the chickens and Burleson rolled out of bed. "If you bought those chickens," he said, "it will be better to wait and let Mrs. Burleson have them nicely fried for breakfast, but if you 'hooked' them, I would advise you to return them at once."

An attempted turkey supper had an even more disastrous ending for students. About a dozen boys had arranged a meeting on "the banks of the Jordan" with an old Negro who brought the turkeys. When President Burleson had learned of the plan, he went early to the assigned place and

[25] Haynes, pp. 204-212.

concealed himself in the ravine. The assembled boys spoke with bravado of what they would do should the president appear. Several threatened throwing him into the water or leaving him tied all night in his underclothes. One boy said, "Well, I would just say, 'Dr. Burleson, walk up and eat some turkey with us.'" At this point, Burleson stepped forward, bowed low and said, "Thank you, sir. As you seem to be the only young man here who has any politeness, I will accept your invitation. Turkey is my favorite fowl." The crowd dispersed in panic, and Burleson found himself with the old Negro and an abundance of turkey.

Two other incidents concerned the president's renowned carriage. On one Friday afternoon of 1856, President Burleson had announced his intent to drive to the country the next morning for a visit with a friend. Two young men decided upon frustration of his plan by hiding his carriage in the woods. Again the Detective Bird was alert. Burleson hurried through supper, rushed to the barn, and concealed himself under a blanket in the carriage. The boys soon appeared and arduously pulled the carriage over a mile into the woods. Then the president arose from his hiding to say to the fatigued pranksters: "Young gentlemen, I am very much obliged for this nice ride, and when you have rested a moment, you can pull me back home."

One morning in the spring of 1858 President Burleson woke to find the renowned buggy on top of the Female College building! His Detective Bird revealed to him the ring leader of the episode. Burleson approached him with: "Robert, here is a bright new ten-dollar gold piece. I will hand it to you if you will go over and bring my buggy home." Robert, anxious to earn the fee, performed the deed. Burleson went out, handed him the gold piece and informed him that it was his own money he had worked for. Students were required to deposit their "pin money" with the president for safe-keeping.

Haynes declared that President Burleson always manifested great interest in the exercises and pastime of his students. On one occasion in 1858 about one hundred boys were playing "hot ball" on the Independence campus. Burleson offered himself as target. Haynes stated that he was pelted a hundred times with solid rubber balls which must have left as many bruises; yet "he was obdurate and un-moved as the sturdy live oak. . . . The sport over, he saluted the boys, and bowed himself from the grounds, his face wreathed in smiles, when he was unquestionably suffering the greatest pain."

Communication between the young men and women *did* exist, despite the difficulties. Autograph albums served as one means of under-ground contact. The albums, frequently containing notes, were passed from boys to their sisters or cousins and hence to the desired recipient. Gossip declared that kinship ties between young men and women were "dis-covered" through an intense interest in genealogy during these days of close supervision, when communication was allowed only between relatives.

Problems of growth and financing again confronted the Baylor trustees. By June 1858 the problem of housing the law department was brought to their attention. A commit-tee was designated to request the Independence Baptist Church to donate church benches in exchange for a release from rents due. The Honorable John Sayles, who had lec-tured during the past session, was added to the staff on June 15, 1858, by a directive of the trustees.

Sayles was one of the ablest men in the legal profession in Texas and garnered fame as a writer—publishing some fif-teen titles, most of several volumes. Two are products of his early Baylor association[26] and were the first texts pub-lished by a Baylor professor.

John Sayles was born in Vernon, Oneida County, New York, on March 9, 1825.[27] His father was Welcome Sayles, an eminent physician from Rhode Island. His mother was

---

[26] John Sayles, *A Treatise on the Practice of the District and Supreme Courts of the State of Texas* (Philadelphia: Kay and Brother, Law Booksellers and Publishers, No. 19 South Sixth Street; Houston: J. S. Taft: Austin: F. T. Duffau), 1858.

John Sayles, *Precedents and Rules of Pleading in Civil Actions in the County and District Courts of Texas* (St. Louis, Missouri: The Gilbert Book Co.), 1882.

In the preface of each volume Sayles declared that the substance of the work was delivered in the summer of 1857 to law classes of Baylor University, "then under the charge of Honorable R. T. Wheeler, Chief Justice of the Supreme Court, and Honorable R. E. B. Baylor, Judge of the Third Judicial District." At the request of these distinguished jurists, the lectures were re-written, with additional material, and read to law classes of 1858 to 1860 and, upon reorganization of the Law Department, again in 1867.

[27] *Hamilton Literary Magazine,* Necrology Notices.

Harriet Sergeant Sayles, the daughter of John Sergeant, a celebrated Presbyterian clergyman famed for his work among the Oneida Indians. The Sergeants, Sedgwicks, and Dwights sustained a consanguineous relationship in the early history of New England and were political, social, religious, and educational leaders. The Sayles family was of English extraction, and one John Sayles came to America in the ship with Roger Williams and afterwards married his eldest daughter, Mary.[28] In 1654 Sayles settled in Providence, Rhode Island, where he was a warden, member of the general council, and deputy to the general court.

The unusually precocious young John Sayles received his early education at an academy in his native town, and at the age of fifteen began teaching, first in New York State, as he attended college.[29] He was graduated from Hamilton College of Clinton, New York, in 1845 with the A. B. degree and was a member of the Alpha Delta Phi fraternity.[30] Sayles received an A.M. degree in 1869.[31] After college, Sayles taught school in Georgia for one year, then came to Texas where he continued to teach—"in a log school house about one-half mile from the [Brenham] court house on the Independence road in 1846."[32] As his teaching duties allowed, young Sayles read law under the supervision of J. D. Giddings and Colonel Barry Gillespie and passed the Texas bar examination.[33] In 1849 Sayles was married to Mary E. Gillespie and became associated with his father-in-law and W. T. McFarland in the practice of law. After the death of Colonel Gillespie in 1851, Sayles formed a partnership in 1857 with Benjamin H. Bassett, which for almost thirty

[28] Reminiscences by C. C. Garrett (friend to Sayles for nearly thirty years) to the *Banner,* Brenham, Texas, May 1897.

[29] Information supplied by grandson, John Sayles of Abilene to Judge Abner V. McCall, March 31, 1953. President McCall has done extensive research on Judge John Sayles.

[30] Edwin K. Tolan, Reference Librarian, Hamilton College, February 14, 1957. Sayles is also listed in the Hamilton College *Alumni Register,* 1812-1932, p. 58.

[31] *Biographical Encyclopedia of Texas* (New York: Southern Publishing Company, 1880), p. 181. The statement is made that Sayles' accomplishment in classical studies was "so comprehensive and thorough . . . that he received the A.B. and A.M. degrees at Hamilton. Toland, however, wrote that he "received the A.M. degree in 1869 but from which college I do not know."

[32] W. G. Wilkins to C. C. Garrett.

[33] *The Handbook of Texas,* II, 576, gives the year as 1846; *Biographical Encyclopedia* gives 1847 as the year Sayles was admitted to the Texas Bar.

years was one of the most successful law firms in early Texas.

Sayles owned a plantation in the Gay Hill neighborhood and a large number of slaves. Renowned for hospitality, the Sayles' home exemplified "refinement, culture, and love," wrote C. C. Garrett. Sayles taught a Bible class in the Presbyterian Church of Brenham and was made a Mason in Baylor Lodge, No. 125 about 1846. He was Master of that lodge and elected Grand Master of Masons of Texas in 1852.[34] In 1855-1856 Sayles represented Washington County in the House of the Sixth Legislature.[35]

One of Judge Sayles' three daughters has transcribed a series of amusing stories about her father. Washington County chuckled over an incident concerning the judge's geese. So dedicated was he to his hobby that he assigned a little Negro boy the job of caring for the geese and keeping them out of the flower beds. Mrs. Sayles one day discovered that some of her prized peaches had fermented. She directed a house-boy to dispose of them. He emptied the large crock in a trough, where the peaches were discovered by the flock of geese. They devoured the tasty repast. About nightfall the little Negro caretaker came running in to report that the geese were all lying around the yard dead. Negro women were called to pick the geese, for even in a home such as the Sayles', frugality was practiced. When Judge Sayles appeared, he was confronted by a flock of denuded geese shivering in a Texas norther! He sent a Negro on horseback into Brenham to buy a bolt of red flannel and ordered mass production of little red flannel jackets for his geese.

This resourceful, erudite scholar liked to keep abreast of the times. He is said to have bought the first sewing machine that came to Texas—intended for leather, it did a devastating job on silk dresses. He also bought the first dish

[34] In 1878 Sayles prepared Sayles' "Masonic Jurisprudence," which became the accepted authority of Masonry in Texas.

A biographical sketch in appreciation of Sayles appears in *Proceedings of the Grand Lodge of Texas,* 1897.

[35] *Dictionary of American Biography,* XVI (1935).

During the Civil War Sayles became brigadier general of the militia and rendered distinguished service under General J. B. Magruder, as adjutant general of his staff. In 1867 he again taught law at Baylor when the law school was reorganized after the war. In 1886 he moved to Abilene and established the law firm of Sayles and Sayles with a son. He died on May 22, 1897.

washer and the first typewriter—"and hired a girl from the North to run it."

Judge Sayles always wore a beard. During the war years, the Yankees burned the bridge over the Brazos, and the train carrying Confederate soldiers fell into the river. Sayles was badly cut across the chin, and henceforth he wore the beard, declared his daughter. The eminent judge brought a colorful career as well as prestige to the Baylor Law Department.

The trustees in June 1858 created a committee to report to the Baptist Convention in October the need of a building for the Male Department, together with a proposed construction plan. Hosea Garrett was appointed General Agent to procure subscriptions for the building at a salary of $1,100 per year plus travel expenses. Garrett immediately subscribed $500 of this amount toward the building fund. President Burleson had been released from his duties to take a trip at the trustees' expense through East Texas as agent for Baylor. Professor Richard B. Burleson was named Chairman of the Faculty during his absence. Dr. W. H. Gant "set forth a synopsis of his plan of organization" for a medical department, but after due deliberation, the board deemed it inexpedient to proceed with such plans. There was much agitation in Texas during the last years of the decade for a school to train young doctors. Some $20,000 had been raised in Houston to establish a medical school under the direction of Ashbel Smith and four teachers.[36] The attempt was abortive, and not until 1865 was Galveston Medical School founded under the direction of Dr. Greenville Dowell.

Of great concern to the community was the completion of the basement of the Female Department building. Dr. Asa Hoxie donated $1,000 for the project, and at the request of Principal Clark, a scholarship for one pupil annually was granted Dr. Hoxie. Dr. J. M. Carroll believed that this circumstance was the beginning of the Burleson-Clark feud, but enmity between the two men had existed from the time of Burleson's plea for state aid "for the Male Department only." The trustees had wanted a two-story building, stated Carroll, but Clark induced a man—a non-Baptist—to supply

<hr>

[36] *Houston Telegraph*, February 6, 1857.

the money for the basement.[37] Another factor adding prestige to the Female Department at this time was the acquisition of a large costly bell of wonderful tone presented by
Trustee A. C. Horton, the first lieutenant governor of Texas.
According to a generally accepted story, Horton gave "fifty
silver Mexican dollars" to be cast into the bell. Students
averred that it could be heard five miles distant.[38]

Population shifting in Texas affected Washington County
by 1858. The *Texas Baptist* described Independence as "unusually quiet and [wearing] the sober appearance of an old
town in one of the older states, where people feel themselves
settled, and live there because they want to."[39] R. B. C.
Howell wrote of his tour of Texas during the fall of 1858,
describing Independence as "a beautiful village of 500 inhabitants with a large and tolerably efficient church, and
Baylor University, the denominational institution of the
State."[40]

Political matters were of much concern in Texas at this
time. Houston made stump speeches during the late summer
at Independence, at Hempstead, and at Washington, where
there was a big barbecue. The *Southern Intelligencer* of
Austin had hoped to get Houston to become head of the
Southern League, but he avoided the states' rights issue entirely.[41] Washington County was divided.

A disturbing factor, also, concerned the Houston and
Texas Central Railroad, which had been completed to Hempstead. Washington and Independence citizens had intended
to build to it, crossing the Brazos River near the old Rock
Island ferry and into the town of Washington for a bonus
of $11,000. The town rejected the proposition and the Cen-

[37] J. M. Carroll, *The History of Texas Baptists* (Dallas: *Baptist Standard*
Publishing Company 1923), p. 391.

[38] The bell bore the inscription "Presented by Hon. A. C. Horton, A.D. 1858.
Ladies Seminary, Independence, Texas."
Girls who accomplished some noteworthy task were allowed to ring the
bell. At one time Virginia Culbertson pulled the rope so vigorously that some
stones from the roof fell, barely missing her head. (Letter from Mrs. Dyess
of Mexia, whose mother, Mrs. Hassell, was a schoolmate of Miss Culbertson.)
Mrs. Eli Moore Townsend, a former member of the Mary Hardin-Baylor
faculty and student of the school at Independence, obtained the bell from the
Hairston family and presented it to the Belton college on February 1, 1917.

[39] The *Texas Baptist*, Anderson, Texas, September 9, 1858.

[40] *Ibid.*, November 20, 1858.

[41] *Southern Intelligencer*, August 18, 1858.

tral built its line on the east side of the river and established a depot at Navasota. Many people felt that this action was the death knell for Washington County, and subsequent events, including the Civil War, confirmed their prognostications. As a result of agitation to move Baylor to a population center, the catalogue carried a paragraph on "permanency," and the trustees issued this resolution:

Resolved, That the Trustees do hereby declare that the removal of this university is both inconsistent with our charter and impracticable and we consider its location permanent and not debatable. [42]

Relationships with the denomination during this period deserve attention. Principal Horace Clark was ordained to the ministry on April 18, 1858, and elected recording secretary of the Baptist State Convention in June 1859. The convention met at Independence in October 1858 with thirty churches and eleven associations represented. Baylor President R. C. Burleson was named convention president and reelected in 1859.

The year brought a change in the calendar of the university. The vacation period was moved to July and August with a ten-day respite at Christmas. The board also designated a Board of Visitors, consisting of fifteen persons for each department, to conduct examinations. (See appendix).

Student discipline again received attention. The trustees "resolved" at the June 15, 1858, meeting "that some of the students of the Male Department in their behavior towards the Female Department are subject of discipline and that we require the faculty of the Male Department to enforce the By-Laws. . . . "

In December President Burleson reported to the trustees that two young men, of previous good conduct, had been induced, "by persons whose business it is to corrupt our students," to get drunk and interrupt the exhibition of the Female Department. The young men were suspended, and since they chose not to appear before the board as requested, they were expelled at a later meeting when the secretary read to the students the minutes relative to the expulsion. [43]

[42] Minutes of the Baylor Board of Trustees, December 1, 1858, p. 159.
[43] Research reveals that one of these young men wrote a letter from a Civil War battlefield telling of his renunciation of the habit of drink. Soon thereafter he died a war hero. Letter, Independence Material, Texas Collection, Baylor University.

Rules and regulations assumed a more definite form with the increase in size of the Female Department and the spacious new building. Young ladies were expected to board in the institution under immediate faculty supervision. The current catalogue stated with formality these rules:

I.   Boarders are required:

1. To occupy the rooms assigned them.
2. To retire and rise at the appointed hours.
3. To be promptly in their places at meals.
4. To have every article of their clothing marked.
5. To keep a record of all articles to be washed.
6. To keep their dormitories in neat order.
7. To deport themselves on all occasions in a lady-like manner.

II.   They are prohibited:

1. From visiting each other after supper or on the Sabbath.
2. From spending nights on the Sabbath abroad.
3. From wearing each other's clothing.
4. From making purchases, excepting under the direction of parents or guardians.
5. From leaving the college grounds without permission.
6. From sending or receiving letters otherwise than by the college post.
7. From communicating with gentlemen or receiving their attentions.[44]

For eight years Principal Clark had managed the school, and it was deemed "a first class Female Institution." The 1858 catalogue carried the commencement program, which indicates the considerations of young women of the era—as well as the endurance of the audience.

December 23, 1858
Commencement Exercises

Oration, W. A. Montgomery, Esq.—Duties of the Educated Woman

Essays: Mary Allcorn—Is Genius Compatible with Domestic Facility?

Emiline Allcorn—The Interest Attached to the Tombs of Distinguished Persons

Sarah H. Chambers—Human Pursuits

Mary A. Eddins—The Conqueror's Trophies

Catherine Clark—Brevity of Human Life

Rebecca S. Skilton—The Hill of Science

Rachael Barry—The Mission of Beauty

Sally A. McNiel—Footprints on the Sands of Time

Bettie B. Carter—Natural Provisions for Human Happiness

⁴⁴ *Catalogue of Baylor University,* Female Department, 1858-59, (Galveston: "News" Book and Job Establishment, 1859), p. 30.

Mary McKellar—Self Culture
Dora A. Pettus—The Religion of Nature
Julia A. Robertson—The Trans-Atlantic Telegraph
Mary A. Whiteside—The Mission of Liberty
Valedictory—Fannie A. Rogers—The Responsibilities of Genius
Address to the Graduates by Principal
Diplomas Conferred
Farewell Song[45]

Classes in the law department listed thirty-three young men in 1858-59, thirteen of whom were graduated in September 1858. During the previous year the students of the law department had organized the Wheeler Law Club to discuss issues of local interest. The catalogues of these years stated that "young men, educated in Texas, will have peculiar advantages . . . of learning fully the genius, character, and wants of the people with whom they are to live and act." It was deemed "a source of regret to see Texians patronizing Northern or distant colleges, where our youth will establish sentiments, habits and tastes antagonistic or alien to ours."

Further notice of strife within the faculty came to the attention of trustees at the last meeting of the year 1858. With the board, President Burleson had "a free and full interchange of opinion . . . touching matters between him and the trustees," and it was unanimously agreed that all differences of opinion heretofore held by each party should be forgotten and that they cooperate and devote all their energies to the building up of the university. President Burleson led in prayer, and the right hand of fellowship was again extended. Then the trustees sent for David R. Wallace, professor of languages, and Elder Clark, the latter accepting the apologies of Wallace who had written a letter to Trustee Garrett which disturbed Principal Clark. The group parted on December 4, 1858, with "mutual good understanding."

A concern of moment to Texas Baptists between 1848 and 1858 was their responsibility to Baylor. Baylor was founded

[45] The class became known as the "Famous Class of '58." Fannie Rogers Harris presided at Ground-Breaking Services for Baylor's Woman's Memorial Dormitory in 1928 as Baylor's oldest graduate. Dora Pettus Hobby was the mother of Texas Governor Hobby; Mary McKellar Herndon was the wife of a congressman and "another graduate was the mother of a congressman." *After Seventy-five Years*, Student League and Alumnae Association of Baylor College, Belton, Texas, 1920, p. 129. Thomas J. Brown, graduate of the 1858 Baylor Law Class, became chief justice of the Texas Supreme Court in 1911.

through the efforts of the Texas Baptist Education Society of the Union Baptist Association. The Texas Baptist Education Society was merged with the Baptist State Convention. At an Independence meeting in 1858 a committee was appointed by the convention to consider the legal relations between the convention and Baylor University. When the convention met in Waco on October 25, 1859, the following report was made:

1. That Baylor is strictly a denominational institution.
2. That the legal title to all its estate, real and personal, is vested in the Board of Trustees.
3. That the Convention in relation to the University possesses no visitorial power.
4. That the Board of Trustees of Baylor University is under the strongest legal, as well as the highest moral obligation to use all its powers, privileges and immunities, and all its trust funds, lands, buildings, endowments and possessions of every description, for the support and maintenance of an institution of learning, under the control of Baptists, and that the law provides the most ample security for such an administration of the trust.
5. That no change in the act of incorporation can increase the obligation of the Trustees or make more secure to the denomination, the tenure by which the trust funds of Baylor University are held.
6. That the only legal relation between the Convention and the University is the power which this Convention has of filling vacancies in the Board of Trustees.
7. That there is a *moral* relation of mutual dependence and support which makes their interests identical, and is a certain guarantee that they will continue to work harmoniously together for the promotion of learning, piety and virtue, so long as there are minds to be enlightened and hearts to be purified, sanctified and made meet for the inheritance of the saints in light.

> All of which is respectfully submitted.
> Signed by the Committee,
> H. L. Clark, Chairman
> H. Garrett
> R. C. Burleson
> W. A. Montgomery
> C. R. Breedlove[46]

Progress at Baylor for 1859 is shown in the report to the Baptist State Convention. Between three and four hundred

[46] *Report on the Legal Relations of Baylor University to the Baptist State Convention of Texas,* Waco, October 25, 1859 (one thousand copies printed and distributed).

volumes had been added to the library in addition to the gifts solicited by President Burleson in the fall of 1858.[47] Apparatus subscriptions totaled about $1,200, of which $500 had been used for purchases. Sale of land donations added $1,000 to the endowment. The institution was valued at $65,000 and boasted fourteen professors and teachers and 275 students. Reported also was the contract for the new stone building for the Male Department at a cost of $4,607.[48] Haynes states that Board President Garrett reported an advanced stage of construction for the two-story stone structure for the Male Department. He also told of the adoption of plans for a three-story building 56x112 feet to cost $30,000, $15,000 of which had been raised. The first story of the building had been completed by Major A. G. Haynes at a cost of $6,500.[49]

The 1859 catalogue explained the plan recommended by the Baptist State Convention at Waco by which Baylor would foster a theological department. "Two pious, intelligent and discreet ministers were to spend two or three months and deliver a short course of familiar lectures on Systematic and Pastoral Theology, Homiletics, Biblical Interpretation and Church History." It was hoped to begin the course in the winter months of 1860 and open it *only* to young men licensed by their churches to preach the Gospel. Nine young ministers were listed in the catalogue as then pursuing their education at Baylor.[50]

Principal Clark was busy maintaining interest in the Female College. The June 30, 1859, minutes of the board show that he was permitted to charge fifty cents admission to a concert, the revenue to be used "for the improvement of the female college." One hundred sixty young women were enrolled in the various classes, with one hundred in the collegiate division. Along with the standard mathematics,

---

[47] The *Texas Baptist*, September 30, 1858, listed "a full set of Gill's *Commentaries* in nine volumes, Greenleaf's *Testimonies of the Gospels,* Scott's *Commentaries* in three volumes, and a complete set of Henry's *Commentaries.*"

[48] *Minutes of the Baptist State Convention,* 1859, p. 10.

[49] Haynes, pp. 292-293.

By 1861 war conditions suspended building operations and subscriptions became valueless. Contractor Haynes is said to have lost 80 per cent of his investment on the venture—about $5,400, a deficit he assumed without complaint. Haynes had used his slaves in construction work.

[50] *Ibid.,* pp. 30-31.

English, history, Latin, German, French, philosophy, physiology, botany, chemistry, astronomy, and meteorology, young ladies could follow cultural pursuits such as music (harp, piano, guitar, voice), painting (water colors—Oriental and Grecian—and oil), ornamental hair work, wax work, and embroidery. Professor Daniel Chase, newly acquired by Baylor from Judson Female Institute, Marion, Alabama, was named Head of the Department of Music in the Female Department.[51] Twelve pianos, a harp, guitars, and other instruments were supplied by the institution.

The chief concern of the Baylor Board of Trustees in 1859 was the completion of plans for the new building for men students. A committee was designated to contract for the stone work of the main structure, and President Burleson and Mr. McKnight were delegated to sell the temporary dormitories as soon as they could be dispensed with.

As in previous years, the catalogue under Burleson publication stated "the earliest age at which it will be advantageous for a student to enter the University classes is at the completion of his fifteenth year." The catalogue also carried the requirement that "every student . . . attend public worship at such place as his parent or guardian may designate." One addition was made to the "Special Laws" governing the institution: "Each professor shall consider himself an official of discipline as much as of instruction" and enforce regulations or "report to the proper authority."[52]

On October 7, 1859, Judge R. T. Wheeler, as requested by the board, supplied the list of the thirteen graduates of the law department the previous September 1858 and submitted the group of sixteen awarded degrees in September 1859 for the minutes of the board. (See appendix). Evidently the re-

---

[51] Professor Chase was highly recommended by Principal M. P. Jewett of Judson Female Institute in Marion, Alabama, where he had taught for the past seven years. Such was his popularity and skill "that I gave him a salary of fifteen hundred dollars for several years, while no other professor of music in Alabama could command over eight hundred or one thousand dollars," wrote Jewett. (Baylor Catalogue, Female Department, 1859-60, p. 24-26.) The Chase family was gifted, and Mrs. Mary E. Chase, Teacher of Harp, Piano, and Vocal Music; Mrs. Carrie L. Chase, Teacher of Drawing and Painting in Oil and Water Colors; and Mr. Oscar P. Chase, Teacher of Piano and Guitar, also joined the faculty. *Minutes of Union Association*, 1858, p. 2. Miss Ella Chase became a student of Latin and French. Baylor Catalogue, 1859, p. 15.

[52] *Catalogue of Baylor University*, Male Department, 1859, p. 24.

quest for the names originated with President Burleson, who was justified in maintaining supervision of the department as a recognized part of the university. Judge Wheeler had bristled under the request and stated in his note that he was presenting the names "in response to the request of Nelson Kavanaugh, Secretary of the Board of Trustees." Wheeler gave assurance that the lists contained "all the law graduates for 1858 and 1859." Burleson's displeasure was evident and rose to a crescendo a bit later when Wheeler resigned and began law lectures in Brenham.

Lost by resignation from the board of trustees was Elder G. W. Baines, and on February 1, 1859, the secretary was asked to notify the Board of Managers of the Baptist State Convention with the request that the vacancy be filled. Baines assumed the editorship of the *Texas Baptist*,[53] with J. B. Stiteler as associate editor.

Newspapers over the state carried the announcement of the Male Department staff for the 1859-60 school year: President Rufus C. Burleson, A.M., Professor of Ancient and Spanish Language; Dr. D. R. Wallace, A.M., Professor of Natural Science and French; Rev. Richard Burleson, A.M., Professor of Mental and Moral Philosophy and Belles Lettres; Mr. O. H. Leland, A.B., Professor of Mathematics and Astronomy; Mr. Lewis Franke, A.M., Professor of German Language and Literature; Mr. J. L. Smith, Principal of Preparatory Division; Wm. Henry Long, Tutor.[54]

President Burleson's health showed the strain of the complicated Independence scene together with his correlated duties as corresponding secretary of the convention for six years, president for two, plus weekly preaching engagements. In the late summer of 1859 he took a trip through the South

[53] Board President Hosea Garrett questioned Brother Baines' reason for resigning from the Board of Trustees: "That the editor of the Texas Baptist should be the free . . . advocate of each and every one of our denominational schools in Texas." His contention was that "the Convention knows nothing of any school but Baylor University." H. Garrett to Bro. Baines, January 1, 1859, Chappell Hill. Texas Collection, Baylor University.

[54] *Dallas Herald*, October 15, 1859.
Long later served as Professor of Natural Science and Spanish at Baylor in Waco, 1885-1893. He also taught at Burleson College in Greenville, Texas, and was an assistant in botany at the University of Texas. He died at the age of eighty on December 10, 1947, at Albuquerque, New Mexico. *Brownsville Herald*, December 11, 1947.

and into the East, writing voluminously along the way. One letter to Mrs. Burleson relates the circumstances of his election to the presidency of Union University at Murfrees-boro, Tennessee. Although he felt that the position would be easier there, "and perhaps more honorable and profitable . . . and we should be clear of taking boarders . . . I am bound to Texas, our church, and Baylor University by a thousand tender ties. . . ."[55] Burleson declined this offer as well as several other lucrative positions.[56] Brother Richard would probably have advised a more realistic decision, for he wrote: "I hope, dear Rufus, that you not return to Texas without getting your money matters streaghtened [*sic*] up. Let our friends and relations know your embarrassment, and I hope they will help you."[57]

On his return trip, President Burleson wrote his brother from Honey Grove, Fannin County. He told of visiting the Red River Association near Clarksville and reported that very little could be done in raising money. Significant, how-ever, is his statement: "There is a vast and rapid change coming over the East in our favor. If I had commenced visiting the East three years ago we might now have 75 young men east of the Trinity River."[58]

The next letter from Burleson to "My dear Brother" came from Waco, during the October 1859 State Convention of the Baptists and shows the unrest that had permeated church affairs. When Burleson was "*elected* [president] *by a large majority* . . . there were many blank faces and un-steady nerves." Reference is made to the alignment of forces and to General Speight, "a strong Gravesman" whom Burle-son quoted: "I am disappointed. This nodding among preach-ers doesn't please me."

[55] Haynes, pp. 137-138.

[56] The *Texas Baptist Herald*, Houston, December 1, 1859; R. C. Burleson to Union University, August 22, 1859. Burleson Papers, Texas Collection, Baylor University.

[57] Richard Burleson to R. C. Burleson, September 15, 1859. Burleson Papers Texas Collection, Baylor University.

[58] Rufus C. Burleson to Richard Burleson, October 12, 1859. Texas Collection, Baylor University.

Burleson also informed his brother that "I have bought you one of the finest buggy horses in Texas. I call him 'Gen. Houston'; also an excellent buggy. I paid some money and am to pay the remainder on the last of Nov. $365 is the price. If you conclude you cannot take them drop me a line at Waco. I can sell them there."

"The fact is," countered Burleson, "his visit here will cause the bauble to burst." Burleson says that he "cannot now unfold the plan that such men as President Campbell, J. B. Taylor, C. D. Mallary and others and I have determined to follow." It is noteworthy that Principal Clark favored Graves. Burleson added this postscript to his letter: *"Keep all money due me till I come."* [59]

A letter of November 1859 to the father of a Baylor freshman student, Jonas Franklin Starr, gives Burleson's report of this extended trip.

Dr. J. H. Starr,

Dear Sir,

I reached home ten days since after an absence of three months and a half. I visited Mississippi, Alabama, Tennessee, Kentucky and Ohio seeking the restoration of strength and health which twelve years incessant toil in Texas had nearly exhausted. My health is greatly improved, and I trust a careful examination of study and modes of teaching in older colleges has prepared me more fully for the direction of our young and flourishing Institution.

I am happy to find that your son had received every necessary aid in selecting a proper boarding house and getting his studies properly classified.

Judge Wheeler and my Brother who is President in my absence had given him special attention.

He boards with my Mother-in-law, who only receives into her family a few of quiet, select boys or young men.

Our facilities here for a thorough education and especially in the department of Modern Languages are superior to any Institution I know in the South.

You may rest assured that your son will have every needed attention in health or sickness in and out of school. I have taken the liberty to insert your name as one of our board of visitors for our examination including 12, 13, 14, 15, 16 days of December. After which we have a recess till January 1, 1860. [60]

[59] Rufus C. Burleson to Richard Burleson, Waco, Texas, October 23, 1859. Texas Collection, Baylor University.
[60] Rufus C. Burleson to Dr. J. H. Starr, November 12, 1859. J. H. Starr Papers, Archives, University of Texas, Austin, Texas.

Student letters during the year reveal interesting things about the school, as these excerpts prove:

I have not been to school for several days. I was out dewberrying last week and had my face poisoned . . . but we put some poultices on it and it is getting well fast.

— — — — —

I am getting along very well in Latin. We have begun to translate sentences. I am to study French next year. I have always thought that I should love French. I should like to learn Spanish if there was any one to teach it.

— — — — —

One of the jubilees here was on 21st of April in commemoration of the Battle of San Jacinto. We had "big doings." Gen. Houston was here and spoke to us. I like very much to hear him speak. He said that there were but two things that he now aspired to—one was to be an overseer of the roads, to see that they were in good order for he knew the ladies did not love to travel over rough roads. The other was to be "Squire" and see that the young ladies did not marry worthless vagabond fellows and that the young gentlemen did not marry slovenly, careless girls. The General has a daughter in school only a few months older than I am. . . . Did I tell you that there is a German gentleman here giving the girls *lessons* in *gymnastics*. [61]

A letter from Jonathan A. McGary, Jr., to his father evidences the parental respect of the day:

I take the present opportunity of answering your kind and welcome letter which came to hand yesterday. . . . I am learning faster than I ever learned in my life. My teachers return their respects to you. We have excellent teachers here. They take all the pains with students that is necessary to advance them. . . . I found enclosed in Mother's letter $10 making $60 which will do me beautifully until I return home. . . . Your excuse for not being willing for me to come to Independence to school is a very good one. If anything should ever happen of that kind, I will be at your service, but I hope that nothing of that kind will ever happen. . . . You must excuse bad writing, for I am in a hurry. I will have to make a speech this evening. . . . [62]

[61] Florence Davis to "My dear Papa," Alfred B. Davis, April 29, 1859. Miss Davis became Mrs. Bledsoe, whose great-niece, Mrs. E. W. Bailey of Austin, gave letters and other memorabilia to Baylor Texas Collection.
President Burleson was listed in the catalogue of the Male Department in 1859 as Professor of the Spanish Language, but classes were not open to young women. The catalogue lists two daughters of Houston: Nannie and Margaret. Home was Huntsville for the Houstons in 1859. Mr. B. S. Fitzgerald taught Latin; Miss Liane De Lassaulx, Modern languages, and Professor W. Willrick was the gymnast mentioned.

[62] Original letter, October 31, 1859, Texas Collection, Baylor University. No explanation of the allusion is available, but the original of a speech on "Christopher Columbus" is filed with the letter.

Characteristic of the entertainment at commencement time is the following scroll-bordered invitation, a bit larger than a calling card:

BAYLOR UNIVERSITY
COMMENCEMENT PARTY
Complimentary to the
Graduating Class
Tuesday Evening, December 13, 1859

Managers:

Erisophian Society
R. T. Wheeler
Cicero Jenkins
T. L. Dunklin

Philomathesian Society
James S. Perry
Ben H. Thompson
M. M. Vander Hurst[63]

Thus closed a decade. By 1860 Texas had witnessed great growth in population: 102,961 in 1846 to 421,411 in 1860. The increase in taxable property was from $34,000,000 to $294,000,000 for the period. The judicial system had expanded from seven to twenty districts. The Baptist denomination also experienced solid growth, for there were approximately 500 Baptist Churches in Texas by 1860 with an aggregate membership of 25,000.

[63] Original in Texas Collection, Baylor University, sent by John Bowen, Waco, to fiancée Miss Emily Grimes of Grimes County. Emily's father was Jessie Grimes, Texas pioneer and a signer of the Texas Declaration of Independence. Letter received from Miss Grimes' niece, Mrs. W. C. Preston, Fort Worth, Texas, on April 3, 1939.
James S. Perry was the nephew of Stephen F. Austin.

CHAPTER VIII

The Disruptive Feud

AT THE FEBRUARY 9, 1860, meeting of the Baylor trustees, Professor Wheeler resigned as professor of law. Unwittingly this action set off a serious dispute, adding fuel to the Burleson-Clark controversy. An anonymous article appeared in the May 10, 1860, *Texas Baptist Herald,* headed: "Brenham Law School, What Does It Mean?" The writer of the article implied denominational prejudice and a desire to injure Baylor in Wheeler's accepting the invitation to lecture at Brenham. The university and the denomination soon became involved, for the letter was attributed to President Burleson; but he had said to his inquisitors: "It is an editorial." A letter from Burleson to Editor Baines clarifies his feeling about the matter, as these excerpts indicate:

I have not the slightest objection to be held responsible for every sentence both yours and mine in the communication of May 10th. . . . I . . . think it better that you as the mouthpiece for the denomination should present these facts to the public. I know there are persons here who would join issue with anything I might write. . . . You commenced your remarks with these words. "We have mentioned these facts and made these remarks." This led me to the conclusion that you had incorporated my facts into an editorial. . . .

Please write to me by Dr. Wallace. There is a great array against our Institution and every Baptist interest in Texas. . . .[1]

An earlier letter from Burleson to Baines, on May 15, 1860, had called attention to local controversy in the matter, in that "Dr. J. B. Robertson is boasting a good deal around here about his reply to your article on the Brenham Law School and is writing a reply." Burleson suggested asking him questions: (1) Is he not President of Board of Trustees for Colonel Forshey's school at Rutersville and does he not send his own son there and influence all his friends in this vicinity to do the same? (2) Did he not threaten to take his daughter away from Baylor if she should go up to the mourners' seat during a revival? (3) Is he not at heart a

[1] R. C. Burleson to Editor G. W. Baines, June 3, 1860. Baines Papers, Texas Collection, Baylor University.

Roman Catholic? (4) "Has he not threatened violence—a whipping—to the author of the piece on the Brenham Law School and does this not show what he and Pope ———— would, if they had the power, do with poor Baptists? It may be well to admit that the Dr. has been a strong friend of the female department, the entire lucrative practice of which he has had till recently." After further advice to the editor, Burleson concluded: "I will say to you confidentially that I believe one reason the Dr. and his friends here are so cut—there is a plan on foot to discontinue our Catholic and Episcopal teachers in the female department into an opposition school and they do not wish much moral indignation excited on the subject."[2]

Concern over the dispute arising from Wheeler's resignation from Baylor and subsequent announcement of lectures in Brenham gained force. Some sixteen men—J. L. Farquhar, A. G. Haynes, A. E. Lipscomb, J. Stribling, B. Blanton, George W. Graves, James L. Smith, both R. C. and R. B. Burleson, D. R. Wallace, O. H. Leland, Jno. McKnight, and others—sent a letter to Editor Baines for publication in the June 7, 1860, *Texas Baptist*. The communication expressed regret over two letters in the *Texas Baptist* of May 24th defending the course of Judge Wheeler in leaving Baylor so precipitately and establishing competitive law lectures.

Dispute arose during the next two months over the signatures attached to this letter, and the gentlemen wrote statements of their feelings, certified by their signatures and printed in the *Texas Baptist* on September 6, 1860. Editor Baines was called upon to referee an argument that undoubtedly lent interest, but certainly not dignity, to the denominational journal.

Feelings erupted at the Sunday evening service of the Independence Church on June 17, 1860. Pastor Ross thought it best to dispense with the usual form of service and to have the church come together as a prayer meeting. Judge Baylor made reference to "dissensions and jealousies in our church." Burleson arose to say that he had felt the "fraternal dagger." In concluding his dramatic speech he told the con-

---

[2] R. C. Burleson to Editor G. W. Baines, May 15, 1860. Baines Papers, Texas Collection, Baylor University.

gregation that "during his recent visit to his native state, while kneeling by the grave of his mother, he had resolved by the grace of God, never to criminate or recriminate any further than was necessary to vindicate his character."[3] Just as the meeting was about to close, Clark arose and said that it was "needless to affect ignorance of the insinuations of President Burleson" and that he had made continued efforts to establish peace—that he had "written a letter to a Brother" inviting him to his office at his convenience in order to effect reconciliation. President Burleson arose to ask if he were "the Brother." With the affirmative answer, Burleson said he had not come for two reasons: one, that Mr. Clark had not come to him, as the Gospel required, but that he had been summoned to his [Clark's] office; secondly, that the letter had charged him with "insincerity and hypocrisy" and thus "placed a wall of fire" between them. Thus ended the unfortunate meeting—but not the feud.

In the *Texas Baptist* on June 18, 1860, there appeared another letter to the editor in which Principal Horace Clark stated his position, quoted in part:

. . . [the article] signed by several respectable gentlemen expressed regret that any friend of Baylor University should not entertain the same opinion that they do in regard to the course of Hon. R. T. Wheeler in severing his connection with Baylor University. In entertaining this opinion they but exercise a right which I have no doubt they will cheerfully accord to me.

Clark attributed no ulterior motives to Wheeler in his resignation from his Baylor position and objected to the published "motives which he [the writer of the May 10th article] could not possibly know to be true."[4]

Soon another circumstance augmented the already tense situation. Principal Clark refused to allow the young ladies to attend the public monthly exercises of the Senior Class of the Male Department and commencement party planned by the young men for the last week in June. The young men then requested President Burleson to announce a meeting after chapel. The purpose of the meeting—"Memori-

---

[3] *Defense of Abner E. Lipscomb*, Addressed to the Baptists of Texas. Independence, Texas, 1860, p. 11.

[4] Horace Clark to Baines, June 18, 1860. Baines Papers, Texas Collection, Baylor University.

alizing the trustees and petitioning them to remedy the existing evils"—was not known by Burleson until the group assembled, at which time he endeavored to persuade the young men to disband. When they declined, he urged moderation in their proceedings. Six young men were appointed to draw up the memorial to be placed before the trustees.

Faced with this circumstance, Clark relented, but the girls were angered at the treatment of their principal and circulated a petition which forbade the signers to attend the boys' party.

The Baylor Board of Trustees again took formal notice of the Burleson-Clark controversy at their extended June 27, 1860, meeting. The record states:

Whereas it is evident that an unpleasant state of feeling exists between Elder R. C. Burleson, President, and H. Clark, Principal of the Female Department, and whereas said controversy is operating injuriously to both departments, be it therefore resolved,

That we ignore anything which may have transpired between these brethren prior to December 1857 at which time was made an adjustment of all difficulties then existing between them in this board. And that we request and *expect* these brethren to make all laudable efforts to adjust any and all matters of controversy generated since above date, and submit said settlement to this board at 8 o'clock Saturday morning next, and in case they fail to do this they will be expected to lay before us all of their aggrievances in writing for an adjustment, and if either of them fail or neglect to comply with the above request, we request his or their resignations, as this injurious state of things must cease.[5]

On the following Saturday, both men presented their written statesments to the assembled trustees.

Principal Clark's charges:

1. I feel aggrieved with Bro. Burleson for compelling me to arise in a religious assembly to reply to what I and others conceived to be a personal attack upon me.

2. I feel aggrieved with him secondly in permitting a disrespectful demonstration toward me on the part of the students of the Male Department.

3. I feel aggrieved with him for permitting to be circulated a certain letter written to him personally many years ago for the purpose of inviting a reconciliation, and which was used not in accordance with its spirit and tenor, but in such a way as to place me in the attitude of an aggressor.

[5] Minutes of the Baylor Board of Trustees, June 27, 1860, p. 176.

4. I feel aggrieved with him for publicly making disparaging remarks of the Female Institution.

5. I feel aggrieved with him for not being willing to submit our differences to the arbitration of mutual friends.

6. I feel aggrieved with him for not manifesting a willingness to settle them upon a basis which I conceive to be mutually honorable.

Respectfully submitted
H. Clark

The Burleson charges against Clark followed:

1. You have publickly on the night of the 17th inst. charged me with being the cause of the dissention and party strife in the church at Independence.

2. You have revived a difficulty that was fully settled in the board of Trustees.

3. In reviving this matter that was settled and buried forever, he has revived a letter casting upon me the imputation of insincerity and hypocrisy, and charging my family and friends with crimes that makes "one sick at heart."

4. You have treated me and my wife with disrespect in not allowing the daughters of my friends and brethren to meet a few select friends at my house.[6]

5. It is currently rumored that you have used your *official position* in a speech before the young ladies *during school hours* to prejudice young and unsuspecting minds against me. All of which I require either to be proven or withdrawn as publickly as they were made.

6. You have grieved me as a member of the Faculty in violating the solemn promise we made the Board of Trustees *not to interfere* with the management of the respective departments committed to our care. You have thus interfered in vindicating and endorsing the course of Judge Wheeler in his resignation as head of the Law Department of Baylor University and his opening a Law School in Brenham June 29, 1860.

Rufus C. Burleson[7]

Burleson and Clark read their charges, which were taken up point by point by the board after the two men retired. Decisions on the Burleson charges were as follows:

The record ignored charges 1 and 2.

The board voted unanimously that Brother Clark be advised to withdraw said letter.

[6] Clark stated that he had not allowed the girls to accept the Burleson invitation because the female teachers in his department were not invited to accompany the girls, as was the respected custom. Minutes of the Baylor Board of Trustees, June 30, 1860, pp. 145-146.

[7] Minutes of the Baylor Board of Trustees, June 30, 1860, pp. 178-179. Also see Harry Haynes, *Life and Writings of Dr. Rufus C. Burleson* (compiled and published by Mrs. Georgia J. Burleson, 1901), p. 215-217.

The explanation given for charge 4 was termed satisfactory to the board.

Charge 5 was sustained in that Brother Clark did address his department on the subject of their differences, but not sustained as to its prejudicial effect against the Male Department.

Charge 6 carried the resolution that "we disapprove of the letter written by Elder Clark to the *Texas Baptist* on the subject of the Law School, but not attributing to him any design of reflecting upon the faculty of the Male Department as is affirmed by him to us.

The charges of Clark resulted in these opinions:

Charge 1 was sustained in that "we disapprove of Brother Burleson introducing it in a religious assembly."

Charge 2 was sustained in that "we disapprove of the conduct of Brother Burleson, but do not believe his conduct was intentional."

Charge 3 was passed by the board.

Charge 4 was sustained and the board "voted that we disapprove of Brother Burleson's remarks about the female department."

Charge 5 was also sustained in that "we disapprove of Brother Burleson in declining to submit the settlement of the difficulty to mutual friends."

Charge 6 was not sustained.

On the following Sunday morning the appointed committee of Barnes, Kavanaugh, and Graves presented the resolutions based on the decisions concerning the charges. Proxy-trustee A. E. Lipscomb requested that his vote be recorded as negative in the first three resolutions; the remaining eight resolutions were carried unanimously. President of the Board, Reverend Hosea Garrett, was requested "to give public notice through the *Texas Baptist* of the adjustment of all our troubles." The members of the faculty were called with Burleson and Clark and "each one present gave full assent and approval to the settlement. . . . "

Judge Wheeler, inadvertently the catalyst in the feud and the person defamed, wrote the following letter to Editor Baines:

Rev. George W. Baines,
Editor of the *Texas Baptist*
Respected Sir,

I have to ask of you the name of the writer of the article in *The Texas Baptist* of the 10th of May last, headed "Brenham Law School: What Does It Mean?"

As the article impugns my conduct and motives, it will be conceded that I have a right to be authoritatively informed who this writer is.

Very Respectfully[8]

Judge Wheeler wrote four other letters to the editor concerning the fiasco. On July 10, 1860, he thanked Baines for the information supplied in the letter just received and stated that he did "not intend to make any use of the information . . . unless it should hereafter become necessary in my own defence." He awaited a communication from Mr. Farquhar and other trustees of Baylor. Upon receipt of it, Wheeler again wrote to Baines:

. . . I have had forwarded me from Independence a communication purporting to be in "explanation" of the indorsement of the article of the 10th of May, designed for publication with my assent. It is quite different from what I anticipated, not less objectionable to me than what it purports to explain. I wish to say to you that I can not consent to its publication.[9]

Wheeler then asked that *nothing* be admitted to the paper from "the source of the former" articles as having his assent. A letter on July 26, 1860, gave Judge Wheeler's presentation of "facts necessary to a proper understanding of my connection with the Law School and the circumstances which led to my acceptance of the invitation to instruct a class here this summer." His letter of August 1, 1860, informs the editor that he has received a copy of the communication which General Brooks sent him for publication. Wheeler stated that "its publication would have done me great service. I have little doubt it would have caused the withdrawal of the indorsement of the first publication.": Wheeler continued:

Moreover, after having been assailed as I have been, am I not entitled to the defence which my friends have seen proper to make? The assault has been made through the organ of the denomination. . . . [10]

[8] R. T. Wheeler to George W. Baines, June 30, 1860. Baines Papers, Texas Collection, Baylor University.

[9] *Ibid.*, July 20, 1860.

[10] *Ibid.*, August 1, 1860. Baines Papers, Texas Collection, Baylor University. A letter from Clark to Baines requested a return of "the communication sent by me to the *Texas Baptist* referring to the Wheeler matter and the publication of which I requested withheld till further advice. . . . Judge Wheeler's letter is just what those would expect who know him intimately: calm, temperate and dignified—sufficient if no more is said. But more will be

Wheeler's professional skill was still sought, despite the Independence controversy. According to John S. Ford, Sam Houston made a fruitless and indirect attempt in November 1860 to get Supreme Court Judges R. T. Wheeler and J. H. Bell to prepare a constitutional argument on the doctrine of secession. He hoped to issue it as a circular to arrest secession agitation. Wheeler evaded the issue.[11]

Despite the prominence of the controversy, the institution did operate in 1858-1860. The trustees were anxious to extend the patronage of the school and appointed a committee to correspond with and visit the East Texas Convention to seek cooperation with the Western Convention in support of Baylor, now that construction of the new building for men was in progress. Closer supervision of school activities is evidenced in the February 9, 1860, board requirements. Officers of the two departments were asked to present the manuscript catalogues to the board for approval before they were printed. A committee was delegated to audit the library and incidental fees of each department. Another committee was directed to visit both departments for a study of course offerings and subsequently to report to the *Texas Baptist*. Names of all faculty for trustee approval were requested from the president and the principal.

Another point of internal concern was the Law Department. After extensive correspondence by the appointed committee "with eminent jurists," the board secured the Honorable R. T. Smyth of Montgomery County and the Honorable James E. Shepherd of Washington County to deliver a course of lectures in law, commencing on July 2, 1860. Both were named professors without salary.

Shepherd, well acquainted with Baylor, had moved to Brenham in 1846 and became a member of the Texas Legislature in 1850. He was born in Mathews County, Virginia, on April 24, 1817, and educated at Miami University in

said—the issue is already made. Let me renew my wishes that you will take no position in the matter (editorially) till you have heard all. I have done my best to reconcile the matter and to stop a newspaper controversy. But a strange infatuation seems to have possessed those in whose power it was to stop it. . . . O, for a gleam of light."

H. Clark to G. W. Baines, August 10, 1860. Baines Papers, Texas Collection, Baylor University.

[11] Llerena B. Friend, *Sam Houston, The Great Designer* (Austin: The University of Texas Press, 1954), p. 331.

Oxford, Ohio. In 1836 he began the study of law with W. R. Beaty at Greenupsburg, Kentucky, and was graduated from the law department of Ohio State University at Cincinnati and admitted to the bar at Flemingsburg, Kentucky, in the spring of 1838. In 1839 he was married to Martha J. Andrews of Flemingsburg.[12]

President Burleson presented four young men for A.B. degrees and two for the B.P. degree at the June 1860 Commencement. Principal Clark presented four young women graduates and two graduates in English. Baylor's first honorary degrees, "A.M. Secundum Gradum," were conferred on June 29, 1860. The recipients were Elder James H. Stribling, Prof. James L. Smith, and Prof. O. H. Leland.[13] At the ceremonies for the Male Department General Sam Houston addressed the assembly and termed Baylor "one of the oldest and most successful colleges in the state."[14]

Baylor University at Independence reached her zenith in 1860. Well known over the South, the institution had attained national and even international notice.[15] The Female Department, despite being relegated to a secondary position, eclipsed the Male Department during the war years. In 1860 the department reported a staff of nine professors and

[12] Shepherd was a member of the secession convention in 1861 and served in the Confederate Army as Lieutenant Colonel of the 16th Regiment of the Texas Infantry. While still on duty he was elected Judge of the Third Judicial District. He was a member of the reconstruction convention in 1866 and re-elected unopposed to the district bench but was removed in 1867 "by the military powers as an impediment to reconstruction." *The Bench and Bar of Texas,* pp. 382-383. Shepherd was named Dean of Faculty, Law Department, in 1879. Baylor Catalogue 1879-1880, p. 16. He formed a partnership with J. G. Searcy of Austin in 1873 and in 1888 returned to Brenham.

[13] Prior to 1872, this type of Master's degree, conferred *in cursu,* was awarded to thousands of baccalaureate graduates of many colleges. The degree was conferred on five of the nine members of Harvard College's first graduating class in 1642. At first Harvard required an interval of two years between the bachelor's degree and the master's degree, *in cursu. Academic Degrees,* U. S. Department of Health, Education, and Welfare. Office of Education (Washington, D.C.: United States Printing Office, 1960), p. 25.

Both Leland and Smith were former Baylor students. Leland joined the teaching staff immediately after receiving his degree in December 1856; Smith was made a teacher in the preparatory school in December 1854. The Reverend Stribling had been identified with Baylor since May 18, 1846, when he served as a proxy for O. Drake at a trustee meeting. In his capacity as a minister he had been asked to serve with other ministers as a voluntary agent for Baylor in 1847 and in 1850. Later, he was appointed on the Board of Visitors for the May 15, 1868, examinations and awarded the D.D. degree on June 7, 1871.

[14] The *Texas Baptist,* Anderson, August 2, 1860.

[15] Haynes, p. 54.

teachers." The library contained standard periodicals plus some of the state newspapers. Under the zealous management of the Clarks, the department was enjoying "a great degree of prosperity."[16] Finances were in good condition for both departments. President Burleson and his faculty received $7,697.62 from the board for the year.[17] Yet despair was evident because of several factors: the year began with an epidemic of yellow fever, causing hundreds of deaths in Texas;[18] the presidential election and the involvement in the war planted fear in the minds of all; then the crescendo of the Burleson-Clark feud gave immediate expression to the general unrest. Baylor indeed faced a crisis.

Evidence that the friends of Burleson and Clark would not let their feud die is seen in the *Defense of Abner E. Lipscomb,* a pamphlet of twenty-four tight pages, released in October 1860 and addressed to the Baptists of Texas.[19] Lipscomb reviewed the affair and the handling of "the settlement" by the board of trustees. He gave the logic behind his sole vote of opposition to their decisions, including other matters which give him cause to condemn Principal Clark. Because "the settlement was not based on Gospel principles," Lipscomb called on both Clark and Elder Ross to clear up matters in the controversy. When the proposal failed, he took the matter to the Independence Church at its regular conference on July 14, 1860. Discussion took several days, and the minutes of the Baylor trustees were read in the

[16] *Minutes of the Baptist State Convention,* 1860, p. 23.

[17] Minutes of the Baylor Board of Trustees, January 10, 1861, p. 188.

[18] A letter from B. H. Carroll to Colonel J. C. Barrow on January 7, 1860, states: "Unwelcome sickness has brooded with its gloomy wings of woe over my father's mansion for months and those dearer to me than life have hovered with all the terror of uncertainty over the dreaded brink of dissolution and the grave. But all are now well and convalescing. The Yellow Fever has carried off hundreds here ('twas not however of that disease our family were sick). . . . For two weeks snow lay on the ground and 'fierce northers' blew; such weather is unprecedented in Texas." Texas Collection, Baylor University.

[19] Author Abner Eddins Lipscomb was a nephew of Judge Abner Smith Lipscomb. He and his wife, Mary Ann Shivers Lipscomb, came from Alabama *via* Mississippi with their family and settled at Independence in 1856. The chief reason for their move was to send their children to Baylor University. Gracey Booker Toland, *Austin Knew His Athens* (San Antonio: The Naylor Company, 1958), p. 14.

Minutes of the Board of Trustees reveal that Abner E. Lipscomb served first as a proxy for Horton on February 9, 1860, and was appointed agent to procure funds to furnish seats for the preparatory department of the institution. He was present as Horton's proxy at the prolonged end-of-June 1860 meeting, as previously indicated.

church. Dr. G. W. Graves and Elder Ross were the center of attacks by Lipscomb. The question of whether Lipscomb had sustained the charges was put to the church and decided in the negative; hence he was asked to withdraw the charges. Upon his refusal, the church withdrew her fellowship from him. Lipscomb concluded the pamphlet with his assertion that

. . . if you think my exclusion was the result of a faithful execution of the laws of Christ, and not the consequence of prejudice and unfairness of those excluding me, if you decide that it was for the honor of the church I will make myself content, with the approval of a conscience that is void of offense toward God and man.[20]

Lipscomb mentioned the fact that eighteen of approximately two hundred members of the church were present at the meeting, with eleven voting for exclusion and seven who did not vote but were opposed to excluding him. He had been advised not to present his case at that particular meeting, but he decided to do so. In March 1861 Lipscomb issued another pamphlet, which was followed by a publication "To the Public" by the Baylor Board of Trustees. In a lengthy, restrained manner an attempt was made to untangle garbled facts and to present circumstances concerning Lipscomb's connection with the Baylor Board merely as a lone, dissenting proxy.[21]

On March 20, 1861, the Baylor trustees held an interview with Principal Clark, who gave assurance that his letter in the fall of 1855 intended no offense to President Burleson, but that if it did, he "withdrew the same." Burleson accepted the apology

. . . and for the sake of peace in this community and the prosperity of the Redeemer's cause, I hope my friends will strive to live in peace so long as a corresponding feeling is manifested, and if I at any time have said or done anything growing out of that letter calculated to injure the feelings of Brother Clark or his interest, I do regret it, and hereby withdraw the same."[22]

[20] *Defense of Abner E. Lipscomb*, p. 24.

[21] Original handwritten copy "To the Public," Texas Collection, Baylor University.

Notice is taken of the fact that Lipscomb "has procured the services of a lady fresh from Yankee land to set up a school at Independence in opposition to the Baylor University, and she is a pedo-Baptist."

[22] Minutes of Baylor Board of Trustees, March 20, 1861, p. 191.

The meeting terminated in singing, extending hands of fellowship and "shedding tears of joy." On the following day the president and professors of Baylor and the principal of the Female Department issued a joint letter in which they denied any ill will, and the document bore all of their signatures.

Even then, the issue caused further controversy. Because of member dissatisfaction, the Independence Church resolved to invite sister churches at Washington, Brenham, Chappell Hill, Bethlehem, Mt. Zion, and Gay Hill, each to send two of their most prudent brethren to sit as a council upon the case. Meetings were held on Friday and Saturday, July 5th and 6th, 1861, and again on July 19-20, 1861. The council decided that the church erred in giving the case a hearing but that the church could not have acted otherwise than it did, after the hearing. The charges were "not fully but partially sustained," and the withdrawal of Lipscomb's charges and pamphlets "by a card in the *Texas Baptist*" *would* entitle him to restoration to the fellowship of the church. Lipscomb took such action in July 1861 and was reinstated.[23]

Haynes records that Burleson was so unnerved by the outcome of the vote against Lipscomb that he "lost his balance." Burleson walked deliberately to the rostrum, thrust his finger into the face of the moderator, and said: "You have been guilty of unfairness, and have used the power of your official position to adopt this motion, and nothing but your gray hairs protect you from the punishment you so justly deserve.' "[24] Elder Ross adjourned the meeting without reply. This incident led to Sam Houston's refusal to "take your [Burleson's] hand until convinced that you have sincerely repented."

During the next month, Baylor graduate James H. Stribling conducted a protracted meeting at the Independence Church. Response was negligible; President Burleson was called upon to pray for the success of the meeting. Burleson,

[23] Report of the Council called by the Church at Independence on the Case of A. E. Lipscomb, July 1861, Bellville, Texas: "Countryman" Print, Texas Collection, Baylor University. During the administration of Dr. Crane, Lipscomb's name appears in the minutes: he was asked to raise $200 from the Good Hope Church for the completion of the new building. Minutes of Trustees, November 4, 1878, p. 270.

[24] Haynes, p. 225.

attired in his black frock coat and trousers, silk plush vest, standing collar and white stock cravat, prostrated himself in the aisle "and poured out his soul to God for a blessing on all he had offended." At the conclusion of the service Pastor Ross, General Houston, and others gave Burleson their hands as a token of reconciliation.

At the November 1860 meeting of the Baylor trustees President Burleson approached the board about an exchange of the Baylor property he owned for "wild lands" belonging to the university. O. H. P. Garrett[25] was appointed to represent the university and Samuel Lusk was to represent President Burleson in the matter. These two were to choose a third person to aid in property estimates. The board held a called meeting on January 9, 1861, ostensibly to act on the matter of property exchange for President Burleson. Then the board hastened to take action on Abner E. Lipscomb, proxy-trustee for A. C. Horton and author of the trouble-making pamphlet. The trustees termed the action discreditable to the board of trustees and some of the faculty of the university; therefore, they unanimously (with the exception of T. J. Jackson, who refused to vote) requested Horton to revoke his proxy.

On the next day Burleson was offered the endowment fund of $3600 in cash and the balance in lands at one dollar per acre to make the sum of $6000 in exchange for his house and all improvements. The board met again at two o'clock, at which time T. J. Jackson was absent. Burleson came to decline the offer and to make his annual report. The board reconsidered and "agreed to give him $6300 and release his liabilities to the endowment fund except his own subscription notes of $400 and the lands at one dollar per acre to make up the sum of $6300 in payment, Burleson paying for the four acres of land lying in the southeast corner of the college land."[26] The trustees agreed to sign the deeds as soon

[25] O. H. P. Garrett was the nephew of Hosea Garrett and married his daughter. Born in South Carolina, he came to Texas on horseback in 1838 at the age of twenty-two and located in Washington County. He laid off the town of Brenham and served as county surveyor and judge. He was clerk of the Gay Hill Baptist Church and later of the Brenham Baptist Church for many years. He served on the Board of Managers of the Baptist State Convention and was made a life member of the Convention in 1857. Frank Elisha Burkhalter, "The Laymen and Their Work," *Centennial History of Texas Baptists,* ed. Harlan J. Matthews (Baptist General Convention of Texas, Burt Building, Dallas, 1936), p. 251.

[26] Minutes of the Baylor Board of Trustees, January 10, 1861, p. 188.

as the land was selected and the deeds were prepared. The property exchange requested by President Burleson was the first indication of his intent to leave Baylor.

Baylor leadership was involved in matters other than local controversy. Feeling about the Civil War was high on the campus. In early January the young ladies at Baylor had raised a Lone Star flag, an incident which caused great discussion and a sheaf of letters to Principal Clark, one with nine signatures. Finally on January 17, 1861, Mr. Clark published a sheet, "The Crisis—Secession." He termed the flag incident "a matter of small import." In a summary statement concerning the great issue facing Southern states, he wrote that there should be "a re-construction of government upon a basis that will guarantee the security of our rights, or separation."[27]

Former law professor, R. T. Wheeler also took his stand early in the conflict, stating that Lincoln's "advocacy of natural and political equality would destroy Southern society, peace, and security." He declared that "it is war upon our institution" [slavery], and that the choice was between defense or submission to utter ruin.[28]

Sam Houston, caught in the Union-Secession controversy, came to Independence and conferred with President Burleson in an endeavor to solicit his aid in "saving Texas." Houston had declared secession to be treason and had stumped Texas between October 17 and 29, arguing against disunion. The Texas press was not of his opinion. Houston's plan was to secure men "in all the great centers of influence . . . to proclaim their unalterable devotion to the South and opposition to the abolition fanaticism, but to declare that our wisest and safest plan is to make our fight in the Union. . . ." declared Burleson. The two men were in agreement and prayed over the proposal.[29] The discussion became a heated controversy on the college campus. Resolutions were read according to the plan suggested by Houston "to remain in the Union and fight for our rights under the Stars and

[27] Circular, Horace Clark, "The Crisis—Secession," Independence, January 17, 1861; Clark Scrapbook, Texas Collection, Baylor University.

[28] R. T. Wheeler, "The Crisis—What is Our Duty?" *The Dallas Herald,* January 16, 1861.

[29] Address by Burleson before the Texas Legislature, March 2, 1893. Printed as an appendix to the House Journal, May 9. Forty-five tight pages, beginning on 1206. Also reported by Haynes, p. 581.

Stripes." A debate ensued, with students John C. Watson and B. H. Carroll advocating the affirmative and T. I. Dunklin and M. M. Vanderhurst the negative. The affirmative won the decision and the Stars and Stripes were suspended from a "fifty-foot-high liberty pole." Opinion in Austin swung the other way, and Houston sent word to President Burleson that "all is lost!" A few days later "Mayor Task Clay cut down our liberty pole and the Stars and Stripes lay tattered and torn in the dust," declared Burleson.

Haynes averred that the heavens told the story of Baylor at Independence.

During the years that the favored town of Independence was passing through this unseemly tumult, there was a most remarkable display of heavenly phenomena.

A great comet came out of the northern heavens. . . .

The following year, (1860), there was a grand auroral display. . . .[30]

The Waco Association of nine churches had been organized on November 16, 1860, and it adopted the Trinity River Association School in Waco, changing the name from Trinity River Male High School to the Waco Classical School chartered on February 2, 1860.[31] President Joseph W. Speight of the school's board conferred "in the earlier part of the year" with President Burleson about coming to the institution. Speight was a former pupil of Burleson in Mississippi. He "elicited the information that a resignation by the entire faculty of the male department of that institution [Baylor] had been seriously contemplated, and that Waco had received their favorable consideration as an eligible point at which to build up a Baptist university of learning."[32]

Among the Burleson papers is a handwritten letter of February 26, 1861, itemizing articles of agreement among the professors of the Male Department:

1. We pledge ourselves to cooperate together to build up a great and flourishing institution at some eligible point in Texas.
2. The basis of cooperation to be our present relations in this institution.

[30] Haynes, pp. 230-232. Haynes recalled that "Ancient Babylon, Jerusalem, Sodom and Gomorrah received warnings of their destruction. . . . We do not maintain that the auroral display was intended to represent the sundered condition of the town, church and university . . . though it looks that way."

[31] Carroll, *The History of Texas Baptists*, p. 224.

In 1861 this school became Waco University. The original school, founded in 1856 with S. G. O'Bryan as first president, was conducted in the First Baptist Church of Waco. Its last president was John C. West.

[32] Report of the Waco Association, September 1861, Marlin, Texas.

3. To secure the end in view more certainly to promise to aid, defend and sustain each to the utmost of our ability.
4. In all matters of interest the will of the majority to rule.
5. In the present difficulties before the Trustees in regard to H. Clark we will stand or fall stay or go together.
6. We will remain here as teachers or go to Waco or elsewhere as the will of the majority of our number decide.
7. We will do all in our power in accordance with justice to promote the pecuniary social and professional interest of each member of this faculty.[33]

Gossip in the town and church would not let the issues of the Burleson-Clark quarrel subside. By March 20, 1861, the trustees again were forced to "inquire into the difficulties between brethren R. C. Burleson and H. Clark." A committee conferred with each man, who expressed his willingness to abide by the decision of the board of last July and asserted that the agreement had not been violated. To support the verbal denial of trouble, the trustees prepared the following statement, which the faculty of both departments signed:

We the President and Professors of Baylor University and Principal of the Female Department certify that
Whereas reports are in circulation that our relations in the above capacity as professors are not of a friendly character.
These reports are unfounded, since the adjustment of difficulties by the board of trustees last July, we have had no cause for a renewal of those feelings which unfortunately had existed, and we do solemnly pledge ourselves for the future that while we hold our present connection with the university, we will do or say nothing directly or indirectly to disturb the friendly and peaceable relations between us as professors of the department or the board of trustees.

> Rufus C. Burleson
> Richard B. Burleson
> D. R. Wallace
> O. H. Leland
> Geo. W. Willrick
> H. Clark
> B. S. Fitzgerald[34]

[33] A revision of this early version was "placed in the hands of President Burleson when he tendered his resignation in June, 1861," with the signatures of the Male Department professors. Haynes, pp. 228-229.

[34] Minutes of the Baylor Board of Trustees, March 20, 1861, p. 156. Original handwritten letter with signatures in Independence Papers, Texas Collection, Baylor University.
A brief penciled letter to Trustee President H. Garrett from President Burleson on March 22, 1861, indicates that he reconsidered a previously determined action: "The matter I wished to lay before the board I have concluded to withhold, at least for the present. We did not hear the church bell or I would have sent this note sooner."

Matters remained unsettled, wounds were too deep to be forgotten, and the periphery of the quarrel extended beyond the limits of the state. Many "private" discussions were held, many letters written, and speculations were rife concerning the intolerable situation.[35] A lengthy letter from Trustee Farquhar to G. W. Baines is evidence of the climate at Independence. First, Farquhar states that Lipscomb compromised himself in stating that he "would withdraw and not sit with the board of trustees as he could not do Clark justice as his prejudices against Clark were too strong." The assertion was made to a prominent member of the Independence Church well in advance of the meeting. Then in a few lines marked "private," Farquhar stated that

. . . the faculty of the male department brought forward their celebrated protest last church conference at Independence and said they did not offer it then but that they would do so after the June meeting of the board of trustees if Lipscomb was not restored to the fellowship of the church. They said they had 33 names to their protest and expected to get some more. Bro. R. C. Burleson was not there . . . he has gone to Waco and I learn he went to give those Waco brethren an answer in regard to moving up there. . . . Bro. B. went by Brother J. G. Thomas of Burleson County and told him that notwithstanding all difficulties between himself and Bro. Clark had been settled yet there was an outside pressure at Independence that he and Bro. Clark could not control . . . and that he had about concluded it was best for him to leave Independence. . . . This I heard from Bro. Thomas myself. Now we must keep this entirely to ourselves and never express any anxiety for them to leave though we would be much gratified if they would. . . .[36]

On February 4, 1861, J. W. Speight, President of the Board of Trustees of Waco Classical School, at the direction of a trustee decision on January 21, 1861, wrote to President Burleson informing him of his election as President of the Faculty of that institution. Also, elected were President Burleson's associates, Professor R. B. Burleson as vice-

[35] One Sunday morning as Mr. Clark led his dormitory students of the Female College to the Independence Baptist Church, a prominent citizen and friend of Burleson stopped his buggy, got out and walked up to Mr. Clark, and spat in his face. Meeting no resistance from Clark, he got back in his buggy and drove away. "Men armed themselves, and appearances indicated that the affairs would be settled *Vi et armis.*" R. C. Crane address at Independence Homecoming, August 1950, with citation of paper by Mrs. Kate Haynes Hudson, about 1890.

[36] J. L. Farquhar, near Washington, Texas, to G. W. Baines, April 27, 1861. Baines Papers, Texas Collection, Baylor University.

president, and Professor O. H. Leland, Dr. D. R. Wallace, and Professor G. W. Willrick. The death of Professor Willrick between the time of the trustee action on January 21 and the writing of the letter prompted President Speight to add that "any choice [for the vacancy] which may be made by the remaining members of the faculty will be approved." Hence on April 15, 1861, President Burleson visited Waco and met with the trustees to state "the conditions of his acceptance and his policy for the government of the institution." He also spoke at a public gathering in which he "gave the essentials of success in an effort to build up a great university" and accepted the position to which he had been elected.[37]

A letter from President Burleson to President of the Board Garrett on April 29, 1861, contains Burleson's resignation.

A law of this Institution says:
"No Professor shall resign without permission of the Board of Trustees, except at the end of a term and after having given two months previous notice of his intention to do so."
In accordance with this law I give notice that at the end of this term on the 27th of June 1861 I expect to resign my office as President and Professor of Moral Science and Belles Lettres in Baylor University.
With my best wishes for the Institution Board of Trustees and especially for yourself. I am as ever Yours Devotedly
Rufus C. Burleson[38]

At a May 15, 1861, meeting of the Baylor Board of Trustees the president presented notices from R. C. Burleson, R. B. Burleson, D. R. Wallace and O. H. Leland "that they would withdraw their connection with the university at the end of the present session." The notices were at once accepted, and it was resolved to take immediate steps to supply their places. Trustee Graves was designated "to confer with Elder Burleson and get whatever notes and subscriptions to the endowment fund may be in his hands." On the next day Graves reported that Burleson was not able to make the report without further time. The matter of subscriptions became another complication. Finally, at the request of

[37] Haynes, pp. 424-25.
[38] Independence Papers, Texas Collection, Baylor University.

Burleson made in a letter of May 15, 1861, a committee of Garrett, Baines, Haynes, Horton, and Graves was appointed to settle all business. Request was made, also, that the faculty hand in their resignations immediately to take effect June 27.

When the trustees came for the regular annual meeting on June 28, 1861, D. R. Wallace tendered his resignation "pursuant with notification given two months ago" with the written request that he be released from a note "held against me due January 1862, for the amount of $50." The request was tabled.

A letter from Burleson presented an ambiguous report on subscriptions with the following statement:

In conclusion we will add that as we raised the above money on our own time and at our own expense except Dr. Wallace's expenses and as we have assurances from some of the donors that the money was given because of personal partiality for us we do not feel at liberty to pay over anything now in our hands either in cash or subscriptions till we learn the wishes of the donors. We are concerned that many of the donors gave their money because of our connection with Baylor University. The reasons and considerations enducing them to donate have now ceased and we do not feel they are morally bound. . . . We hope also you will have published this in the Texas Baptist as we are anxious that our actions may be critically examined by the whole denomination and if we have made any omission will take great pleasure in fully correcting. [39]

The Board's action in this matter was immediate:

Resolved that the amount obtained on subscription for the endowment fund by President R. C. Burleson in the vicinity of Cold Spring, Polk County, or at any other place, be placed on the endowment for the presidency of Baylor University, as President Burleson was expressly authorized to collect this fund for that expressed purpose. [40]

Professor Richard Burleson and President Burleson, as well as Professor Wallace, ignored the request of the trustees for earlier resignations and submitted them at this meeting. O. H. Leland's resignation did not come to the board until September 2, 1861. President Burleson concluded his with this statement: "Let it suffice to say that I expect ever to cherish a devout affection for Baylor University, to the pre-

[39] Rufus C. Burleson, June 26, 1861, Independence Papers, Texas Collection, Baylor University.
[40] Minutes of the Baylor Board of Trustees, June 28, 1861, p. 197.

cise extent that it is made auxiliary to the great Interest of Texas and the Church of God."

Even this was still not the end of unpleasantness and vindictiveness. The trustees directed H. Garrett to inquire of President Burleson the reasons why the examination and commencement of the Male Department were not held. He was also instructed to inquire "what disposition has been made of the *library* belonging to the two literary societies connected with the university."

Burleson, in reply to the above letter "just handed me," lists:

1. The Civil War which has suspended most of the best endowed colleges in the South

2. A Local war was threatened between some of the citizens of this place and our students

3. You advised me to adjourn the University rather than have an outbreak so seriously threatened.

4. The Senior Class, the largest we ever had informed us in writing that they had determined not to present themselves for Graduation, but will apply for, and no doubt receive their Diplomas from Waco University on the 4th of September 1861.

On which occasion we will be rejoiced to see our old friends.

As you never furnished the literary Societies with such rooms as is usual in all Colleges, they never had any part of a Library. [41]

The seven members of the senior class "unwisely yielding to the influence of the president" declares Dr. Eby, were granted degrees from the month-old Waco University in what he termed "an academic monstrosity."[42]

In *The Life of Dr. Burleson* appears the statement that Burleson "had been discredited by his church, and it may be said also, by the Board of Trustees of Baylor University, but his over-towering personality and character enabled him to overcome much of the opposition." Then mention is made of his "triumph over General Houston," in that they remained trusted friends. In a resumé of the administration of Burleson at Independence, Haynes lists these facts:

The only building on the campus in 1851 was a two-story stone structure 40x60 feet, Graves Hall. By 1861 a two-story

---

[41] Minutes of the Baylor Board of Trustees, June 29, 1861, p. 199.

[42] Frederick Eby in *Centennial Story of Texas Baptists,* p. 148.

Members of the class were M. M. Vanderhurst, Willis B. Darby, Boling Eldredge, John C. Watson, Mark A. Kelton, James L. Bowers, and Henry F. Pahl.

stone structure 40x80, the building on the women's campus called "the College Edifice," and the first story of the main university structure 56x112 had been completed. Three wooden buildings 16x32 contained a total of twelve large recitation rooms, a chapel and halls. The three-story "Octagon" of twenty-five rooms had received an eight-room annex for more boarders.

In 1851 there was no library. Haynes states that by 1861 the library contained 2500 volumes and adequate apparatus "for chemical and philosophical experiments and demonstrations."

Enrollment had risen from 27 in the Male Department and 25 in the Female Department in 1851 to 280 in the Male and 200 in the Female in 1861. Receipts also increased from approximately $2000, including $336 interest on endowment notes, in 1851, to $7,467.79 reported by Burleson for the Male Department in 1861.

Haynes concludes his assessment by saying that in 1851 Baylor was "an uncertain educational enterprise," but by 1861 it was known in every state of the union and catalogued by the London *Times* among the leading institutions of learning in America.[43]

The Baptist State Convention, which met at Huntsville on October 26-29, 1861, in its fourteenth annual session, upheld the Baylor Board of Trustees in all of its actions on the Burleson-Clark imbroglio. In his report Board President H. Garrett acknowledged that Baylor University

. . . in common with similar institutions of the country, is suffering on account of the present national troubles. . . . Youths . . . have joined the army in defence of the liberties and rights of our Government; and where others are yet left at home, the unprecedented money crisis will, in many cases, prevent their entering college. . . . The Board has found it necessary to furnish a new faculty for the Male Department . . . electing for one year Elder G. W. Baines, President and Professor of Natural Science; Elder J. F. Hillyer, Professor of Mathematics; and J. C. Anderson, Professor of Modern and Ancient Languages. . . . The wing building, reported as nearly completed . . . has since suffered from a partial giving way of the walls, and is being reclaimed at small expense. . . .[44]

[43] Haynes, pp. 234-235.
[44] *Report of Baptist State Convention of Texas,* 1861, (Houston: Texas Printing House), p. 11.

The "giving way of the walls" was symbolic. Baylor indeed faced depression and anxiety, for the controversy had wreaked vengeance on the institution.

CHAPTER IX

The Administration of President George Washington Baines
July 1861–Summer 1862

THE MID-JULY 1861 meeting of the Baylor Board of Trustees was a troubled one. Texas had seceded from the Union and joined the Confederacy by action of a convention on January 28, 1861, and ratified on February 23 by a state-wide vote. Governor Houston, who strongly opposed secession, had been deposed. Independence and Baylor University were extremely conscious of political affairs, yet the trustees felt the urgency of proceeding with as much normality as possible. The chief business before the group was to fill the vacated chairs of the Male Department. On July 17, 1861, the trustees named Elder G. W. Baines president and professor of natural science, Elder S. G. O'Bryan professor of mathematics, and John C. Anderson professor of ancient and modern languages; the secretary was instructed to notify these gentlemen of their election. They were to be "allowed the whole endowment and tuition fees, rating the president's salary at fifteen hundred and the professors' twelve hundred each, making thirty-nine hundred dollars. If the tuition fees and endowment should yield more or less than that amount, the same proportion would be observed." They were requested to meet the board of trustees at Independence on Friday the 26th, at 3 P.M.

In view of recent complications, the board also thought it wise to exercise some control over the matter of proxy trustees. It was decreed that after July 1861 no member of the board should have more than one proxy.

Settlement of affairs with Mr. Burleson was in the hands of a committee composed of Garrett, Horton, Barnes, Haynes, and Graves, to which was added M. D. Anderson, a proxy. This committee was empowered to take possession of all buildings and property of the university and to rent the dwelling house and lot.

[197]

At the second July meeting, on the 26th, Mr. John C. Anderson appeared to accept his appointment, but Mr. O'Bryan declined. The services of John F. Hillyer were subsequently secured. The report to the Baptist State Convention at Huntsville in the fall of 1861 stated that President Baines "in the Male Department, was given two strong assistants" in the persons of J. F. Hillyer, A.M., M.D., professor of mathematics; and J. C. Anderson, professor of ancient and modern languages. On the second day of the board meeting Mr. Baines came before the board and submitted the following communication:

> In answer to the proposition of the Board of Trustees now on record requesting my acceptance of the Presidency of Baylor University, I respond that I accept the proposition, provided that (it) be so changed as to make my salary to bear the proportion to the salaries of the other professors that sixteen bears to twelve and that I be assured by the Board that my salary shall not be less than twelve hundred dollars.[1]

The board acquiesced and the communication was filed. Then the board moved to confer the degree of Master of Arts on Elder Baines and Mr. Anderson.

Because the Burleson faculty had failed to settle with a committee of trustees after frequent efforts on the trustees' part and because the faculty was about to leave for Waco, "without settling with us for several items yet due, and whereas the failure may be cause of irritation and much misrepresentation, and believing also that they are indebted to us ... " the trustees appointed B. Blanton, J. L. Farquhar and G. W. Graves to agree upon disinterested referees to whom all unsettled business should be submitted. Such was the board's disposition of the irksome problem resulting from the Burleson resignation.

Preparations were made for the following school year. The building committee was requested to deepen the well at the college building, and necessary repairs were ordered to put the male college building in order.

President Baines was well-known to the board of trustees of Baylor University. He had served as pastor to many of

---

[1] Original manuscript, Baines Papers, Texas Collection, Baylor University.

them at Independence in 1851-52; he and Mrs. Baines had operated one boarding house for the Female College Division and Principal and Mrs. Clark another in those years; they had read his editorials in the *Texas Baptist* for years; and they had served with him on the Baylor Board. He had taken his seat as a board member on June 17, 1851, at the famous candlelight meeting in the Independence Church when Rufus C. Burleson was made president. His committee service had been frequent and effective: on June 18, 1851, he was on the committee which appointed James Huckins agent and on the first building committee; on August 2, 1851, he served with Judges Baylor and Lipscomb to make out the course of study for the Male and Female Departments; and he was made treasurer of the endowment fund, to be "bonded when he has in hand $1,000"[2]; on November 4, 1851, he was named to a committee to organize a theological department, the result being a request for him to lecture at Baylor; on December 16, 1852, his committee selected the visitors to conduct the examinations and adopted a code of laws for the university; on July 24, 1856, he served on the committee for rules and regulations for the graduating classes.[3] On various occasions he opened the meetings with prayer and also served as secretary pro-tempore on December 15, 1851, and July 30, 1952, and president pro-tempore on December 1, 1858. His attendance at board meetings had been remarkably regular, and he was represented by D. D. Crumpler, A. Daniels, G. W. Graves, J. F. Hillyer and O. H. P. Hill as proxies in his absence. Baines had offered his resignation as trustee to the board on August 30, 1858, but the board tabled the request, and he served until February 1, 1859.

George Washington Baines was born near Raleigh, North Carolina, on December 30, 1809. He was the eldest son of the Reverend Thomas Baines and the grandson of the Reverend George Baines, a Baptist minister who came from Ireland and adopted the English spelling of the name with an "e."

[2] Minutes of the Baylor Board of Trustees, p. 58.

[3] On October 28, 1856, Baines signed a note for $50 ($25 had been struck out and $50 inserted above) which he borrowed from the treasurer of Baylor University and repaid January 1, 1858. Baines Papers, Texas Collection, Baylor University.

In 1817 the family moved to Georgia and thence to Alabama. On a farm near Tuscaloosa young George spent his youth with little opportunity for formal education. When he became of age, he cut and dressed timber for funds to attend the University of Alabama. Because of failing health, he left school in 1836, his senior year. A college mate, ex-Governor O. M. Roberts, described him as "a modest, painstaking, hardworking student, greatly respected by all who knew him."

Baines took a teaching job in the fall of 1832. In September, when twenty-three, he was converted in a revival conducted by the famous pulpiteer T. J. Fisher about ten miles south of Tuscaloosa. He was baptized by Reverend Robert Guthrie into the Salem Church. At twenty-five he was licensed to preach by order of the Philadelphia Church, Tuscaloosa County, on July 20, 1834, and the following license was issued soon thereafter:

State of Alabama
Tuscaloosa County
>   The Philadelphia Baptist Church
>   To all to whom these presents shall carry greeting.

This is to certify that Brother George W. Baines is licensed to preach the gospel wherever God in His Providence may direct him. Signed by order and in behalf of the church in conference July 25, 1834.

>   Holland W. Middilow
>   Thomas Baines[4]

Two years later, Baines was ordained at Grants' Creek Church on August 7, 1836, as indicated by this paper:

>   Alabama
>   Tuscaloosa County

To all to whom it may concern, these are to certify that the bearer hereof Brother George W. Baines was at the call of the Grant's Creek Baptist Church humanly set apart this day by the imposition of hands, and ordained by us to the Gospel ministry: He not being at present invested with any particular pastoral charge but fully authorized to minister at large in the Lord's vineyard wherever Divine Providence may direct his course, and to administer the special as well as more common ordinances of the Gospel on every proper occasion.

[4] Baines Papers, Texas Collection, Baylor University.

And we do hereby recommend him to the affectionate regard, confidence and respect of all Christian people, but most especially of those who pertain to the Baptist denomination.

Given under our hands this 7th day of August, 1836.

Robert Morse, Pastor, Grant's Creek Baptist Church
Thomas Harris, Pastor, Mt. Pleasant Church
James H. Devotie, Pastor, Tuscaloosa City Baptist Church
Wm. Hood, Pastor, Big Creek Baptist Church
Thomas Baines, Pastor, New Bethel Baptist Church[5]

The ordination sermon on the text of II Timothy 4:5, 6 was delivered by Reverend J. H. Devotie. The signature of the father of Baines appears on both his license and ordination papers, and Robert S. Foster, Church clerk signed his credentials on November 5, 1837.

In 1837, Baines went to Carroll County, Arkansas, in hopes of reclaiming his health and founded three churches, baptizing 150 in what Link termed "wilderness country." He became a pioneer—built his cabin in the forest, hunted turkey, bear, and deer, and took a bride among the people. On October 20, 1840, Baines married Melissa Ann Butler, and she rode behind him on his horse to their new cabin for their wedding journey. Melissa Ann (born in 1824) was the daughter of Nealy Butler (born in 1796) and Amy Butler (born in 1799).[6] Nine children were born to George W. and Melissa Baines.[7]

Baines was referred to by his church members as "the best preacher that ever was in North Arkansas" and they described him as "a lithe, medium-sized man, having wonderful powers of endurance, with deep blue eyes, and coal black hair." During the seven years of his Arkansas sojourn,

[5] *Ibid.*

[6] Information supplied by granddaughter, Janet Baines Brockett, Mansfield, Texas, February 7, 1945.

[7] In *A Family Album* (New York: McGraw-Hill, 1965), pp. 131-2, Rebekah Baines Johnson listed them as follows:
1. Thomas Nealy (1841-1861). Died in Captain John William Hutchinson's Co. of Greys, 17th Brigade, C.S.A.
2. William Martin (1842-1912). Service in C.S.A.
3. Mary Elizabeth (1845-died in infancy).
4. Joseph Wilson (1846-1906), whose daughter Rebekah (Mrs. Sam Johnson) was the mother of United States President Lyndon Baines Johnson.
5. George Washington Baines II (1848-1923). Minister and educator.
6. James O'Neal Baines (1852-died in infancy).
7. Annie Melissa (1854-1897). Married William Edwin Rosborough, lawyer.
8. Taliaferro (1859-1870).
9. Johnnie Paxton (1863-1865).

Baines held a commission for parts of three years from the Baptist Home Mission Board of New York City.[8]

At the earnest request of friends he ran for representative from Carroll County to the Fourth Legislature and was elected to serve with Robert Fencher for the term of November 7, 1842, to February 4, 1843.[9]

In 1844, yielding to conviction, Baines settled in July at Mt. Lebanon, Louisiana. He preached there and at Minden, Laline, and other churches in the area, where his reputation was great and "among the Baptists his counsel was law." During the six years in Louisiana he served for a time as superintendent of schools in the Bienville Parish and visited Texas to assist John Bryce in the organization of the Baptist Church of Marshall in 1847.

After a seventeen-day journey across country in 1850 Baines moved his family, in the company of a young Englishman, Professor Thomas George Edwards, to Huntsville, Texas. He pastored the church there for a year and began a lifelong friendship with the Maxcys, Wilsons, and Sam Houstons. Baines exerted his influence in urging old friend Sam Houston to make a public profession of his religious faith. This Houston did, and President Burleson administered the ordinance of baptism on November 19, 1854.[10] Houston held Pastor Baines in high esteem and understood the travail of ministers of the gospel during pioneer days in Texas, as this excerpt from a letter shows. Houston asked

[8] A letter of August 20, 1956, from Mrs. Milo E. Wenger, Secretary, American Baptist Home Missions Board, reveals that Mr. Baines is listed on the missionary roster of 1838, residence, Crooked Creek, Arkansas. He had worked there for three months in the year 1838. His record reads: "January 21st, Since my arrival the church has called a meeting. Yesterday and today I attended and tried to preach . . . and had the pleasure of baptizing one man. Many other settlements are destitute of a preached gospel." Brother Baines was highly recommended by his former acquaintances, and the committee hoped much from him. He is again mentioned by the record of 1839 as having worked all of the twelve months at Crooked Creek. His report to the Board stated: "The brethren in this state have been restricted by sickness, and other causes, in the performance of their duties."

[9] Marcus Holbrook, Director, State of Arkansas Legislative Council, Little Rock, Arkansas, July 9, 1956.

[10] A photostatic copy of p. 166 of Haynes' *The Life and Writings of Dr. Rufus C. Burleson* which belongs to Mrs. E. D. Brockett (Janet Baines) reveals a marginal note of interest: "In this pool I was baptized by my father [George W. Baines, Sr.] in 1862. Miss Nannie, the eldest daughter of General Sam Houston, was the only other person baptized with me. Geo. W. Baines [Jr.]" The note refers to the baptismal pool in Little Rocky.

Baines, who owed him $300, to renew the note and wrote that he had

> . . . knocked off the interest for 6 years at 8% amounting to over $140. This I am not loath to do, as you have the luck to minister to congregations who think you can afford to preach to them gratis. If you do not devise some plan to change their practices, they will think that you ought to pay them a good salary for attending church. . . . I allude to plain old-fashioned honesty of paying what they subscribe! They ought to know that paper currency will not pass in Heaven. Cotton fields and cotton bales will find no market in Paradise![11]

Immediately after his coming to Texas, Baines began his service with the Baptist State Convention, first as recording-secretary, preacher of the convention sermon, and representative to the Southern Baptist Convention. President W. C. Crane stated that he was "intimately connected with every good enterprise of the denomination" for thirty-two years—until his death in 1882.[12]

Baines came to Independence as pastor in 1851 and remained for one year. In 1852 he moved to Anderson—then a town of 1200 to 1500 people—as pastor and editor of the first Baptist paper in Texas, a post he held until shortly before he became president of Baylor University.[13]

One of the great problems facing Baines as member of the Baylor Board of Trustees from June 17, 1851, to February 1, 1859, as well as editor, was the Burleson controversy, which he handled with a high degree of objectivity. Nevertheless it brought him anxieties and misunderstandings that lasted years. Baines did not feel that journalism was his forte and had assumed the editorship under coercion. The original plan called for J. B. Stiteler to edit the paper in Independence, but he declined because no publisher could be

[11] Sam Houston to G. W. Baines, November 23, 1857. Baines Papers, Texas Collection, Baylor University.

[12] J. B. Link, *Texas Historical and Biographical Magazine* I, 1891, p. 483.

[13] After several convention committees had failed to work out a satisfactory plan for a Texas paper, the ambition was achieved with the establishment of *The Texas Baptist* in January, 1855. George W. Baines was named editor, with J. B. Stiteler assistant editor. The format consisted of four closely printed pages, approximately twenty-two by thirty inches. The subscription list ran as high as 2,600. Rupert Norval Richardson, "Literature and Scholarship," *Centennial Story of Texas Baptists* (Dallas, Texas: Baptist General Convention of Texas, Burt Building, 1936), pp. 350-351.

found in the locale. Since one was available at Anderson, Baines was named to the post.[14]

R. B. C. Howell in a letter to *The Tennessee Baptist* said that Baines was "one of the most cautious, prudent men living . . . a man of few words, but of much hard, earnest labor, who is also pastor of a large church in his town."[15]

General J. W. Barnes of Anderson lauded the work of Baines as editor and termed him one of the ablest men of the denomination. He was a natural choice to assume the presidency of Baylor at such a hazardous time as 1861. This was not the first time Baines was recognized as presidential material. Through W. Ikard, the trustees had offered him the presidency of the Brazos River Institute.[16] In the face of insurmountable odds, Baines maintained the fledgling Baylor University for two years at great sacrifice of his health.

President Baines could not have found a more demanding position in Texas than the one which he was coerced into accepting. The Burleson-Clark problems were far from being settled and feeling ran high in the locale. The Civil War made all Texans apprehensive. The Baptist denomination had experienced great growth, however, and numbered about 50,000 in Texas.[17] Churches had multiplied and had pastors of marked ability, and with the appointment of former editor Baines to the presidency of Baylor University—"the fountain source of missionary supply"—the twenty-four associations felt a bit more secure. Yet Carroll, in writing on the Baylor University Board of Trustees' report to the Baptist State Convention in Huntsville, 1861, described the situation skeptically: "Baylor University, in common with similar institutions of the country, is suffering on account of the present national troubles through which we are passing."[18]

The president entered upon his duties immediately. At the September 2, 1861, meeting of the board the resignation

[14] J. M. Carroll, *A History of Texas Baptists,* ed. J. B. Cranfill (Dallas, Texas: Baptist Standard Publishing Co., 1923), p. 286

[15] R. B. C. Howell to *The Tennessee Baptist,* November 20, 1858.

[16] W. Ikard to Elder G. W. Baines, November 20 (no year), Weatherford, Texas. Baines Papers, Texas Collection, Baylor University.

[17] J. M. Dawson, "Missions and Missionaries," *Centennial Story of Texas Baptists,* p. 40.

[18] Carroll, p. 239.

of Professor O. H. Leland was belatedly presented and accepted. The committees to settle with Burleson and administer building problems begged more time. A committee of five was appointed to study the laws of the university and make such amendments as necessary. President Baines was requested "to visit as many associations and public meetings this year as he can, consistent with his duties at the University." The low ebb of finances is indicated by the board's declining to accept B. S. Fitzgerald's proposal "to sell his house and lot to the university for a boarding house for the Female Department" in the present "pecuniary embarrassment of the country."

Further indication of the economic state of Washington County is seen in the fact that on February 12, 1862, President Baines secured from Sam Houston a young Negro boy (Charles, about 14) and promised to pay Houston $70 on the next December 25th. He also contracted to give the boy "one suit of winter clothes and two suits of summer clothes, a pair of shoes and a blanket and to treat him in a humane manner."[19]

The effects of the Civil War are shown in the trustees' resolution on March 13, 1862, that military drill be taught in the Male Department. Professor Hillyer was requested to conduct the class.

Hillyer, well-educated and experienced, brought a broad background to Baylor. He was born in Wilkes County, Georgia, on May 25, 1805.[20] His parents were well-educated people and desired that their children have similar advantages. The two older sons, John and Junius, were sent to a boarding school, and "Little Granby," age seven, was sent to an old field school, where he boarded with the teacher from Monday through Friday.[21] John F. entered the University of Georgia in 1821 and received the A.B. degree in 1825, at which time he was the commencement speaker.[22] Link records that he attended the Georgia Medical College

[19] Baines Correspondence, Texas Collection, Baylor University.
[20] J. B. Link, *Texas Historical and Biographical Magazine,* II, 372.
[21] S. G. Hillyer, *Reminiscences of Georgia Baptists* (Atlanta: Foote and Davies Company, 1902). The last chapter, written by daughter Louise C. Hillyer, is the source of this information.
[22] W. M. Crane, Jr., Alumni Secretary, The University of Georgia, Athens, Georgia, March 14, 1955, to Mrs. Lily M. Russell. Extensive research has failed to establish other earned degrees.

and practiced medicine for two years.[23] Descendant, Mrs. Lorene Hillyer Fox, states that faculty members taught a few students in the hospitals before the opening of the Georgia Medical College and that John F. Hillyer was probably one of these who were later licensed. Family records confirm the suggestion.[24]

With his conversion to the Baptist faith in 1825, Hillyer gave up medicine and began preaching. Salary contracts were unknown in Georgia at the time, for it was not deemed right "to preach for money"; so he was forced into the schoolroom to earn subsistence. Yet he preached nearly all his life—as a Baptist minister sixty-seven years of his eighty-nine year life-span.[25]

From 1835 to 1839, under the presidency of Billington Sanders, John Hillyer taught mathematics in Mercer University, Penfield, Georgia.[26] He preached and taught in Eatonton, Georgia, until 1847 when he accepted an appointment from the Domestic Mission Board as missionary to Texas.[27] He arrived in Galveston on November 11, 1847. Through the solicitations of James Huckins, a new church had been built in the Crescent City and William M. Tryon of Houston had preached the dedicatory sermon in September. Huckins was too ill to attend the services and resigned on September 26, 1847. Hillyer was elected to succeed him on January 3, 1848, and served until September 24, 1848, when he resigned.[28]

On November 11, 1848, Hillyer moved to a farm near Goliad, Texas, to supply more profitable employment for his slaves. There he took charge of the Goliad school. Hillyer Female College, established in December 1848 under the patronage of the Baptist Church, occupied a three-story building on a twenty-acre tract which included the grounds of the mission of Nuestra Senora del Espiritu Santo de

[23] Link, II, 372.

[24] Mrs. Jesse E. Fox (Lorene Hillyer), Austin, Texas, November 4, 1957, to Mrs. Lily M. Russell.

[25] R. J. Massey, "John F. Hillyer," *Atlanta Constitution*, November 12, 1903.

[26] C. D. Mallary in *Memoirs of Jesse Mercer* lists Hillyer among the instructors at Mercer. Spright Dowell, President Emeritus of Mercer, recorded this service from 1834 to 1837 in a letter to Mrs. Lily M. Russell.

[27] Hillyer's missionary sermon delivered on the fourth Sunday in August 1840 is printed in the *Georgia Pulpit* I, Sermon XII, (ed.) Robert Fleming.

[28] Link, I, 166.

Zunige. Hillyer opened the first ten-month term on February 1, 1849, offering courses in Greek, Latin, music, drawing, "and other branches proper for female education." The school continued operation until 1852, when Aranama College opened in the building with Hillyer as one of the first trustees.[29]

Hillyer also established the first Baptist church to be organized west of the Guadalupe River.[30] Indicative of the pioneer nature of the sparsely settled country was an Indian raid and the loss of many possessions at the Hillyer homestead. Yet Hillyer continued his ministry, encompassing Victoria and Clinton, until August 1852.

Gonzales College, chartered on February 16, 1852, by an act of the Texas Legislature as a non-denominational, privately owned school to be operated by the Gonzales College Association, induced Hillyer to become its first president. Thomas J. Pilgrim was president of the board of trustees, and the initial enrollment of fifty students studied under four teachers.[31]

At Gonzales College Hillyer gave a series of scientific and philosophical lectures, raising $1,000 through small admission fees. He "went North" to purchase "the first set of philosophical and chemical apparatus ever brought into the state,"[32]

[29] Walter Prescott Webb and H. Bailey Carroll (eds.), *The Handbook of Texas*, p. 816.
   In 1852 the Presbytery of Western Texas through the efforts of William C. Blair established Aranama College in the old Aranama Indian Mission building. It was chartered by the Fifth Legislature on January 25, 1854. Frederick Eby, "Education in Texas, Source Materials," *University of Texas Bulletin*, #1824, April 25, 1918.

[30] Link lists original members as Reverend and Mrs. John Hillyer, daughter Kate (later Mrs. J. A. Robbins, who with her husband taught music at Baylor College), son H. B. Hillyer; Judge Pryor Lee; a Mr. and Mrs. Brightman; "Uncle Jacob" and "Aunt Liza," servants of the Hillyers. Link, II, 373.

[31] The school acquired four leagues of land from the defunct Guadalupe College, the sale of which netted the new college $2,150.60. The town of Gonzales gave a music building in 1853 and a Female Seminary in 1855. Enrollment steadily increased, reaching 276 students in 1859-60; about eighty per cent of the students were in the preparatory school, but the college division offered four years' work leading to a degree. The Civil War reduced the student body, and a storm severely damaged the Male Department building. It was demolished and the stones used in a fortification against a possible attack by Federal gunboats. In 1874 the college property was acquired by the city and eventually became a part of the Gonzales public school system. *The Handbook of Texas*, I, 707.

[32] Link, II, 373.

a statement disputed by J. A. Kimball, who brought such equipment to Texas in 1850.[33]

While at Gonzales, Hillyer's wife, formerly Mary Biscoe, died, and after two years he returned to Georgia to preach. There he married Mrs. D. Storey and returned to Texas in 1857, supporting himself as he preached a free gospel. On July 27, 1861, Hillyer was elected to the chair of mathematics at Baylor University and came before the board on September 2, to accept the appointment. On December 18, Hillyer was asked to add natural science and military tactics to his schedule, then in March he added military drill.

The present faculty was asked to continue in service for the spring term of 1862, but indications of a feeling of temporary status is evident in the reactivating of the old committee to recommend a permanent faculty with the request that it "act energetically in finding suitable persons for said duties."[34] The Convention report on Baylor University in the fall of 1861 termed enrollment "small at present."[35] The Convention records for 1862 are silent concerning the activities of the two Baylors, but it is known that the student body was greatly reduced in both schools.

In the spring of 1861 young men in the senior class petitioned the university president, asking to be relieved of their academic pursuits so that they might enlist. Of course the petition was granted.[36] Records reveal that 151 young men who had attended Baylor University enlisted in the Confederate Army.[37] Baylor graduate and teacher, Oscar H. Leland, left school to serve the Confederacy as adjutant of Colonel E. J. Gurley's regiment, and Dr. D. R. Wallace, Baylor teacher, was surgeon of Colonel Speight's regiment. Professors Rogers, Sayles, and Shepherd of the Baylor Law Department also served with the Confederate forces, as did Professor Fitzgerald of the Male Department. Baylor classrooms were hard hit by the war.

[33] J. A. Kimball, "Editor's Drawer," *Texas Historical Biographical Magazine,* II, 434.
[34] Minutes of the Baylor Board of Trustees, March 13, 1862, p. 207.
[35] Report of Baylor Trustees at Baptist State Convention; 14th Annual Session, at Huntsville, 1861.
[36] Margaret Royalty Edwards, "A Sketch of Baylor University" (unpublished Master's thesis, Department of History, Baylor University, 1920), p. 89.
[37] *The Baylor Bulletin,* ed. A. J. Armstrong, XXI (December 1918), 50-53. See Appendix for complete list.

A state of crisis was evident in schools all over the land. President Rufus C. Burleson left the infant Waco University in the hands of his brother, Professor R. B. Burleson, and joined Colonel Speight's regiment near Millican. An impassioned letter from President Burleson to the *Houston Telegraph* states that "all of our professors capable of performing military service and all our students over eighteen are now in the army." Yet, he declared that Waco University, as reported, was not suspended, but that between 90 and 100 students were in daily attendance, with 123 students matriculated during the spring 1862 session. Male students received military training in the University Guards.[38]

The young women at Baylor at Independence were emotionally involved in the war, as evidenced by a letter to the Soldiers of the Southland Braves accompanying a resplendent flag. Among the signatures of six patriots are those of Sam Houston's daughter, Nannie; Ella Tryon, daughter of one of Baylor's founding fathers; and Dora Pettus, later the mother of Texas Governor Hobby.

Captain W. R. Sullivan of Waul's Legion wrote a gallant reply:

> In behalf of the "Southland Braves," we tender you our utmost thanks for the presentation of one of the most beautiful Confederate Ensigns that has ever been thrown to the breeze upon our tented fields. . . . [39]

At the outbreak of the Civil War, Baylor University was sixteen years old and had graduated twelve classes. The male population was drastically reduced, as in all Southern areas. One young lady moaned: "You can drive all across town and not see a single young man." But "the coed provided the necessary safeguard against economic demise."[40]

Significant in Baylor history is the recommendation of the board of trustees on June 25, 1862. Principal Clark of the Female Department presented four names: Mary Ella

[38] Burleson Letter to Editor, *The Tri-Weekly Telegraph*, XXVIII, No. 44, Houston, Texas, June 27, 1862.
[39] Letter to Soldiers of the Southland Braves, July 2, 1862, from Ella Tryon, Clara Mason, Kate Clark, Mary Mason, Nannie Houston, Dora Pettus, Baylor University.
Captain W. R. Sullivan, Camp Waul, July 3, 1862, to Six Young Ladies, Baylor University. *The Tri-Weekly Telegraph*, XXVIII, No. 55, Houston, Texas, Wednesday, July 23, 1862.
[40] Frederick Eby, "Education and Educators," *Centennial Story of Texas Baptists*, p. 151.

Chase, Virginia A. Cleveland, Addie Haynes, and Anna Goodwin "for graduation." The board moved that the degree of Bachelor of Arts be conferred on them. Heretofore such recognition had not been accorded.[41]

Again Mr. Fitzgerald had approached the board about the purchase of his property, and a committee had been requested to confer with him following the June meeting. The December 18, 1862, meeting failed to have a quorum present, but the four members and two proxies agreed to proceed with business subject to the ratification of the next session. Proposal was made to accept the proposition of A. G. Haynes to sell him the dormitory for $120. Agreement was made to rent the boarding house for $300, the renter to board students for $20 per month. For the year 1863 President Baines and Mr. Hillyer were re-elected, and Mr. W. W. James of Grimes County was named professor of ancient languages.

President Baines sent the following letter to the board of trustees before their June 25, 1862, meeting, and it was "laid on the table for the present":

Independence June the 24th 1862

To the Board of Trustees of Baylor University

Dear Brethren,

The time, for which I accepted the Presidency of Baylor University, expires with the present collegiate year.

At your last meeting, I am informed, that you passed an order, requesting me to continue my services until the end of the present year. It is my desire, that you allow me to decline this offer. My principal reason is that my state of health will not justify the confinement which is necessary to teach and control a school of little boys, seven or eight hours every day. If we could employ a competent teacher, to take charge of the primary classes I could then hear recitations four hours, as it is usual in colleges, and have time for literary preparations and relaxation. But as I see no prospect of this, I prefer that you should obtain the services of some one that is able to fill the place as things are now. I have other reasons for declining which I will communicate if you desire to hear them. Hoping that you will be able to procure suitable men to carry on the School through these trying times, and that Baylor University may always be the best, and most useful college in Texas.

I remain with feelings of confidence and esteem, your humble servant.

Geo. W. Baines[42]

[41] Oberlin College awarded the A.B. degree to three women in 1841. Oberlin College *Bulletin,* Oberlin, Ohio, 1966.

[42] Baines Correspondence, Texas Collection, Baylor University.

A committee was then appointed to procure a teacher for the primary classes of the Male Department, and every effort was made to cooperate with President Baines, who had sacrificed himself to maintain the university during this perilous time. At the June 24-26 meeting B. S. Fitzgerald was named professor of ancient languages in the Male Department "with the provision that he is to look to the endowments and tuition for his salary," and a tuition raise was allowed in both divisions—"at the [professor's] discretion so as not to exceed one hundred per cent of the present terms." Another indication of the calamitous condition of the school was the trustee directive to have the boarding house of the Male Department occupied and cared for "to prevent it from going to destruction." One bright spot, however, was the presentation by Principal Clark of six young ladies as candidates for degrees.

During the summer a trustee committee of correspondence entered into negotiations with Dr. William Carey Crane to fill the presidency vacated by the Reverend Mr. Baines.

After resigning as president of Baylor, Baines moved to a farm about two and a half miles from Fairfield, Freestone County, and pastored churches at Fairfield, Springfield, Butler, and one in the Cockrell area. These were difficult years, for his wife and youngest son, Johnny Paxton, died; yet Baines accepted his grief with Christian fortitude. Granddaughter Janet Baines Brockett wrote: "Since the Civil War made appropriate facilities unavailable, Grandfather himself had to make the coffin grandmother was buried in."[43]

On June 13, 1865, Baines married Mrs. Cynthia W. Williams, with former Baylor President H. L. Graves performing the ceremony. In the fall of 1866 Baines gave up his churches to travel until the next October as agent for the State Convention. Then he settled at Salado, Bell County, as pastor of that church and several others, including Florence in Williamson County.[44] A letter from President Crane of Baylor shows that his interests were still with the university.

[43] Janet Brockett letter to Mrs. Lily M. Russell, February 7, 1945, Mansfield, Texas.
[44] The minutes of the Salado Baptist Church show that Rev. Geo. W. Baines, Sr., his wife, Mrs. Cynthia Baines, and their daughter Anna M. Baines joined the church on November 16, 1867, by letter from the Fairfield Baptist Church.

Crane requested him to deliver a series of four or five lectures on themes of his own choice in Polemic Theology some week in March. Then followed some words about son George W. Baines, Jr., a Baylor student.[45]

In 1877 Baines accepted an agency for the Education Commission, but in 1881 the Salado Church insisted that he re-enter the pastorate there. In January 1882 his wife, Cynthia, died at Belton and was buried at Salado. Thereafter Baines made his home in Belton with his daughter Anna (Mrs. William Edwin Rosborough) until he died of malaria fever on December 28, 1882. Reverend M. V. Smith conducted the funeral services, with interment at Salado by the side of his wife and ten-year-old son, Taliaferro.

The first issue of *The Texas Baptist* after the death of Baines carried two columns by Z. N. Morrell in praise of his beloved co-worker who "came to Texas fifteen years after the author." He said Baines' name first appeared in Baptist minutes in 1850, that he was "naturally fond of metaphysics, and frequently was referred to as the 'hairsplitter' by brethren after sermons and debates" because of his logical, profound thinking. A manuscript on "The Object of Mental Science and the Probability of Its Success" is evidence of President Baines' faith in the field of psychology.[46] Morrell recalled the staunch position taken by Baines against having Ledbetter preach the missionary sermon at the Seventh Session of the Trinity River Association in 1854, when Ledbetter was under a charge of heresy. Morrell characterized Baines as "faithful, steady, modest, persevering, intelligent, manly, charitable, prudent, and successful in raising a family." He concluded his tribute with the transcription of his last conversation with Baines—at the October meeting of the Baptist State Convention in Belton, where they both stood for "compromise in all that was consistent with the word of God, but no more." He was justly termed "a good soldier of Jesus Christ."

Numberless tributes have been paid to President Baines. Reverend M. V. Smith termed "his love of peace among his brethren his most prominent characteristic" and said he

[45] W. C. Crane to G. W. Baines, December 8, 1873. Baines Papers, Texas Collection, Baylor University.
[46] Baines Papers, Texas Collection, Baylor University.

was ". . . one of the best and most remarkable men I ever knew. Not a stain rests upon his name. . . . He could see as far into the subject as it fell to the lot of man to do, and he was wonderfully gifted in seeing the difficulties in the way of reaching the correct conclusions. Fortunate was the young preacher who had him for counselor when in deep theological waters or in the midst of fiery trials. I never went to him without getting instruction and comfort."[47] Dr. F. Courtney of Arkansas and Louisiana wrote: "I never knew a man more beloved and honored by the people he served."

The sons of President Baines filled worthy places in Texas: Joseph Wilson Baines was appointed Secretary of State by Governor Ireland; G. W. Baines, Jr., was appointed missionary by the Board of the Baptist State Convention to El Paso—one of the most important posts in Texas.[48] He also taught at San Marcos Baptist Academy and received an A.M. degree from Baylor in 1875 and the D.D. in 1900. Baylor records list many members of the Baines family as students at the university.[49]

Great-grandson, Huffman Baines, Jr., of Austin, as a Baylor trustee (1963-to date), has given dynamic leadership to the all-important Development Committee.

Great-grandson, Lyndon Baines Johnson, President of the United States, was awarded a Doctor of Laws degree

[47] Article in *The Home and Sunday School,* Dallas, Texas, February 2, 1886, based on Reverend M. V. Smith's article in *Texas Baptist Herald* in January 1883.

[48] Notes of sermon by Elder George W. Baines, Jr., at Oak Grove, Bell County, November 29, 1874. Baines Papers, Texas Collection, Baylor University.

[49] Descendants of President Baines who attended Baylor include:
Anne Baines, San Marcos, A.B. 1913 (Mrs. J. P. Reesing, Gatesville).
George Washington Baines, Jr., Independence, A.M. 1875, D.D. 1900; San Marcos.
George W. Baines, III, Waco, 1901; Alpine.
Janet Baines, San Marcos, B.S. 1909 (Mrs. E. D. Brockett, Fort Worth).
Joseph Baines, San Marcos, 1913-1917; Dallas.
Joseph Wilson Baines, Independence, 1851-1852; Blanco.
Myra Baines, Rockdale, 1879-1880 (Mrs. J. H. Hearn, Beeville).
Rebekah Baines, 1901 (Mrs. Sam Johnson, Johnson City).
Thomas Nealy Baines, Independence, 1851-1852.
William McIntosh Baines, Alpine, 1901-1904; San Antonio.
George Baines Rosborough, 1901-1907.
Frances Reesing, Gatesville, A.B. 1945 (Mrs. R. H. Woolridge, Jr., Waco).
Mary Baines, B.A. 1942 (Mrs. Arthur Sheeran, Palacios).
John P. Reesing, Jr., Gatesville, A.B. 1941; Professor of English, The Georgetown University, Washington, D.C.

by Baylor University at the May 28, 1965, Convocation. The elaborate program carried this reference to President Johnson's great-grandfather, Baylor's President George Washington Baines:

" . . . he could have had any office within the gift of the people, however, he chose to preach. . . " (*Texas Baptist Herald*, 1883.)

Through the efforts of Mrs. Lily M. Russell, the Texas Collection has many articles—furniture, personalia, and correspondence which belonged to President Baines. The Baines collection was secured through purchase and gift.

Grandson Joseph Baines of Dallas declared that President Baines was a Mason.

On May 1, 1966, at three in the afternoon at the First Baptist Church of Fairfield, Texas, a program was held to dedicate a Texas Historical Marker for Reverend George Washington Baines. President Abner V. McCall of Baylor University made the dedicatory address, and Mr. Huffman Baines, Jr., great-grandson of the Reverend Baines, unveiled the marker. Others in the program were Mr. H. D. Whitaker, Miss Joan Hill, Reverend Bob Parker, Mrs. Joe Lee Kergan, Professor P. D. Browne, Mr. J. D. Hudson, Jr., Reverend Jack McDaniel, and the Fairfield Boy Scout Troup No. 68.

The plaza of the Moody Memorial Library was given in memory of President Baines, and a handsome plaque bears this legend:

Dedicated to the memory of George Washington Baines, Third President of Baylor University 1861-1863. Given by his Descendants and Relatives.

President Henry Lee Graves

College Hill Home of President Graves

Dress of Mrs. Henry Lee Graves on Mannequin

Graves Hall

President Rufus C. Burleson

Burleson Wedding Picture

Judge Abner S. Lipscomb
Baylor Law Professor

First Faculty

Dr. R. C. Burleson
Prof. O. H. Leland

Prof. R. B. Burleson
Prof. J. L. Smith

Prof. D. R. Wallace
Prof. G. W. Willrick

Principal Horace Clark

General Sam Houston

Independence Baptist Church

Baptismal Pool

Mary Gentry Kavanaugh
First Woman Graduate, 1855

Stephen Decatur Rowe
First Baylor Graduate, 1845

Thomas J. Brown
L.L.B., 1858

Reverend Adolf Fuchs
Early Baylor Music Teacher

"Female Building"

Desks from 1854 Catalogue

Girls' Dormitory

Tryon Hall

President George Washington Baines

William Henry Long
Tutor in the Male Department

Judge John Sayles
Law Professor and Author

Reverend J.W.D. Creath
Baylor Agent

Reverend Jacob Beverly Stiteler
Professor of Natural Sciences

President William Carey Crane

Drawing of Early Baylor Campus at Independence

Reverend Hosea Garrett
Long-Term Trustee

Major Moses Austin Bryan
Baylor Trustee

Harry Arthur McArdle
Baylor Artist

T. J. Jackson
Early Trustee

Reverend P. B. Chandler
Baylor Agent

Charles Wedemeyer
Vice President

President Reddin Andrews

Old Baylor Columns at Independence

CHAPTER X

President William Carey Crane's
First Five Years

O^{N AUGUST} 5, 1863, Baylor trustees met at a called session. Board President Hosea Garrett announced that the Committee of Correspondence had been in communication with Dr. William Carey Crane, who was then "in town on invitation of the committee." R. E. B. Baylor, H. Garrett, and G. W. Graves (brother of Baylor's first president) were designated to confer with him about the presidency of Baylor University and to report at a meeting at 7 o'clock the following morning. In compliance with a request from the Houston Baptist Church, written by Mrs. M. J. Young, at the instance of Colonel John S. Sydnor, Crane and his eldest son came by buggy from Keachi, Louisiana. The Cranes were located there on the plantation of brother-in-law Charles J. Shepherd of New Orleans.[1] En route Dr. Crane spent a day or so with General James W. Barnes, who had called on him at Mount Lebanon to discuss the presidency of Baylor University. Subsequently an invitation to Baylor had been forwarded to him, backed by a letter from Michael Ross.[2]

All along the route from Keachi to Anderson he heard statements extremely prejudicial to Baylor; yet he promised Barnes that he would visit Independence. At Houston he was received cordially and was issued an invitation to become pastor of the church at a flattering salary. On the eve of accepting the invitation, a committee from Independence, composed of Trustee Graves and B. S. Fitzgerald, who had held the school together during the recent crisis, came to Houston and insisted that he go to Independence before making a decision. Crane had been told of "a terrible dif-

---

[1] In a speech delivered before the Texas Baptist State Convention at Galveston in 1869, Dr. Crane reviewed the circumstances which brought him to Texas.

[2] Michael Ross, Pastor of Independence Baptist Church, June 1, 1863; George W. Graves, representing the Baylor Trustees, on June 18, 1863, to Ross. Crane Correspondence, Texas Collection. "This invitation had been recalled, of which I had no knowledge, however, for months thereafter," stated Crane.

ficulty there—a state-wide schism," that the institution was defunct, that it had been removed to Waco (as published in the *Richmond Religious Herald*), "that it was entirely under Northern influence, and other things touching sad church and state difficulties," that individuals owing the institution would not pay, and that the interest on the endowment could not be collected.

Despite these discouraging statements, Dr. Crane preached at the Independence Church every night for over two weeks in a very successful meeting. Recorded in his chronicle is a list of the eleven whom he baptized. During this period he stayed in the home of George W. Graves—just behind the church. Judge Baylor was a guest there also and joined Graves in influencing Crane to consider the presidency of Baylor University. The trustees first offered the position "based on the past receipts of the institution," but the appointment was declined. The school at the time had only fifteen students.

On August 11, 1863, Crane wrote to his wife:

When I think merely of personal enjoyment, I feel that I should settle at Houston, but when I consider the condition of the children, cheapness of living, and health, I am for Independence. I think I shall preach a while at Houston, try to get that church right, get acquainted with the people, and then, when things are ready for removal, move you all here.[3]

Since the trustees and Dr. Crane reached no agreement, they adjourned to meet at Plantersville in Grimes County during the approaching Baptist Associational meeting. There on August 16, 1863, the Baylor Board of Trustees unanimously elected Dr. Crane "President of the Faculty of Baylor University to take effect from the first of January next with a salary of three thousand dollars." At a candlelight meeting on the same day Dr. Crane came before the board to accept the offer. Public notice of the action was made through the issuance of a circular by the president and secretary of the board:

The Board of Trustees of Baylor University
August 29, 1863

The trustees are happy to announce to the public that the Rev. Wm. Carey Crane, D. D., has accepted the Presidency of this in-

[3] Letter in Crane Correspondence, Texas Collection, Baylor University.

stitution. He enters upon his duties on the first day of January, 1864. Of his qualifications as a theologian and scholar, his extended reputation as an instructor and his high standing give occasion to the trustees to congratulate the friends of Baylor University upon his accession to the faculty.[4]

Descended from early New England settlers, William Carey Crane was born on March 17, 1816, at Richmond, Virginia. There his father established the William Crane & Company, Hide and Leather Dealers, in 1820. Intensely religious and missionary in conviction, Crane named his first son William Carey, the second Adoniram Judson, and the third Andrew Fuller. Father William Crane was a Sunday School teacher and deacon for fifty years; he initiated the plan and advanced the first money for the *Religious Herald*; he was one of the founders of Richmond College; he served as a trustee and supporter of Columbian College; he worked for the organization of the Southern Baptist Convention and became one of its first officers; and he worked all his life "for the uplift of the African race."[5]

The Crane children were given the advantages afforded by the time and locale. William Carey began his education in Richmond and continued in Baltimore, where his family established a branch business in 1834. Because the lad showed signs of superior intelligence, he was sent to Mt. Pleasant Classical Institute in Amherst, Massachusetts, where he received thorough preparatory training. Here one of his schoolmates was Henry Ward Beecher. Here also

[4] Dr. Crane recalled that he was to receive in addition to the salary "corn and meat for the first year and expenses of removal from Keachi." Major A. G. Haynes, George W. Graves and Reddin Vickers sent their wagons and brought as much "of my effects" as could be transported. The rest remained until the close of the war and were sold to assist in paying for the removal of Dr. Crane's library from Shreveport, where it had been stored in the Warehouse of the Confederate Bureau of Clothing for three years.

[5] C. H. Wedemeyer, "William Carey Crane," *Baylor University Bulletin*, XIII (January 1910).

William Crane took an active part in the movement sponsoring colonization of Liberia and helped educate his Negro friend Lott Carey who eventually became President of Liberia. In appreciation Carey sent Crane an ivory-headed ebony walking cane, which fell to eldest son William Carey Crane when Crane died in 1867. Although he did not need a cane, Dr. Crane carried this cane until his death in 1885. As the property of his eldest son, W. C. Crane, Jr., it was lost in a fire. See Hazel Montgomery, "An Historic Cane," *Baylor University Bulletin*, XIII (January 1910), 11.

Crane was converted and consecrated his life to the ministry.[6]

Among youthful reminiscences Crane listed those involving Lafayette, Thomas Jefferson, James Madison, and James Monroe, all of whom he saw during his school years or at sessions of Congress where he heard Calhoun, Clay, and Webster debate. His diary records experiences at receptions given by President Jackson at the White House.

As a young ministerial student Crane returned to Virginia and entered Richmond College as one of the first fourteen students. A year and a half later he entered Columbian College, the national Baptist institution in Washington, D.C., where he took the A.B. and A.M. degrees. Then he enrolled as a student of theology at Madison University (later Colgate) in 1836 and studied for three years.[7] Howard College awarded him the D.D. in 1860.[8] Baylor University honored him with the LL.D. in 1873.

In 1837 Crane went to Georgia to enter upon his teaching career as co-principal of the Classical School at Talbottom.[9] Immediately upon his arrival in Georgia, he began to write for the *Christian Index*, the general subject being "collegiate education as bearing upon Baptist influence."[10]

On June 18, 1838, Crane was married to Alcesta Flora Galusha of Rochester, New York. On September 23 of that year he was ordained to the ministry at Baltimore, Maryland, and became pastor of the Baptist Church at Montgomery, Alabama, the following year. There he became friends with the Lea family, who preceded him to Texas. A few miles distant from Montgomery was Wetumpka, where William

[6] Frederick Eby, "Education and Educators," *The Centennial Story of Texas* (Dallas, Texas: Baptist General Convention of Texas, 1936), p. 154.

[7] *First Half Century of Madison University*, p. 228. From this institution also came T. J. Pilgrim, Henry L. Graves, J. B. Stiteler, and J. V. E. Covey to labor in Texas.

[8] President H. Talbird, Howard College, Marion, Alabama, to President W. C. Crane, President of Mt. Lebanon University, July 3, 1860. Texas Collection, Baylor University.

[9] A letter of October 25, 1837, from William Crane to son William Carey on his departure contained the older man's "Lesson's of Life": admonishments concerning the care of money; the habits of ministers (lying abed and too long devotionals); "don't ask others to do what you can do yourself"; read the Bible through yearly; use your own thoughts, not commentaries. Texas Collection, Baylor University.

[10] Rufus W. Weaver, address on "The Founders of Baylor University," June 13, 1944.

Tryon was pastor. Crane performed the ceremony when Tryon was married to Mrs. Higgins on April 26, 1840. On the following day Crane accompanied his wife to Tuscaloosa. Mrs. Crane, quite ill, went on by easy stages to her parents' home in Rochester, New York, where she died on June 23, 1840. On June 9 Crane wrote her a lengthy letter—which she was destined never to receive although it followed her East—telling of a week's visit of

> . . . Brother Huckins, whom I accompanied to Wetumpka, and saw Tryon and his lady. . . . He thinks a little of going to Texas and took up a collection and subscriptions to the amount of $96. The church passed a resolution last night directing that I be made a life director of the American Baptist Home Mission Society. . . . Brother Huckins is a very good man indeed and preaches pretty well. He went from here to Marion.[11]

As a member of the Domestic Mission Board, Crane undoubtedly had a part in sending Huckins and Tryon to Texas, and hence in the founding of Baylor University.

While traveling for the Virginia Track Society, Crane married Jane Louise Wright of Rome, New York, whom he described as "a young lady of rare accomplishment and a worthy member of the Presbyterian Church."[12] She, too, experienced a brief married life, for she died at Richmond, Virginia, on December 26, 1842.

In 1844 Crane began his pastorate in Columbus, Mississippi, and on April 26, 1845, was married to Catherine Jane Shepherd of Mobile, Alabama. She was "a young lady of wonderful beauty, fine native endowment and fascinating manners."[13] The seventeen-year-old bride and her husband went to live at the leading hotel of Columbus, where they became close friends of a young lawyer, Henry Dickinson, and his wife, Annie.[14] The Cranes became the parents of nine children, eight of whom lived to maturity.

[11] William Carey Crane to wife, Texas Collection, Baylor University.
[12] *Biographical Encyclopedia of Texas*, p. 138.
[13] *Ibid.*
Catherine Shepherd's father, of Scottish descent, was a tobacco planter and owner of the "Crossroads Store" in Northumberland County, Virginia. He moved his family to Mobile when Kate was about ten years old and died soon afterwards in a yellow fever epidemic.
[14] Royston C. Crane recorded that District Judge Dickinson wrote to his parents, asking if they might visit them. Doctors had advised them "to get in the buggy and travel" with their ailing infant son. The Cranes welcomed their old friends, and Mrs. Crane, who had a baby girl of her own, nursed

Crane held other Mississippi pastorates: Vicksburg in 1847; Yazoo City in 1848; Hernando, January 1851 to 1857. In addition to his ministerial duties, he was Principal of Yazoo Classical Hall from 1843 to 1851 and President of Mississippi Female College from 1851 to 1857; President of Semple Broaddus College at Centre Hill, Mississippi, from 1857 to 1860; President and Professor of Theology at Mt. Lebanon University in Louisiana from 1860 to 1863. In 1845 Crane, his father and his brother, James C. Crane, were prominent in the organization of the Southern Baptist Convention. From 1851 until 1863 Dr. Crane served as one of its secretaries and later, in the '70's and '80's as a vice-president. "His opportunities had enabled him to become a profound scholar, ranking among the most useful and able Baptists in the Southern States."[15]

For twenty-two years—from August 1863 to February 1885, Dr. Crane served as president of Baylor University at Independence and for most of that time pastor of the Independence Baptist Church. Carroll termed him "the best equipped college man that had ever been in Texas," stating that he could teach anything taught in a full college course—"all the languages, ancient or modern, all the sciences. . . ."[16]

Crane believed in a broad-based curriculum with specialization only on the graduate level after students' powers had been "harmoniously developed." Otherwise study produced only "intellectual bigots" and "splinters of straw," he contended.[17]

One can hardly imagine a more herculean task than the one that faced Dr. Crane as the new president. Independence—which had been incorporated in 1852 with the strange boundary of "one mile in all directions from the center of the public square"—had felt the effects of the Civil War. At the outbreak of the conflict, Washington County, with a population of 5,424 white people, listed 5,853 slaves—worth

the little sick boy until he showed decided improvement in about a week. A few days after the guests departed, little Kate Crane died. The little Dickinson boy became Secretary of War in the Taft Administration.
[15] *Baptist Encyclopedia*, ed. William Cathcart (Philadelphia: Louis H. Everts, 1881).
[16] J. M. Carroll, *The History of Texas Baptists* (Dallas: Baptist Standard Publishing Company, 1923), p. 379.
[17] W. C. Crane, *Education: Theory, Practice, Position, and Benefits.* Pamphlet (n.d.).

on the tax rolls over $500 each. Cattle were listed at $6 per head, horses at $55, and land at $6 per acre; flour sold at $55 per 100 pounds and calico at $4 to $5 per yard. The greatest wealth of the county was in slaves; hence the freeing of the slaves was a great blow to the economy of the county. Moreover, the action revolutionized agriculture and family life in the area. The town of Independence at the beginning of the war had less than 400 people, of whom more than half were slaves. Only fifty-seven citizens were qualified voters. Young men who would have been Baylor students enlisted, and Confederate troops occupied the Baylor buildings. All colleges suffered, many closed, and Baylor was again declared dead by many contemporaries. Yet Crane wrote that the area of Independence was "one of the most beautiful sites in the South."

In competition with attempts to resurrect Baylor at the time was the newly-founded Waco University (1861) under the patronage of the Waco Baptist Association and under the direction of President Rufus C. Burleson. Fairfield Female College, in Freestone County, was headed by Reverend Henry L. Graves and boasted eight instructors; Bosque Male and Female College, eight miles from Waco, had Reverend S. G. O'Bryan as president. Each of these men previously had served at Baylor University at Independence and were followed with interest by the Baptist State Convention of Texas.[18]

The Sixteenth Baptist State Convention, meeting at Independence in October 1863, resolved to raise $10,000 to send missionaries to the Army. The convention also passed a plan for the free tuition education of disabled soldiers and the children of deceased soldiers, but no money was allocated for the implementation of the order.[19]

The Union Association Report on Education in 1863, just as Dr. Crane came to Baylor, carried a statement which Crane thought highly prejudicial and served to defeat his early efforts:

---

[18] Announcements of these schools appear in the inside cover of the Convention minutes for 1864.

[19] *Minutes of Baptist State Convention of Texas* 1863 (Houston: Telegraph Book and Job Establishment, 1864), p. 16.

The Female Department of Baylor University retains its usual patronage, while the Male Department, from various adverse circumstances, has fallen far below its former high position. "Bretheren, why is this?"

W. W. James, Chairman.

The report was anything but helpful and reflected on the judgment and observation of the chairman. In the wake of a disrupting feud and a Civil War, mere survival of the Male Department now seems astonishing.

Officially the new president was to assume responsibility at the beginning of the new year, but he began activities earlier. The president's domicile, supposed to be the residence of Dr. Crane, was filled with soldiers. Crane had written to Brother Graves about this circumstance on October 30, 1863, adding: " . . . besides I have a large and expensive family." Subsequently Crane found it necessary to apply to the Confederate general in command of the region to gain possession of the college buildings.[20] In the meantime the new president purchased a home in Independence about a block from the home occupied by Mrs. Sam Houston.[21] Here he installed his wife and six children, with a seventh due in five months. Dr. Crane's diary reveals his depression at the time:

---

[20] The Minutes of the Board make no reference to the use of the buildings by the military. A letter from Crane to General W. R. Boggs on December 18, 1863, reveals that Baylor had aided the cause of the South by drilling students who were exempt from active service and that the buildings of the university had been used as barracks for Confederate soldiers. Dr. Crane asked that, if possible, the buildings be made exempt from further use by the army. The university expressed willingness to bear the property damage estimated at $1500. Dr. Crane's request for the release of the buildings was referred to General J. B. Magruder, in command of the Trans-Mississippi Department. His favorable reply is recorded on the back of the letter. Crane Correspondence, Texas Collection, Baylor University.

[21] Dr. Crane's diary reveals that he met Mrs. Houston on the train when he came to Independence in August 1863 to confer with the Baylor Board for the first time. As pastor of the First Baptist Church at Montgomery, Alabama, he had known Mrs. Houston—then Margaret Lea. Shortly after the train conversation, Mrs. Houston, whose famous husband had died in Huntsville the previous month, moved her family to Independence to place her children in Baylor University. Houston had returned to Independence after his ejection from the governor's chair in March 1861 because of his refusal to take the oath of allegiance to the Southern Confederacy, but feeling that Baylor could not survive the traumatic Burleson-Clark feud coupled with the war crisis, he moved his family to Huntsville. Mrs. Houston returned to Independence to be near her mother and to educate her children. The second Houston daughter, Mary William, was already a Baylor student in 1883 and was joined by the third, Antoinette Power (born January 21, 1852). Antoinette developed her poetic talents and had verses published in Scribner's and the New York

November 24, 1863 . . . borrowed $1500 from F. W. Robertson of Dallas before coming to Texas.

Dec. 30, 1863 . . . mind much disturbed about personal affairs. Everything looks dark indeed, with reference to the country's prospects, Baylor University, and all the surroundings.

In anticipation of President Crane's first term at Baylor, Texas newspapers carried glowing announcements.

President Crane opened his first term at Baylor on January 11, 1864. His inaugural address, "Mind is the Standard of the Man," was termed philosophical by contemporary newspapers. Twenty-five students present at the opening increased to fifty by January 25 and to seventy-five by the end of the session. The convention report listed two hundred in both men's and women's departments.

The Baylor Board of Trustees did not meet after the mid-August 1863 session until February 5, 1864. At that time B. S. Fitzgerald was appointed collecting agent on a ten per cent commission basis for the income on the endowments and the tuition of the Male Department, but next day he was instructed "not to collect the interest on the endowment for the present." In view of the depreciation of currency, the faculties of each department were allowed to raise the tuition to three times the old rates. In line with this order, the salary of the president was increased to $4500 for the scholastic year. A special committee was ordered to have the boarding house put in good condition and to engage a person to operate it. President Crane was also authorized to employ Mr. John N. Henderson as teacher of English.[22]

Evening Post. See R. Henderson Shuffler, *The Houstons at Independence.* (Waco, Texas: Texian Press, 1966), p. 71. Son Temple Lea Houston took a Ph.B. degree at Baylor in 1878.

[22] Henderson was a member of the freshman class at Baylor in 1858 and an active Erisophian, serving as editor of the weekly club paper. At the end of his junior year in 1860 he enlisted in the first company to leave Washington County for military service in Virginia as a private in the Fifth Regiment of the Texas Brigade. At the Battle of Sharpsburg he lost an arm and returned to Independence.

In addition to his academic work at Baylor he conducted a military company—all the boys under sixteen years of age. When General J. B. Robertson was detailed to Texas in command of a Military District, he gave Henderson a place on his staff with the rank of captain. After the war when Baylor's law department was reorganized, Henderson attended. Judge James Shepherd of Brenham appointed an examining board which granted him a license, and he opened a partnership with J. S. Perry in Millican and later moved to Bryan. In 1872 he was elected district attorney "in one of the most lawless communities in the state" and persevered undauntedly to make it "among the most orderly and law-abiding districts in the state." J. S. Perry, Rockdale,

It seemed that the school was in business again, after a decline to fifteen students and facilities "without doors, without floors, without windows." Yet Dr. Crane had recorded in his diary just two days before: "Do not like the course of affairs at all. B. U. is nothing but a day school for Independence boys."

The president's duties were arduous. He taught classes for six or seven hours daily—"all of the branches of a course of college study, besides preaching twice, or often three times each Sabbath." (Dr. Crane was pastor of the Independence Baptist Church from 1864 to 1867, and from 1869 to 1884 and served as supply in the interim. He also preached monthly at Houston from July 1863 to May 1866.) During the first year of his Baylor presidency, ninety students were enrolled. The term ended in June 1864 and one young man, W. C. Crane, Jr., was awarded the A. B. degree.[23]

Assisting President Crane as faculty were William T. Etheridge, professor of languages, and L. G. Lea, principal of the pre-college department. Professor B. S. Fitzgerald was on leave to serve with the Army of Virginia.

Reverend James E. Carnes delivered "a very able, erudite, chaste and appropriate" commencement address for the Male Department of June 15. The Honorable Horace Cone delivered the address for the Female Department on the following day, with six young women composing the graduating class.

Salary adjustments were made for the following year,

Texas, March 18, 1908, to Hon. T. S. Henderson, Cameron, Texas. By permission of Judge Frank M. Wilson. President of Baylor Board of Trustees, 1967.

[23] A letter from Baylor student Belle Wallace to cousin Georgia Burleson at Waco University on July 13, 1864, is critical of this degree to Dr. Crane's son "who only went to college here not more than two months. He joined the army two months before the examination. He came home on a furlough to the examination but was not examined." President Crane was aware of "a war waged against [his] son during the full period of his continuance . . . as teacher." Crane address before Texas Baptist Convention at Galveston, 1869.

Belle also told Mrs. Burleson about her slim chances of "getting Harriet" who spins a fine thread, for "Ma was a twin too and she says she feels attached to [Harriet] and cannot sell her for any price."

See Burleson Correspondence, Texas Collection, Baylor University, also Merle Mears Duncan, *The Southwestern Historical Quarterly,* LXIV (January 1961), 368-372.

Anti-authoritarian criticism from non-boarding student Margaret Lea Houston was directed against Professor Horace Clark of the Baylor Female school: "[he is] so mean to the girls sometimes that I just want to beat him!" Margaret Lea to Lt. Sam Houston, Jr., February 18, 1864. Xerox copy, Texas Collection, Baylor University.

with the president's salary fixed at $1750, that of the professor of ancient languages at $1000, and that of the tutor at $600. It was agreed that any excess in the proceeds be divided among the faculty. President Crane later wrote that he received only $45 of the $3000 promised as his first year's salary, and that in an adjustment he compromised for $1700 specie or equivalent, payable in tuition fees which had already accrued, and four acres of land. During this session of the board Willet Holmes was appointed Bursar of the Male Department and ordered to pay to the faculty semi-annually funds accruing from tuition or the endowment fund. Tuition rates were returned to a "before the war" basis. The board established a Chair of Theology and requested the Baptist State Convention to take steps to endow the chair.[24] The following announcement released by President Garrett is significant:

Baylor University

The next Session will open on the first Monday in September and continue nine months, divided into two terms, one closing at Christmas, the other the first week in June. This University furnishes all the means for a complete education, and its standard of scholarship is as elevated as any other on the continent. Whole number of pupils entered from September, 1863, to May, 1864, 90 students. Instructors will be added to the faculty as the wants of pupils may demand it. The course of study embraces English studies, Mathematics, all the branches of Natural Science, Greek, French, Spanish, and Hebrew Languages. Lectures will be delivered by the President on Natural Philosophy, Geology, Physiology, Rhetoric, and Ethics, and by others on Chemistry and other subjects. Daily prelections will be given upon all studies by each instructor. Students are drilled one hour each day in military tactics.

Terms

Tuition $50; $40; $30 per year, Modern Languages extra. Board—including lodging, washing, table and fuels, $15 per month; Incidental Tax, $2 per year. Disabled soldiers and children of deceased soldiers, tuition free. Currency taken at commercial rates. Produce received.

Independence is unsurpassed for health, salubrity of climate, good water, high-toned citizens and religious privileges.

H. Garrett, Pres. Bd. Trustees

[24] Baptist State Convention President, Henry L. Graves, had requested the Convention Board of Tuition to make arrangements for theological instruction of "each young minister as repaired to that Institution for that purpose." April 2, 1864.

At this convention session Dr. Crane reported on Bible operations, suggesting that one-tenth of all contributions sent up to the convention be set apart to procure Bibles and Testaments to be sent through Mexico or the blockade runners for gratuitous distribution among our soldiers. Independence was to serve as the depository.

The session opened on September 5, 1864, with forty-six students, the number increasing to ninety-three by October 31. Teaching was resumed in the new stone building, and Dr. Crane recorded that he was "unwell, over-taxed with labors."[25] Nevertheless, by the end of the session, he had accepted 140 students and added W. Carey Crane, Jr., to the staff as tutor. The school was saddened by the deaths of original trustees A. C. Horton and Aaron Shannon during the school year. Horton died at his home on the Matagorda coast on September 1, 1865. Shannon died in July 1865 at his Grimes County plantation. The two trustees who supplied Baylor with school bells died the same year—after twenty years of service as trustees.

When President Crane came to Independence, he was well aware of the situation into which he stepped. He was determined to avoid any complicity in the aftermath of the Clark-Burleson controversy, which "old timers chose never to forget." In August 1863 Dr. Burleson wrote Dr. Crane a very cordial letter welcoming him to Texas as pastor of the First Baptist Church of Houston—a position he himself vacated to become president of Baylor University. Shortly thereafter when he heard that Crane had been persuaded to accept the presidency of Baylor instead of the Houston pastorate, he wrote him another letter, blunt and tactless, assuring him that Baylor was dead and that his labors would be fruitless, terming the venture "Icabod!"

In October 1864 Dr. Crane and Dr. Burleson had their first meeting in Texas[26]—at Providence Church in Burleson County. Characteristic of his meticulousness and sense of history, Crane recorded and preserved a complete memorandum of the visit. One paragraph of the recorded conversation may have had its influence on President Burleson:

[25] J. M. Carroll, *A History of Texas Baptists* (Dallas, Texas: Baptist Standard Publishing Company), 1923, p. 382.

[26] Dr. Crane was pastor of the First Baptist Church of Columbus, Mississippi, when Burleson—about ten years his junior—was teaching school in the vicinity in preparation to attend Western Baptist Theological Institute at Covington, Kentucky. The two men became friends and Crane loaned Burleson books from his personal library. (Reminiscences of Mrs. Catherine Crane, Sweetwater, Texas, Texas Collection Baylor University.) Letters written by Burleson and now in Baylor's Texas Collection reveal the satisfaction the younger man derived from the friendship. On June 8, 1845, at Starkville, Mississippi, Dr. Crane preached the ordination sermon when Burleson was ordained and, as previously noted, Crane's signature appears on the Burleson credentials.

Dr. Burleson said he could not consent that Waco University should be ignored as a Baptist school. I repeated the position of my letter to him in September 1863 written from Houston to the effect that there was room enough for both universities in the state; that I was willing to pass resolutions in favor of Waco University, but could not consent to taking it under the Convention on an equality with Baylor University, as that would work badly. I instanced Mississippi College and Semple Broadus College and said that it would be better for him to have a Northern organization if one was needed for his university.[27]

In 1868 the Baptist General Association, embracing Waco Association and what was formerly Trinity Association, was organized with Dr. Burleson as one of its leaders and officers. Haynes, in his Burleson biography, stated that "the real reason for changing the name of the East Texas Convention" and extending its jurisdiction to include the Waco Association was to "give the new Body the undisputed right to foster Waco University. . . ." Haynes concluded that Dr. R. C. Burleson was "largely instrumental in inducing the East Texas Convention to practically dissolve and surrender the situation to the new organization."[28]

No explanation is given in the Baylor board minutes for failure to convene at the designated September 1 meeting. On December 4, 1864, however, the board assembled pursuant to the call of the president. Evidently funds were not available to pay salaries, for "the committee to settle with professors was allowed further time." W. T. Etheridge was named associate professor of ancient languages and L. G. Lea's continuance as tutor was referred to a committee. The next meeting was scheduled for January but did not convene until April 5, 1865. The committee appointed at the June meeting reported the following indebtedness: to President Crane $80.76 plus $2760 previously due; to B. S. Fitzgerald $157.67, and to John N. Henderson $150.00. The committee recommended that collections be made on the dues to the endowment funds in order to discharge the claims. Evidently Hillyer resigned at the end of the June 1865 term, for B. S. Fitzgerald was named professor of mathematics on July 8, 1865.[29]

[27] Crane Papers, Texas Collection, Baylor University.
[28] Harry Haynes, *Life and Writings of Dr. Rufus C. Burleson* (Compiled and published by Mrs. Georgia J. Burleson, 1901), p. 403.
[29] Minutes of the Baylor Board of Trustees, p. 191.
Hillyer suffered the loss of his slaves and all of his property during the

Dr. Crane's detailed report shows the fees collected by the faculty members to pay their own salaries. The board also considered a long-due bill of $179.41 to Mr. Ross for lime furnished B. S. Fitzgerald for the East building. The board failed to meet in June, but on July 8, 1865, the lime bill was referred to a special committee. The matter was delayed until June 1866, when Mr. Ross was finally paid $1.25 per bushel for 114 bushels, with interest from the time of delivery.

The school year had presented myriad problems for President Crane, as the following excerpts from correspondence with Baylor patrons indicate:

... son anxious to come ... have only Confederate money ... have heard expenses must be paid in specie. ... [30]

... wish to know if your institution comes under the order of the Secretary of War respecting students between the ages of 17 and 18. Also can cotton pay tuition ... have it on hand and may not be able to sell without great loss—can give any security you wish. [31]

Then fate and the weather seemed to hamper the barter-business:

... son is ill and can't return ... with regard to the hams I was saving for you, the weather has been so unfavorable that I have saved no meat with the bone in it. As yet the cold spells have been too short. ... [32]

war years. He moved to Lockhart and taught and preached for about twenty years in Bastrop, Travis, Burleson, and Milam Counties. In 1865 the Baptist State Convention passed resolutions supporting his intention "to work among the colored population." (See Carroll, p. 341). Hillyer was active in Baptist organizations, helping to organize the Georgia Baptist Convention, the Southern Baptist Convention at Augusta in 1845, and the Texas Baptist State Convention at Anderson in 1848. He served as Moderator of the San Marcos Association and Chaplain for the House of Representatives of Texas from January 12 to May 4, 1874, and from January 12 to March 15, 1875. (Lorene Hillyer Fox to Lily M. Russell, April 12, 1955). Baylor University awarded former mathematics Professor John F. Hillyer the LL.D. degree on July 9, 1883. (See Minutes of the Board of Trustees, p. 328).

John F. Hillyer died on December 12, 1893, at Belton, Texas. Judge R. E. B. Baylor ranked him "among our ablest preachers." He also praised his love for mechanics, stating that he could make anything out of iron or wood. During the war he made looms and spinning wheels for the women. (See R. E. B. Baylor, "Sketch of Hillyer," MS in Texas Collection, Baylor University.) Hillyer's brother, Shaler Granby Hillyer, also taught at Mercer and served as a trustee. His second wife was Elizabeth Dagg, daughter of Mercer's president, Reverend J. L. Dagg. Brother Junius was a member of Congress and also a Mercer trustee. (See *Mercer University Centennial Brochure*.) Many descendants of John F. Hillyer have attended Baylor University.

[30] Wm. Herndon to President Crane, January 6, 1865. Crane Correspondence, Texas Collection, Baylor University.

[31] W. L. Cochran, Colita, Polk County, to President Crane, January 16, 1865.

[32] J. J. Anderson, Wharton, Texas, to President Crane, January 8, 1865.

. . . as to potatoes, I was absent from home when they were dug and nearly all were destroyed before I reached home and many that were put up rotted for want of attention. . . . As for the La. money, I spent it at 3 for 1 on the Mississippi River so the $40.00 La. money will be worth $14 in specie. This was the best I could do which I hope will be satisfactory to you. [33]

. . . regretted very much that we missed Mr. Grant's wagon . . . had enough provisions to defray nearly all of the expenses. . . . We still have the butter . . . could have sent some down on horseback but we received a note from Mrs. Ross that there was no sale for old butter down there . . . (that dreadful Yegua was out of banks) . . . if we can't succeed in sending you provisions Mama is perfectly willing to give you her note if she fails in collecting some money owing to her. [34]

Other letters solicited President Crane's support of controversial issues:

. . . I would make no terms with the Yankees . . . We have no right to free our slaves. God has placed them in their present condition, and all past experience proved it to be the best condition for the African race and it is our duty to contend for it to the bitter end. Can't you write one or two short articles for the papers on this subject. [35]

Appeals of young men seeking education were always answered by Dr. Crane; he usually found some way to resolve their problems. His diary, which he kept from about his eighteenth year, reveals many of these "trades." On one account he took a black milch cow as tuition; from a boy named Kirk (who became a doctor), he took a span of gray horses. These—"Rob" and "Roy"—Crane hitched to his old "rockaway" bought at Baltimore for $400 out of his father's estate. Eggs became the commodity of barter for a German named Dreese, who brought the eggs wrapped in tree moss and packed in saddle bags. A young man, John G. Boyle, just discharged from the Federal Army, came to Dr. Crane

[33] J. L. Farquhar to President Crane, January 20, 1865.

[34] Ella Hill, Brazos Bottom, Texas, to President Crane, February 9, 1865.

[35] A. S. Broaddus, Caldwell, Burleson County, to President Crane, January 28, 1865. Mr. Broaddus desired a new Baptist paper, as did M. I. Young of Houston, who wrote to Crane on January 17, 1865, concerning the possibility of another publication, with the "hope that our people are prepared for better things than *The Texas Baptist*."

R. N. Richardson in "Literature and Scholarship," *Centennial Story of Texas Baptists*, p. 349, terms *The Texas Baptist*, established in January 1855, "the first denominational newspaper" in the state. *The Texas Baptist Herald*, also a weekly, became the successor of *The Texas Baptist* in 1865 under the editorship of J. B. Link. The *Texas Baptist Standard* established in 1892 under editorship of M. V. Smith and J. B. Cranfill attained the distinction of the greatest circulation of any Baptist paper in America.

penniless but ready to work for an education. Crane gave him work, schooling, and board.[36] A student reported that the president of Baylor University said that "the sons of deceased soldiers would receive their education there free of charge" and cites two cases: Wm. J. Rutledge and Robert Edward Rice.[37]

Dr. Crane acquired some half dozen tracts of land in exchange for "schooling." One, a tract of eighty acres in the bend of the Guadalupe River between Kyle and San Marcos, paid for the education of Sam H. Dixon, Texas historian; another, in Coryell County, paid for "the schooling" of William S. Graves until he went to West Point and subsequently became a major general in the U. S. Army.[38]

Several Baylor men achieved high m i l i t a r y honors. Lawrence Sullivan Ross, a Baylor student in 1855-1856 (who transferred to Wesleyan University of Florence, Alabama) enlisted with the Texas troops as a private. In three years he became a brigadier general on December 21, 1863, for his outstanding service at Corinth, Mississippi, in 1862. Then he commanded the Sixth Texas Regiment.[39] Baylor man Felix H. Robertson, who went from Baylor to West Point, at twenty-five became the youngest Confederate brigadier general. He served under General Joseph Wheeler at Charleston Harbor and at the Fort Sumter bombardment.[40] Charles Isaac Evans, sophomore at Baylor in 1861, enlisted as a private in the Second Texas Infantry in July 1861. At the end of the war he was artillery lieutenant in Jones' Texas Battalion and gave the order to fire the last shot at Palmito Ranch—the final skirmish of the war.[41]

President Crane's son Willie enlisted on May 21, 1864, and Crane endeavored to maintain military training for the under-age boys left at Baylor. Early in 1865 he wrote the Confederate military regional headquarters requesting rifles

---

[36] This young man became assistant attorney general of Texas and United States District Attorney for the Galveston District.

[37] E. C. Warton letter to "Dear Uncle," Houston, February 1, 1865. Crane Correspondence, Texas Collection, Baylor University.

[38] Reminiscences of R. C. Crane, Texas Collection, Baylor University.

[39] Victor M. Rose, *Ross' Texas Brigade* (Louisville: Courier Journal Book and Job Rooms, 1881), p. 168.

[40] Margaret Royalty Edwards, "Baylor's Generals," MS in Texas Collection, Baylor University, 1963, p. 38.

[41] *Ibid.,* p. 5-9; 18-21.

for the college military training program. On February 18, 1865, he received this terse reply: "There are no arms in the hands of the military authorities here that can be opened to you."[42]

An unfortunate incident occurred in the schoolroom some time in April 1865. Fifteen-year-old John L. Creek, ward of O. H. P. Garrett, "misbehaved in recitation hall, pulled out his knife, and ran downstairs." The faculty, composed of Dr. Crane, Professor W. T. Etheridge, and Mr. John W. Harris (pro tem), suspended him until Monday, "requiring him to keep to his room." The young man defied suspension, went uptown and attended a concert at the Female College. He was then suspended until the end of the session in June.

Crane's memorandum r e c o r d s that President Hosea Garrett called the faculty together and proposed "that Crane whip him [reference not clear]" but the proposal was rejected. Crane did not soon forget the circumstance, for he recorded: "Neither prior to that time, nor since, during the present presidency has Hon. O. H. P. Garrett patronized either this or any other Baptist School in the U. S. by sending his sons there." Crane later noted, however, that Garrett did not refuse to pay his interest "as per bill made"—the last being in July 1868 to the chair of Natural Science.[43]

A letter from Dr. Crane to Board President Garrett the following month, May 1865, revealed further complications. "Brother Clark without conference has announced that he would have no examination." Since Baylor University and Baylor Female College were interdependent in many ways, communication between the two would have been highly desirable. Crane stated that many boys would leave with their sisters and that under the circumstances he would be compelled to close school on Friday, June 2. He planned to examine all pupils present and hold an "exhibition" Monday night "if we can have any appearance of success." He requested a trustee meeting on Friday and concluded his note with "Confusion reigns in this region."[44]

[42] Confederate Regional Command to President R. C. Crane, February 18, 1865. Crane Papers, Texas Collection, Baylor University.

[43] Crane Papers, Texas Collection, Baylor University.

[44] Crane to Garrett, May 25, 1865. Crane Correspondence, Texas Collection, Baylor University.

One small matter brought a compliment to the heavily burdened president. On January 6, 1865, the Office of the Provost Marshall General sent him a General Pass for the year for the District of Texas, New Mexico, and Arizona.

At the July 8, 1865, meeting of the Baylor Board of Trustees, members agreed to sell to President Crane "that portion of the Male College lot lying between Roberts' lot and a line drawn from the line between Burleson's lot and the Round House lot, maintaining the same width up to the town lots, at fifty dollars per acre," thereon to build a suitable president's residence.[45] The balance due Dr. Crane on his salary to July 1864 ($183.46) was to be taken as part payment, with his note for the remainder.

Then the following appointments were made for the ensuing year:

W. T. Etheridge, Professor of Ancient Languages, $1000
B. S. Fitzgerald, Professor of Mathematics, $1200
Wm. C. Crane, Jr., Tutor in Preparatory Dept., $400

A committee was appointed to correspond with gentlemen to fill the chairs in the law department, and President Crane was authorized to employ instructors in music for the Male Department without expense to the board.

Principal Horace Clark presented the names of three young women who were awarded degrees. The degree of Master of Arts was conferred on Horace Clark and Ben S. Fitzgerald by order of the board.

The first term of the 1866 school year brought President Crane added anxiety because of a decline in enrollment. In a letter to Trustee A. G. Haynes he stated that "Texas was not in the theatre of the war" and that the trustees should be active in building student enrollment.[46]

A circular on the Female Department of Baylor University announced the faculty for 1866, stating that the institution was now in its twentieth year—fifteen under the same principal—and had graduated ten classes. Attendance for the past year was listed as 180, with the present senior class as

[45] An interlinear insertion in the minutes in the handwriting of Dr. W. C. Crane states that the president's home built in 1881-2 was not placed on this property, but on land purchased from W. A. Baldwin.

[46] Crane to Haynes, March 29, 1866. Crane Correspondence, Texas Collection, Baylor University.

11. Board, exclusive of washing and lights, was $12.50 per month. The following quotation was added inducement:

Peculiar advantages are offered to young ladies of energy and talent who wish to qualify themselves for *Teachers*. A diploma from this institution is a passport to any position as an educator of youth.[47]

The trustees were due to convene on February 8, 1866, but a quorum was not present. The members in attendance agreed to hold an informal meeting subject to ratification or rejection at the next regular meeting. Judge W. P. Hill was appointed principal professor in the law department at a salary of $1000, and Judge R. T. Smyth associate with a salary of $600; Judge James E. Shepherd and the Honorable John Sayles were named associates without salary.[48] The annual sessions of the law department were designated as three and a half months in duration. The resignation of Professor Fitzgerald was received and accepted at this meeting, and the books of the endowment fund were handed over to President Crane. He was authorized to make collections to repair buildings and get subscriptions to the endowment funds. These actions were ratified by the board at the June 6, 1866, meeting.

Trustee resignations added discouragement to Baylor officials. In May, W. A. Montgomery wrote Reverend Garrett, Board President, that he felt that he could "not be of any benefit to the University or to the Denomination by my position as a trustee." He extended his respect, esteem, and entire and hearty sympathy.[49] Another resignation came

[47] Circular, Clark Papers, Texas Collection, Baylor University.
A writer for *The Galveston News* at this time applauded the young women of Baylor Female Department, stating that they "all wrote the same kind of 'hand,' read alike and possessed the same kind of demeanor." Credit was given to Professor Clark, whom the girls revered.

[48] J. S. Perry wrote that the law department was placed in charge of Judge Smyth of Montgomery County in 1866. He was a member of the class with J. N. Henderson, N. R. Green, I. J. Newman, a Mr. Robinson, Bledsoe Davidson, John Roberts, M. M. McCraw, and A. P. Perry. He termed Smyth "a very painstaking and accurate instructor." Before the opening of the second term Smyth was forced to give up his work with the class because he "had almost entirely lost his eyesight." See J. S. Perry to T. S. Henderson, *loc. cit.*
Judge William Pinckney Hill was mayor of Bastrop in 1839. An able attorney, he became district judge after secession when Confederate courts replaced the U. S. District Courts in Texas. See *The Handbook of Texas* (Austin: The State Historical Association, 1952), II, 815.

[49] W. A. Montgomery to Rev. H. Garrett, May 7, 1866. Garrett Letters, Texas Collection, Baylor University. His resignation was accepted at the Oct. 10, 1866, meeting.

from A. S. Broaddus, who gave reasons of "ill health and pecuniary affairs" and included warmest interest in success.[50]

At the June 6, 1866, trustee meeting President Crane was granted leave to travel "either to the North or South" without abridgement of salary as an authorized agent to receive funds for the university. He was also to receive travel expenses and the payment of "any deficit which may accrue on account of his absences from churches under his charge."

President Crane missed the closing exercises of June 1866. In a letter to Reverend Garrett he states that he left all papers "expected of me" with Trustee George W. Graves. The following excerpt from the letter indicates the seriousness of the breach between Crane and Garrett:

> . . . I feel greatly wronged in the allegation made as to the government of B. U. and can hardly think that friendship for me or regard for the cause of Christ and education in Texas could have dictated it. I forgive those who meant no harm. Twenty-five years' experience should save me from such imputations. Please converse *freely* when you next visit Independence with Brother Haynes and Brother McKnight. I have striven for harmony at Independence and I shall always strive for it. . . . I hope the denomination generally will reach the conclusion that Texas has room enough for two or three excellent colleges.[51]

President Crane's report listed 106 students in the Male Division, including 14 in the law department, enrolled for the term ending June 1866. Principal Clark reported 80 in the Female Division and presented 9 young ladies who had earned degrees. Examinations were held in both departments from June 1 to 7. Colonel Ashbel Smith, who delivered the commencement address for the Female Department, and Professor Clark, who delivered the baccalaureate sermon, were requested to give the board copies for publication in the *Houston Telegraph*.

Finances continued to be the chief concern at the June 1866 trustee session. Mr. Etheridge presented his resignation, the reason for which undoubtedly was absence of salary. The resignation was tabled; then at a third session of the trustees, it was accepted "with the understanding with

[50] A. S. Broaddus, Burleson County, to Rev. H. Garrett, June 4, 1866. Garrett Letters, Texas Collection, Baylor University.
[51] Crane to Garrett from Galveston, June 6, 1866. Garrett Letters, Texas Collection, Baylor University.

Professor Etheridge that the salaries of the president and faculty be paid from the tuition fees and endowment fund as agreed upon."[52] Trustees A. G. Haynes and M. A. Bryan were requested to witness the settlement between President Crane and Professor Etheridge.

Principal Horace Clark of the Female Department was granted a leave of absence for twelve months on condition that he procure the services of B. S. Fitzgerald and a sufficient number of teachers to operate the department during his absence. Since Mr. Clark received all the tuition fees, he was requested to keep the building and fences in good condition and to repair "the defect now in the walls and chimney before further damage results to the building." President Crane was given authorization to collect funds and to receive donations of land or other property "for the repairs of the old buildings and the completion of the one partly erected and for additional apparatus, furniture, books."

The committee to select law school personnel reported that R. T. Smyth, as resident professor at a salary of $600, was now holding classes for nine young men. The calculated financial loss on the session was $150. Honorable John Sayles had agreed to deliver a course of lectures on pleadings during the month, with voluntary assistance from Honorable James Shepherd. Both men served without remuneration.

One fortunate circumstance became a high hope for Baylor. Moses Austin Bryan offered to give the sorely plagued university a choice of several tracts of land. The trustees decided on the one containing about 1107 acres lying between Old Caney and Bernard Creek on Cedar Lake and passed

---

[52] Another indication of the destitute treasury is the correspondence between English teacher John N. Henderson, President Crane, and H. Garrett. President Crane gave Henderson notes on Mrs. Hatfield "netting only $66, leaving a balance due of $65." Then the interest on a note against Thomas N. Henderson was given, leaving still an unpaid balance of $32. Henderson wrote to Board President Garrett requesting "other good paper of the university" in payment. See John N. Henderson to Garrett, Chappell Hill, June 18, 1866. Garrett Letters, Texas Collection, Baylor University.

As late as 1869 correspondence about the matter continued, for Dr. Crane wrote to him: "Baylor U. promised me $3000 for the year 1864 . . . I compromised with the Trustees for what I could get of tuition fees. I was promised $1750 for 1865-6 and it has stood nominally at that sum ever since, although I have not annually received one-half of the amount. Besides that I have advanced $1200 in gold for repairs, for which I *may* get lands. I paid also $50 in gold to make up Judge Smyth's salary." See Crane to Henderson, April 26, 1867. Crane Correspondence, Texas Collection, Baylor University.

resolutions of gratitude to Major Bryan for his liberal donation, estimated to be eight or ten thousand dollars. Again the
board ordered its president to write and publish a circular
"setting forth the conditions and prospects of the university."
And the building committee was allowed to use part of the
endowment fund for the Chair of Natural Science due from
the estate of Dr. Hoxie and $100 paid recently by Mr.
Hubbard for the purpose of repairs.

Life at Independence was not all grim. The old Baptist
church was the scene of many brilliant weddings in early
Texas days. On August 1, 1866, Houston's first daughter—a
Baylor student—Miss Nancy Elizabeth Houston and Cap-
tain Joseph Clay Stiles Morrow were united in marriage by
Dr. William Carey Crane, President of Baylor University.
Mrs. Crane made the wedding dress—"a white moire silk
with real Valenciennes lace, which was featured in a current
magazine." After the wedding, friends assembled in the
Houston home. "Nannie in her wedding gown took her seat
at the piano. Tenderly she caressed the keys and sang . . .
'Sad Hour of Parting,' " wrote Mrs. W. A. Wood.[53]

The second Houston daughter, Margaret Lea, was married
at the Independence Baptist Church on October 17, 1866,
to Captain Weston Lafayette Williams. Dr. Crane again
was the celebrant.[54] Another wedding uniting two prominent
Washington County families was that of Miss Blue and
Colonel Ben S. Rogers.

---

[53] Mrs. W. A. Wood, "Sad Hour of Parting," *The Century* (November
1940), Baylor University, p. 7. The wedding dress is in the Houston Memorial
Museum in Huntsville.

The Steinway No. 4079, a gift from General Houston to his eldest daughter
on her fifteenth birthday, September 6, 1861, was shipped from New York to
Augusta Santleleen of Galveston; then by schooner it crossed the Bay to
Cedar Point, and by wagon to the Houston home. Successive moves finally
brought the piano to Georgetown in 1876 with the bride, where it remained
for thirty years. In 1896 Nancy offered the use of the piano to her cousins,
Mr. and Mrs. William Morrow of Taylor. In 1903 Mrs. Nannie Elizabeth
Morrow presented the beloved instrument to Baylor University's Texas Col-
lection through President S. P. Brooks.

[54] Reminiscences of Sallie Trice Thompson, Baylor Class of 1892.

The Williams' daughter Madge was married to Roy Hearne in a double
wedding ceremony many years later in the same setting. The other couple was
Adele Robertson and Hoxie Williams. Dr. Burleson was the minister.

CHAPTER XI

Land Grant Proposal and Two Baylors

PRESIDENT CRANE WAS WELL acquainted with the program of grants to denominational schools in the state of Louisiana, where some $200,000 had been distributed to Catholic, Episcopalian, Methodist and Presbyterian schools. Aware of the repeated efforts of Baylor officers to acquire a land grant, he resurrected the proposal of Texas land grants to colleges. Austin College had repeatedly sought the collaboration of Baylor in such an endeavor; now Houston Academy joined in the effort. Dr. Crane, abetted by Independence support, went to Houston in early July 1866 to confer with ministers and educators. He was named chairman of a committee to serve with M. J. Hancock of Houston Academy and Samuel McKinney of Austin College to memorialize the Texas Legislature to establish a public school system, a normal college and a state university. The bill was drawn up with the help of friend Ashbel Smith, H. M. Rospton, and C. L. Robards. It embraced these provisions: (1) that 10,000 acres of land should be appropriated to each college and university in the State of Texas which had a chartered existence during the past ten years (1855-1865) and was now in successful operation with not less than three officers in its faculty; (2) that 5,000 acres of land be granted for each five years of operation.[1]

Undoubtedly Board President Garrett was unaware of the action, for a letter from Crane to Garrett contains the following illuminating excerpts:

Yours of 16*th* instant is before me.

In reply, I take pleasure in saying first that at the instance of James W. Baines, A. G. Haynes, G. W. Graves, and M. A. Bryan, upon the money of Montgomery, F. W. Morris, W. A. Baldwin, Capt. Williams and other half of my own, I went to Austin to secure an appropriation of land for all chartered colleges and universities of Texas. Rev. Samuel McKinney, E. E., Pres. of Austin College, Huntsville, suggested the plan. He was joined by M. J. Hancock,

---

[1] Original Bill in Archives, Texas Collection, Baylor University. Undated clipping in Crane Scrapbook, "Legislative Aid to Existing Colleges and Universities." Crane Papers, Texas Collection, Baylor University.

Principal of Houston Academy. After consulting with all the prominent members of the Legislature, all the Departments, and the Governor (who aided in maturing the bill) I drew up a bill. . . .

My consultations with members of the Legislature satisfied me that separate female institutions at Chappell Hill, Waco, etc., would apply for lands, and that our institutions were at present organized [so that] those places would obtain twice as much as we would. I, therefore, upon consulting with J. D. Giddings and Bro. Shaw of Colorado, drew up a bill in conjuncting Baylor Female College, in accordance with views expressed and conversed about which we intended to present at Convention between H. Clark, A. G. Haynes, W. A. Montgomery, J. McKnight and others. This bill places its instance in the Enacting clause upon the words "by and with the consent of Trustees of Baylor University." Its closing clause reads nearly as follows:

The Baptist State Convention of Texas shall maintain a supervisory power over said Baylor Female College, and at its next session after the passage of this bill shall appoint fifteen citizens of Texas Trustees of Baylor Female College who shall be divided into three classes. . . .

To make the system uniform and place Baylor University in the same relation to the Convention . . . a bill adopting the same trustee plan was devised.

I assume all the responsibility under the extraordinary circumstances of obtaining appropriations for both institutions of drawing up *act of incorporation for Baylor Female College*, subject to the satisfaction of the Trustees of Baylor University and of getting the other bills as part of whole plan before the Legislature.

I made a full statement of these matters to Church here—and to all Trustees whom I have met—and from Bro. Baylor, last Sabbath received his most hearty affirmal. Hoping these facts will be an answer to your enquiries.

I am yours in Gospel bond.

Wm. Carey Crane.[2]

Before Garrett could receive a reply to his letter to Dr. Crane, he received a letter from J. W. Barnes informing him that he had seen a notice in the proceedings of the Legislature relating to charter changes and trustee elections of Baylor University. "How is that?" he queried, and then wrote "Knowing that the institution has its enemies I sense apprehensions of *foul play*." Barnes requested a reply and suggested that he stop the proceedings by "Telegraph" until he can see the object and *"who* it is at work on this delicate subject."[3]

[2] President Crane, Independence, to Reverend Hosea Garrett, September 19, 1866, Texas Collection, Baylor University.
[3] Article alluded to appeared in the *Daily Telegraph*, September 13, 1866. Barnes letter to Garrett, September 17, 1866, Garrett Letters, Texas Collection, Baylor University.

A second letter from Barnes to Garrett states that "His [Crane's] excuse to me for proposing to separate the Institution was to take advantage of the donation of lands—very good if he accomplishes it."[4]

The Baylor Board of Trustees filed no minutes for the designated meeting on July 10, the next meeting being held on October 6, 1866. Then the trustees requested the Baptist State Convention—in session at Independence—to appoint a committee of seven to confer with the Baylor trustees "relative to a proposed change touching the interest of Baylor University." J. W. D. Creath was appointed to convey this request to the convention. Nine, instead of seven, were named to meet with the Baylor trustees.[5]

After the joint session, the committee reported to the convention their sanction of the two bills passed on September 28, 1866, by the Legislature of the State of Texas relating (1) to the separation of the Male and Female Departments of Baylor University and (2) to the classification and election of the Board of Trustees.[6] The convention adopted the report and recommended it to the Baylor Board, which approved the legislative act authorizing the Board of Trustees of Baylor University to divide itself into three equal classes and regulate their election.[7] Then the trustees at this four-day meeting approved the act of the Legislature "to incorporate the Board of Trustees of Baylor Female College and to regulate the mode of their election."

Trustee Garrett submitted the detailed report of his agency, showing a balance of notes on hand of $2876.73 after deduction of $568.44 for salary and expenses. At his request, Mr. Garrett was relieved of his responsibility. A

[4] Barnes to Garrett, September 24, 1866, Garrett Letters, Texas Collection, Baylor University.
[5] The Baptist State Convention appointed J. J. Sledge, G. W. Baines, P. B. Chandler, J. B. Link, F. M. Law, P. Harris, T. S. Allen, W. A. Montgomery, and C. R. Breedlove, who sat in joint session with the Baylor Board of Trustees.
[6] Gammel's *Laws*, V, 1265.
[7] By ballot the board divided itself in the following manner:
First class: G. W. Graves, J. L. Farquhar, N. Kavanaugh, J. S. Lester, and vacancy (resignation of W. A. Montgomery). Members of this class were to serve one year. (Upon the resignation of Lester, Dr. Joseph A. Holland was elected and took his seat at the December 6 meeting.)
Second class: R. E. B. Baylor, J. W. Barnes, T. J. Jackson, J. G. Thomas, and E. G. Mays. Members were to serve two years.
Third class: H. Garrett, A. G. Haynes, J. W. D. Creath, A. S. Broaddus, and M. A. Bryan. Members were to serve three years.
Minutes of Baylor Trustees, October 10, 1866, p. 238.

committee was appointed to confer with F. M. Law about accepting the agency.

While the Baylor trustees and the convention were in session, President Crane received the news of the failure of his great plan. The Texas Legislature reached the unfavorable decision because they termed it unwise to enter into denominational affairs,[8] but Dr. Crane felt that "the enemies of Baylor" had defeated the proposal.

Before the end of the year the Board of Trustees of Baylor Female College was duly organized and reported to the Baylor University Board on December 6 that they "were ready to receive any communication it might wish to make." Immediately a committee was appointed to confer with the Board of Baylor Female College to adjust property and other matters.[9] Elder F. M. Law declined the appointment of General Agent and A. E. Vandivere was named for one year. Every effort was to be made for the collection of interest due on the endowment funds for the presidency and the chair of natural science in order to assure the faculty of support. Thanks were extended to Professor Wm. A. Montgomery, and he was asked to continue as professor of political economy and English. John B. Berryman was appointed professor of mathematics and natural science, and W. C. Crane, Jr., (who tendered his resignation) was thanked for his able execution of duties as tutor.

With the legal separation of Baylor Female College, Baylor University published a catalogue for her twenty-first year (from January 1886 to January 1887).[10] Several things of interest were announced: the Board of Visitors to conduct the annual examination in June 1867 included Governor J. W. Throckmorton, and a Lowe Printing Press was "attached to the institution." Buildings then in use were Graves Hall, a stone structure with four study-and-recitation rooms; the two-story Houston Hall with five study-and-recitation rooms, a library and apparatus rooms; the incomplete Tryon Hall also in stone, and the twelve-room

[8] F. F. Foscue to Dr. Crane, October 8, 1866, Crane Correspondence, Texas Collection, Baylor University.

On December 7, 1866, a news story by W. C. Crane appeared under the title, "Legislative Aid to Existing Colleges and Universities." Crane Scrapbook, Texas Collection, Baylor University.

[9] This committee consisted of G. W. Graves, J. McKnight and J. A. Holland.

[10] Baylor University Catalogue, 1866-1867 (Houston: Gray, Smallwood and Company, Book and Job Printers).

cedar octagonal Burleson Domicile. Mention was made of the current newspapers and periodicals in the library and the daily mail and railroad facilities available by stage connections.

A slight change had been made in the education of ministers. Candidates for the ministry might receive free tuition upon examination and approval by the Directors of the Texas Baptist State Convention. Funds appropriated by churches were to be donated to them in sums not exceeding $150 per year.[11]

University regulations affecting students deserve notice. President Crane held weekly faculty meetings, where he requested a report on the standing of each student. Students were required to attend religious services each morning and evening in the chapel. The twenty disciplinary laws listed were much the same as those in earlier catalogues except for Sabbath observation. Students were expected to attend public worship on Sunday morning or report to the faculty. Attendance at any church was considered a failure if the student entered after the services began or left it before the close: "imperious necessity alone will be taken as an excuse."[12]

Despite the dejection resulting from the failure of the land grant bill, Baylor opened auspiciously in September. Pretense was short-lived, however. On September 16, 1867, Dr. Crane recorded in his *Diary*: "Terrific panic on account of yellow-fever at Brenham." Again on September 20, he wrote: "Panic over town, half the people did take flight. Students dispersed until it was necessary to suspend classes." Dr. Crane took his family to Sulphur Springs. When the scare subsided after a few weeks, classes were resumed.

Although two years had passed since the war, the pangs of reconstruction were daily demonstrated on the college scene. The following responses to bills sent out by the president indicate the state of affairs in the Baylor constituency:

. . . not in my power to send any money . . . until I can force collections of moneys now due me. I will not be able to pay anything.[13]

[11] *Ibid.*, p. 15.

[12] *Ibid.*, p. 26.

[13] David Ferguson to Dr. Crane, March 15, 1866, Crane Correspondence, Texas Collection, Baylor University.

. . . for the school bill I will try to trade you land for I have no money . . . and my salary [is] only thirty a month.[14]

. . . I may possibly attend next session. And I will settle [previous bill] at the end of the year . . . that is if I can draw on my crop.[15]

The policy of paying the faculty on a percentage basis of the tuition collected was the unsatisfactory but necessary method used. Many who could afford the luxury sent their children to out-of-state schools. President Crane decried the fact and wrote an article for *The Ranger,* declaring the action a "bitter reflection upon the scholars of Texas . . . and a questionable patriotism."[16]

Of significance at the first trustee meeting of the year on January 8, 1867, was the communication from President Crane and R. T. Smyth, resident professor of law, recommending the LL.B. degree for John N. Henderson and D. R. Bledsoe, who had completed the prescribed course of study. They were the last law degrees conferred by Baylor at Independence, making a total of thirty-one awarded.

At the June 18, 1867, meeting an executive committee was appointed to act for the board when a quorum was not present, their acts to be submitted to the board for ratification.[17] Extremely discouraging to Dr. Crane had been the difficulty of assembling the trustees, and the executive committee seemed an expedient measure. The yellow fever epidemic and other illness affected meetings. During the year 1867 Trustee T. J. Jackson was lost by death.

At the June commencement Colonel John Kerr Connally delivered the address and Reverend H. F. Buckner the sermon.

Reddin Andrews, student at the time, recalled many years later his impressions of this spectacular affair. Colonel Connally, a Virginian then practicing law in Galveston, had lost an arm in a Civil War battle. The subject of his commencement address was "The Burial Ground of the Nations," which the student characterized as "painfully eloquent." His graphic recollection of the address gives a vivid sample of the oratory of the age:

[14] J. M. Tryon to President Crane, February 19, 1867.
[15] J. I. Hill to President Crane, April 27, 1867.
[16] Article in Crane Scrapbook, Texas Collection, Baylor University.
[17] The executive committee was composed of A. G. Haynes, John McKnight, M. A. Bryan, G. W. Graves, and J. A. Holland.

"I have to thank you for the invitation you have given me, a stranger, to speak to you on this delightful occasion. Stranger, did I say? If to have been born of a Southern mother and fondled by a Southern sire; if to have fought, aye, to have bled (touching the stump of his lost arm) in the same glorious cause, be a bond that unites us, then I am no stranger here, but, with a heart for any fate, am one amongst this people.'

Andrews said that he then sketched the history of the rise and fall of the nations: when Greece was buried, "the ghost of Miltiades still stalked across the Plains of Marathon; . . . Ireland was The Emerald Isle, a dimple in the broad face of the deep; and lastly . . . the new-made grave—the expiration and burial of the young Confederacy—and bedewed with our tears." The subject, the occasion, the circumstances made the orator transcendently great and overpowering in his eloquence, declared Andrews, and every eye was suffused with tears.[18]

Again arrangements were made for the publication of the addresses. The A.M. degree was conferred on William Carey Crane, Jr., and Elder H. F. Buckner of Independence. The D.D. degree was awarded William Shelton, President of West Tennessee College, and Daniel P. Bester of Columbus, Mississippi. This occasion was the first on which the university went afield for recipients of honorary degrees. The action brought prestige to the school. Of interest, too, was the commencement of Baylor Female College "across the Jordan" where General William Gibbs McAdoo delivered the literary address on Thursday, June 13, 1867.

A circular by Major J. H. Whittlesy of the U. S. Army to the Colleges of the United States was pondered by the board. The concern was military education, and the Baylor trustees decided to await further development of congressional action and to inform Major Whittlesy at Winchester, Virginia, of their decision.

This had been another gruelling year for President Crane. His report to the trustees showed that he received $553 in salary, $375 for preaching, and $560 in board bills—a total of $1388 for six to seven hours of teaching for nine and one-half months, preaching three times a Sabbath for twelve months and for boarding five young men. "I state these

---

[18] Reddin Andrews, "The Baylor I Knew," *The Baylor Bulletin*, XVIII (December 1915), 40-54.

things to show that neither I nor any other man can keep up this institution without the interest on the endowment fully paid, debts liquidated, and suitable buildings and apparatus furnished," wrote Dr. Crane.[19]

The report to the convention by the president of the board confirmed the feelings of Dr. Crane:

[Baylor] closed its session of 1866-1867 with an examination and commencement exercises unsurpassed in all respects by any in its previous history. . . . Besides the Academic, four regular college classes were formed. . . .

The President of the University continues faithfully, successfully, and most acceptably to discharge his duties with great sacrifice and inadequate support.[20]

Hosea Garrett, president of the Baylor Board of Trustees for twenty years, resigned, and the following resolutions were passed at a called session of the Board on February 13, 1868:

Whereas our highly esteemed and venerable brother Reverend Hosea Garrett, in view of his age and desire to be relieved of weighty responsibilities in the evening of life, has seen fit to resign the office of President of this Board, which he has held for twenty years. Therefore:

Resolved, That we accept the resignation of our long cherished companion in the cause of education with deep regret and here tender to him our hearty thanks for the zeal, devotion, unflagging and tireless energy, which have always characterized him as a Trustee and President of the Board.

Resolved, That the cause of general and ministerial education in Texas owe our late President a debt of gratitude which we earnestly hope every friend of Baylor University will ever cheerfully unite in rendering to him with cordial interest.

Resolved, That whenever the Buildings are so far completed as to furnish the Chapel promised in the plan, then shall be placed over its main entrance the following inscription: "Hosea Garrett Chapel."

Resolved, That a copy of these resolutions be forwarded to our late President, and to the *Texas Baptist Herald, Galveston News,* and *Houston Telegraph* for publication.

Hosea Garrett, although not an original trustee of Baylor University, was one of the founders present at the organizational meeting and served as president pro-tempore. He was elected to the board of trustees in 1845, made president in 1848 and served until 1868, missing only one meeting during

[19] Report to Trustees of Baylor University by President Crane. Crane Papers, Texas Collection, Baylor University.

[20] J. M. Carroll, *The History of Texas Baptists* (Dallas: Baptist Standard Publishing Company, 1923).

that time. He "retired" from the board, but was again elected and made president in 1870, serving until his death in 1888. He served as a trustee 37 years—longer than any other man —and probably gave more money to Baylor than any other person.[21]

Garrett, a seventh son, was born in Laurens District, South Carolina, on November 26, 1800. He was baptized in 1830 and ordained in 1834, serving his first pastorate in his native area. On September 20, 1841, the Reedy River Baptist Association, meeting at Cedar Shoals Church in Spartanburg District, gave him a commendation, executed in fine penmanship and signed by clerk John S. Canish and moderator Joseph Babb. He left South Carolina with this letter because of his "disgust with the superstition that brought people to him for healing by the 'laying on of hands.' "[22]

Chappell Hill, east of Washington-on-the-Brazos, became the scene of his activities for half a century. He was a preacher-farmer, pastoring churches in Washington, Burleson, and Austin counties. He traveled from place to place on horseback or in a buggy, and the only time he ever accepted remuneration for his preaching was the occasion when he lost his horse and saddle in a swollen stream on his way to a service. He allowed the congregation to make replacement.

At the age of nineteen Garrett had married his first cousin, Mary Garrett (1805-1862), who was fourteen. They came to Texas with their two daughters—Nancy Matilda (born January 22, 1827) and Sarah Harris (born July 26, 1829) in oxen wagon trains, bringing along their household furnishings. Their first home at Chappell Hill was a log house with high portholes for Indian fighting. Garrett was a good manager, and his holdings grew richer and richer. He soon built a large home on his plantation, with slave quarters, smokehouses, and even lye vats. He gave the original place to daughter Sallie, who at eighteen married Captain Claudius Buster. Daughter Nancy, at fourteen, married her cousin Oliver Hazard Perry Garrett, also from Laurens District,

[21] Carroll, p. 203.

[22] Mary Nicks, *Garrett-Buster-Estes Family History*. Privately printed, December 1956, p. 3.

South Carolina, who came to Texas in 1838. The three home locations formed a triangle, and Father Hosea could direct activities on each from the vertex.

The sons-in-law eventually escaped Garrett's watchcare, however. O. H. P. Garrett built a colonial mansion with tall white columns, and wide steps. A fan of peacock feathers—a punkah—operated by a mechanical contrivance turned with a crank by a little Negro boy gave tone and comfort to the dining room. Claudius acquired his father's land near Brenham and gave the farm near Father Hosea to his daughter, Mary Buster, upon her marriage.

The three Garrett families kept their slaves (150 freed) together, not permitting any "mixing" with neighboring plantation slaves. Hosea dictated laws of social decorum to the slaves and insisted upon marriage ceremonies. Claudius Buster said that the slaves handed down their legends from generation to generation—even "crocodile worship" from the Nile, and "occasionally a planter would lose a black baby, pitched into the Yegua."[23]

The Garrett plantation had field workers and a retinue of house servants. A Negro man in livery drove the family carriage (upholstered in watered silk) to church at Chappell Hill each Sunday. With pomp and ceremony he would tie the horses to the hitching post, open the doors, and let down the folding steps. Although lacking formal education, Garrett tolerated no informality. On special occasions he served wine at his table, but if a guest asked for a second glass, he was never a guest again.

Even in his daughters' romances Garrett was not permissive. A young man of another community paid court to one of the girls, and Reverend Garrett voiced his objection in a definite manner, as was his custom. On one Sunday morning he went to preach at a church near the young man's home and found his buggy horse tied up in the pulpit with his mane and tail shaved off. About a hundred years later Mollie Buster Estes related the story at a Baptist Missionary Society meeting in Tulsa, Oklahoma, and an elderly woman in excitement said, "And it was my father who did that to the horse."

[23] *Ibid.*, p. 6.

Mary Garrett died of cancer, after three operations in Tennessee, on November 14, 1861, at age 57. On July 9, 1862, Hosea Garrett married Nancy, the widow of General T. D. Woolridge.[24]

On June 8, 1870, Trustee Garrett was in attendance at the board meeting and named president pro-tempore. The minutes of April 5, 1871, list Reverend Garrett as president. Subsequently, John McKnight sometimes served as proxy for Garrett, but the devoted man lived to attend most of the trustee meetings and to serve his beloved Baylor University for almost another score of years.

Newly named Board President J. W. D. Creath presided at a called session on May 15, 1868, with Z. N. Morrell as a guest. Twenty-two outstanding Texans were named to a board of visitors to conduct the June examinations. (See Appendix) The trustees gave attention to the propriety of connecting the university to the Manual Labor System. Further deliberation on the subject came at the June 8, 1868, meeting and again on October 7, when it was decided that adoption of the system was impractical at the time. A committee of three trustees was designated to investigate the possibility of re-opening the law department. The services of the Honorable John Sayles and the Honorable J. E. Shepherd were again sought, with the addition of John Alexander.

Of primary consideration at this called session of the board was the petition of a committee of "medical gentlemen of Galveston" for the organization of a medical department to be located at Galveston under the name of the Texas Medical College. It met favor, and the Baylor Board of Trustees passed resolutions establishing the school, naming Dr. Thomas J. Heard the president with the following as members of the original faculty: Dr. Willam D. Kelley, Dr. Edwin H. Watts, Dr. Samuel L. Welch, Dr. George W. Teete, and Dr. Ferdinand E. Daniels. The medical school

---

[24] Nancy was born March 9, 1804, and died October 17, 1879, at age 75. On May 20, 1880, Garrett was married to Mrs. Mary Hartzog, with President William Carey Crane performing the ceremony. Garrett had predicted that he would live to be a hundred, but he was thrown from a horse and received injuries which shortened his life. He died on September 4, 1888, and was buried in the Prairie Lea Cemetery. Wife Mary Hartzog Garrett survived him several years.

was to be a separate financial venture, with Baylor University in no way responsible for its expense.

As if to indulge in self-deception, faculty and students made commencement of the year 1868 a gala occasion. Colonel George W. Carter delivered "a masterly address on The Philosophy of Life before the Erisophian and Stonewall Societies and the citizens generally." Reverend J. B. Link delivered an excellent commencement sermon on May 31.

The close association of Baylor University and Baylor Female College is seen in the trustees' appointment of two committees at their June board meeting. One committee was to confer with a similar committee already appointed by the trustees of the sister school relative to fixing the times for the commencements and the college calendars. Another committee was to confer with a similar committee from the Female College on the adoption of textbooks.

The hopeless financial state of the school cast an understandable pall on its president, who had made this recording on his fifty-second birthday:

> Tues. 17th . . . I have very little in the past for which to look and feel satisfied. My labors in life have been varied. I have toiled hard; so far as accumulating property, so far my life has been a failure. I have preached with but little interruption for nearly 31 years, and prefer to preach rather than engage in any other work. The cares of life and a dependent family requiring education have shaped my course to a great extent.[25]

Among his papers, President Crane, ever faithful in recording his thoughts, left this summary of his "survival of his first years" at Baylor University:

1. Trying political condition, removal of people, bankruptcy, tendency to ignore old obligations.
2. Direct efforts to take students from Baylor.
3. Failure of persons to pay pledges for building repairs.

Hosea Garrett presented the first report of the Baylor Board of Trustees to the Baptist State Convention of Texas in 1854. He served as president of that convention and as vice-president of the Southern Baptist Convention. The Texas Collection preserves a small, leather-bound notebook containing the subscription list for Baylor's early "Endowment of the Presidency" and for the "Professorship of Natural Science." Garrett subscribed $200 a year to the Presidency; sons-in-law O. H. P. Garrett $100 and C. Buster $50.00 per year. They also registered pledges and payments for the Professorship, the first entry dated October 1, 1852. Payments lagged for many donors, for the agents affixed explanations opposite unpaid amounts, such as "His wife won't let him."

[25] Crane Diary, March 17, 1868, Texas Collection, Baylor University.

4. Reports of insufficient number of teachers untrue.
5. Reports that Crane is in debt to all teachers untrue.
6. Personal opposition in Independence.

As so often the case in the analysis of difficult circumstances, a conscientious, responsible individual internalizes his anxiety. Such was the case with President Crane, and his burden became even heavier because of his suspicions and fears.

With the coming of fall, Dr. Crane relentlessly assumed his responsibility, determined to make academic progress, if no other. Under his direction the student body was organized into two senior classes, two middle classes, and ten junior classes with "sundry small classes."[26]

Finances were the chief concern of the trustees at their October 7, 1868, meeting. Subscriptions to the endowment fund were ordered placed in a trust fund "which cannot be applied to the liquidation of any debt." Subscribers to the fund were held responsible for their notes—"as binding as any other obligation," and the treasurer was authorized to collect principal and interest.

In his report to the Union Association in 1868 Dr. Crane reviewed educational advancement in the United States during the past fifty years, during which time the increase was from one college to thirty-five, with over three hundred male and female high schools in the U. S. He stated that Baylor University had 140 students at the close of the war and 72 at the close of the current year.

The Baylor Board of Trustees met in a called meeting again on October 22, 1868, but the only business transacted was the appointment of a committee to secure Willet Holmes as agent for the school. The next meeting reported in the minutes of the board is for March 19, 1869. Nevertheless, during this interim there was great cause for concern in Independence. An unpaid bill of $200 for shingles purchased in 1859 during the Burleson presidency was the cause of a suit against the institution and the subsequent sheriff's sale of the buildings of the university. The university was bought by C. R. Breedlove of Brenham for $250 on January 5, 1869. President Crane in desperation begged for funds

[26] Crane Diary, September 4, 1868, Texas Collection, Baylor University.

among friends and acquaintances and finally "closed the affairs by giving a check for $100 on his father's estate."[27]

The trustees, after concern with other matters, appointed Dr. Crane and M. Austin Bryan as a committee "fully empowered to settle with Charles R. Breedlove for all claims held by him against Baylor University upon condition of his reconveying [it] to this Board of Trustees."

The use of part of a subscription by James Cooper was authorized by the board to satisfy the claim of Breedlove. Then at the June meeting the committee designated to settle the claim reported "that said claims were all satisfied by payment and presented deeds and certificates legally authenticated showing that Baylor University had been reconveyed to the Board of Trustees in trust for the Baptist Denomination."[28] And that was precisely where the denomination left it—without support.

As traumatic as the sale of the university must have been to President Crane, whose house was sold along with the university, he received yet another blow. In lieu of salary payment he had received a tract of land in Lavaca County, only to find that it had previously been conveyed to R. C. Burleson. Hence at the March 1869 board meeting, the trustees voted to surrender to Dr. Burleson the note they held against him for $56 plus interest, "in the event the said R. C. Burleson make over and secure to W. C. Crane the eighty acre Nathan Fuller tract of land in McLennan County."

Perhaps this transaction served as the stimulus for a cutting letter which Burleson sent to Crane on May 23, 1869. Burleson wrote that he rejoiced that scores and hundreds

. . . of the brethren who are above me in success and merit . . . I rejoice that you have accomplished so much; for I had never regarded you as a successful preacher or teacher. You are regarded as one of the finest Belles Lettres scholars in America and as an indefatigable worker. But the impression prevails among many of your admirers and all of your opponents that your extraordinary *claims* and your most unfortunate way of manifesting them fearfully lessens your influence and defeats your incessant toils and necessitates frequent removals on your part.[29]

[27] *Biographical Encyclopedia of Texas,* p. 139.

[28] Minutes of the Baylor Board of Trustees, June 7, 1869, p. 221.

[29] Letter from President Burleson to President Crane, Crane Correspondence, Texas Collection, Baylor University.

Distressed as he was over conditions at Baylor, Dr. Crane was probably influenced by Dr. Burleson's letter in his determination to stay with the university. His reply, with its insinuation, was dated June 4, 1869:

. . . I am content that history and my contemporaries in college from 1831 to 1838; my associates in the ministry from 1838 to 1869 may say when I am gone whether your statements as to myself have any foundation or not. As to yourself or any effort to wrong you, I know nothing and assuredly abhor it.

I shall not undertake to imitate your candor in giving an estimate of your personal character. I *have* understood some things. I understand more now. It has been my aim to act in concert.[30]

Burleson had said that the means used to send him from Baylor were so foul that "they will certainly call down the vengeance of God on all the perpetrators and the university." This exchange of letters did nothing to ameliorate the deep injury.

Another anxiety for President Crane was occasioned by the request of Margaret Lea Houston that he write the biography of General Sam Houston. Opposition to the undertaking appeared early in the *Galveston Civilian* and the *Lavaca Commercial*. Critics declared that his school duties should absorb his time, together with his preparations for the pulpit. Then the charge of unsympathetic understanding was hurled: "Crane is an Old Line Whig"; Houston "an Old Jackson Democrat." Crane was a "fine Virginia gentleman . . . who had spent the larger part of his life in elegant parlors and cushioned pulpits"; Houston was "a plain, rugged frontiersman." This unnamed critic declared that Crane would gain "but few laurels in writing the life of a man so antipodal to himself."[31] Crane's friend, J. W. D. Creath, wrote a defense of Crane's position, stating that he was the authorized biographer and would gladly submit his manuscript to a committee of "five or fifty of the best writers and most devoted friends of General Houston from Maine to California. . . ."[32] Then followed charges of political involvement and professional jealousy. One writer indicated that he

[30] Copy in Crane's handwriting, Crane Correspondence, Texas Collection, Baylor University.

[31] Newsclipping, Crane Scrapbook, August 16, 1869, Texas Collection, Baylor University.

[32] Newsclipping by J. W. D. Creath, September 1869, Crane Scrapbook, Texas Collection, Baylor University.

guessed the identity of the Crane critic as coming from a malicious source "being sanctioned by an individual prominently connected with a rival institution."[33] Nevertheless, Crane decided to attempt the biography since Mrs. Houston "gave him the materials for the complete works of her distinguished husband." He planned three volumes, but "nineteen years filled with delay and disappointment passed before the manuscript was published."[34] This volume, *The Life and Select Literary Remains of Sam Houston*, published by J. B. Lippincott of Philadelphia in the spring of 1884 was listed by Sterling North along with J. Frank Dobie's *Coronado's Children* as the two Texas books "adding another dimension to our view of America."[35]

During the year, as might be supposed because of the financial crisis, there was much agitation for the removal of Baylor from Independence. The *Bryan News Letter* of May 22, 1869, carried a story—most likely based on conjecture—from which the following excerpt comes:

> Preliminary efforts are being made to locate Baylor University at Bryan, and it is argued by many, that the transfer . . . will make it a more successful enterprise than it has been at Independence. . . .
>
> The Baylor University has been a failure at Independence, cut off, as it is, from all public thoroughfares, and surrounded by a belt of creeks with bottoms impassable at certain seasons of the year. We have no doubt but what this institution would be successful here, and with proper efforts its transfer can be effected. . . .

President Crane answered the story, saying that if Baylor had been a failure, so had been—with few exceptions—all Southern institutions. Responsibility for the location of the university at Independence rested with the Legislature of the State of Texas, the trustees, the Baptist State Convention, and the donors to the school; and with them should rest the question of permanence, he contended. Truth demanded that he state that Baylor was in better condition in June 1869 than it had been since 1860, he concluded. Dr. Crane estimated the cost of removal at $36,000 in property

[33] Letter in *Lavaca Commercial,* December 1869.

[34] Dwain Perry, "William Carey Crane, A Biographer of Sam Houston," Seminar Paper for Dr. Bruce Thompson, Chairman, Department of History, Baylor University, p. 6.

[35] Sterling North, "A Literary Map of the United States" *Holiday,* February 1947, p. 138.

loss at Independence "plus 1700 acres of good cotton land."

The Baylor Board of Trustees was disturbed that rumors persisted concerning the removal of Baylor University, and a committee was appointed to draft resolutions for a report at the next meeting. On the following day, June 8, 1869, no meeting was held. Commencement did take place, however, and among the Crane papers is a newsclipping of a baccalaureate address by W. C. Crane, "To Think, To Feel, To Act," given June 9, 1869. Daniel McIntyre and Charles Judson Crane were awarded A.B. degrees, and the honorary D.D. was conferred on three ministers: William Howard, A. Paul Ripeton, and A. W. Chambliss.

The catalogue for the year June 1868-June 1869—Baylor's twenty-third—listed the Medical Department—Texas Medical College with seven faculty members. The Erosophian [*sic*] and the Stonewall were the two societies listed. Enrollment for the year was given as eighty-nine. During the Crane administration, one student had been graduated in 1864, one in 1868, and two in 1869.[36] President Crane's report to the Convention for 1868-1869 gave a final total of 129 students enrolled during the year. The faculty consisted of:

W. A. Montgomery	I. N. May
R. T. Smyth	J. G. Boyle
President Crane	W. C. Crane, Jr.

Physical facilities were in sad repair: Houston Hall had two portions of rock wall fall; Graves Hall needed repairs, and the Burleson Domicile "leaked like a sieve." The president reported that tuition fees amounted to $907.50 with over $500 still due; the interest on the endowment was $138.13. Dr. Crane had received $553.00 and was personally responsible to Mr. May and Mr. Montgomery for their salaries, the only responsibility of the kind he had ever assumed and "such as I do not desire again to assume, he wrote."[37]

A note in Crane's papers makes reference to a public meeting in behalf of the institution. President Crane termed it a

[36] *Baylor Catalogue*, 1868-1869 (Baltimore: John F. Weishampel, Jr., No. 8, Under the Eutaw House).

[37] Original Report June 7, 1869, Crane Papers, Texas Collection, Baylor University.

"respectable meeting with some enthusiasm," but if there were any concrete results, they are yet to be discovered.

Crane's defense did not end the removal problem, however. A communication from Trustee J. L. Farquhar, dated September 3, 1869, alerted Dr. Crane about rumors in Navasota "that Baylor University was in bad hands and that at the next meeting of the Baptist State Convention at Galveston" the university would be moved to Bryan.[38]

Friends of Crane assured him of their support, as indicated by this statement: "We will carry the war [removal] to Africa if need be and give them a jolly time before they remove Baylor or the President."[39] Among Dr. Crane's papers is an undated address in which he questioned the legality of the proposed removal. He also urged that the historic associations not be overlooked in impetuosity.

By October 4, 1869, when the convention met, the supporters of the removal movement had dwindled to a very few. The following resolution was passed:

> Resolved, that after full and free discussion, we are satisfied that it is impractical now or at any future time to remove Baylor University or Baylor Female College.

The *Lavaca Commercial* commented on the action:

> The Convention very promptly determined to extend its fostering care to Baylor University and . . . to seek to build it up as the most deserving object of their organization. This action . . . will concentrate public support and secure that large patronage for Baylor which it so justly deserves.[40]

These proved to be false hopes. Not until November 10, 1870, did the trustees confirm the convention decision and term it "final."[41] President Crane said the agitation had cost him and the university thousands of dollars in subscriptions. He also expressed vexation at the convention which did nothing to support the school except "commend it to the demon by resolutions." Crane's opinion was verified in an 1871 convention action to strike out of the report "everything calculated to convey the idea that any past, present,

---

[38] Letter in Crane Correspondence, Texas Collection, Baylor University.
[39] James W. Barnes to President Crane, September 18, 1869, Crane Correspondence, Texas Collection, Baylor University.
[40] Crane Scrapbook, Texas Collection, Baylor University.
[41] Original copy of resolution in Archives, Texas Collection, Baylor University.

or future action of this Convention can impose upon Baptists any moral obligation" for support.[42] This action was later modified to show no intent to "disparage the claims of Baylor to the sympathies and prayers of the Baptist denomination of Texas." But colleges have found it difficult to operate on sympathies and prayers, however devout.

A loyal group, nevertheless, gave support as indicated by these notes:

> There seems to be a desire among some to divorce the Convention from her schools, but I am far from having such a desire.[43]

> I will certainly do all in my power for Baylor and regret exceedingly any want of patronage on the part of the Denomination.[44]

President Crane, weary of waiting, summed up the situation in his *Diary*: "Duties in college are enough to discourage any mortal man in the snail pace and the lethargy of the fancied workers for Baylor University.[45]

Not until November 3, 1869, did the Baylor trustees reconvene after the June 1869 meeting. Then they voted their belated thanks to the late William Crane of Baltimore and his sons for their contribution in 1866 which supplied glass, sash, and paint for the old college edifice to make it usable. Gratitude was also paid President Crane "for his untiring exertions and success in his voluntary efforts to relieve Baylor University from legal embarrassment.[46] It was resolved that "the first monies collected, not appropriated to repairs, be used to pay President Crane for the Theodolite and Mathematical instruments which he purchased with his own funds and have been used by the University over two years past."

The dire need for operating funds brought forth several proposals from the board:

1. That every lady in Texas be requested to contribute one dollar a year for five years to provide means for the completion of the College buildings.
2. That the superintendent of every Sunday school in the Texas Baptist State Convention solicit contributions of twenty-five cents

[42] Carroll, p. 386.

[43] H. F. Buckner to Dr. Crane, November 10, 1868, Crane Correspondence, Texas Collection, Baylor University.

[44] Wm. Howard to Dr. Crane, November 13, 1869, Crane Correspondence, Texas Collection, Baylor University.

[45] Crane *Diary*, January 10, 1870, Texas Collection, Baylor University.

[46] Minutes of the Baylor Board of Trustees, p. 222.

for each teacher and scholar during the year to raise a fund for the support and education of candidates for the ministry.

3. That the General Financial Agent of the Convention J. W. D. Creath present the claims of Baylor University at each place he visits and that each pastor do the same at the churches.

4. That Willett Holmes, the newly appointed agent, secure the renewal of all notes and subscriptions on printed legal notes; that he be authorized to secure contributions of money, land, stock or produce. Holmes was also directed to sell scholarships to complete the endowment of the chairs of the President and Professors of Languages, Mathematics, and Natural Science.

5. That the president be instructed to renew his exertions to secure from the Legislature when in session an appropriation in land for endowment purposes.

6. A list of thirteen ministers was drawn up, each being requested to spend at least one month during the year in canvassing his respective neighborhood.

7. That the secretary of the board prepare a circular letter, to be printed in letter form, disclosing the above board actions, and sent to Baptist ministers and friends of education generally.[47]

At this meeting the trustees recommended that the D.D. degree be conferred on Reverend Henry F. Buckner "now of this place, but under appointment as a missionary to the Creek Indians."

A committee of seven was named to request the use of the County Court House and make other necessary arrangements for the 1869 session of the law department in the town of Brenham.

These *were* times that tried men's souls. The war between the States had brought disaster to many, even though Texas was not in the theatre of war. Population growth had halted. The decade of 1860-70 shows the smallest population increase in any of the nine decades for which enumeration had been made. An increase of 94.5 per cent is recorded for the 1870-80 decade,[48] but for half a century Texas had been looking to an uncertain future.

[47] *Ibid.*, pp. 222-24.
On November 9, 1869, Board President Pro-Tempore and Secretary George W. Graves issued a circular—*To the Friends of Baylor University*, urging "everybody in Texas to contribute one dollar a year for five years to provide for the completion of our college buildings . . . and that every Sunday school superintendent in the Texas Baptist State Convention solicit 25 cents from each member "to educate candidates for the gospel ministry." No results of the campaign were reported.
[48] *Texas Almanac 1849-50* (Dallas: *The Dallas Morning News*), p. 91.
Texas population rose from 604,215 in 1860 to 818,579 in 1870. By 1880 population reached 1,591,749.

Another unprecedented action was the trustees directive that Agent W. Holmes borrow from the Trustees of the Texas Baptist State Convention "one half of the amount of the bequest of Mrs. E. Vickers ($110 currency) to be used immediately for repairs of the buildings." Security was to be given and interest paid. Even this seemingly reasonable hope was destined to end in futility, however. Emissary Holmes reported at the next board meeting, February 8, 1870, that he was denied "the loan of the Vickers Fund to the Board by the Trustees of the Baptist State Convention." As a result the board was instructed to loan all sums paid for the endorsement of the several chairs to solvent parties at the rate of ten per cent interest, all loans being secured by a deed of trust on real estate.

Dr. Crane addressed the Texas Baptist State Convention at its Galveston meeting in 1869. In a highly personalized manner, he recounted his term of office as president of Baylor University. He made a point-listing of factors which had operated against him in the execution of his duties: the post-Civil War gloom; trying political and personal conditions; removals and bankruptcy of many; failure in payment of interest on endowment and the feeling that all obligations to the university should be cancelled; efforts, personal and by letter, particularly on the part of law students, to dissuade students in their attendance; the resignation of a professor termed by many as vital to the institution and "his acceptance of a place on a railroad train" in November 1865; buildings had fallen into disrepair because of unpaid subscriptions; the false report of inadequate number of teachers, which influenced churches and individuals to withhold their subscription payments,[49] animosity toward Wm. Carey Crane, Jr., graduate and later tutor at Baylor; a formal complaint to the board of trustees against him by a professor who resigned in June 1866 and a prejudicial speech by a trustee against him; the necessity of teachers' having to collect their own salaries; the yellow fever epidemic of 1867

---

[49] Galveston Baptist Church was one to which Crane referred. Church Treasurer W. A. Kunklin wrote to Dr. Crane in response to his letter about the interest on the Endowment for the Chair of Natural Science: "The church declined to pay because they felt it not binding because that chair had not been filled *in the manner contemplated* when the subscription was made." W. A. Kunklin to President Crane, from Galveston, December 30, 1868.

and the lack of confidence in health conditions at Independence; personal opposition to his presence at Baylor and to his holding jointly the presidency and the pastorate of the Independence Church; the vindictive defeat of his proposed legislative land grant bill; and derogatory newspaper and Union Association publicity; the backwash of the Clark-Burleson feud; and finally the sheriff's sale of the university.

This is a damning list, particularly for an institution which depends on public esteem for its existence. No doubt the suspicions and sensitivity of Dr. Crane added some exaggeration to the case, but the statements were essentially true. Solution of the problem was an heroic task, if not an impossible undertaking. Baylor University was not alone in facing financial disaster. Enrollment had slumped in well-established colleges over the nation.[50] Many colleges closed, while others maintained a struggling existence. Dr. Crane asserted that Baylor had incurred no debt since the War nor had the school met salary obligations. President Crane had sustained the school through his own efforts. The success the institution did achieve seems almost miraculous.

[50] *The American Baptist Yearbook for 1869* reported these enrollment figures: Richmond College, Virginia, 147; Mercer University, Georgia, 77; Georgetown College, Kentucky, 115; Howard College, Alabama, 90; and William Jewell College, Missouri, 104.

CHAPTER XII

Visionary Plans and Baylor Fortitude

THE FIRST HALF OF THE DECADE of 1870-80 was fraught with further turmoil for the Baptists of Texas. They were well aware of the unsatisfactory condition of their schools, and leaders evolved varied plans to solve the problems.

General J. E. Harrison of Waco became the leader in a movement to create "a great central Baptist University."[1] Both Burleson and Crane faced a common threat and were wary of the proposal. In an effort at conciliation, a secret arrangement was worked out by Waco backers of the plan by which Baylor and Waco Universities would become a part of the proposed institution with Burleson as president and Crane as Professor of Theology. A letter from Burleson to Crane early in the planning declares, "I would rejoice to be associated with you during our last days and mightiest struggles for our blessed Savior's cause."[2] Confirmation of the arrangement came in a letter from J. W. Speight to Dr. Crane shortly thereafter, revealing the plan of making Waco University the central university. "It would be exceedingly gratifying to have you with us . . . but advise no promulgation of the plan at the present time."[3]

The proposal came up in the Texas Baptist State Convention for the first time in late 1870 at Bremond. The plan was presented as an effort to concentrate Baptist loyalties on an entirely new university, free from previous animosities. General J. E. Harrison, F. M. Law, J. B. Link, and General J. W. Speight were the strongest advocates of the proposal. Supporters of the plan mustered sufficient approval to win about seven-tenths of the forty-seven members pres-

[1] J. E. Harrison, Waco, to Crane, August 16, 1870. General Harrison wrote the first article outlining the proposal. He declared that ambition, prejudice, and jealousy had divided Baptists in the support of two universities and that the solution was to have one central university. Speculation ran high concerning what was to be done with Baylor and Waco Universities. Were they to be abandoned or converted into high schools?

[2] Burleson to Crane, October 27, 1870. Crane Correspondence, Texas Collection, Baylor University.

[3] J. W. Speight to Crane, November 21, 1870. Crane Correspondence, Texas Collection, Baylor University.

ent. Rivalry between Baylor University and Waco University was pronounced.[4]

The next convention meeting was scheduled for July 19-21, 1871, at Fairfield. Reverend J. W. D. Creath advised President Crane to avoid participation in the controversy—"let others do the talking and writing."[5] For this occasion the proponents of the movement presented an expansive plan which included the establishing of good primary schools in every neighborhood, assistance by moral support of every denominational school in the state, the establishing of one or more academies or high schools in every association, and finally the establishing of an institution of higher learning. The financing of this grandiose plan was to be accomplished through the sale of shares in a stock company.

A minority committee, headed by J. C. Mott, offered the following amendment to the plan: accept as the first objective assistance to the existing institutions—$50,000 to each declared on a secure basis; then if necessary found the central university. Nevertheless, enthusiasm for the plan ran high and $7,000 in subscriptions was pledged at Fairfield. Groups continued their activity, and at a called meeting at Bryan on August 7, 1872, the Educational Union was organized and chartered under the general incorporation act. Agents were assigned the task of selling $200,000 worth of stock—the amount designated to begin a new school. J. B. Link lent active support to the campaign through the *Texas Baptist Herald* and even wrote to President Crane urging his support.[6] Arrayed in opposition to Link were Tom Compere,[7] R. C. Buckner,[8] W. W. Harris,[9] and other prominent Baptists.

Controversy continued for years. During January 1874 several Baptist papers rallied to the support of the existing

[4] A letter from H. F. Buckner to Dr. Crane on January 10, 1871, states that the writer was tickled "half to death at seeing Dr. Burleson's and Speight's crawfishing as soon as they discovered that the *place* and *men* did not suit." Crane Archives, University of Texas.

[5] J.W. D. Creath to President Crane, July 11, 1871. Crane Correspondence, Texas Collection, Baylor University.

[6] J. B. Link to President Crane, November 27, 1872. Crane Correspondence, Texas Collection, Baylor University.

[7] Thomas H. Compere to Dr. Crane, August 11, 1871.

[8] R. C. Buckner to President Crane, August 2, 1871.

[9] W. W. Harris to Dr. Crane, August 22, 1871. Crane Correspondence, Texas Collection, Baylor University.

institutions. An agreement to hold a fraternal conference was reached, with Crane of Baylor, Burleson of Waco, and Link of the Educational Union selecting two representatives each to join in the meeting. It was held at Navasota in the home of Judge John R. Kennard. Dr. J. M. Carroll, then a Baylor student accompanying President Crane, reported dramatically of the meeting that lasted all night and until ten the next morning. The aggressive Educational Union trio put the other two groups on the defensive, but "a sort of distinctly unsatisfactory compromise" resulted. Baylor and Waco were to become parts of one Baptist university in the state. Baylor was to have the theological department, to have a high school in conjunction, and to receive the first $25,000 endowment. Waco, to be called "Baylor University," was to have the literary department and the greater part of the endowment of several thousand dollars. B. T. Kavanaugh wrote President Crane that he believed "all Protestant denominations [should] unite and advocate the plan."[10]

By June 25, 1875, at the Bremond meeting of the Baptists, aspects had changed again. Dallas had inaugurated a Baptist college and demanded equal consideration with Waco, Baylor, and the Educational Union. The Navasota agreement was scrapped! Then the problem was referred to a committee, the "Immortal Fifteen," composed of three friends each from Baylor, Waco, Dallas, and the Educational Union and three appointed by moderator J. H. Stribling. The hundreds attending the meeting waited for n e a r l y twenty-four hours for the committee report. The recommendation was to make Baylor University the one school of the State; that rejected, the same proposal should apply to Waco University. Provision was made for a Central Baptist Education Commission of Texas, composed of thirty members, to raise $250,000 of which $100,000 was to be collected and invested. The donors were to locate the school where they could secure the largest bonus with the best eligibility. The Educational Union was to be dissolved and its assets turned over to the Commission.[11] The p r o p o s a l s were adopted, and at an October 2, 1875, meeting of the Commis-

[10] B. T. Kavanaugh to Dr. Crane, December 31, 1874. Crane Correspondence, Texas Collection, Baylor University.
[11] J. B. Link, *Historical and Biographical Magazine*, II, 685.

sion during a session of the Baptist State Convention at Calvert, F. M. Law was named agent. In the next two years, he and his aides raised $80,500 in notes and lands. Nevertheless, there was not complete unanimity among the Baptist leaders. R. C. Buckner told Dr. Crane that he was "heartsick and opposed to the combination of the schools" in the proposed plan.[12]

After seven years, the assets of the Commission totaled $96,673.60, and the Commission was dissolved. According to the wishes of the donors, the assets were to go to Baylor or Waco University or back to the contributors. So ended the Texas Baptist effort of resolving their problem of collegiate education.

In the meantime, Baylor University proceeded with her own affairs. At the first board meeting of the new decade on February 23, 1870, the trustees of Baylor resolved to send representatives to the General Baptist Educational Convention. The meeting had been called by the Educational Commission of New York and New Jersey to meet in Brooklyn, New York, on April 19. A committee was designated to raise funds for expenses to send President Crane and Trustees J. W. D. Creath and J. W. Barnes. At the April 6 trustee meeting M. V. Smith of the faculty was also named a delegate to the convention. Attendance at the meeting was fruitless in so far as its effect on Baylor policy was concerned, for no mention of it has been found in university documents, but Dr. Crane was influenced concerning university and state relationships in education.

On March 22, 1870, original trustee Albert G. Haynes died. President Crane conducted the funeral service, using this opening sentence: "Albert Gallitan Haynes is dead, and no ordinary man has fallen." In tribute to his long, dedicated service and as a testimony to his sterling character, fellow citizens erected in the Independence cemetery a stone monument so "that his many virtues might not lightly pass away."

Commencement was held in June with one A.B. graduate. Sixty young men constituted the year's enrollment, and the law school, suspended since 1866, had resumed in May at Brenham. Honorary degrees, A.M. and M.P. respec-

[12] R. C. Buckner to Dr. Crane, June 1, 1875. Crane Correspondence, Texas Collection, Baylor University.

tively, were conferred on James F. Lannear, Professor of Mathematics at William Jewell College of Liberty, Missouri, and on Charles Shepherd Webb, teacher of mathematics at Baylor.[13]

The perennial problem of the agency came up again in the June 8 trustee meeting. Mr. W. Holmes had been serving in the position, and a committee of two was appointed to cooperate with the president to procure an agent. The board also decided to place money matters in the hands of a Standing Finance Committee, composed of G. W. Graves, M. A. Bryan, and John McKnight.

The next meeting of the trustees was set for June 17, undoubtedly because of the urgency of financial matters. At that time the committee reported the willingness of President Crane to assume the responsibility of agent. He was directed to obtain substitutes to conduct his campus duties in his absence and he was to be paid $600 and travel expenses "out of any money which he may collect." The board reaffirmed their confidence in President Crane in the form of a resolution and designated an unprecedented *third* trustee meeting in one month on June 25.

A complete, analytical report on the Endowment Funds for the Presidency and the Chair of Natural Science was examined. Death, change of fortune, and other causes made many of the subscriptions uncollectable. Frequently those paid had been by barter system—a due-note from someone else in lieu of subscription, land, cotton, and even Confederate currency. Since Mr. Holmes had served as representative for both Baylor University and the Female College, he turned over to each one-half of his collection—$157.25 for the year 1869-70.

Exemplifying his maxim, "Genius never discards routine," President Crane gave a detailed annual report of university affairs to the board of trustees:

[13] Mr. Webb resigned from his position at the next board meeting, and the trustees entered their regrets in a resolution transcribed in the minutes. He was termed an "interesting, accomplished gentleman . . . a scholar and pious Christian." Ill health necessitated his resignation. The board owed Mr. Webb $400 in salary, and at a subsequent meeting ordered agent W. Holmes to continue his efforts to raise money for this deficit. Dr. Crane reported that Mr. Webb had received one-fourth of the tuition fees and his board "and other necessities."

1. He listed the number of students as 60, with three or four never attending. In the main, good order prevailed; although a few were suspended for rule violations, none for "grevious vices."

2. Dr. Crane complimented Professor Charles S. Webb's marked ability.

3. Professor F. Constet, teacher of French, Spanish and German taught for four and a half months, and substituted for Dr. Crane as teacher of Latin and Greek during his absence at Brooklyn and Louisville. (He was paid $20 extra.) Dr. Crane gave him board for instructing the two Crane sons in Spanish. He resigned after one term.

4. Reddin Andrews, Jr., was termed an "usher," who heard recitations of a class in etymology and instructed primary classes in Latin and Greek. Andrews, a licentiate, was charged nothing for tuition and only $10 for board and lodging. Sam Ellis served as an usher for one month and was not charged tuition.

5. Nearly all of the students, all of the officers, and the president's family belonged to an organization known as "Friends of the Council of Temperance," dedicated to the abolition of beverage use of all intoxicating drinks.

6. The Law School had resumed in Brenham on the first Monday in March, with Mr. R. T. Smyth as active professor, aided by Judges Sayles and Shepherd.

7. Two concerts produced $105, which was used to purchase fifteen "new style double seats" now in transit to Brenham.

8. In the realm of science, these purchases were made and paid for, most resting now at the office in Brenham awaiting payment of express charges: "an entirely new electrical apparatus, a chemical apparatus, new globes, a new clock, some important instruments for measurement of rain and temperature." (The president also noted that he had not yet been reimbursed for his theodolite and mathematical instruments).

9. A few library acquisitions had been made, and the president personally paid postage on the newspapers which came to the Reading Room.

10. Prospects for enrollment for the next term were better than in the spring, according to student comments and "other concurrent circumstances."

11. The president held a bill of $20 due on subscriptions.

12. He had borrowed $150 from the Presidential Endowment and $50 from the Natural Science Chair Endowment "for purchase of apparatus, sash and glass."

13. Dr. Crane reported that he had collected $1303 since 1863 and paid it out for repairs, fixtures, apparatus, and to release the buildings from the sheriff sale in January 1869. One half the sum was contributed by his relations and himself. About $500 was expended on Houston Hall.

14. Collections since 1865 of interest on the endowments of the Presidency amounted to $363.50—about $73 per year. Collections of interest on the endowment of the Chair of Natural Science were $642.95—$128.59 per year. About $150 in collections were assigned to other uses, the total being $1156.45 in five years.

15. Crane estimated about $800 endowment for the Presidency and about $1350 for the Chair of Natural Science "that could be relied upon."

16. The institution owed the Tryon monument Fund $55 plus $12 to Mr. Leek, stone mason. Only $20 of $400 had been collected for the Professor of Mathematics; nothing collected in Washington County "except this $20."[14]

President Crane presented a factual, realistic survey of the college situation and recommended that "all the objects resolved on March 9, 1869" (involvement of all churches, women, and Sunday schools) be considered as vital to the prosperity of Baylor University.

The president had spent a busy year. Frequently the young ladies of Baylor College wanted some course not in their curriculum. President Crane would organize a class and teach the girls after his eight-hour day of Baylor University instruction. After school hours and on Saturdays a Negro man met President Crane in his library for an extended period in order to benefit from Crane's teaching. He afterwards became Reverend Mose Johnson, a prominent Negro Baptist minister.

President Crane had a great library, and he filed his books, papers, magazines, and letters so systematically that each was readily available. He was an omnivorous reader. His diary reveals that in January of 1870 he read Darwin's *Origin of Species*, Murray's *Outline of Hamilton's Philosophy*, and Warburton's *Divine Legation of Moses*. Dr. Crane also read the complete Bible every year. Titles of his lectures evidenced the breadth of his interests and knowledge: Mineralogy, Hygiene, Geometry, Hydrostatics, Mental Depth, Mind the Stand of Man, Cluttered Intellect, Hebrew Poetry, and Rationalism and Supernaturalism.[15]

He wrote many letters each day in an unusually fine hand with marvelous speed. He was never known "to idle away a single moment." He did all of his clerical work (the books for

[14] Minutes of Baylor Board of Trustees, June 25, 1870, p. 240-3.
[15] Newsclipping, *Brenham Banner* (n.d.), Texas Collection, Baylor University.

the university and his own household) in his living room on a 3 x 4 foot table.[16]

Dr. Crane was a prolific writer, serving as editor or co-editor of the *Banner and Pioneer, The Mississippi Baptist, The Louisiana Baptist, The Christian Repository,* the *New York Chronicle,* and *The Baptist* of Nashville, Tennessee.[17] Before coming to Texas, Crane had written *A Collection of Arguments and Opinions on Baptism,* published at Montgomery, Alabama, in 1839, and *Literary Discourses* in 1853. In his chronicle he listed some thirty newspapers and magazines to which he contributed.[18]

When school opened in the fall of 1870, President Crane was encouraged. He had travelled for two and a half months during the summer and collected $194.45 and $25 in pledges for building repairs. His diary records "thirty students and prospects good for many more."[19] His report to the trustees was also optimistic in that he felt the prospects better than in the past five years.

A brief trustee meeting on October 3, 1870, resulted in the appointment of Colonel F. W. Adams as agent "to collect funds for the Board."[20] At the following meeting on November 10 the trustees conferred an honorary law degree on Noah K. Davis, President of Bethel College, Russellville, Kentucky. Then they passed resolutions affirming the fact that "the legal connection existing between the convention and Baylor University has imposed a high moral obligation on the constituents of the convention to sustain by contributions, patronage and moral support the institution under its

---

[16] The table was constructed of cedar without a single nail by Allen Warren, husband of the Crane's cook, Ann, who had been brought to Independence by Reddin Vickers. "Allen was in the penitentiary during most of the time I was growing up for burning up the business part of the town," wrote R. C. Crane.

[17] *The First Half Century of Madison University,* 1819-1869, Jubilee Volume (New York: Sheldon & Co., 1872), p. 228; *Colgate University General Catalogue,* I, 62.

[18] R. N. Richardson, "Literature and Scholarship," *Centennial History of Texas Baptists,* pp. 351-364.

In 1878 Dr. Crane's *Baptist Catechism* was printed in lesson form for use in Sunday schools. During that year, too, Dr. Crane wrote the introduction for Sam H. Dixon's *The Poets and Poetry of Texas,* thus showing something of the scope of his literary interests.

[19] Crane Diary, September 20, 1870, Texas Collection, Baylor University.

[20] Mr. Adams' tenure was brief. Resolutions on his death were passed at the April 5, 1871, board meeting and ordered published in the Brenham *Banner* and the *Texas Baptist Herald.*

charge," and secondly that every consideration of denominational policy and moral honor "forbid the acquiescence of its Trustees in any scheme which may lower its aims or surrender it to others differing in sentiment from its founders."

These resolutions bore some connection to "the Educational Plan" fomenting discussion over the state and were an effort to reinforce the position of Baylor University—the Baptists' first college in Texas. An order was given for their publication in the *Baptist Herald*, the *Galveston News*, and *Flake's Bulletin*.[21] Again a committee was appointed to mature plans to raise funds for the endowment of the chairs of the university, with a mass meeting called on October 24 to start the project.

The report of Dr. Crane to the Baptist Convention in the fall of 1870 contained some strong statements.[22] He emphasized the organic connection of Baylor University and Baylor Female College to the convention in that "you elect their board of trustees . . . and virtually control them." Hence the institutions look to the convention for financial support and the sending of Baptist children to educate. He urged the appointment of a commission to visit Independence and make a thorough and judicious examination of the institutions, "the object being to make a truthful and unvarnished report of the conditions, advantages, defects and wants of these institutions." The convention president then appointed seven men to visit Baylor and seven to visit Baylor Female College.

The pressure of the Baylor supporters had been strong out of necessity, but it had an adverse psychological effect on many members of the convention, particularly when the moral obligations of ownership were stressed. In 1871 the convention passed what Carroll termed "some strange resolutions."[23] The first was a renunciation of "moral support":

[21] *Flake's Bulletin* was published by Ferdinand Flake, Galveston mayor, and Colonel John S. Sydnor. It was one of the leading newspapers in Texas during the reconstruction period. Flake also published the German *Die Union*. Fornell, *The Galveston Era* (Austin: The University of Texas Press, 1961), p. 150.

[22] J. M. Carroll, *The History of Texas Baptists* (Dallas: Baptist Standard Publishing Company, 1923), p. 384.

Reports of yellow fever just as the convention adjourned stopped all rail travel, and people "had to get home as best they could," wrote J. A. Kimball. Negroes with guns guarded the ferryboat crossing at Washington, and travel was possible only by pass issued by a health officer.

[23] *Ibid.*, p. 386.

Resolved, that there be stricken from the report of the trustees of
Baylor University everything calculated to convey the idea that any
past, present or future action of this Convention can impose upon
Baptists any moral obligation.

The resolution was adopted, but during the same session,
after some reflection, the blow was softened in the following
ambiguous, evasive resolution:

Resolved, that in the discussion as to whether this Convention
rested under moral obligation to aid and sustain Baylor University,
there was no intention to disparage the claims of that institution to
the sympathies and prayers of the Baptist denomination of Texas,
but to maintain a great truth.[24]

At the Texas Baptist Association meeting in 1870, J. W.
D. Creath gave a report on the Education Convention of
Texas, organized in October 1869 (and destined to live
three years) with a three-fold purpose: to aid indigent young
ministers in securing an education, to prepare competent
and efficient teachers, and to arouse a general and deep interest in the cause of education. Creath expressed a fear of the
inroads of Roman Catholicism. Ministerial aid had been
given to several young Baylor men; in 1866, $130 had been
raised to assist A. F. Perry; in 1867 both Perry and Reddin
Andrews, Jr., received aid; in 1868 only Andrews was the
recipient of $102.60 from the Colorado Association.

Money-raising efforts by Baylor trustees were still un-
productive, for at an April 5 meeting a committee was appointed "to devise some plan to keep up the repairs of the
university buildings," and an urgent appeal was made for all
subscribers to the endowment fund to pay interest up to
June "as the wants of Baylor University imperatively demand money to sustain its teachers." The president was directed to communicate these resolutions to the *Texas Baptist
Herald*.

In the wake of the Educational Union Movement came
another disturbing incident. The governor had appointed
commissioners to locate an Agricultural and Mechanical College "contemplated by act of Congress." The Baylor trustees
appointed a committee composed of M. A. Bryan, R. E. B.
Baylor, and Dr. Crane to confer with the designated officials.

[24] Idem.

President Crane was much disturbed over educational provisions in Texas. State Superintendent Jacob C. DeGress (May 6, 1871 to January 20, 1874) instituted an autocratic system[25] of which Dr. Crane gave frank criticism to the press.[26] He was convinced of the wisdom of a dual system of colleges, one denominational and one state-controlled. Yet he believed that the state should extend financial assistance to denominational schools, since it is the state "which profits most from the endeavors of private and denominational schools."[27]

President Crane, a knowledgeable educator, advocated a modification of the New York system of university operation, with a board of regents charged with the administration of educational funds for the state. He proposed that denominational colleges, such as Baylor University, Austin College, Waco University, and others, maintaining their autonomy, become a part of a great Texas University, with the graduate and professional schools at Austin. Admittance was to be free. Presidents Burleson of Waco University, Samuel McKinney of Austin College, and B. T. Kavanaugh of Houston rallied to the support of the plan. Some observers saw the humor in the reconciliation of old enemies and facetiously referred to it as "a positively sublime spectacle."[28]

President Crane's identity with the denomination brought forth rigorous attacks from the secular press in the form of letters signed fictitiously. Personal motives and private reasons were credited for his efforts. Supporters were termed "reverend drummers for ecclesiastical schools scrambling for spoils." Dr. Crane continued his support of the idea the rest of his life, although he was constant in his defense of religious-oriented colleges.[29] But even the Baptists were reluctant to lend support, and the *Baptist Herald* and denominational leaders such as O. H. Cooper and O. N. Hol-

[25] Eby, Frederick, "Education and Educators, *Centennial Story of Texas Baptists,* ed. Harlan J. Matthews (Dallas, Texas: Baptist General Convention of Texas, 1936), p. 152.
[26] W. C. Crane, "The Present Free School System," September 21, 23, 1871. Newsclipping, Crane Papers, Texas Collection, Baylor University.
[27] W. C. Crane to *Galveston News,* September 22, 1871.
[28] Anonymous Letter, *Democratic Statesman,* Austin, (n.d.), Crane Scrapbook, Texas Collection, Baylor University.
[29] W. C. Crane, "Shall Christians Surrender to the State the Secular Education of Their Children?" Clipping, (n.d.), Crane Scrapbook, Texas Collection, Baylor University.

lingsworth led overt opposition to doom the plan to failure.

Two interesting communications from Waco University President Rufus C. Burleson came to President Crane when the central university plan was still fomenting interest among both denominational and secular groups. First, a postcard:

> Your commission article has the right ring at last. We must move out total on that line or we are ruined.
> There is no time for delay. The AnaConder has been coiling his deadly coils around us for years and crying all the time peace peace peace.
> The people are with us and for the right.

Then came a letter:

> Let us demand that "The Texas University" be made the grandest thing on this continent . . . organized like "London University" and be composed of all the Institutions of the State reaching a certain grade, whether owned by Masons, Odd Fellows, Denominations or local corporations provided they bind themselves to teach no "sectarian religion."
> Under this plan Waco and Baylor and the Georgetown Methodist school could all become a part of "The Texas University" and receive state aid and send up students for final examinations to the Regents of "The Texas University."[30]

Despite the denominational discontent, the school year at Baylor ended on June 6, 1871, with a "public day," and two young men received degrees at the evening exhibition. Honorary degrees were conferred: the LL.D on J. F. Cook, President of LaGrange College in Missouri, and the D.D. on Reverend James H. Stribling.[31] The trustees appointed Hugh C. McIntyre as treasurer of the institution, to hold all papers, vouchers and documents belonging to the university. Board President Hosea Garrett, who had retired in 1866, had resumed his position of leadership and reported to the convention that the year had been marked with divine favor. Ninety-four students, mostly in advanced grades, attended. The law school operated until Christmas and was then suspended. One graduate of the year was pursuing theological training at Greenville, South Carolina, and the other was teaching.[32]

[30] R. C. Burleson to Dr. Crane, January 3, 1878. R. C. Burleson to Dr. Crane, February 20, 1878. Crane Correspondence, Texas Collection, Baylor University.

[31] Reverend Stribling had been awarded an honorary A.M. in 1860.

[32] Reddin Andrews, Jr. was the theological student; J. A. Lipscomb, the teacher.

In December 1871 President Crane received a much appreciated grant to the university: an authorization to use the Brockway and Fredrick's patented improved fence for the grounds of the institution "for the full time for which said patent may be extended." The treasurer of the university was admonished to collect all sums due the institution "which he can prudently, so as not to prejudice the interests of the Institution." The board had decided to "soft-pedal" soliciting for the university. It must have been difficult for President Crane, for on May 3, 1872, the newspapers in the area carried this letter over his signature:

The silence of the undersigned and of the friends of the institution over which he presides must not be constructed into indifference about the question of higher education now occupying the minds of the great educators of the world. We were never wider awake, never more resolute, never more full of hope, never with greater evidence of general sympathy and support, irrespective of sect or party. Our forthcoming catalogue will confirm these statements. The design of the founders of this institution will never be abandoned. The undersigned will take all proper occasions during the coming summer and fall to represent this general interest at all suitable convocations.
Wm. Carey Crane.

The closing action of the year was the indefinite suspension by the board of a young man termed by President Crane as "still insubordinate."

The trustee report to the convention for the year 1871-72 showed 120 students enrolled with an average attendance of about 70. There were almost twice as many boarding students as in the previous year. An enlarged endowment was solicited and subscriptions were taken for $7,200. One young man earned a B.P. degree, and honorary A.M. degrees were conferred upon Daniel McIntyre and Charles Judson Crane. This commencement was the first to award the "Hiram Woods" prize for elocution. (See Appendix for list of award winners.)

Stringent financial measures were enacted at the year-end board meeting. The treasurer was authorized to institute a suit against "some one of the parties refusing to pay principal or interest on the endowment" and to compromise the claim held by the board against the estate of John H. Allcorn. The board was indebted to the president $367.14 for the current year, and the treasurer was ordered to pay him "the first money coming into his hands not otherwise appropriated." Then Judge Baylor presented a resolution tendering thanks to President Crane "for the untiring energy, zeal, and devotion with which he has managed the affairs of Baylor University and for the sacrifices he has made in the interest of our beloved Institution."[33]

During August 1872 Baylor University issued a circular announcing the following staff: Crane, President and Professor of Theology and Belles Lettres; Fitzgerald, Professor of Mathematics and Natural Science; Etheridge, Professor of Languages; C. J. Humphreys, Tutor; and Willet Holmes, Bursar. Three courses were optional to students: English, scientific, or classical. The student was required to have preparatory work in the area chosen and be at least thirteen years of age to enter the upper division. Pupils were received in the Academic Department at seven years of age. Military tactics were taught and practiced. Tuition was $30, $40, and $50, depending on choice of curriculum, but it was free to all candidates for Gospel Ministry and sons of disabled soldiers or those who died in service. Board was from $10 to $20, with pupils providing their own linens and lights. "The number of times a student is tardy, absent, excused, sick or whispers" was to be checked in the appropriate column!

The law department was suspended at this time, but the Baylor Catalogue of 1871-1872 has an appended note stating that "nearly twenty law students and lawyers attend special lectures in Brenham whose names are not registered [at Baylor] . . . six of the young men would have been graduated in June 1871 [had the department been in operation]."

For the benefit of students wishing to read law before the department was resumed, the following books were listed:

Junior Class: Blackstone and Kent's *Commentaries*
                Stephens on *Pleadings*
                Greenleaf on *Evidence*

Senior Class: Parsons on Contracts; *Bills on Exchange and Promisory Notes*
                Storm on *Equity, Jurisprudence, Evidence Conflict of Laws*
                Pascall's *Digest of State Laws*

[33] Minutes of the Baylor Board of Trustees, June 16, 1872, p. 250.

In mid-August the president of the Baylor Board of Trustees called a meeting at the Oakland Baptist Church in Grimes County, where Judge Baylor served as president pro-tempore. The purpose was to appoint a committee of three "to nominate some qualified brother commanding the confidence of the denomination" to act as General Financial Agent of Baylor University. Then it was resolved to request Brother J. W. D. Creath to present the claims of Baylor University to the Baptist State Convention at its next meeting. The board met again, on October 3, 1872, in Independence, and appointed two men to confer with convention officials to set a time for Brother Creath to address the assembly in the interest of Baylor University. On the following day at an Independence mass meeting the old Texas Baptist Education Society was revived with Henry L. Graves as president.[34] In the first annual report of the society in 1873, Corresponding Secretary Crane listed the beneficiaries at Baylor. Then in November the executive committee of the board appointed H. C. Schmidt an agent to canvas among the Germans for the endowment of a Chair of Modern Languages. In January the board thought it expedient to have one agent serve both the university and Baylor Female College and appointed a committee to investigate the possibility.

At the June 26, 1873, commencement Dr. Crane delivered the baccalaureate address "without manuscript" and it was pronounced his best effort of this kind. The trustees paid tribute to their own: the LL.D. degree was conferred upon President Crane; Horace Clark, former president of Baylor Female College; and J. F. Hillyer, former professor of mathematics. Two young men earned the A.B. degree.

Finances were still the great unsolved problem, and President Crane was credited with $367.14 (a two-year-old debt) on his note of endowment in lieu of funds owed him, and a committee sought another agent. Resolutions were passed upon the death of J. L. Farquhar in appreciation of the long term of service of this original trustee, "a true man, a true Christian, a true patriot, and a true friend of education, contributing liberally of time, influence and money."

[34] J. M. Carroll stated that "because of this society" he came to Baylor. *A History of Texas Baptists,* p. 376.

Of significance is the statement in the minutes of this meeting that President Crane "was authorized to avail himself of any advantage of the present school law."[35]

The Baylor Catalogue for May 1872 to May 1873, the university's twenty-seventh year, showed 81 students in attendance—ages ranging from 10 to 34 years, the average age being 17. The following young ministers were listed:

Charles B. Hollis	James M. Carroll	James R. Horne
Charles F. Jensen	T. Judson Chandler	Milton F. Miller
A. Frank Ross	M. M. Haggard	Julian K. Pace
George W. Baines, Jr.	James A. Bell	Arthur W. Robbins[36]

An entry in President Crane's diary revealed a note of disappointment concerning the opening of the fall term of 1873:

B. U. opened with about 40 pupils. Nine of them are candidates for the ministry. No money has been paid me lately to feed or to sustain these young men. A sad state of affairs exists in Texas.

Baylor graduate Reddin Andrews, Jr., just back from the Greenville Seminary, was selected as the new agent. He had just begun his work when a money panic throughout the country made his efforts almost fruitless. In January 1874 President Crane reported to the trustees that he had given tuition to 26 students. Four teachers assisted Dr. Crane. He needed help, both financial and instructional. On March 31, 1874, he issued a printed appeal to 200 persons for $10 each to secure a residence for a professor of natural science.

No young men were graduated from Baylor University in 1874, but a D.D. degree was conferred upon Reverend J. T. Zealy, pastor of the Houston Baptist Church, at the June commencement.[37]

Finances grew increasingly worse, and at the October 4, 1874, trustee meeting, Dr. Crane's property notes for $600 were cancelled, in lieu of salary payments. Then the board called in six outsiders—J. B. Link, F. M. Law, Horace Clark, H. L. Graves, G. W. Pickett, and J. W. Terrell—for

[35] Minutes of the Baylor Board of Trustees, June 9, 1873, p. 254.

[36] *Baylor University Catalogue*, 1872-1873 (Houston: A. C. Gray.)

[37] Recommendations were made for the granting of an LL.D. degree to Leslie Waggoner, Chairman of the Faculty of Bethel College, Russellville, Kentucky, but Crane correspondence reveals that the recipient was unable to come for the award.

consultation on the subject of aid to the university. The result was the search for another agent, to be paid "not more than twenty-five per cent of the amount which he may collect." President Crane was given authority "to take such steps as he may deem proper to raise $100 for covering of the roof of one of the university buildings."[38]

Another result of "the consultation" was a circular in very small penmanship evidently sent to J. B. Link for publication. It listed the faculty: Wm. C. Crane, Louis Polk, H. A. McArdle, H. C. Schmidt; assistants Charles F. Jensen and T. Judson Chandler. The school enrollment was eighty students with an average age of sixteen, eleven of whom were ministerial students. Alumni of the collegiate branch numbered thirty-nine; of law thirty-one. Link's comment across the copy was this: "It will be impossible to get it up unless you write it in plainer style. The names, many of them being strange, cannot be read with certainty." The affair did little to ameliorate feelings between Crane and Link, who opposed each other in the Educational Union Plan.[39]

The responsibility evolving on President Crane during this year must have been unusually heavy, for his diary contains the following entry on the New Year:

I am surprised that a year has passed away and not a line has been written in this book. I have labored very hard . . . preached 119 sermons, delivered many lectures . . . taught six or seven hours daily with considerable success. My reading has been various and generally thorough and my work generally more acceptable to my feelings.[40]

The report to the trustees for the year listed $1371.96 collected from tuition, fees, and endowment. J. M. Carroll, a student there at the time, wrote that the president's livelihood came from what he could make out of some twenty boarders at $12.50 per month each and a possible $700 per annum received as pastor of the Independence Church.

[38] Board of Trustees' Minutes at this time are in the handwriting of President Crane.

[39] Manuscript Circular, Crane Correspondence, Texas Collection, Baylor University.

[40] Crane Diary, January 1, 1875, Texas Collection, Baylor University.
The university library in 1874 was said to contain 1000 volumes and that of President Crane 2500. The *Brenham Banner* (n.d.) stated that "the library of W. C. Crane of Independence is perhaps the largest owned by any private individual in the state—four or five thousand volumes." Crane Scrapbook, Texas Collection, Baylor University.

Two young men received A.B. degrees at commencement on June 2, 1875. The LL.D. was conferred on Reverend R. B. Burleson, brother of the president of Waco University. The student body for the year numbered seventy-five "above the average age of seventeen."[41]

[41] Carroll, p. 388.

CHAPTER XIII

President Crane's Last Years

THE CONSTANTLY recurring agency problem was the subject of discussion when the Baylor Board of Trustees met October 4, 1875, at Calvert in conjunction with the Baptist Convention. A month later on November 10 at Brenham, T. J. Chandler, June graduate, was appointed agent for the university. A motion was made that an agent be appointed in every church in the bounds of the convention, but it was reconsidered and dropped.

Oddly, the minutes of the trustees carry no mention of the death of founder R. E. B. Baylor, in December of 1873, but at this meeting the treasurer was instructed "to inquire and if necessary to take legal steps to collect amount due by the R. E. B. Baylor estate to Baylor University."

The faculty for the year 1875-76 was President Crane, Reddin Andrews, Jr., C. H. Wedemeyer, James W. Dallas, Bennett Hatcher, and H. A. McArdle, the renowned Texas artist.

Harry Arthur McArdle was born on June 9, 1836, in Belfast, Ireland, of French-Irish parentage. His father died when McArdle was three, and his mother when he was eleven. She taught him the rudiments of art; and after her death, he studied with the accomplished French artist, Sanneur, frequently sketching ships in Belfast harbor. At the age of fourteen the youth came to the United States with a maiden aunt, who died shortly after arrival. He studied art under Baltimore Professor D. A. Woodward, who did the famous portrait of the Prince of Wales—later Edward VII of England. McArdle's first recognition came when in 1869 he won the Peabody first prize and medal at the Maryland Academy of Design—considered the best art school in the United States at the time.

With the start of the Civil War, McArdle enlisted in the Confederate Army in Richmond, Virginia, and later served as draughtsman for gunboats for the navy and as engineer on the staff of General Robert E. Lee in West Virginia. At the close of the war, he married Miss Jennie Smith of Albermarle County, Virginia, and began his study for his painting, "Lee at the Wilderness."

Doctor's orders in 1869 caused his move to Texas in the hope of aiding his tuberculosis-stricken wife. McArdle established his home in Independence, but Mrs. McArdle died in 1870. McArdle was professor of art at Baylor until the college was moved in 1886. In Texas the artist used men of Hood's Brigade as his models, and Jefferson Davis is said to have wept when he viewed the canvas "Lee at the Wilderness" in 1875. The painting was lost when the Old Capitol burned on November 9, 1881. Although the Legislature had passed a bill appropriating $8,000 for it, the artist suffered the loss.

At Independence, many participants and knowledgeable individuals a i d e d McArdle in research for his renowned "Dawn at the Alamo" and "The Battle of San Jacinto," among them being his neighbor, Mrs. Maggie Williams, the daughter of General and Mrs. Sam Houston, and Major Moses Austin Bryan, the nephew of Stephen F. Austin. These two paintings, valued by Dr. Samuel E. Gideon and artist Wayman Adams at $50,000, hung for twenty-five years in the Senate Chamber at Austin without remuneration to the artist. Finally $25,000 was appropriated for purchase of the two masterpieces. Other paintings include "Ben R. Milam Calling for Volunteers to Storm San Antonio," "Henry Karnes Breaking through the Walls with Crowbar," "Deaf Smith Announcing the Destruction of Vince's Bridge," and a smaller painting of "The Battle of San Jacinto"—the last four being commissions for Mr. James T. DeShields, in addition to portraits of Juan N. Seguin, Baron de Bastrop, Collin McKinney, James A. Sylvester, Samuel M. Williams, General Houston and others. DeShields also purchased the large canvas of "The Settlement of Texas by Anglo-Americans," now hanging in the Hall of the House of Representatives, and commissioned the Houston full-length portrait based on the pen-and-ink sketch made from life by the Hungarian artist Ivonski. The Senate Chamber contains two other McArdle canvases: a portrait of Reuben M. Potter, author of "Hymn of the Alamo," presented to the State by the Texas Veterans' Association; and the magnificent full-length portrait of Jefferson Davis, presented by several citizens of Brenham, Texas. Later McArdle completed portraits of Travis, Judge J. W. Stayton of the Supreme Court, and Judge Pleasants of Cuero. In the library of Southwestern University, Georgetown, Texas, hangs the portrait of Dr. Francis Asbury Mood, founder of the university. Finished in 1905, this canvas is considered his last work.

McArdle's wife, formerly Isophene Lucy Dunnington of West Virginia, died on June 18, 1907, and he on February 16, 1908.[1] The McArdles brought a heightened artistic interest to Texas and Baylor was fortunate indeed to claim the artist, who identified so thoroughly with the campus.

Commencement of 1876 came with two young men as candidates for the A.B. degree. Dr. Carroll noted that more boarders had entered than in any similar period since the close of the war and that twenty-nine young ministers had attended the university since 1870. Eleven were in residence in 1875-76 in a student body of 113. Former Lieutenant Governor George Washington Jones delivered the annual address before the literary societies, Reverend W. H. Dodson the commencement sermon, and Reverend W. W. Keep the baccalaureate sermon before the Richard Fuller Theological Society.[2] The coveted Hiram Woods Gold Medal for oratory this year was won by J. M. Carroll,[3] and Hosea L.

[1] The McArdle's daughter, Marie F., became Mrs. George Linn Bland of Weston, West Virginia. Three sons lived in Texas: Marmaduke P. in Houston, and Phil H. and Willet A. in San Antonio; the fourth son, Ruskin, was librarian of the Senate Library in Washington, D. C. Mr. Willet McArdle gave to Baylor a portrait of his father, which was placed in the McArdle room of Pat Neff Hall. The Texas Collection has seven McArdle paintings: Sam Houston, Judge Baylor, Presidents Crane, Andrews, Graves, Baines, and Burleson. Dr. J. B. Smith, Chairman of the Baylor Art Department, opened the McArdle Art Gallery on April 27, 1967, in honor of Baylor's first artist. See *Texas Outlook*, July 1936, pp. 37-38; *Year Book for Texas*, 1901; Walter Prescott Webb and H. Bailey Carroll (eds.), *The Handbook of Texas*, II, 190; Phamphlet, *McArdle, Texas' Historian-Artist;* Dayton Kelley, "H. A. McArdle," *Southwestern Art*, I, No. 4 (1967), 6-13.

[2] J. M. Carroll, *A History of Texas Baptists* (Dallas: Baptist Standard Publishing Company, 1923), p. 521.

The Richard Fuller Society, organized in 1873, continued its service during Baylor's years at Independence. M. M. Haggard was the first president, Charles F. Jensen, secretary and J. M. Carroll treasurer.

[3] Carroll listed President Crane as "the most helpful friend I ever had" in his *A History of Texas Baptists*. Carroll became President of Oklahoma Baptist College at Shawnee, and was awarded the D.D. degree by Baylor University, Waco, in 1903.

Garrett won the President Crane Silver Medal for best scholarship.

The Texas Baptist Convention, impressed by the report on Baylor, had adopted this resolution:

> Resolved, that Baylor University, one of the cherished objects of this convention, shall continue to receive our influence, our benefactions and our prayers until it shall be placed upon a foundation as firm and as enduring as that of any other institution in our land.

The influence, the benefactions, and the prayers failed to reach their destination, for President Crane's diary confided:

> . . . The carrying on of this institution is a serious burden to me with very little profit. I have had to raise the money the best way I can and from all sources imaginable. The state of things, educational and religious, in Texas, is anything but agreeable . . . with repudiated endowment, unpaid pledges and delinquent tuition payers.[4]

Positive urgency appears in the trustee minutes of August 21, 1876, under resolutions marked A, B, C, D, and E. The treasurer was to collect "as quick as possible" endowment funds from J. W. D. Creath and G. W. Graves and any other subscriptions owed and "commit into the best interest bearing securities State or National." A committee was ordered to settle with new agent T. J. Chandler and "to receive any reports of work done in securing Centennial [United States] funds." The board also restricted the use of university rooms to the Grange and Temperance organizations, other than the regular use for literary or benevolent purposes. In the same effort, J. McKnight was asked to remove his office and fixtures as soon as convenient and that he be charged no rent, except "$30 receipted by W. C. Crane for repairs and plastering." (The landmark drugstore of Mr. McKnight on the main street of Independence had burned.) At the September 30 meeting Mr. McKnight was instructed to make out a balance sheet with agent Chandler and to sell the saddle and pony, which belonged to the trustees.

On Christmas Day 1876 Dr. Crane made another despondent entry in his diary:

> . . . great difficulties have been experienced in business affairs and very little aid has been received from any quarter. The situation of my family has been and is very difficult.

[4] Crane Diary, Monday, June 12, 1876. Texas Collection, Baylor University.

Despite the impossible financial situation, President Crane did rejoice in one thing—the success of his 117 students enrolled for 1877. At commencement on June 6, three young men received the A.B. degree, and seven the B.P.[5] An honorary A.M. was given to George W. Baines, Jr.,[6] who preached the annual missionary sermon. Reverend S. A. Beauchamp delivered the commencement sermon and S. M. King the sermon before the Richard Fuller Society. This year J. M. Carroll received the scholarship award and Robert J. Andrews, brother of Reddin Andrews, was runner-up.

At the annual board meeting President Crane recommended that the next session commence on the second week in September and continue for sixteen weeks to the first of January with the second session of twenty-four weeks to continue into June. Dr. Crane was asked to secure a special agent to collect all subscriptions on "the Centennial Dollar Roll," which had originated on July 4, 1876.

At the December board meeting in Brenham, President Crane and recent graduate J. M. Carroll (who attended the board meeting as proxy for G. W. Pickett) were requested to act as agents to take subscriptions and notes for the completion of the unfinished main building, begun prior to the Civil War. The convention abetted the effort, as evidenced by President Crane's statement:

Elected president [Baptist State Convention] seventh time. Large attendance—$2725 subscribed for completion of buildings for B. U. [only first floor completed]. More hopeful in Texas than I have ever been before.[7]

But despair soon followed for the moody president, as indicated by his entry on the last day of the year:

Many hardships this year. I am compelled to work almost alone. I work harder than ever before in my life, and at more points and in more ways. I hope that I do good, but I feel *unsupported* and too dictated to by those who do little except plan and talk. But my desire is to work on until life ceases.[8]

[5] Carroll states that four of these graduates attended the Baylor Seventy-fifth anniversary in 1921.

[6] Baines, son of former President Baines, became a professor in the Baptist Academy at San Marcos, Texas.

[7] Crane Diary, October 6, 1877, Texas Collection, Baylor University.

[8] *Ibid.*, December 31, 1877.

Dr. E. Bruce Thompson calls attention to the "lamentable flaw in character which often nullified [Crane's] splendid academic and religious achievements"—his lack of humility, his hypersensitivity to criticism, his relish of controversy and his evident persecution complex.[9] The combination of Crane's genteel background, superior education, and very manner seemed to make his associates feel inferior and even defensive. Letters and other records reveal that Crane was frequently misunderstood, misinterpreted, and even maliciously slandered. Professional jealousy as well as Crane's inability to cope with things which he considered beneath his dignity contributed to his unhappiness. His sensitivity was a long-standing trait. Thompson makes reference to it in a letter from father William Crane to his twenty-six-year old son:

You are so touchy . . . take your Bible and learn humility. . . . I am very much afraid that you will experience far more unhappy feeling in future life from an unnecessary high estimate of yourself than from any other source.[10]

Fifteen years later a similar reaction was recorded by M. W. Philips: "You are so easy to be miffed."[11] The tragic flaw seemed indelible and hampered straight-forward communication during all of Crane's life.

Nevertheless, President Crane operated a highly successful college and was ever alert to bring recognition to it. The degree of A.M. *pro Honoris Causa* was conferred on Colonel William Winston Fontaine of Austin by the trustees on March 6, 1878. Then at commencement on June 12, 1878, four young men were granted A.B. degrees,[12] six the B.P., with the following honorary degrees being awarded: A.M. to Phil A. Pointer of Trenton, Kentucky; the D.D. to Reverend C. C. Chaplin of Austin, Texas; Reverend J. D. Murphy of Bryan, Texas; Reverend C. E. W. Dobbs of Bowling Green, Kentucky.

[9] E. Bruce Thompson, "William Carey Crane and Texas Education," *The Southwestern Historical Quarterly,* LVIII (January, 1955), 407.

[10] William Crane to son William Carey Crane, December 7, 1842. Crane Papers, Texas Collection, Baylor University.

[11] M. W. Philips to William Carey Crane, November 8, 1857. Crane Papers, Texas Collection, Baylor University.

[12] Two of these graduates, T. J. Dodson and F. S. Roundtree, were ordained ministers.

The school year of 1878 was considered one of the greatest in Baylor's history. That year the Baptist State Convention increased the subscriptions for the completion of the Baylor building to $5,372 and expressed the hope of attaining $12,000.

Regrettable, however, was the resignation of Reddin Andrews at the end of June 1878. A letter from him to Dr. Thomas Meredith of Corsicana detailed the activities of the pastor-teacher and expressed a perennial hope:

I preach eight times every month and teach school five long days in every week. I am my own woodman, fireman and waterman. I have been assistant cook a part of the time and assistant nurse all of the time. I have looked after household affairs and have been, in large measure, my own errand boy. . . .

Our school has been small, not more than forty pupils at a time, and four teachers to live on the fees promised by students. I wish to serve my generation faithfully; perhaps I am trying to do too much. I live in faith; and believe very strongly, I think, in the providence of God. This faith is my stay amid all my duties and trials. I am longing to see the day when we, as Baptists, will have a college, and when we will be united in head, heart and means to maintain one worthy of our name, or commensurate with the increasing demands of the age. . . .[13]

President Crane added the work of Andrews to his own at the behest of the trustees. By November he was able to secure the services of recent graduate T. Judson Chandler as professor of natural science and English, and the board conferred on him the A.M. degree.

During the summer Dr. Crane made a significant address before the Mexia Education Convention titled: "Who Ought to Support and Control the Education Needed by the People?" Noteworthy among his statements was his declaration that "the denominational school recognizes religion as the basis of education; the State and non-denominational school generally recognizes reason as the basis. . . ." Among the advantages of a denominational school he listed (1) a faculty supporting a fixed standard of study in ethics, based upon admitted principles of religion; (2) the insinuation into the minds of students a higher veneration for pure truth, a loftier sense of the supernatural and superhuman, and a

[13] Andrews to Meredith, February 19, 1878. Cited by Marjorie Rogers, *The Dallas Morning News*, November 2, 1944.

grander view of individual responsibility; and (3) association with students of moral fiber and students preparing for Christian ministry.[14]

In order to facilitate the completion of the construction of the building, the trustees designated individuals in various areas to be responsible for raising listed amounts of money.

Brenham: $2,000—Cr. R. Breedlove, C. C. Garrett, W. H. Carroll
Chappell Hill: $2,000—Q. T. Simpson, E. M. Chapel, H. Garrett
Burton: $----—L. N. Halbert, W. H. McCuthen
Long Point: $300—J. V. Matson, Chauncy B. Shepard
German and Ebenezer Churches: $300
Washington: $100—J. G. Heard, T. J. Chandler.
Gay Hill: $200—W. T. Veazey, J. L. Kirk, J. B. Goodlot, F. W. Carroll.
Good Hope Church: $100—A. E. Lipscomb, C. A. Walling.
Mt. Zion Church: $100—G. S. Chandler, T. J. Chandler
Houston: $600—J. M. C. Breaker, O. C. Pope
Galveston: $----—Wm. Howard, W. H. Stewart, Guy M. Bryan
Navasota: $200—G. W. Pickett, J. W. Terrell, J. H. Owen
Courtney: $100—J. M. Calloway
Hempstead: $50—D. E. Taylor, W. A. Heard
Bryan: $500—J. B. Hardwicke, F. M. Law, J. B. McCleland
Austin: $1,000—C. C. Chaplin, W. Haral, F. W. Chandler
Anderson: $500—J. M. Carroll, P. Hawkins, W. R. Howell
Oakland Church—$150
Calvert: $200—S. B. McJunken, Wm. McIntosh, Wm. Hanne
Caldwell: $400—John Alexander, F. S. Hudson, A. S. Broaddus
La Grange: $400—B. F. Dunn, John T. Duncan, Robt. J. Andrews, Wm. Scallorn.
————————: $250—L. G. Holloway, L. C. Cunningham
Seguin: $100—T. J. Dodson
Bastrop: $150—A. W. Moore
Blanco Assoc.: $200—J. W. Baylor.[15]

The secretary was requested to solicit free passes over the railroads for the president of the university while attempting to raise funds for the completion of the building.

Characteristic of the benevolence of aged J. W. D. Creath is the following note written on the back of a Crane letter to Creath. He was hopeful for the success of the building campaign.

Let us all work together—and God will bless. My poor heart is made to rejoice at the prospects of our schools at Independence.

[14] Reprint of August 6, 1878, address. Crane Papers, Texas Collection, Baylor University.
[15] Minutes of the Baylor Board of Trustees, November 4, 1879, p. 269.

Pray three times where we have prayed once and the Lord will yet more and more smile upon our poor efforts.[16]

At the next board of trustees meeting on April 10, 1879, a committee was appointed to compute specific costs on the completion of the building. Plans were made for a special appeal for subscriptions and money at the next commencement. It was also agreed that Treasurer H. C. McIntyre handle all funds without compensation.

At the June 10 commencement the A.B. degree was awarded one student and the B.P. given to six. During the school year seven ministers had been brought in as lecturers to the ninety-one students, twelve of whom were preparing for the ministry. For the year February 1878 to February 1879 there was a catalogue which contained a picture of the campus.[17]

Yet occasional disrupting circumstances made President Crane's position of leadership difficult, as evidenced by this statement:

Thurs. 6 . . . one brother threatened to part with me and to withdraw support to young men studying for the ministry here; another to form a new organization separate from the State Convention; another to withdraw his subscription—all because I proposed that the "Commission" (the most unfortunate mistake ever made in Texas) shall change its figures. . . . [18]

J. B. Hardwick was appointed agent by the trustees in early November 1879 with an agreement to pay him 33⅓ per cent of money collected, so anxious were they to complete the construction of the buildings. Then, on the next day they drew up a lengthy building contract with Willet Holmes, agreeing to pay $2100 in installments: "$600 in cash, $1000 collected from the denomination and friends of Baylor University, by the said Holmes or some one else." Date of completion was December 1, 1880. The forfeit was set at $500 should either party fail in his contract.

Baylor University published a catalogue for this the thirty-fifth year. It carried a listing of the three classes of trustees and 119 students, among whom were 11 ministers and 9

[16] Letter in Crane Correspondence, November 15, 1879. Texas Collection, Baylor University.
[17] Catalogue of Baylor University, 1878-1879. (Cincinnati: Elm St. Printing Companies, Nos. 176 and 178 Elm St.).
[18] Crane Diary, February 6, 1879, Texas Collection, Baylor University.

young men in the reopened law school at Brenham.[19] By this date Baylor University had contributed to the education of 3,000[20] young men, over 80 of whom were ministers.

The catalogue named two societies for ministers: the Richard Fuller Theological Society and a Missionary Society. There were also two debate societies, unnamed. These groups were under faculty direction: (1) all proceedings were open to inspection of faculty and trustees; (2) no society could hold meetings or appoint lecturers without the advice and consent of the faculty; (3) none but active students could hold membership—former students, alumni, and other worthy ones could hold honorary membership.

A called session of the trustees on April 8, 1880, resulted in a special convocation for distinguished lecturers. President Crane reported that a procession was a part of the affair in honor of the recipients of the honorary degrees. The D.D. was conferred on Reverend W. D. Bailey of Galveston and Reverend O. C. Pope of Houston; the LL.D. on Professor H. H. Smith of Sam Houston Normal Institute at Huntsville and Professor T. N. Clark of William Jewell College at Liberty, Missouri; and the A.M. on Charles H. Wedemeyer of the class of '78, who was appointed Professor of Pure Mathematics for the following year. "A grand gathering" was held at the president's home in the evening, which Dr. Crane said was enjoyable in every way and there was "pleasant conversation" with all parties.[21]

A disciplinary matter resulted in another called session of the board of trustees on May 29. The president presented a petition from eleven students concerning the decision

[19] Catalogue of Baylor University, February 1879-February 1880, (Moawequa, Illinois: F. M. Hughes, Printer).

The catalogue announced the faculty of the Law Department as John Sayles and James E. Shepherd. There were no seniors among the nine students for the October 4, 1879, opening of the eight-months term. Occasional lectures were given by Hon. D. C. Giddings, Hon. Seth Shepard, Hon. J. D. McAdoo, J. T. Swearingen, Esq., C. R. Breedlove, Esq., E. F. Ewing, Esq., T. W. Morris, Esq., C. C. Garrett, Esq., B. H. Bassett, Esq., of the local bar, and by distinguished gentlemen from other cities. (pp. 15-16). Breedlove, Ewing, and Morris were graduates of the Baylor Law Department. Communications concerning the law classes were to be addressed to Hon. James E. Shepherd, LL.D., Dean of the Faculty.

Later catalogues continued to list Sayles and Shepherd as law faculty members along with the statement: "Law Department at present not in operation." Baylor Catalogue, 1882-3, p. 11.

[20] Carroll, p. 523.

[21] Crane Diary, Texas Collection, Baylor University.

of the faculty and executive committee in refusing to grant them an honorable dismissal. Facts were presented and discussed; then Dr. C. C. Chaplin was commissioned to talk with the students in an endeavor to induce a change of intent. The conversation was ineffective, and the young men were asked to return to their university duties or else suffer suspension.

At the June 8 annual board meeting Dr. Crane was asked to make a complete statement of the facts, upon which the board resolved unanimously not to grant honorable dismissal. Furthermore, "in as much as the eleven students have refused obedience to the commands of the Faculty and Trustees, they are hereby expelled."[22]

At the June 1880 commencement one young man received the A.B. degree and four the B.P. An honorary D.D. degree was conferred on Reverend Justin A. Kimball of Larissa, Texas, and the LL.D. on J. C. Long of Chester, Pennsylvania.

In an effort to push to completion the planned construction, the board employed F. W. Carroll[23] to collect funds. C. H. Wedemeyer was asked to solicit endowment for the Chair of German. At the beginning of the year the report to the convention had offered congratulations to the friends of Baylor on its improved prospects since the war. "It only needs the strong fostering hand of the Baptist denomination and friends of higher education to make it all its originators designed it to be," the report read. But the hopes were not realized; President Crane wrote that the denomination is "torn to tatters in the State" and that poor headway was being made on the construction of the Main Building.[24]

The trustees gave an order that Dr. Crane's and Thomas McKnight's bill for material furnished for the repair of Graves Hall be paid out of the first money received. The executive committee was authorized to negotiate sale of lands belonging to the trust funds of the university. The

[22] The students were D. Roy Magee, E. S. Banks, James S. Evans, W. F. Nichols, J. T. Haile, J. W. Anderson, E. C. Ralston, B. Hatcher, Wm. S. Banks, J. C. Muse, and E. L. Fouts.

[23] Francis Wayland Carroll, brother of J. M. Carroll and a ministerial student, died during this year at Baylor University.

[24] Crane Diary, November 29, 1880, Texas Collection, Baylor University.

A Crane letter to Trustee Garrett on September 1, 1880, stated that the Treasurer's book shows that "nearly everything collected for the Main Building has been through *yourself* or *myself*. . . ."

trustees were sufficiently hopeful of success to ask Board President Hosea Garrett to have his picture painted for placement in the Garrett Chapel of the new building.

For the thirty-sixth year at Baylor, February 1880-February 1881, the catalogue reported 120 students, with three law students and six ministers.[25] At the time the campus covered thirty-two acres. Tragedy hit the boarding school, however, in the deaths of two students, an exceedingly rare occurrence at Baylor. Depressing also was the slow collection of subscriptions to the building fund, and work on Tryon Hall was again suspended. Commencement in June 1881 honored one A.B. graduate and the following ministers who received doctorates; the D.D. degree to J. C. Maple of Mexico, Missouri, and E. T. Winkler of Marion, Alabama, and the LL.D. to C. H. Carey of Richmond, Virginia.

The *Baylor Aegis* of August 1881 carried an article describing the sacrificial work of President Crane. In addition to his labor, often without salary, he "had paid $500 to endowment and $1200 to general repairs and subscribed $250 for the new building, plus $200 for mathematical instruments." He also kept his splendid library open to students. Reference is made to the new house he was at last building for his family—"with means acquired before coming to Texas."[26]

The fall convention report for 1881 showed an increase in students. President Crane listed sixty-six at the end of the third week in September,[27] the number increasing to 100 after Christmas and to 126 as a total for 1881-1882. Baylor Female College reported 111 students for the same period. Attendance at most colleges was erratic, with enrollment highest in the spring session. Comparative enrollment in Southern colleges was the concern of President Crane. For

---

[25] President Crane's personal catalogue with penned notes. Texas Collection, Baylor University.

[26] *Baylor Aegis,* I (August 1881), Independence, Washington County.

The monthly magazine, begun in February 1881, was published alternately by the Societies. The name was suggested by Professor Wedemeyer, who, upon request contributed an article—"The Debating Society As A Means of Mental Culture"—to the second issue. He had delivered the oration on February 26, 1880. The first issue carried a "salutatory" announcing the purpose of the periodical to be the development of truth, science, and eloquence . . . and to shield and help forward the interest of an institution whose past history proves her well worthy the praise and encouragement of all lovers of education within the broad domain of our Empire State."

[27] Crane Diary, September 20, 1881, Texas Collection, Baylor University.

this same period he listed Howard College as having 203 students, Judson Female Institute (also at Marion, Alabama) with 143, Mississippi College (Clinton, Mississippi) with 239, the Central Female Institute (also at Clinton) with 119 students, Waco University Male Department with 205 and the Female Department with 116.[28]

Just as hopes were bright for the future, calamity came in the form of a destructive cyclone in Independence on February 27, 1882. The newly completed walls of the main building, the roof of Graves Hall, another of the rock buildings, and the president's home—the dormitory—were seriously damaged. President Crane stood forth "almost alone, and with unfaltering trust said: 'we can and must repair the damage. Baylor University must succeed.' "[29] Because of Crane's work in collecting funds and rallying support for the stricken institution, the buildings were better than before, and the year was termed the best of Crane's presidency.[30]

The trustees gave authorization to sell 640 acres of land in Lee County and a strip of land on the south of the college grounds to relieve immediate financial distress. Reverend H. Nabring was employed as financial agent and was to receive one-third of his collections as salary.

By the end of the school year the main building was "not internally finished, but the chapel was used for commencement.[31] Three young men received the A.B. degree and two the B.P. Honorary D.D. degrees were conferred on four ministers: J. B. Taylor, Wilmington, North Carolina; George W. Pickett, Dallas, Texas; F. M. Law, Giddings, Texas; and W. H. Vernor, Little Rock, Arkansas.

University buildings listed in the catalogue as in use at this time were Graves and Houston Halls, the President's Domicile and Creath's Mansion. At the annual business session of the trustees President Crane reported and paid over money he had collected in Baltimore and was empowered to solicit other subscriptions.

[28] W. C. C., "Facts and Figures About Higher Institutions," *Baylor Aegis,* II (December 1882).
[29] T. J. Chandler, "Reverend Wm. Carey Crane in His Relation to Education," *Texas Baptist Herald,* June 18, 1885.
[30] Ford Hoyt, "The Life and Works of Dr. William Carey Crane," (unpublished Master's thesis, University of Texas, 1926).
[31] *Baylor Catalogue, Thirty-eighth Year, February 1882-1883* (Brenham: Banner Steam Book Print).

A trustee committee conferred with a committee of Baylor Female College and changed the school session from forty weeks to thirty-six weeks, beginning on August 28. Professor C. H. Wedemeyer was then allowed to use a hall to teach a preparatory school during the vacation.

Dr. Crane was constantly alert to stimulate interest in higher education, and his information was broad. In a newspaper article in December 1882 he reviewed the collegiate situation among the "ivy-league schools" and the state university issue then before Texas people. In defense of the denominational school he wrote: "[I] honestly believe denominational schools are the hope of the world; that moral education, imparted by religious minds, is superior to mere intellectual education, conducted by minds avowing the independence of free thought." Then followed his earnest plea for endowment and an analysis of "education of the sexes," based on *The Teacher,* published by Eldredge & Brother of Philadelphia. [32]

In order to complete the construction of the main building, Baylor trustees had "borrowed" endowment funds. At the April 5, 1883, meeting they executed two notes—one for $1150 and one for $1250—to President Crane, with interest to be paid each March 1. Because of the financial condition of the institution, the resignation of Professor C. H. Wedemeyer was accepted, and the position not filled. Two tracts of land belonging to the university were sold to J. W. Webb—a total of 960 acres for $1500. [33] Then J. T. Hairston and Harry Haynes were requested to present the matter of the endowment of chairs to the Texas Baptist Convention to meet in San Antonio in October.

Commencement of 1883 came with the celebration of the acquisition of some drawings for the university by Baylor artist, Professor H. A. McArdle. Two former students of the Class of 1877, L. R. Bryan of Brenham and James M. Carroll of Lampasas, received honorary A.M. degrees but

[32] W. C. C., "Facts and Figures About Higher Institutions," *loc. cit.*

[33] Some complications resulted in the sale. Minutes of the Trustees for November 18, 1885, reveal that Trustee Hosea Garrett paid Webb $500 "in full satisfaction for a tract of 320 acres of land, sold to said Webb on his contract for work done on main building, the title to which upon investigation appeared to be defective." The board extended their thanks to Garrett for his generous donation.

there were no earned degrees this year. [34]

George Parkin, uncle of Sarah Vickers Chancellor, was to receive his degree at the June 1883 commencement, but he died in December 1882 at school. "President Crane conducted his funeral, Baylor girls sang, and young men of his class carried him to the cemetery," wrote Gertrude Osterhour to her family.

Enrollment for the year was 120, ten of whom were young ministers and one student was the son of William B. Travis, Commander at the Alamo. [35] Student life at this time was limited and the only meeting place for boys and girls was the church—except one day in the winter of 1883 when Independence experienced a snow storm. Also students maintained a secret postoffice in the back of a garden, where boys and girls posted notes in a turnip patch. [36]

An announcement of a small happening on the campus in 1882 appeared in a local sheet:

Dr. Crane has moved the bell from the place where it has stood so long to a position near Houston Hall so that he will not have to walk so far when he taps the bell for class changes. [37]

Baylor property was valued at $60,000 in 1883. Arrangements were made for seats in Tryon Chapel at an August meeting of the trustees. At this time they also designated official names for existing buildings:

the main building [to be] known as Garrett Hall, the Chapel as Tryon Chapel; the oldest building as Graves Hall, the second building Houston Hall, the wood building (purchased by Texas Baptist Education Society with funds contributed by J. W. D. Creath) as Creath Hall, and the octagonal building as President's Mansion.

A layman, George B. Davis, Esquire, was appointed agent for Baylor University on November 20, 1883, by the Baylor trustees. His salary was fixed at $1500 and necessary travel expenses not to exceed $300. At the January 9, 1884, meet-

[34] The Minutes of the Baylor Board of Trustees, May 7, 1883, state that the same degree was awarded to Reverend W. D. Powell of Saltillo, Mexico, but he is not listed by Carroll or the Alumni Directory 1854-1911.

[35] Mrs. Georgia J. Burleson's personal Baylor Catalogue (39th year) 1883-1884, (Dallas: Texas Baptist Steam Print). Notation is made that Charles E. Travis received the LL.B. in 1859.

[36] Information supplied by Isabella Hester, later Mrs. Engelhart of Livingston.

[37] In 1934 Baylor President Neff, walking over the old campus, found the bell, identified by Independence citizens, and moved it to the Waco Campus. It is the smaller of the two bells around which "Ring Out" is held each year.

ing Agent Nabring sent in his report of $415 (less commissions collected since May 7, 1883). Subscriptions of about $2000 were still due. Trustee Breedlove was instructed to inform Mr. Nabring that his commission as agent was revoked, and if he "refused to deliver up all said subscriptions," the facts should be published in the *Texas Baptist Herald*. Agent Davis reported $417.50 paid on endowment notes during the year. Thirteen ministerial students were among the 103 enrolled during the school year.[38]

Commencement was a gala affair in June 1884 with A.B. degrees earned by three young men and the B.P. by one. Each graduate delivered an original oration, and His Excellency, John Ireland, Governor, addressed the Philomathesian and Erisophian societies of the university and the Royal Society of Baylor Female College. Honorary doctorates were awarded Reverend W. J. Mitchell of Marshall, Texas, and Reverend A. E. Owens of Portsmouth, Virginia. The Independence Methodist Church loaned the university seats for use in Garrett Hall for the occasion and received the thanks of the trustees. The Sub-Junior Exhibition on June 2, 1884, was held at seven o'clock; the program and music consisted of thirty-seven numbers!

Indebtedness to President Crane again came to the attention of the trustees, and it was resolved that the amount of $383.20 paid out by Dr. Crane for fences, repairs, books, etc. be "paid out of any subscriptions already made or to be made, not appropriated to pay notes now held against the institution."

President Crane issued an announcement on August 1, 1884, about Baylor University. The course of study included Classical, Scientific, and Business. The location was termed "on a parallel with Austin and unsurpassed for health, society, and attractive scenery." Hacks came daily from Brenham; the nearest depot was four miles; board, tuition, lights, fuel and washing were $178, $188, $203, according to grade and habits of economy; books were $5 to $10. Students for the ministry "can mess in Creath Hall by clubbing to purchase room furnishings and provisions."

Inserted in the minutes are memorial resolutions passed at a called meeting at Brenham on November 18, 1884,

[38] Carroll, p. 524.

honoring Trustee Charles C. Chaplin, Pastor of the Brenham Baptist Church and President of the Texas Baptist State Convention.[39]

February 27 proved to be a fateful day for Baylor University. Just three years after the disastrous cyclone on that day President William Carey Crane died on February 27, 1885. Dr. J. M. Carroll wrote that he had never known Crane to be ill, but that a sudden attack of pneumonia caused his death.

Shortly before his terminal illness, Dr. Crane received word of his last brother's death. Evidence of the depth of his depression can be seen in his diary recording:

> . . . mine has been the hardest lot. Far from blood relations, among strangers and often among enemies, open or concealed, faced by difficulties, misunderstood or misrepresented; my lot has been a hard one. . . . I have made some sad mistakes and erred at times and ways numberless. God grant that the remainder of my days be free from error and sin; that success may crown my last exertions, to do good, secure comfort for my family and success to my children. To this end may God grant me grace and enable me faithfully to discharge every duty and live in accordance with His will.

These are the words of an acutely sensitive, humble, dedicated man. The greater portion of Crane's days at Independence were dark, yet he remained philosophical and felt that the Baptist denomination would "exist and flourish so long as the memory of Jesus Christ exists on earth."[40]

Soon after he had graduated his sixth and last son, with his last child, Hallie, due to be graduated at the end of the year, death came for President Crane. He had completed a self-assigned task—the education of his children. He was buried in the old community cemetery at Independence. As he directed, a modest marble slab bore the inscription, "He gave his life for the cause of education and religion in Georgia, Alabama, Mississippi, Louisiana, and Texas." In 1937 the Texas Centennial Commission had President Crane's remains reinterred in the State Cemetery, the inscription bearing this legend:

William Carey Crane, 1816-1885
President of Baylor University
1st President of Texas State Teachers Assn.

[39] The memorial resolution terminated Dr. Crane's handwriting on the Minutes of the Trustees, which he began executing on December 7, 1877.
[40] William Carey Crane, "Facts and Figures," *The Baylor Aegis, loc. cit.*

Despite his frequent despondency, Crane took an avid interest in community affairs, as well as those of church and school. He participated in activities of the Masons, Odd Fellows, the State Legislature, and organized the Band of Hope in Independence and the State Council of Friends of Temperance in Waco. In a report on his activities during his first two decades in Texas he wrote:

. . . in addition to my literary labors, I have preached 2064 sermons, given 1000 lectures, baptized 309, married 89 couples, conducted 78 funerals, attended five-sixths of the funerals [in the area], assisted in ordaining 13 ministers and 14 deacons, and raised $23,000.[41]

During the last year of his life, Dr. Crane continued this exhaustive pace. Besides teaching eight hours a day, he paid fifty-two pastoral calls, preached 107 sermons (some as far away as Baltimore and others at Dallas, Waxahachie, Tyler, and Lancaster), married three couples, conducted ten funerals, delivered two Masonic Corner Stone addresses (at Belton and Brenham), and raised over $4,500.00 for the completion of the main building at Baylor, kept all books and accounts for the institution, and wrote numerous letters for the press and religious journals.

Life weighed heavily on Dr. Crane—and frequently with good reason. Dr. Frederick Eby declared: "The tragedy of the situation lay in the fact that Dr. Crane was wasting the ripest years of his noble career on a situation which was foredoomed to end in failure." Eby felt that Crane had no peer as an educator in the South.[42] Carroll termed him "the prince among school presidents" and the best equipped college man in Texas. He termed his death the beginning of the end for Baylor at Independence, for "the master mind, spirit and personality had gone."[43]

Historians have agreed that Crane's heroic struggle to maintain Baylor—at the cost of his most productive years and his fortune[44]—was a sacrifice for a lost cause. Baylor

[41] William Carey Crane, "Twenty Years in Texas," Texas Baptist Herald, February 14, 1884.
[42] Frederick Eby, "Education and Educators," Centennial Story of Texas Baptists, p. 154.
[43] Carroll, p. 525.
[44] T. J. Chandler estimated that Crane spent $7,000 of his personal funds on Baylor, in addition to his family's gifts and his salary losses. "Reverend Wm. Carey Crane in His Relation to Education." Texas Baptist Herald, June 18, 1885. J. M. Carroll added that Crane gave $10,000 in room and board to struggling students. Waco Times-Herald, June 2, 1909.

at Independence was doomed to failure. Eby enumerates a series of causes: "denomination wrangling, the ugly competition of other Baptist schools, changes in sociological conditions, lack of funds, the rise of the public school system, and financial depression after the War."[45] Small consolation rested in the fact that other denominations had experienced similar disasters: the Methodists at Chappell Hill, the Presbyterians at Gay Hill and Huntsville, and the Episcopalians at Anderson. Despite the fact that Baylor at Independence was ultimately closed, it must be agreed that the school rendered a great service, both to the Baptist denomination and to Texas, even in its denouement as attested to by fifty-nine young men who were graduated under Crane's tutelage, with numerous others in attendance. Chandler stated that hundreds of young men were "fired with a generous ambition and noble principles by the example of their venerable preceptor."[46] Well over three thousand students attended Baylor at Independence, with nearly half of that number during the administration of Dr. Crane, the largest graduating class being in 1877-78.[47]

The sacrifice of Dr. Crane as president of Baylor at Independence was monumental, and his maintenance of the institution during the decades 1865-1885 provided for the ultimate unity of Baylor University and Waco University as the foremost Baptist university. An accurate assessment of the work of President Crane at Baylor is impossible to make. He gave the school scholastic dignity and purpose while on the verge of financial catastrophe during the entire period. Dr. E. Bruce Thompson, in the most comprehensive summation of Crane's work in Texas, describes his effort to save Baylor "an educational epic."[48]

Credit must also be given to Dr. Crane's diligence and foresight in working for the establishment of the state university and the normal college—Sam Houston Normal

[45] Eby, p. 155.

[46] Chandler, *op. cit.*

[47] Prior to the coming of Crane, thirty-four young men were graduated in the literary department, counting the seven who received their degrees at Waco University. Twenty-nine young men received law degrees in the classes of 1858 and 1859. During Crane's administration only two law degrees (1866) were granted. R. C. Crane Correspondence. Texas Collection, Baylor University.

[48] E. Bruce Thompson. "William Carey Crane and Texas Education," *The Southwestern Historical Quarterly*, LVIII (January 1955), 405-422.

College in Huntsville in 1879.[49] He also served as the first president of the Texas State Teachers Association, founded in Austin on January 28, 1879, and worked for an improved public school system.

The annals of Texas Baptists attest to the denominational service of William Carey Crane. He was president of the Texas Baptist State Convention ten consecutive years and was a member of several boards and committees.[50] Before coming to Texas he had served as president of the Mississippi State Convention for two years and for three years as president of the Louisiana State Convention.[51] For twelve years he was secretary of the Southern Baptist Convention and vice-president for four years.

A staunch champion of women's activity, Dr. Crane worked diligently for the organization of women for missions. The first Texas Home Mission Society was organized at Independence in 1878 with Baylor women as officers: Mrs. Fannie Breedlove Davis, president, and Miss Anne Luther, secretary. Subsequently in October 1880 in Austin where the Baptist State Convention was in session, the Women's Missionary Union of Texas was organized, with Mrs. Davis as the first president.[52]

Harlan J. Matthews declared that Crane's ability as a preacher equaled his strength and effectiveness as an educator. His sermons presented "unanswerable logic and fascinating sermonic literature." His dignified, majestic, and even dominating presence in the pulpit and on the platform caused some to regard him as egotistical, but such was not the case, declared Matthews, who wrote of Crane's "beautiful humility and . . . dependence upon God and the prayers of his brethren."[53] Long-time Texas minister Jeff D. Ray also wrote that many considered Crane "pompous and ego-

[49] R. C. Crane, "Dr. William Carey Crane's Activities in the Establishment of State University, Normal College and Improved Public School System," *The Baylor Monthly*, March 13, 1929.

[50] J. M. Carroll, "William Carey Crane," *The Baylor Monthly*, V (April 1929), p. 3.

[51] C. H. Wedemeyer (Belton), "William Carey Crane," *Baylor University Bulletin*, XIII, No. 1. (January 1910).

[52] Mrs. B. A. Copass, "The Women and Their Work," *Centennial Story of Texas Baptists*, pp. 208-210.

[53] Harlan J. Matthews, "Preaching and Preachers," *Centennial Story of Texas Baptists*, p. 98.

tistic," but intimates considered him a man of "simple tastes and most beautiful humility of spirit."[54]

In an analysis of the man William Carey Crane, C. H. Wedemeyer (who taught in both Baylor at Independence and at Waco University) wrote: " . . . tenfold greater than was Cicero's debt to Achias is mine to William Carey Crane." He explained the secret of Crane's power and commanding personality as resulting from ancestors of heroic mold; brains and a spirit of magnanimity that made him one of nature's noblemen; the best of training and education; patient toil and matchless expedition under thoroughly disciplined faculties; the power of discovery and inspiration; and finally his devout humility as a Christian. Wedemeyer recorded that Crane was often misunderstood and maligned, but that he had the courage to overlook and to forgive. Annoyed greatly by petty things, amid real disasters he was undismayed.[55]

Various posthumous honors have been paid this heroic pioneer Texas educator-minister. Crane County on the Pecos River in West Texas was created by the Texas legislature in 1887 and organized in 1927 with the town of Crane its county seat.[56]

As a part of Baylor's Centennial Celebration, Baylor alumni of Austin, Texas, paid tribute to President William Carey Crane on Sunday, May 27, 1945. Dr. W. R. White (later to become president of Baylor) devoted the morning service of the First Baptist Church to the honor of Dr. Crane. At three o'clock former students and friends of Baylor met at the cemetery—fifteen paces west of the Stephen F. Austin statue—and placed a wreath on his grave. Texas University historian, Dr. Frederick Eby, formerly of the Baylor faculty, and John Henry Johnson, Clerk of the Supreme Court of Texas, spoke.[57] On May 28, 1949, the Baylor University Historical Society paid tribute to President Crane. The guests of honor were members of the Crane

[54] Jeff D. Ray, "William Carey Crane," *Fort Worth Star Telegram*, September 26, 1937.

[55] C. H. Wedemeyer, "William Carey Crane," *The Belton Journal*, December 3, 1909.

[56] *Texas Almanac* (*The Dallas Morning News* 1956-1957), p. 623.

[57] John H. Johnson, "Report," May 20, 1945. Texas Collection, Baylor University.

family, including grandsons Dorset and Davis Crane, and son, Judge Royston C. Crane, who wrote of his illustrious father: "If Baylor, Huckins and Tryon were the founders of Baylor, then Crane was its Saviour."[58]

In the Texas Collection of Baylor University hangs the McArdle portrait of President William Carey Crane, and the archives contain the great bulk of his work—scrapbooks, diary, letters and papers—meticulously executed and preserved by him and conferred to Baylor University by his son Royston C. Crane, as well as personal items.[59]

William Carey Crane, who declined the presidency of eleven colleges to expend his life at Baylor University, justified his illustrious heritage and education in his "magnificent crusade for Christian education in Texas."[60]

Baylor Board of Trustees resolutions on "the decease of our beloved President" declared it a public calamity and an irreparable loss to the Baptist denomination of Texas. Directions were given for a memorial sermon to be delivered by Dr. William Howard at the next Baptist State Convention.

Minutes of the 38th Annual Session of the Baptist State Convention also contained a report on the death of President Crane:

> On the 27th of February last the usual quiet routine of this institution was suddenly interrupted by the death of Dr. William Carey Crane, then in the twentieth year of his administration. This was a severe loss, because for years, the one aim of his life, the one hope

[58] Royston C. Crane (Sweetwater, Texas), "Mission-Minded Men Laid Plans for Baptist Future in Texas," *Baptist Standard,* November 11, 1948, p. 18.

[59] The Crane Collection contains the handcarved, ebonized Emerson piano purchased by Dr. Crane about 1880. In Independence the piano was the center of student social activity, for the young people promenaded around the old octagonal veranda to the strains of "Old Black Joe," "Swanee River," and "Monastery Bells." The fine instrument was presented to Baylor by Judge Royston C. Crane of Sweetwater in 1928. *The Dallas Morning News,* January 19, 1941. The Collection also contains Dr. Crane's chair, washstand, and the historic Lea dresser. It was inherited by Nancy Lea, mother of Mrs. Royston and Mrs. Sam Houston—all three widows and good friends of Mrs. Kate Crane, the wife of President Crane. At the death of Mrs. Lea the dresser went to Mrs. Royston, who had just lost a son in a Virginia battle. (A Crane son was named Vernal Royston Campbell Crane on February 16, 1864). Mrs. Royston gave the dresser to her son's namesake and it went to the Crane home where it was kept in the Crane family until 1895. President Pat M. Neff acquired it from Mr. V. R. Crane in January 1945. R. C. Crane letter, February 5, 1945.

[60] Thompson, p. 421.

of his heart, has been to build firm the foundation and to make sure the future of the institution he loved so well. [61]

The trustees then proceeded to the election of a successor to Dr. Crane. Dr. Pickett nominated Reverend Reddin Andrews, who received a majority of all votes cast and on March 4, 1885, was named President of Baylor University. [62] Professor T. J. Chandler and the staff had carried on the work at the university until March 4, when President Andrews accepted the responsibility.

[61] Minutes of Baptist State Convention, 1885, p. 29.
[62] Minutes of Trustees henceforth are in the handwriting of Harry Haynes.

CHAPTER XIV

Baylor's Denouement

R EVEREND REDDIN ANDREWS, pastor of the Tyler Baptist Church, accepted the call to the presidency of his alma mater and appeared at the March 9, 1885, trustee meeting to discuss plans. Reddin Andrews knew Baylor and the great service the university had rendered under the most difficult circumstances throughout the years of its existence. During his childhood an idealized vision of the university had stimulated his thinking. His oldest half-sister, Mrs. Mary J. Ellis, widow of pioneer Baptist preacher Richard Ellis conducted a boardinghouse at Independence in the 1850's and sent her twin daughters to Baylor. Several of his younger half-sisters attended, and others of his extended family visited the school. He observed "that there was a sort of polish, finish, and dignity about those who had been favored with the opportunity of going to school at Baylor University."[1] The probability of his attending "the heaven-favored" institution was so remote that it did not occur to him.

As a young man of fifteen Andrews first saw Baylor University on July 2, 1863, as he and Isaac Sellers went off to join the Confederate Army. He was awed by the imposing rock buildings—the biggest he had ever seen, except at Monterrey and Saltillo, where he had visited three years before. After the war Andrews attended "a double-log house" school near the Fayette-Colorado county line. The teacher was George L. Chandler, Baylor graduate, who revived his dreams of the university. In 1866 Andrews attended school at Rutersville for five months; then in 1867, at age twenty, the young scholar went by stage coach to Brenham and mail hack to Independence and spent the night in the old wooden inn—the Hood House—to await enrollment at Baylor University.

Andrews' venture was typical of the times, for he took the customary letters of introduction to the notables of the place. One was from William Harris, a minister and former Baylor

[1] Reddin Andrews, '71, "The Baylor I Knew," *Baylor Bulletin,* XVIII (December 1915), 41.

student, to Asbury Daniels (father-in-law of Dr. D. R. Wallace). Daniels was the current justice of the peace and left the three-room concrete cottage [2] to walk with him to the octagonal house on the Baylor campus. There he presented to Dr. Crane a letter of introduction from his former pastor, P. B. Chandler. Thus began a long friendship. For four years Andrews was a member of the Crane household. He praised President Crane's "extensive knowledge of the whole range of human learning" and declared that Crane "knew more about more things than any other man of my acquaintance"—in fact he termed him a bit "book-heavy."

Andrews was a diligent student, a member of the Erisophian Society, and a serious public speaker. He recalled the June commencement of 1871 as "the crowning day of my life, up to that time." As valedictorian he spoke on "The Demands of the Times." A natural sequence of events brought Andrews back to Baylor as agent, then teacher; and at the death of President Crane, he was the logical choice to direct the affairs of the troubled institution.

Compensation for staff members was a significant matter, as usual, and Reverend F. Kiefer was directed to act as temporary agent to collect funds for the president's salary. Dr. J. H. Luther, President of Baylor Female College, volunteered to canvas the town of Independence.[3]

Three months later on June 3, 1885, President Andrews submitted his report to the board of trustees:

. . . I need not refer to the sad circumstances that brought me to this place. . . . I have done what I could to carry on the work. There have been 64 students during the scholastic year, with perhaps a daily average of forty. The order has been tolerably good. The faculty has been *compeled* to suspend 3 or 4 students indefinitely, and inflict less severe punishment in other cases. I say nothing . . . concerning the condition of the buildings (choosing) rather to make some verbal statements. I present herewith the resignation of Professor Chandler, who for the last 7 years has faithfully discharged

[2] Later the cottage was owned by Andrews' mother-in-law, Mrs. Virginia Vickers. Some eight years later Andrews and Bettie E. Eddins were married there by President W. C. Crane.

[3] President Luther telegraphed Andrews the stunning news of President Crane's death on February 28, 1885. Some of the trustees en route to Brenham for their meeting wired Andrews that he was to be chosen president. Andrews stated that he was elected with only one dissenting vote. Andrews, *op. cit.*, p. 44.

the duties of Professor of Natural Science. He has been driven to this step by failing health.

I have made no arrangements for teachers next year. I did not feel justified in doing so without a knowledge of the financial condition of the university. Of this I know nothing. . . . I know of several first class teachers whom I could get if I could assure them of support.

My own support has been only partially attended to since I came into my present position. I shall expect you to take some steps with reference to this matter so important to myself. We have one graduate for this year, F. M. Newman, who earned the B.P.[4]

At two o'clock on June 3, 1885, the Baylor University trustees met in joint session with the trustees of Baylor Female College. Harry Haynes introduced a strong resolution against removal of the schools from Independence—an idea long supported by the press, both religious and secular, and individuals over the state. The controversy had damaged the efficiency of the schools and certainly affected the patronage. Action on the matter, however, was deferred until June 16, when a second joint meeting of the trustees was arranged at Brenham.

The Reverend Garrett was called to the chair at the joint session, with J. B. Link serving as secretary. The business at hand was the Haynes resolution. Dr. William Howard offered the following resolution:

Whereas the changes wrought in the Providences of God by time, changes in population, centers of influence, accessibility, etc., it sometimes becomes necessary to remove institutions of learning to more favored localities . . . therefore be it resolved

First . . . that these institutions should be removed from Independence at as early a day as the preservation of their interest will admit. . . . Fealty to the mental interests of the rising ministry and to Christ require it.

Second, that it is the sense of this body that the locality offering the largest amount for one or both of them, other things being equal, ought to be given the preference.

Third, that it would be unwise to take any final step until the voice of the Convention is heard, and that a committee be appointed to present the matter. . . .

Much discussion followed, various changes were made and amendments proposed, but the whole question was referred to the convention to meet in October 1885 at Lampasas.

[4] Minutes of the Baylor Board of Trustees, June 3, 1885.
Frank M. Newman, later a lawyer at Brady, Texas, was the last graduate of Baylor University at Independence.

Regardless of the proposed removal of the Baylors from Independence, the trustees of Baylor University had many problems before them. In a June 12, 1885, session they requested publication of resolutions on the resignation of Professor Chandler in *The Texas Baptist* and *The Baptist Herald*. It was decided that President Andrews had been paid in full for his past services as president, and Dr. Howard was requested to correspond with President Andrews concerning a continuation in office "under the present circumstances." A committee was appointed to confer with the heirs of Dr. Crane. The next meeting was scheduled for July when the Sunday School Convention met in Houston, at which time President Garrett was to bring to the convention the question of the removal of Baylor.

Arrangements were made on September 10, 1885, with President Andrews to conduct affairs at Baylor for the year 1885-1886. He was to be allowed all receipts for tuition fees, incidental tax, library fees, and all interest accruing from the endowment fund, the sum not to exceed $2,000 to be raised by him. Out of these sources he was to pay all salaries and the current expenses of the school. Professor C. H. Wedemeyer was named vice-president and professor of natural science.[5]

At the Lampasas meeting on October 22, 1885, this cryptic statement appears in the minutes of the Baptist State Convention:

There has been much agitation in the bounds of this Convention on the subject of the removal of Baylor University from Independence, therefore

Resolved, that this matter be placed before the Convention for the action of said body on the question.[6]

Trustee A. W. Dunn offered the resolution for the removal of the two schools from Independence. The resolution was adopted, and thus terminated the long struggle. It was agreed that Baylor University and Waco University merge.

[5] Wedemeyer was an A.B. graduate of Baylor in 1878 and had joined the staff as professor of mathematics in September of 1880, having been awarded an A.M. in April. He remained at Baylor until April 1883, when he was forced to resign because of unpaid salary. Into Professor Wedemeyer's hands fell the old book containing the minutes of the trustees, later obtained by R. C. Crane.

[6] *Baptist State Convention Annual*, 1885, p. 30.

A committee of fifteen was appointed to work with trustees of the two schools. Buildings, grounds, libraries, furniture, etc. of Baylor at Independence were tendered to Union Association. Endowment, where the donor was dead, should remain with the old school; but when the donor was living, he could elect its placement. Dr. J. M. Carroll estimated the holdings of the two Independence schools as "very large . . . easily worth $300,000, and the whole debt not in excess of $5,000—probably not over $2,500. The property became a total loss to the denomination."[7]

The Baylor trustees designated a committee of three— Harry Haynes, A. W. McIver, and L. R. Bryan—to work with a similar committee from the Female College to procure the change in charter necessitated by the proposed move of the institutions.

The history of Baylor University is closely linked to that of Baylor Female College. In the beginning, from the granting of the charter, provisions were made for the education of girls and young women. Under Baylor's first teacher, Henry F. Gillette, girls and boys were taught together. With the coming of President Henry L. Graves in 1847 boys and girls were taught in separate rooms, but shared teachers. When Principal Horace Clark assumed direction of the Female Department in 1851, the separation was complete in instruction, but President Burleson maintained a supervisory responsibility. The fact that the Female Department was given a secondary role contributed to the disagreement between Burleson and Clark. Course offerings in the two schools differed and women were granted diplomas instead of degrees until June 1862. The two departments had the same board of trustees until the separation by an act of the Texas Legislature in September 1866; then a separate board was organized and the Female Department became Baylor Female College.

The decade of 1851 to 1861 was a period of distinct growth under the direction of Principal Clark. At first the department shared the cramped quarters of Baylor's one frame building—two stories, four rooms. For the 1851-52 school year, the Male Department moved into the new stone build-

---

[7] This estimate was given in the last years of Dr. Carroll. He was pastor of the Lampasas Church when the removal was decided upon.

ing, leaving the frame structure to the Female Department. Here, actually, begins the separate history of the Female Department. Reports to the trustees came from each department and a certain amount of autonomy was recognized. In 1857 through the diligence of Principal Clark and contractor J. P. Collins the Female Department moved into what has been termed "a gem of beauty and utility and probably at that time the best school building in Texas."[8]

Young women lived in a large dormitory originally owned by W. H. Cleveland and enlarged by Clark, who operated it with the assistance of his faculty. Upon the resignation of Clark in 1866 after fifteen years of dedicated and effective leadership, the dormitory was operated by his brother-in-law George B. Davis. This structure was the only dormitory for women during the forty years Baylor was at Independence. Bright in the memory of all Baylor and Independence people of these years was the great bell given to the women's department by Trustee A. C. Horton in 1858.[9]

When Baylor Female College began its operation as a distinctly separate institution in 1866, B. S. Fitzgerald became the first president, with former Baylor University president George W. Baines, Sr., as president of the board of trustees. Mr. Clark returned to the presidency in 1868 at which time Judge R. E. B. Baylor made the report to the Baptist State Convention. The 1869 report made by Dr. William Howard, Galveston pastor, emphasized the wide area from which the school drew its students—at one time numbering 280 young women. Emphasis was placed on "a thorough and practical education."

Proponents of female education were extremely conscious, however, of the steady emphasis upon the educational opportunities for men. Texas was more liberal than most states, although convention records throughout the early years and school practice witness the attention given to the education of men over that of women. In view of this fact, the trustees

---

[8] J. M. Carroll, *A History of Texas Baptists* (Dallas: Baptist Standard Publishing Company, 1923), p. 391.

[9] Pranks by students often involved the bell. At one time the boys tied a long rope to it, with the other end tied to a cow grazing on the college green. As long as she moved about, the bell tolled on the front porch of the dormitory. (Undated letter written by Mrs. Tommie L. Fleming, Kingsbury.) The bell now rests on the Mary Hardin-Baylor Campus in Belton.

of Baylor Female College in session at Brenham on October 3, 1870, proposed that the school be separated from the Baptist State Convention, "in view of the embarrassments in which the Convention is involved in having under its control and patronage two institutions of learning, while it has scarcely means of providing for one. . . ." The plan was to place the school under the Union Association, and a committee was appointed to make application to the convention. Agitation for the removal of both Baylors from Independence quelled the proposal.

In 1871, former Baylor University President Henry L. Graves succeeded President Horace Clark and served for one year. Dr. Francis Marion Law, President of the Board of Trustees, reported the election of Colonel W. W. Fontaine as the new president in 1872. Debt against the school was liquidated and $6,000 was raised for the endowment fund. Course offerings were up-graded to conform to the university plan. President Fontaine resigned in 1874 and was succeeded by Reverend William Royall, who continued to board young ladies "at the unprecedented low price of $10 per month." During his term of office, Board President Law reported to the convention that Baylor Female College was "the only purely female college in the state" and that no better educational facilities for young women could be found in Texas. The college building underwent thorough repairs in 1877 and the school was reported to be in the best condition in years.

Dr. Royall resigned in 1878. Dr. John Hill Luther came to the presidency in 1878 and served for thirteen years. Enrollment doubled in 1880, despite "the giving away" of one wall of the main building, which necessitated great inconvenience and extensive repair. By 1881 the college was in excellent condition, boasting an enrollment of 125 students, 50 of whom were boarders. At the 1882 commencement further progress was noted: six young women were graduated and an honorary doctorate was conferred on Board President Dr. F. M. Law. Of great service to the college was the work of Miss Eli C. Moore, who raised money to enlarge the dormitory capacity of the college. Progress continued at Baylor Female College until the great agitation for removal of Baylor reached a climax with the death of President Crane in 1885. The trustees made a strong appeal to the convention to settle the question, many feeling that the decision would not affect the Female College. Unity came for the two schools when joint annual services were held in 1885, with Reverend J. A. Hockett of San Antonio and M. V. Smith of Belton delivering addresses.

After the decisive Baptist State Convention meeting at Lampasas in October 1885, a sub-committee of the appointed committees on the Consolidation of Educational Interests of the Baptists of Texas recommended that "as very many Baptists oppose co-education, Baylor Female College be located at some other central point, the place where located to give a bonus. . . ."[10] A committee of F. M. Law, A. W. Dunn, H. W. Waters, C. R. Breedlove, G. W. Capps, J. B. Link, R. J. Sledge, R. Andrews, O. H. P. Garrett, S. F. Styles, M. V. Smith, Harry Haynes, G. W. Breedlove, Hosea Garrett, A. W. McIver, William Howard, J. H. Stribling, S. A. Beauchamp, W. R. Maxwell, and C. C. Garrett advertised for bids. Belton's offer of $32,000 was accepted and the school was located on a commanding eminence one mile northwest of the courthouse. Erection of a building was begun, the cornerstone of which was laid April 21, 1886, by the Masonic Lodge with Dr. B. H. Carroll delivering an address on Christian education. The cornerstone of Burnet marble bears the inscription:

Independence 1845   Removed to Belton 1886

The following table shows the changes in organization of the Women's Department of Baylor at Independence:

BAYLOR FEMALE COLLEGE AT INDEPENDENCE

Woman's Department organized—	1850
Dr. Horace Clark, Principal of Woman's Department—	1851
Separate Charter for Baylor Female College	1866
Professor B. S. Fitzgerald, President	1866-1867
(during Clark's leave of absence)	
Reverend Horace Clark, President	1867-1871
Reverend Henry L. Graves, President	1871-1872
Colonel W. W. Fontaine, President	1872-1875
Dr. William Royall, President	1875-1878
Dr. J. H. Luther, President	1878-1886

[10] Mrs. Elli Moore Townsend, *After Seventy-five Years* (Baylor College, Belton, Texas: Student League and Alumnae Association, 1920), p. 20.

President Andrews and his co-workers at Baylor University carried on under adverse circumstances following the announcement of the school's removal. Enrollment dropped to about forty for the term, but the school was maintained.

Andrews realized that his position was a critical one, and he later declared that "a real sense of depression caught me in its grasp. I said little, suffered much and did all that I could in the face of a forlorn hope."[11] He was well aware of the heated discussions among Baptists concerning the removal of the Baylors from Independence. Aligned against the thinning ranks of the Old Guard—Crane, Creath, Baylor, Breedlove, Law, Smith, the Garretts—were the less sentimental, more realistic advocates for removal. Andrews could hear the death-knell, and he acted accordingly: "I resigned at the close of the [fall] session and removed to Waco to enter upon my duties as vice-president and teacher in the united school, under the old title of Baylor University." His course excited suspicion, his motives were impugned, and he was criticized, he declared. Yet he felt that "new conditions render new demands imperative and every generation has its peculiar idea of expediency and necessity," and he moved with confidence blended with regret.

Board President Hosea Garrett sent his last report on Baylor University to the Baptist State Convention for the June 29-July 2, 1886, Waco meeting. It was read by G. W. Pickett at the First Baptist Church. He stated that President R. Andrews reported to trustees that he had planned to continue operation of the school at Independence and had employed two teachers. He commenced the session and continued for some time, "but without informing the trustees of his intentions, he and Professor Pace left." Professor Wedemeyer ably conducted the school for the remainder of the year. "Commencement," with student speeches, was held. Garrett also reported on the condition of buildings and their planned transfer to the Union Association and the indebtedness against the school—perhaps $1600 in notes for building repairs and $250 due Mrs. Crane.[12]

The Baptists of Texas recognized the claim of $1000 against Baylor by H. Hudgins and authorized resigned

[11] Andrews, *op. cit.*, p. 49.
[12] *Texas Baptist Annual,* 1886, pp. 26-27.

trustees at Independence to make a conveyance of part of the property of Baylor at Independence to satisfy the debt.

In the minutes of November 18, 1886, is the statement that "our resignations as trustees of Baylor University take effect when the Baptist General Convention have appointed a new board for the consolidated university." Nevertheless, the board of trustees met from time to time in order to satisfy debts of the institution. The book containing the proceedings of the Baylor University Board of Trustees was placed in the custody of Harry Haynes.[13]

The Union Association, the original sponsor of Baylor University at Independence, received the property of the institution. In hopes of rallying South Texas support they opened a new school, William Carey Crane College. W. W. Fontaine, a former president of Baylor College, and Professor Binford headed the two departments, but it, too, could not continue operation.

On June 1, 1887, the remnants of the Baylor Board met in Brenham and appointed a committee to make a schedule of the assets and liabilities of the institution and to determine what arrangements could be made with creditors. No quorum responded for a designated January 1889 meeting in Brenham, but on January 26 a meeting was held there. L. R. Bryan was called to the chair, for beloved Board President Hosea Garrett had died on September 4, 1888. Bryan was then named president. The claims of the Crane heirs were settled by compromise, the estate receiving 195 acres of land in Montgomery County, patented to A. McCowan.

During the first two months of 1889 the Baylor trustees met six times in the office of Bryan and Campbell in an effort to close out claims against the institution. Finally on

[13] Minutes of the Board and a record book were in the possession of President Crane at the time of his death on February 27, 1885. In the summer Board Secretary Haynes called for the minutes, and the president's son, R. C. Crane, gave them to him. Then they fell into the hands of Professor Charles H. Wedemeyer who returned to Crane College. The later minutes were recorded in the penmanship of Harry Haynes, son of original trustee A. G. Haynes. (Recorded information by R. C. Crane, Minutes of Baylor Board of Trustees, p. 342, Sweetwater, Texas, January 27, 1934.)

The Texas Collection received the Minutes of the Board of Trustees at Independence from Berry Wedemeyer.

After the official consolidation of Baylor and Waco Universities and their location in Waco, the Baylor Board at Independence held the following meetings in order to terminate affairs: June 1, 1887; January 26, 1889; February 5, 1889, at Brenham, and November 15, 1897, and November 22, 1897, at Independence.

February 27—again a fateful day—the board executed a deed conveying all the real estate of Baylor University located at Independence, consisting of 30 acres of land, two frame buildings and one of stone, to T. C. Clay. Clay in turn was to pay off the promisory note held against the university for $1670 (principal and interest) by H. Hudgins. Hudgins subsequently sold the property to F. M. Huhn.[14] The library, maps, charts, furniture and apparatus were not to be conveyed.

On April 5, the trustees conveyed lots 9 through 14, Smith and Woods Division in Rockport, Texas, to C. C. Garrett as a result of H. Garrett's payment of J. W. Webb's claim of $450 for work done on the main building. Finally two meetings in November 1897 at Brenham closed the affairs of Baylor University at Independence. Abram Weaver reported on expenditures in the prosecution of a suit against F. M. Huhn—an effort to recover the Baylor University property sold to T. C. Clay—on the basis of illegality of sale. The case went to the Court of Civil Appeals in Galveston but was lost.[15] The sale of three pianos—to W. E. Clark, Lucy Bailey, and Dr. Burford—concluded the business transactions of Baylor University at Independence.

The university property eventually went into the hands of the Catholics, who established there a Negro orphanage. It too has passed. The site now holds only stone columns to memorialize "the most romantic history ever chronicled by the Baptists of this or any other state."[16]

Postlude

An accurate assessment of the effectiveness of Baylor University during its forty years at Independence is impossible to make. Since history is a "witness of the times," one must consider the locale and the era in perspective—as the period of infancy in a new civilization. Pioneers exhibited stalwart character in founding the Republic of Texas against staggering odds. A traveler in Texas at the time, Mrs. Matilda Houstoun, declared that "no one is stopped in this country

---

[14] A. E. Lipscomb to Dr. S. P. Brooks, July 31, 1929.

[15] *Southwestern Reporter*, XXVI, 755.

[16] J. M. Carroll, *A History of Texas Baptists* (Dallas: Baptist Standard Publishing Company, 1923), p. 527.

by anything short of a bowie knife or a rifle shot." She also wrote that Texans were impatient—"that they drive to their end with greater velocity than any individuals" that she had ever seen or heard of. The courage and impatience of Baptists in infant Texas are readily seen. Determination and disregard of difficulties were demonstrated in the first organized religious body in the state of Texas—the Union Baptist Association, which began functioning in 1841. Out of its early meeting came the Education Society, following the precedent set by such church-affiliated organizations in New England, familiar to Huckins and Tryon. The stated objective of the Education Society was to found a school for the education of a native ministry and to place the entire body of Texas Baptists behind it for support. Such was the plan of a mere handful of men in an area where living itself was hazardous, where transportation was primitive, and where there was little homogeniety among the settlers except in their deprivations. Settlements presented ludicrous incongruities: bookcases of classics in log cabins, tobacco-spitting men in cotton flannel shirts quoting Latin, coffee in tin cups on Dresden saucers, guests using barrels for chairs as they listened to Beethoven on a grand piano!

Circumstances produced an unusual breed of pioneers. The early Texan was termed talkative—particularly about money and business. Yet there was no lack of basic refinement either in conversation or demeanor among many of the early settlers. Mary Austin Holley remarked on the spontaneous gaiety of the women of the Austin Colony and marvelled that they would sometimes ride horseback fifty miles to a ball with their silk dresses tucked in their saddlebags. Twenty years later men found the ladies of "the Brazos bottom" still particularly noticeable for their winning qualities. Despite the primitive living conditions, they were acutely conscious of the amenities—a consciousness which sometimes led to amusing pretentiousness. Life was made easier for the planter class by the holding of slaves. In 1847 one-third of the Texas population were slaves. Baylor founders, Judge Baylor, the Reverend Huckins, and the Reverend Tryon were slave-holders (the last receiving his through marriage to Mrs. Higgins).

These early Texans felt that education was a debt due from the present generation to the future generation and that it was a matter of immediacy. They measured their ability by the strength of their convictions. The Reverend McCalla, a Presbyterian minister living in a tent on Galveston beach in 1840, delivered an elaborate address in favor of a university at Galveston. According to tradition, most plans for education emerged from church-connected groups. The leaders remembered that the motivation force for the founding of Harvard in 1636, Yale in 1700, Princeton in 1746, Columbia in 1754, and Brown in 1760 was the need for a trained ministry. Hence the Union Association took a vigorous stand on behalf of an educated ministry and identified education with evangelism. In fact, evangelism took priority over school support if a choice had to be made. The Sixteenth Baptist State Convention (October 1863) went on record to raise $10,000 for missionaries to the Confederate Army and destitute areas of the state, although their Baylor University was in dire need of support.

By 1845, when Baylor was chartered under the Republic of Texas, the Union Association, the sponsoring group, had grown from four churches with forty-four members to nineteen churches with six hundred members and ten ministers. This group represented a scattered population of pioneers intent on cultivating virgin land and building homes on the prairies. There were no railways, few roads, and few bridges —merely small communities isolated from civilization. Dr. Burleson emphasized the primitive nature of the area in his famous story of his visit with the family of Colonel Aaron Shannon as a missionary out of Houston in 1849 when he "sang solos to the wolves."[17] Nevertheless, this small group dared to found a college. Burleson registered his amazement in his declaration that "six hundred Baptists, surrounded by eight million hostile Mexicans on the west and sixty thousand hostile Indians on the north, resolved to found a grand university to equal any on this continent." During the entire period of its existence at Independence, the school was closely identified with the Baptist denomination. Financial support was never adequate. The Baptist constituency was small and

[17] J. H. McCuiston, *What Happened in 1865 to 1936 to J. H. McCuiston,* (Guthrie, Oklahoma: Co-operative Publishing Co., 1936). p. 85.

far from affluent, and the feeling that the institution should be self-sustaining seemed to be prevalent. Minutes of the Union Association and the Baptist State Convention usually carried announcements of the sessions of Baylor on their covers, and a report on the condition of the school comprised the Report on Education, after which speeches were usually made to encourage the members to give the school their patronage and prayers. The Union Association and then the Baptist State Convention appointed the Board of Trustees, who exercised close supervision over the school, but the president faced the necessity of financial management. Continual bids were made for state aid from the time of Burleson's presidency, but the state legislature rejected the memorials, not because of the lack of merit in the requests, but because of their denominational origin and the consequent obligation to all such religious-affiliated schools.

Baylor began as a co-educational, non-sectarian venture, with Episcopalian Gillette serving as the first teacher. President Graves began the tradition of having a minister as the head of the school, and usually the president was pastor of the Independence Baptist Church. Expediency was the determining factor in many decisions during this cradle period of Baylor, as in most of the early schools of the state. Young President Burleson separated the departments with provision for the education of girls and young women under the direction of Principal Clark. President Burleson at that time believed in the traditional classical education. Recently Frank A. Rose wrote that most people of that day considered higher education "a privilege of rank, aiming at producing 'gentlemen' to fill the pulpits, sit on the benches of justice, deliberate in the state houses, or control agrarian and industrial empires."[18] The curriculum, basically the same for all students, aimed at disciplining the mind to create habits of clear and deep thinking. The general public did not feel that women were actually fitted for such an educational process, although early Texans did feel that women should be given the "cultural" advantages of college.

In a comparatively recent study Wreathy Aiken states that "evidently the denominational institutions, particularly

[18] Frank A. Rose, "The University Today," *The Baptist Faculty Paper,* XI (Spring 1968). Nashville, Tennessee.

Baylor University, provided educational opportunities which were remarkably superior to those of all other institutions in Texas at the time."[19] Most Texas institutions required young women to be fourteen to enter college, but Baylor University and Chappell Hill Female College specified sixteen and seventeen respectively *plus* a testimonial of good character. These female applicants for admission could present a certificate of attainment in lieu of an examination, as was the custom in most schools.[20] The Baylor University women were allowed to substitute courses in science for courses in ancient languages for the A.B. degree in 1850. The Male Department, modeled on the traditional curriculum of the best Eastern and Southern schools, was also a respectable institution for the time. During the ten-year Burleson administration, Baylor University experienced its greatest physical growth and gained academic recognition as a college. The unfortunate rift between President Burleson and Principal Clark resulted in Burleson's withdrawal from the institution; the railroad by-passed Independence; the Civil War claimed the male students; and then came the difficult days of reconstruction. In 1865 the school initiated the policy of payment in advance. Aid from the denomination became less and less, for people could hardly help themselves.

Presidents Baines and Crane labored heroically with uncertain support from organized Baptists. Almost single-handedly, Crane operated Baylor University for twenty years, surviving flood, yellow fever, the by-pass of the railroad, the auction of the university, and finally a cyclone. The death of President Crane became the final blow in what may appear to be the tragic history of Baylor at Independence. It remained for President Andrews to close the book. Yet the history cannot be dismissed so summarily. Imagining Texas *without* Baylor University at Independence from 1845 to 1886 points out immediately some immeasurable values. The mere existence of a college dating its founding to the days of the Republic is a prestige factor. During the entire period the school served as a focal cultural point for hundreds of individuals beyond the realm of its immediate

[19] Wreathy Aiken, *Education of Women in Texas* (San Antonio: The Naylor Company, 1957), p. 46.
[20] *Ibid.*, p. 102.

constituency of staff, students, and patrons. It was the uni-
fying link with the Baptist ministry and denomination,
the news media, and the many educated individuals in
sparsely settled Texas who came to serve on the Visiting
and Examining Boards. Biographical study of these people
shows the tenor of their lives, their aspirations, and the high
esteem in which they held Baylor University. They rightly
considered themselves builders and felt that the richest
legacy that parents could leave children is "a cultured mind
and a pure heart." They thoroughly justified religious-oriented education. C. H. Wedemeyer stated that "state schools,
of any character, cannot supply the place of private and denominational institutions nor supercede them."[21] It was not
enough that the intellect be trained; the moral nature must
be cultivated. The great mass of students who attended
Baylor at Independence have attested to this fact in their
speeches, their letters, their diaries, and their publications—
along with eloquent tributes to the various faculty members
who inspired them. Baylor University was a dynamic force
to the individuals schooled within her walls and also to the
church and state. The history of Baylor University is actually
a history of her people.

The primary purpose of the founding fathers of Baylor
University was to train ministers. How well was this intent
fulfilled? In the 1883 Report on Education, R. A. Massey
stated that forty-nine men had been educated for the ministry at Baylor. "Thirty-two are now pastors and evangelists,
one is a missionary to Brazil and one to the Indians. Of all
thus instructed, only three have failed to fulfill the purpose
of their training," he continued.[22] At the Baptist State Convention of the next year, President Crane reported that ten
licensed ministers were enrolled at Baylor and that "as yet
nothing has been received to pay their expenses."[23] Certainly
Baylor lived up to the expectancy of her founders in pro-

[21] C. H. Wedemeyer, Committee on Education Report, Union Baptist Association, Sealy Baptist Church, August 14, 1885.
[22] R. A. Massey, Report on Education, Union Baptist Association, Minutes
of the Forty-Third Annual Session, Held with the Baptist Church of Brenham,
August 17, 18, 1883, p. 6-7.
[23] Dr. Crane listed J. H. Harrott, George Hamman, Benjamin Miller, M. M.
Hitchcock, J. T. Stanton, M. S. Lackey, M. D. Bullock, Peter Rhynard, E. J.
Seale, and C. F. Maxwell. Dr. Crane added that there were as many more
applicants for fellowships.

viding education for young ministers, although much of the credit goes to the generous-hearted presidents and faculty rather than to the denomination.

Only four stone columns mark the place that was Baylor University at Independence. Graves Hall, Tryon Hall containing the Hosea Garrett Chapel, Houston Hall, the President's Octagonal Domicile and Creath Hall are no longer on Allen Hill, the men's campus.[24] The memorial columns now marking the locale were the stately entrance of the Female College edifice, erected in 1857. The girls' dormitory, the principal's residence, the kitchen and storehouse, and dining hall are dim memories.

Baylor at Independence is no more, but the devotion of those who loved the school carried over to succeeding generations to build a new Baylor on the Waco campus. The vision of the founding fathers served as the guiding star in the continuation of that early plan—"a Baptist university in Texas built upon a plan so broad that the requirements of existing conditions would be fully met, and that would be susceptible of enlargement and development to meet the needs of all the ages to come." This intent—through the hands of Providence—was to be implemented in a new era in a new setting. Baylor University at Waco, a union of Baylor at Independence and Waco University, was to become the focal point of interest and prayers for Texas Baptists in the reaffirmation of its motto, "For Church and State."

[24] In December 1901 Graves Hall was destroyed by fire, Letter from N. N. Vickers, Hamshire, Texas, May 31, 1955, to Mrs. Lily M. Russell.

Bibliography

Unpublished Material

Baines, Elder George W. Notes of sermon delivered at ordination service of George W. Baines, Jr. at Oak Grove, November 29, 1874. Baines Papers, Texas Collection, Baylor University.

Baylor, R. E. B. "Sketches of Men." Allen, Anderson, Reddin Andrews, Barnes, Baxter, Bell, Breedlove, Buffington, Rufus Burleson, Burrows, Buster, Crane, Cantwell, Thomas Chilton, Clabaugh, Clark, Cleveland, Cole, Creath, Davis, Dodge, Eave, Ellege, Fisher, Fitzgerald, H. Garrett, P. Garrett, Glise, George Graves, Henry Graves, R. F. Harris, Harvey, A. G. Haynes, Hillyer, Heisig, Horton, Keifer, Law, Mason, Mercer, Z. N. Morrell, Paseton, Pickett, Ross, Sledge, Smith, Stribling, Taliaferro, Teasey, Thomas, Tryon, Williams, Witt, Woodruff.

——————. Collection and Papers. Texas Collection, Baylor University.

Baylor University. "Minutes of the Baylor Historical Society," May 29, 1948+.

——————. "Minutes of the Baylor University Board of Trustees, Independence, Texas, April 7, 1845 to 1897." Original Handwritten Book.

Browne, Philip Dale. "The Early History of Freestone County to 1865." M.A. thesis, The University of Texas, 1925.

——————. "Henry Lee Graves at Fairfield." Baylor Historical Society Waco: May 25, 1956. (Typewritten.)

Bryant, C. E., Jr. "A Brief Biographical Sketch of Judge R. E. B. Baylor." M.S., Texas Collection, Baylor University.

Campbell, John T. "The Bible Revision Movement and William Carey Crane." Baylor University, 1956 (Typewritten).

Clabaugh, John. "Theology on Horseback." MS, 1887. Tidwell Library, Baylor University.

Crane, Catherine. "Reminiscences." Texas Collection, Baylor University.

Crane, William Carey. "Literary Discourses." W. C. Crane Papers. Texas Collection, Baylor University.

——————. "Reminiscences." Texas Collection, Baylor University.

——————. Papers, Ledger, Registers, Roll books, 4 vols. Crane Papers. Texas Collection, Baylor University.

Davis, Hugh Charles. "The Origin, Development, and Decline of Anti-Intellectualism Among Baptists of the South, 1820-50." M.A. thesis, Baylor University, 1956.

Dickinson, William Calvin. "Baylor University, a Century of Discipline 1845-1947." M.A. thesis, Baylor University, 1962.

Duncan, Francis Higginbotham. "The Life and Times of R. E. B. Baylor, 1793-1846." M.A. thesis, Baylor University, 1954.

Edwards, Margaret Royalty. "A Sketch of Baylor University." M.A. thesis, Department of History, Baylor University, 1920.
————. "Baylor's Generals," MS, Texas Collection, Baylor University, 1963.
Ferguson, Roberta Scott. "The Education of Women and Girls in Texas before the Civil War." M.A. thesis, University of Texas, 1925.
Ford, Hoyt. "The Life and Works of Dr. William Carey Crane." M.A. thesis, University of Texas, 1926.
Gambrell, Herbert P. "The Early Baylor University 1841-1861." M.A. thesis, S. M. U., 1924.
Grusendorf, Arthur August. "The Social and Philosophical Determinants of Education in Washington County Since 1835." Doctoral dissertation, University of Texas, 1938.
————. The Baptists and Education in Washington County, 1845-1875." MS, Texas Collection, Baylor University.
————. "A Century of Education in Washington County, Texas, 1845-1875." MS, Texas Collection, Baylor University.
————. "Henry Flavel Gillette," MS, San Marcos. Sent to Prof. E. H. Sparkman, Baylor Spanish Department, November 21, 1939.
Guemple, John Robert. "A History of Waco University." M.A. thesis, Baylor University, 1964.
Gunn, Jack Winton. "The Life of Rufus C. Burleson." Ph.D. dissertation, University of Texas, 1951.
Hale, Joseph W. "Judge Baylor in Perspective." MS, Texas Collection, Baylor University.
Hardy, Ruth Gillette. "Brief Memoir of the Reverend Charles Gillette." MS prepared at 35 Garden Place, Brooklyn, New York, 1946.
Hearne, Madge W. "Washington County." M.S. (n.d.), Texas Collection, Baylor University.
Hesler, Samuel B. "Rev. Zachariah N. Morrell, The Texas Baptist Minister." History Senior Seminar 492B, Fall 1967-68, Houston Baptist College.
Huffstutler, Ernest Vaughn. "A Study of Public Law 874 and Its Operation in Texas." Waco, Texas, 1959.
Hyden, Elmer E. "The Relation of William Carey Crane to the Bible Revision Movement in the Antebellum South." Waco, Texas, 1949. (Typewritten.)
Johnson, John H. "Report." Texas Collection, Baylor University, May 20, 1945.
Klipple, Mrs. Georgia E. "Francis Judith Somes Trask." (Biography) M.A. thesis, University of Texas, 1939.
Ledlow, William Franklin. "History of Protestant Education in Texas." Doctoral dissertation, University of Texas, 1926.
Lacy, G. R. "A History of Gonzales College." M.A. thesis, University of Texas, 1936.

McCormick, William W. "History of Early Education in Concrete." MS done at Cuero, Texas, March 1950.

Mason, Zane Allan. "The Baptist Missionary Movement on the Texas Frontier," 1865-1885. Ph.D. dissertation, Texas Technological College, Lubbock, Texas, 1958.

Martin, James Lee. "History of Goliad from 1835 to 1880." M.A. thesis, University of Texas, 1937.

Nelson, Guy T., Jr. "Baylor University at Independence, 1861-1886." M.A. thesis, Department of History, Baylor University, 1961.

Nichols, John. "The Influence of Freemasons in Baylor University, 1845-1861." History 420 Paper, Baylor University, 1961.

Perrin, E. A. "History of Education in Goliad County." M.A. thesis, University of Texas, 1933.

Perry, Dwain. "William Carey Crane, A Biographer of Sam Houston." Seminar Paper for Dr. Bruce Thompson, Baylor University.

Radney, Imogene Burleson. "A History of the Peabody Education Fund for the Southern and Southwestern States." (Typewritten.)

——————————. "Richard Byrd Burleson, Biography." MS.

Smiley, David Leslie. "The Ante-bellum Professor as Seen in the William Carey Crane Collection." M.A. thesis, Baylor University, 1948.

Snapp, Harry Franklin. "The Mississippi Career of William Carey Crane." M.A. thesis, Baylor University, 1953.

Standard, Jack. "Historical and Biographical Sketch of the Baylor Family." MS, Texas Collection, Baylor University, (n.d.).

Thompson, Sally Trice. "Reminiscences, Baylor Class of 1892." Texas Collection, Baylor University.

Tubbs, Walter Louis. "Elder Joseph L. Bays, A Pioneer Texas Baptist Preacher." M.A. thesis, William W. Barnes Collection, Fleming Library, Southwestern Baptist Theological Seminary Fort Worth, Texas, 1916.

Walker, Thad. "Mary Hardin-Baylor College, 1845-1937." Doctor of Education dissertation, George Peabody College, Nashville. August 1962. Microfilm-Xerography by University of Michigan, 1963.

Wallace, David R. "Life of Sam Houston, by a Personal Friend," (n.d.). MS, Texas Collection, Baylor University.

Watson, Bert Allan. "Baylor University: A Military History." A.M. thesis, Baylor University, 1968.

Williams, Earl Francis. "History of Baylor University." M.A. thesis, Baylor University, 1941.

Wilson, Carl Bassett. "A History of Baptist Educational Efforts in Texas, 1829-1900." Ph.D. thesis, University of Texas, Austin, Texas, 1934.

Wolfshill, Casper George. "The Educational Philosophy of William Carey Crane." M.A. thesis, Baylor University, 1947.

Wood, Neil. "Burleson at Houston." Baylor University, 1957.

Books and Pamphlets

Academic Degrees. U. S. Department of Health, Education and Welfare, Office of Education, Washington, D. C.: U. S. Printing Office, 1960.

Adair, Garland (ed.). *Texas Pictorial Handbook.* Austin: Austin News Agency, May 1957.

Adams, George F. *A Brief Sketch of the Life and Character of the Late William Crane of Baltimore.* Baltimore: John F. Weishampel, 1868.

Adkins, Mary Grace Muse, and Allen, Corrie Walker. *Pioneering in Texas.* Dallas: The Southern Publishing Co., 1935.

Aiken, Wreathy Price. *Education of Women in Texas.* San Antonio: Naylor Co., 1957.

Aldrich, Armitstead Albert. *The History of Houston County,* together with Biographical Sketches of Many Pioneers. . . . San Antonio: The Naylor Co., 1943.

Allan, Francis D. (ed.). *A Collection of Southern Patriotic Songs Made During Confederate Times.* Galveston: J. D. Sawyer, 1874.

Allbritton, Joe L. (ed.). *George Washington Baines, Sr.* Compiled from His Papers in the Baylor University Texas Collection by Elizabeth Hale Steakley under direction of Joe L. Allbritton. Houston, Texas, 1965.

Allen, Clifton J., and Cox, Norman Wade (eds.). *Encyclopedia of Southern Baptists,* I, II. Nashville: Broadman Press, 1958.

Allen, J. Taylor. *Early Pioneer Days in Texas.* Dallas: Wilkinson Printing Co., 1918.

Allen, O. F. *The City of Houston from Wilderness to Wonder.* Temple, Texas: Privately printed, 1936.

American Baptist Yearbook 1869. Philadelphia: The American Baptist Publication Society, 1868-1940.

Armstrong, Zella (compiler). *Notable Southern Families.* Chattanooga: The Lookout Publishing Co., 1928.

Atkinson, Wm. B. (ed.). *Biographical Dictionary of Contemporary American Physicians and Surgeons.* Philadelphia: C. S. Brinton, 1880.

Backus, Isaac. *An Abridgment of the Church History of New England from 1602 to 1804.* Boston: E. Lincoln, 1804.

Baker, DeWitt Clinton. *A Texas Scrap Book.* New York: A. S. Barnes, 1875.

Barker, Eugene Campbell, and Winkler, Ernest William. *A History of Texas and Texans.* 4 vols. Chicago: American Historical Society, 1914.

Barker, Eugene C. (ed.). *History of Texas.* Dallas: The Southwest Press, 1929.

——————. *The Life of Stephen F. Austin, Founder of Texas, 1793-1836: A Chapter in the Westward Movement of the Anglo-American People.* Nashville: Cokesbury Press, 1926.

——————. (ed.). *Readings in Texas History.* Dallas: The Southwestern Press, 1929.

Barkley, Mary Starr. *History of Travis County and Austin, 1839-1899.* Waco: Texian Press, 1963.

Barnes, William Wright. *The Southern Baptist Convention 1845-1953.* Nashville, Tennessee: Broadman Press, 1954.

Baylor, Orval Walker. *Baylor's History of the Baylors.* Le Roy Journal Printing Company, 1914.

Baylor University Annual, 1896.

Baylor University. *Report on the Legal Relations of Baylor University to the Baptist State Convention of Texas.* Waco: October 25, 1895.

Baylor University *Round Up,* 1945 Centennial Edition.

Beale, George W. *Semple's History of the Rise and Progress of the Baptists in Virginia.* Richmond: Pitt and Dickinson, 1894.

Benedict, David. *A General History of the Baptist Denomination in America.* New York: Lewis Colly & Company, 1848.

Biographical Directory of the American Congress, 1774-1949.

Biographical Directory of the Texan Conventions and Congresses 1832-1845. Austin: Book Exchange, 1941.

Biographical Encyclopedia of Texas. New York: Southern Publishing Co., 1880. (Crane's Personal Copy)

Blackford, James Baylor. *The Story of the Episcopal Church in Texas.* Austin: Episcopal Theological Seminary, 1964.

Boatright, Mody C. (ed.). *Mexican Border Ballads and other Lore.* Publication of Texas Folklore Society, XXI. Austin: Capital Printing Co., 1946.

Boddie, John Bennett. *Southside Virginia Families.* Redwood City, California: Pacific Coast Publishers, 1955.

Boswell, Harry James (ed.). *The American Blue Book.* Texas Attorneys. Minneapolis: 1926.

Bronson, B. F. *et al. The First Half Century of Madison University.* The Jubilee Volume. New York: Sheldon & Co.,; Boston: Gould & Lincoln; Philadelphia, Chicago, and St. Louis: Bible and Publication Society, 1872.

Bruce, Henry. *Life of General Houston.* New York: Dodd, Mead, and Company, 1891.

Burke's Texas Almanac and Immigrant's Handbook . . . with incorporation of Hanford's Texas State Register. Houston: J. Burke, (n.d.).

Burkhalter, Frank E. "The Laymen and Their Work," *Centennial Story of Texas Baptists.* Baptist General Convention of Texas. 1936.

————. *A World-Visioned Church.* Nashville, Tenn.: Broadman Press, 1946.

Burleson, Rufus C. *My Life Work and Sixty-Third Birthday.* Waco: Privately published, 1886.

Burleson, Georgia J. (compiler). *The Life and Writings of Rufus C. Burleson, D.D., LL.D., Containing a Biography of Dr. Burleson by Harry Haynes.* Waco: 1901.

Burleson, Solomon S. *A Brief History of the Burleson Family.* Waco: University Printing Co., 1889.

Carroll, B. H. *History of Houston*. Knoxville: H. W. Crew and Co., 1912.

Carroll, H. Bailey. *Masonic Influences on Education in the Republic of Texas*. Waco: Texas Lodge of Research, A.F. & A.M., 1960.

Carroll, J. M. *A History of Texas Baptists*. Dallas: Baptist Standard Publishing Co., 1923.

Carson, Jane. *James Innes and His Brothers of the F. H. C.* Williamsburg Research Studies. The University Press of Virginia, The Rotunds, Charlottesville, Va., (n.d.).

Carter, James D. *Masonry in Texas*. Waco: Committee on Masonic Education, 1955.

Cathcart, William (ed). *The Baptist Encyclopedia*. Philadelphia: Louis H. Everts, 1881.

Cattell, J. McKeen (ed.). *American Men of Science,* a Biographical Directory. New York: The Science Press, 1906.

Chamberlain, Joshua L. (ed.). *Universities and Their Sons*. I & II. Boston: R. Herndon Co., 1898.

Cole, J. P. *The First Baptist Church of Galveston, Texas*. Galveston: News Steam Job Press, 1871.

Commissioner of Education. [Texas] *Annual Report,* 1900-1901.

Cossitt, P. S. *The Cossitt Family*. Pasadena, California: F. H. White, 1925.

Coulter, E. Merton. *College Life in the Old South*. New York: Macmillan Co., 1928.

Crane, William Carey. *Education: Theory, Practice, Position, and Benefits*. Pamphlet, (n.d.).

——————. *History of Washington County*. Reprint, Brenham: Banner Press, 1939.

——————. *Life and Select Literary Remains of Sam Houston of Texas*. Philadelphia: J. B. Lippincott and Company, 1884; also Dallas: William G. Scarff and Co., 1884.

——————. (Essay) *Who Ought to Supply and Control the Education Needed by the People*. Galveston: Shaw and Blaylock, 1878.

Cranfill, J. B. *From Memory: Reminiscences, Recitals, and Gleanings from a Bustling and Busy Life*. Nashville: Broadman Press, 1937.

Davis, Ellis A., and Grobe, Edwin H. *The Encyclopedia of Texas*. Dallas: Texas Development Bureau.

Dawson, Joseph Martin. *Baptists and the American Republic*. Nashville: Broadman Press, 1956.

——————. *Give Me Texas,* a Dramatic Pageant . . . Depicting a Hundred Years of Baptist History in Texas. Script by J. M. Dawson, Staged by Paul Baker, Music by Robert Markham, Consulting Director, Sara Lowrey, (n.d.). (1945).

——————. "Missions and Missionaries," *Centennial Story of Texas Baptists*. Dallas: Baptist General Convention of Texas, 1936.

——————. *A Century with Texas Baptists*. Nashville: Broadman Press, 1947.

Dewees, W. B. *Letters from An Early Settler in Texas*. Louisville: (n.p.), 1858.

Dietrich, Wilfred O. *The Blazing Story of Washington County*. Brenham, Texas: Banner Press, 1950.

Dixon, Samuel Houston. *The Poets and Poetry of Texas* (Introduction by William Carey Crane). Austin: Sam H. Dixon Co., 1885.

Dowell, Spright. *History of Mercer University 1833-1953*. Macon, Georgia: Mercer University, 1958.

Durfee, Calvin. *Williams Biographical Annals*.

Durse, (Mrs.) Harriet M. Jamison. *Early Days in Texas*. Reprint of articles for *Houston Post*. Pamphlet. Okla. City: Parry Printing Co., (n.d.).

Duval, John Crittenden. *Early Times in Texas*. Austin, Texas: H. P. H. Gammel & Co., 1892.

Early, C. Y. *Walker-Smith Company—1894-1944*. Dallas: Harben Spotts, (n.d.).

Eby, Frederick. *Christianity and Education*. Dallas: Baptist General Convention of Texas, 1915.

—————. *The Development of Education in Texas*. New York: The Macmillan Company, 1925.

—————. *Education in Texas*. University of Texas Bulletin, April 25, 1918.

Edgar, J. W. (ed.). *Centennial Handbook, Texas Public Schools, 1854-1954*. Austin: Texas Education Agency, (n.d.).

Ellet, Elizabeth Fries (Lummis). *Pioneer Women of the West*. Philadelphia: Porter & Coates, (n.d.).

Estep, W. R. *A Baptist Chapter of Texas History*: The Story of Baptist Influence as a Young Republic Gains Religious and Political Freedom. Dallas: The Baptist Standard Publishing Co., 1957.

Fields, F. T., and Schiwetz, E. M. *Texas Sketchbook*. Houston: Humble Oil & Refining Co., 1952.

Fitzhugh, Bessie Lee. *Bells over Texas*. El Paso, Texas: Texas Western Press, 1955.

Flangan, Sue. *Sam Houston's Texas*. Austin: University of Texas Press, 1964.

Fleming, Robert (ed.). *Georgia Pulpit*, I, Sermon XII.

Foreman, Grant. *Pioneer Days in the Early Southwest*. Cleveland: Arthur H. Clark Company, 1926.

Fornell, Earl Wesley. *The Galveston Era*. Austin: The University of Texas Press, 1961.

Frantz, Joe B. *Gail Borden*. Norman: University of Oklahoma Press, 1951.

Friend, Llerena B. *Sam Houston, The Great Designer*. Austin: The University of Texas Press, 1954.

—————. "Sam Houston," *Heroes of Texas*. Waco, Texas: Texian Press, 1964.

Fuller, B. F. *History of Texas Baptists*. Louisville, Kentucky: Baptist Book Concern, 1900.

Gambrell, Herbert. *Anson Jones, The Last President of Texas.* Garden City: Doubleday and Company, 1948.

Gammel, H. P. N. *The Laws of Texas,* 10 vols. Austin: Gammel Book Co., 1898.

Gingrich, Dorothea L. (compiler). *According to His Purpose:* Mary Hardin-Baylor College and Student Christian Life. Baylor College, Belton, 1945.

Godbold, Adbea. *The Church College of the Old South.* Durham, N. C.: Duke University Press, 1944.

Goeth, Ottilie. *Was Grossmutter Erzaehlt,* Cypress Mill, Texas; (n.p.), 1915.

Graves, Louise, (ed.). *Dr. Henry Lee Graves and Family.* Dallas, Texas: Privately printed, 1960.

Gray, William Fairfax. *From Virginia to Texas, 1835.* Houston: Gray, Cillage & Co., 1909.

Gregory, Winifred (ed.). *American Newspapers, 1821-1936.* New York: The H. W. Wilson Co., 1937.

Griffin, S. C. *History of Galveston, Texas.* Galveston: A. H. Cawston, 1931.

Harden, Henry Winthrop. *Huckins Family.* Privately published, 1916.

Harlow, Ralph. *The Growth of the U. S.* New York: Henry Holt & Co., 1923.

Haynes, Harry. Part I "Biography of Rufus C. Burleson," *The Life and Writings of Rufus C. Burleson.* Compiled and published by Georgia J. Burleson, 1901.

The Herald, Centennial 1840-1940. Pamphlet. Galveston: First Baptist Church, Harold L. Fickett, Pastor, January 28, 1940.

Hewitt, John H. *Williams College and Foreign Missions.* Pamphlet, (n.d.).

Hillyer, S. G. *Reminiscences of Georgia Baptists.* Atlanta: Foote and Davies Company, 1902.

Historical Sketch of the First Baptist Church of Galveston, Texas. Pamphlet. Galveston: News Steam Job Establishment, 1871.

History of Texas, Together with the Biographical History of the Cities of Galveston & Houston. Chicago: Lewis Publishing Co., 1895.

Hogan, Wm. Ranson. *The Texas Republic.* Norman: University of Oklahoma Press, 1946.

Hotten, John Camden (ed.). *The Original Lists of Persons of Quality 1600-1700.* New York: G. A. Baker & Co., Inc., 1913.

Houston, Samuel Rutherford. *Brief Biographical Accounts of Many Members of the Houston Family.* Cincinnati: Elm Street Printing Co., 1882.

Houstoun, Matilda Charlotte (Jesse) Fraser. *Hesperos: or Travels in the West.* 2 vols. London: John Murray, 1844.

Independence. Report of the Council called by the Church at Independence, on the case of A. E. Lipscomb July, 1861. Beeville, Texas: "Countryman" Print. Texas Collection, Baylor University.

James, Marquis. *The Raven,* a Biography of Sam Houston. New York: Blue Ribbon Books, 1929.

Jemison, E. Grace. *Historic Tales of Talladega.* Talladega, Alabama: (n.p.), 1959.

Jennings, John Melville, Director of Virginia Historical Society, 428 N. Blvd. Richmond, Va. Bulletin No. 9, October, 1964.

Jester, Annie Lash (ed.). *Adventurers of Purse and Person, Virginia, 1607-1625.* Order of First Families of Virginia, 1956.

Johnson, Charles D. *Higher Education of Southern Baptists.* Waco: Baylor University Press, 1955.

Johnson, Rebekah (Baines). *A Family Album.* New York: McGraw-Hill, 1965.

Jones, Anson. *Memoranda and Official Correspondence to the Republic of Texas,* Its History and Annexation. New York: Appelton & Co., 1859.

Jones, J. A. *The Lone Star Baptist History of Texas.* Bowie, Texas: Privately published, (n.d.).

Jones, Mary Callaway. *Mercer at Penfield, 1833-1871.* Pamphlet. Centennial Celebration, May 27, 1933.

Kemp, Louis Wiltz. *The Signers of the Texas Declaration of Independence.* Houston: Anson Jones Press, 1944.

Kennedy, Mary Seldon. *Seldons of Virginia and Allied Families.* Pamphlet. Privately published, (n.d.).

Langworthy, Asahel. *A Visit to Texas*: Being the Journal of a Traveller through Those Parts Most Interesting to American Settlers. New York: Goodrich & Wiley, 1834.

Laws of the Baylor University, 1854, 1872, 1880. Independence, Washington Co., Texas. Austin: J. W. Hampton, State Gazette Office, 1854.

Lester, C. Edwards. *Life and Achievements of Sam Houston, Hero and Statesman.* New York: Hurst and Company, 1883.

Lipscomb, Abner E. *Defense of Abner E. Lipscomb.* Addressed to the Baptists of Texas. Pamphlet. Independence, Texas, 1860.

Ludlow, N. M. *Dramatic Life as I Found It:* A Record of Personal Experience, with an Account of the Rise and Progress of the Drama in the West and South. St. Louis: G. I. Jones and Co., 1880.

Lynch, James D. *Bench and Bar of Texas.* St. Louis: Nixon-Jones Printing Co., 1885.

Mallary, Charles Dutton. *Memoirs of Elder Jesse Mercer.* New York: American Baptist Publishing Society, 1844.

Malone, Dumas (ed.). *Dictionary of American Biography,* XVI. New York: Charles Scribner's Sons, 1935.

Marquis, Albert Nelson (ed.). *Who's Who in America.* Chicago: The A. N. Marquis Co., 1938.

Matthews, Harlan J., et al. *Centennial Story of Texas Baptists.* Dallas: Baptist General Convention of Texas, 1936.

Mercer University Centennial Brochure, (n.p.), 1933.

Miller, Edmund T. *A Financial History of Texas.* University of Texas *Bulletin No. 37.* Austin: A. C. Baldwin and Sons, 1916.

Millis, William Alfred. *The History of Hanover College from 1827 to 1927*. Greenfield, Ind.: Wm. Mitchell Printing Co., 1927.

Moore, Doris D. *Biography of Dr. D. R. Wallace*. Dallas: Timberlawn Foundation, 1966.

Moore, Francis, Jr. *Map and Description of Texas*: Containing Sketches of Its History, Geology, Geography and Statistics. . . . Waco, Texas: Texian Press, 1965.

Morrell, Zachariah Nehemiah. *Flowers and Fruits of the Wilderness*. Third Edition, St. Louis: Commercial Printing Company, 1882; Fourth Edition, Dallas: W. G. Scarff and Co., 1886. (original 1872).

Murphy, (Mrs.) E. M. *History of the Woman's Missionary Union of District Four*, Auxiliary to District Four of the General Baptist Convention of Texas. Houston: Jackson Printery, (n.d.).

McCalla, W. L. *Adventures in Texas 1840*. Philadelphia: Privately printed, 1841.

McCuistion, J. H. *What Happened in 1865 to 1936 to J. H. McCuistion*. Guthrie, Okla.: Co-operative Publishing Co., 1936.

Newton, Lewis A., and Gambrell, Herbert P. *Social and Political History of Texas*. Dallas: Southwest Press, 1932.

——————. *Texas Yesterday and Today*. Dallas, Texas: Turner Co., 1948.

Nicks, Mary. *Garrett-Buster-Estes Family History*. Privately printed, December, 1956.

Nixon, Pat Ireland. *A History of the Texas Medical Association 1853-1934*. Austin: University of Texas Press, 1953.

North, Thomas. *Five Years in Texas 1861-1866*. Cincinnati: Elm Street Printing Co., 1871.

Olmsted, Frederick Law. *A Journey through Texas*: or, a Saddle-Trip on the Southwestern Frontier. New York: Dix, Edwards & Co., 1857.

Orr, Lyndon. *The Wives of General Houston*. New York: Harper & Bros., 1912.

Parisot, Pierre Fourier. *The Reminiscences of a Texas Missionary*. San Antonio: Johnson Bros. Printing Co., 1894.

Paschal. *History of Wake Forest College*. Wake Forest, N. C., 1935.

Patterson, Roberta Turner. *Candle By Night*, A History of Woman's Missionary Union, Auxiliary to the Baptist General Convention of Texas, 1800-1955. W. M. U. of Texas, 1955.

Pennington, (Mrs.) R. C. *History of Brenham and Washington County*. Houston: Standard Printing Co., 1915.

Phelan, Macum. *A History of Early Methodism in Texas, 1817-1866*. Nashville: Cokesbury Press, 1924.

Pickrell, Annie Doom. *Pioneer Women in Texas*. Austin: E. L. Steck Co., 1929.

Pollard, Edward B. *Luther Rice*. Edited and Completed by Daniel Gurden Stevens. Philadelphia: The Judson Press, 1928.

Provence, Mrs. E. W. "Historical Sketch of Baylor University," *The Diamond Jubilee Record of the Founding of Baylor University*. Waco: The Baylor University Press, 1921.

Ragsdale, Bartow Davis. *The Founders of Mercer University*, Address at Penfield Chapel, Centennial Mercer University, May 27, 1933.

——————. *Story of Georgia Baptists*. Atlanta: Foote and Davis Co., 1932.

Ramey, Wm. Neal (ed.). *The Texian Annual or Ramey's Texas Almanac*. Austin, April 21, 1886.

Ramsdell, C. W. "The Frontier and Secession," in *Studies in Southern History and Politics*. New York: Columbia University Press, 1914.

Rankin, Melinda. *Texas in 1850*. Boston: Damrell and Moore, 1850.

Ray, Worth S. *Austin Colony Pioneers*. Austin: Privately printed, 1949.

The Record of Southwest Texas. Chicago: Goodspeed Brothers, 1894.

Red, William Stuart. *A History of the Presbyterian Church in Texas*. San Antonio: The Steck Company, 1936.

Reid, Captain Mayne. *Wild Life or Adventures on the Frontier*, A Tale of the Early Days of the Texas Republic. New York: Carleton Publisher; London: Richard Bentley, 1873.

Richardson, Rupert Norval. "Literature and Scholarship." *Centennial Story of Texas Baptists*. Dallas: Baptist General Convention of Texas, 1936.

——————. *Texas, the Lone Star State*. New York: Prentice-Hall, 1943.

Richardson, Thomas Clarence. *East Texas, Its History and Its Makers*. New York: Lewis Historical Pub. Co., 1940.

Robinson, Duncan W. *Robert McAlpin Williamson*. Austin, Texas: (n.p.), 1948.

Rose, Victor M. *Ross' Texas Brigade*. Louisville: Courier Journal Book and Job Rooms, 1881.

Sallee, Annie Jenkins. *Friend of God*. San Antonio: The Naylor Company, 1952.

Santleben, August. *A Texas Pioneer*. Early Staging and Overland Freighting Days on the Frontiers of Texas & Mexico. New York and Washington: Neale Pub. Co., 1910.

Sayles, John. *Precedents and Rules of Pleading in Civil Actions in the County and District Courts of Texas*. St. Louis: The Gilbert Book Co., 1882.

——————. *A Treatise on the Practice of the District and Supreme Courts of the State of Texas*. Philadelphia: Kay and Brother, Law Booksellers and Publishers; Houston: J. S. Taft; Austin: F. T. Daffaw, 1858.

Schmidt, Charles S. *The History of Washington County*. San Antonio: The Naylor Co., 1949.

Schmitz, Joseph William. *Thus They Lived*: Social Life in the Republic of Texas. San Antonio, Texas: Naylor Co., 1936.

Shuffler, R. Henderson. *The Houstons at Independence.* Waco, Texas: Texian Press, 1966.

Sibley, Marilyn McAdams. *Travelers in Texas 1791-1860.* Austin: University of Texas Press, 1967.

Simmons, Laura. *Out of Our Past.* Texas History Stories. Waco: Texian Press, 1967.

Sjolander, John P. (compiler). *Semi-Centennial History of Cedar Bayou Lodge No. 321, A.F. and A.M.* Goose Creek: (n.d.).

Smith, (Mrs.) W. J. J. *A Centennial History of the Baptist Women of Texas.* Houston: The Baptist Missions Press, 1933.

Smither, Harriet (ed.). *Journals of the Fourth Congress of the Republic of Texas, 1839-1840.* Austin: Von Boeckmann-Jones Co., 1931.

——————. (ed.). *Journals of the Sixth Congress of the Republic of Texas,* 1841-1842, II. Austin: Von Boeckmann-Jones Co., 1940.

Smithwick, Noah. *The Evolution of a State.* Austin: Gammel Book Company, 1900.

Sprague, William B. *Annals of the American Pulpit,* Commemorative Notices of Distinguished Clergymen of the Baptist Denomination in the U. S. New York: Robert Carter & Brothers, 1860.

Spell, Lota M. *Music in Texas.* Austin: (n.p.), 1936.

Streeter, Thomas Winthrop. *Bibliography of Texas, 1795-1845.* Cambridge: Harvard University Press, 1955.

Student League & Alumnae Association Baylor College. *After Seventy-five Years.* Belton, Texas: (n.p.), 1920.

Stuart, Ben C. *The History of Texas Newspapers* from the Earliest Period to the Present, 1917. Archives Collection, University of Texas Library.

The Texas Almanac for 1854. New Orleans: Jarvis & Woodman.

Texas Almanac. 1949-1950. Dallas: A. H. Belo Corporation.

Texas Almanac. 1956-1957. Dallas: A. H. Belo Corporation.

Texas Almanac. 1964-1965. Dallas: A. H. Belo Corporation.

Texas Almanac & State Industrial Guide 1857. Galveston: A. H. Belo & Co., 1857.

Texas Newspapers, 1813-1939: a Union List of Newspaper Files.... Houston: San Jacinto Museum of History Association, 1941.

Thompson, Henry. *Texas: Sketches of Character, Moral and Political Conditions of the Republic, the Judiciary. . . .* Philadelphia: Brown, Bicking & Guilbert, Printers, 1839.

Thrall, Homer S. *Brief History of Methodism in Texas.* Houston: E. H. Cushing, 1872.

——————. *A Pictorial History of Texas.* St. Louis: N. D. Thompson & Company, 1879.

Toland, Gracey Booker. *Austin Knew His Athens.* San Antonio: The Naylor Company, 1958.

Torbet Robert George. *A History of the Baptists*—Early Days of Baptists & Roots Abroad. Valley Forge: The Judson Press, 1965.

——————. *Venture in Faith*—a Story of the American Baptist Foreign Mission Society, 1814-1854. Philadelphia: The Judson Press, 1965.

Townsend, Elli Moore (ed.). *After Seventy-Five Years*: A History of Baylor College, 1921.

Trantham, Henry. *The Diamond Jubilee*, a Record of the Seventy-Fifth Anniversary of Baylor University, 1845-1920. Waco: The Baylor University Press, 1921.

The Union Baptist Association, Centennial History 1840-1940. Brenham: Banner Press, (n.d.).

Vandever, John Wellington. *Talledega County History.* (n.d.).

Wade, Houston. *Masonic Dictionary: Republic of Texas.* La Grange Journal, 1935.

Wallis, Jonnie Lockhart, and Hill, Laurance L. *Sixty Years on the Brazos: The Life and Letters of Dr. John Washington Lockhart.* Los Angeles: Privately printed, 1930.

Walker, James L. *History of the Waco Baptist Association of Texas.* Waco: Bryne-Hill Printing House, 1897.

Weaver, Rufus W. *The Place of Luther Rice in American Baptist Life.* Washington, D.C.: Luther Rice Centennial Commission, 1936.

Webb, Walter Prescott and Carroll, H. Bailey (eds.). *The Handbook of Texas.* Austin: The Texas State Historical Association, 1952.

Weyland, Leonie, and Wade, Houston. *Early History of Fayette County.* La Grange, Texas: La Grange Journal Plant, 1936.

Williams, Alfred M. *Sam Houston and the War of Independence in Texas.* Boston: Houghton Mifflin, 1898.

Williams, Amelia W., and Barker, E. C. (eds.). *The Writings of Sam Houston* 1813-1863. Austin, Texas: The University of Texas Press, 1938.

Williams, Charles Richard (ed.). *Diary and Letters of Rutherford Birchard Haynes.* 5 vols. Columbus: Ohio State Archaeological & Historical Society, 1922-1926.

Winkler, E. W. (ed.). *Secret Journals of the Senate of the Republic of Texas* (1911). Austin: Austin Printing Co., 1911.

Wood, Mrs. W. A. *The Little Church in the Dell, Independence, Texas,* (n.d.).

Woody, Thomas. *A History of Women's Education in the United States.* 2 vols. New York: Science Press, 1929.

Wright, David R. (Church Clerk) *Account of Organization of First Baptist Church of Galveston,* February 15, 1840.

"Historical Sketch of Washington County," *The American Sketch Book,* IV (1878). Austin: Texas Capital Printing.

White, Michael Allen. *History of Baylor University, 1845-1861.* Waco: Texian Press, 1968.

Year Book for Texas. 1901.

Yoakum, Henderson. *History of Texas,* From Its First Settlement in 1685 to Its Annexation to the United States in 1846. 2 vols. New York: J. S. Redfield, 1855.

Articles and Periodicals

Adair, Anthony Garland. "The Capitols of Texas," *Texas Pageantry,* I, No. 1 (Austin, Texas), April 1946.

Andrews, Reddin. "The Baylor I Knew," *The Baylor Bulletin,* XVIII (December 1915).

Armstrong, A. J. (ed.). *The Baylor Bulletin, Patriotic Edition,* XXI (December 1918).

Babcock, R., Choules, John O., and Peck, John M. (eds.). *The Baptist Memorial and Monthly Record,* IV, No. 5 (May 1845).

Barker, Eugene C. "The Annexation of Texas," *Southwestern Historical Quarterly,* L (1946/47).

Baylor Aegis (Independence, Texas) February 1881-April 1883. (Published by Baylor Literary Societies.)

Baylor Literary Annual (1897).

Baylor, Orval W. *Baylor's Quarterly.* Louisville, Kentucky: The Baylor Publishing Company, April 1930.

Biblical Recorder. Raleigh, N. C., October 5, 12, 19, 1836.

Bragg, J. D. "Baylor University 1851-1861," *Southwestern Historical Quarterly,* XLIX (July 1945).

Bryan, Lewis R., Dodson, W. H., Muse, E. B., Newman, F. M., Wedemeyer, Charles H. "Appreciation of William Carey Crane," *Baylor Monthly,* V (Crane Memorial Edition) (April 1929).

Burkhalter, Frank E. "Judge R. E. B. Baylor," *Texas Bar Journal,* VIII (March 1945).

Burleson, R. B. Letter Concerning Baptism by a Pedo-Baptist Minister, *Western Baptist Review* (Louisville), February 25, 1848.

Burleson, Rufus C. "Baylor University, Waco, Texas," *Round Table,* II, No. 1 (May 1890).

———————. "The Baylor Image," *Texas Baptist* (July 15, 1856).

———————. "The Lights and Shadows of Baylor University for Fifty Years," *The Guardian,* XI, No. 5 (May 1892) ; also XI, No. 6 (June 1892).

Carroll, J. M. "William Carey Crane," *The Baylor Monthly,* V (April 1929).

Carter, James D. "Free Masonry and Texas History, 1800-1835," *Southwestern Historical Quarterly,* LVI (January 1953).

Chandler, T. J. "Reverend Wm. Carey Crane in His Relation to Education," *Texas Baptist Herald* (June 18, 1885).

The Christian Index. Atlanta, Ga.: (February 2, 1838 and November 19, 1841).

Cox, Norman (ed.). "Luther Rice, Builder of the Baptist Denomination," *The Quarterly Review.* Nashville: Baptist Sunday School Board, October-December, 1952.

Crane, R. C. "Dr. William Carey Crane's Activities in the Establishment of State University, Norman College, and Improved Public School System," *The Baylor Monthly,* (March 13, 1929).

———————. "Mission-Minded Men Laid Plans for Baptist Future in Texas," *Baptist Standard* (November 11, 1948).

—————. "Texas Baptist History Made at Independence," *Baptist Standard,* LIX (February 6, 1947).

—————. "Tryon Hall—The Main Building at Old Baylor—Independence," *The Baylor Monthly,* V (April 1929).

Crane, W. C. "Facts and Figures About Higher Institutions," *Baylor Aegis,* II (December 1882).

—————. Letter to Editor, *Christian Watchman and Reflector* (Boston), December 12, 1865.

—————. "Twenty Years in Texas," *Texas Baptist Herald* (February 14, 1884).

—————. "Read and Remember," *Baylor Aegis* (August 1881).

Culberson, Charles A. "General Sam Houston and Secession," *Scribner's Magazine,* XXXIX (May 1906).

Dawson, Joseph Martin. "Henry Lee Graves: A Major First," *The Baptist Standard* (February 28, 1962).

"Diary of Adolphus Sterne," *Southwestern Historical Quarterly,* XXX.

Dodson, T. J. "A Tribute to William Carey Crane," *The Baylor Monthly,* V (October 1929).

Duncan, Merle Mears. "David Richard Wallace, Pioneer in Psychiatry," *Texana,* I, No. 4 (Fall 1963).

—————. "An 1864 Letter to Mrs. Rufus C. Burleson," *Southwestern Historical Quarterly,* LXIV (January 1961).

Eby, Frederick. "Education in Texas, Source Materials," *University of Texas Bulletin,* No. 1824 (April 25, 1918).

Ferguson, Dan. "Forerunners of Baylor," *Southwestern Historical Quarterly,* XLIX (July 1945).

Galveston *First Baptist Church, Bulletin,* John W. Salzman, Pastor (June 15-22, 1958).

Garwood, Ellen. "Early Texas Inns: A Study in Social Relationships," *Southwestern Historical Quarterly,* LX (October 1956).

The Guardian, Vols. I-V (Devoted to Education, Literature and Texas History. Published monthly and edited by Dr. R. C. Burleson, Waco University, Waco: Ivy & George) 1884.

Hamilton Literary Magazine. Hamilton College, Clinton, New York.

Hannum, Sharon Elaine. "Thomas Chilton, Lawyer, Politician, Preacher," *The Felson Club Historical Quarterly,* XXXVIII (Louisville, Kentucky) April 1964.

Harris, Fannie R. "Baylor at Old Independence," *The Baylor Monthly,* III (March 1928).

Haynes, Harry. "Dr. Rufus C. Burleson," *Southwestern Historical Review,* V (July 1901).

Hiden, Mrs. P. W. "The Graves Family of Spotsylvania County," *Tyler's Quarterly Magazine,* No. 18.

Holland, J. K. "Reminiscences of Austin and Old Washington," *Texas Historical Association Quarterly,* I (October 1897).

Hoxie, Asa. Letter to R. M. Williamson, *Quarterly of the Texas State Historical Association,* IX (December 2, 1832).

The Home and Sunday School (Dallas, Texas), February 2, 1886. Article based on Reverend M. V. Smith's article in *Texas Baptist Herald*, 1883.

Huckins, James. Letter. *The Christian Index.* (April 28, 1843).

———————————. Letter from Reverend James Huckins. First Baptist Church, V, No. 39. (March 22, 1963).

Kelley, Dayton. "H. A. McArdle," *Southwestern Art,* I, No. 4 (1967).

Kenney, M. M. "Recollections of Early Schools," *Quarterly of the Texas State Historical Association,* I.

Kimball, J. A. "Editor's Drawer," *Texas Historical and Biographical Magazine,* II.

———————————."Recollections of Early Days in Texas." *Historical and Biographical Magazine,* II.

Knowles, J. D. (ed.). "The History of Columbian College, District of Columbia," *The Christian Review,* II (March 1837).

Link, J. B. (ed.). *Texas Historical and Biographical Magazine,* I & II. Austin, Texas (1891).

Lively, Hiram F. (Grand Master of Texas). "Masonic Education in Texas," *The Master Mason,* VII (March-April 1930).

Miller, R. F. "Early Presbyterianism in Texas," *Southwestern Historical Quarterly,* XIX (1915-1916).

Montgomery, Hazel. "An Historic Cane," *Baylor University Bulletin,* XIII (January 1910).

North, Sterling. "A Literary Map of the United States," *Holiday* (February 1947).

"Pioneer [Z. N. Morrell] Reinterred in State Grave," *Southwestern Historical Quarterly,* XLVIII (April 1945).

Priestly, Philander. "Texas," *American Farmer,* XIV (June 29, 1832).

Reckless, Harry. "Passage of Life in Texas," *Knickerbocker Magazine* (March 1846).

Red, W. A. "Allen's Reminiscences of Texas, 1838-1842," *Southwestern Historical Quarterly,* XVIII (1914-15).

Saxon, Charles E. "Molly Buster Estes," *Baylor Monthly,* V (October 1929).

Schmitz, Joseph (ed.). "Impressions of Texas in 1860," *Southwestern Historical Quarterly,* XLII (1938-1939).

Shuffler, R. Henderson. "The Signing of Texas' Declaration of Independence: Myth and Record," *The Southwestern Historical Quarterly,* LXV (January 1962).

Smiley, David Leslie. "William Carey Crane, Professor of Old Mississippi," *Journal of Mississippi History,* XII (April 1950).

Smither, Harriet (ed.). "Diary of Adolphus Sterne," *Southwestern Historical Quarterly,* XXX-XXXVIII (1926-35).

South-Western Baptist Chronicle. New Orleans, Louisiana: January 8, 1848.

Southwestern University Bulletin, 1964-5.

Strecker, John K. "The Crane Piano," *The Baylor Monthly,* (April 1929).

Sweeney, William Montgomery. "Captain Thomas Graves and Some of His Descendants," *William and Mary Quarterly,* (1935).

Tennessee Baptist (Nashville) Nov. 20, 1858.

Texas Outlook. July, 1936.

Thompson, E. Bruce. "William Carey Crane and Texas Education," *The Southwestern Historical Quarterly,* LVIII (January 1955).

Tidwell, D. D. "Reverend Z. N. Morrell," *Texas Grand Lodge Magazine,* XXXI (March 1961).

——————. "Where is the Creath Collection?" *Baptist Standard* (April 17, 1941).

Virginia Magazine of History and Biography, XXII (January 1914).

Weaver, Carl, "Oscar J. Fox and His Heritage," *The Junior Historian,* XXIV (December 1963) p. 19.

Wedemeyer, Prof. C. H. (Belton) "William Carey Crane," *Baylor University Bulletin,* XIII (January 1910).

Wilson, Mrs. A. Randolph. "Old Independence," *The Lone Star Gardener,* I (September 18, 1941).

Wood, Mrs. W. A. "Prof. Henry F. Gillette Lives in His Deeds," *Gulf Coast Baptist* (September 18, 1941).

——————. "Sad Hour of Parting," *The Century.* Waco, Texas: Baylor University, November 1940.

Records and Documents

Ainsworth, Fred C. *The War of Rebellion: A Compilation of the Official Records of the Union and Confederation Armies.* Washington: Government Printing Office, 1902.

Alabama. Records of Grand Secretary of Grand Lodge of Alabama Masons. Montgomery, Alabama.

Baines, G. W. signed note for $50. October 28, 1856. Texas Collection, Baylor University.

Baines Papers, Texas Collection, Baylor University.

Barker, E. C. *The Austin Papers,* October 1834-January 1837, III. Washington: Government Printing Office, 1924.

Baylor, R. E. B. Papers, Records. Archives, Texas Collection, Baylor University.

——————, Hosea Garrett, and A. G. Haynes. June 15, 1847. Handwritten contract. Archives, Texas Collection, Baylor University.

Baylor University. *Alumni Directory* (1854-1911). Baylor University Bulletin, XIV, No. 4, 1911.

——————. Baylor University Charter. State Archives, Austin, Texas.

——————. Circular: Announcing Coming of Wm. Carey Crane to Baylor University. August 29, 1863.

——————. Circular. Female Department of Baylor University, 1866. Clark Papers. Texas Collection, Baylor University.

——————. *Circular of the Law Department,* Baylor University. Printed at the American Office, Washington, 1857. Texas Collection, Baylor University.

—————————. Circular. *To the Friends of Baylor University.* November 9, 1869.

—————————. Commencement Program, Male Department of Baylor University, June 25, 1856. Texas Collection, Baylor University.

—————————. Diplomas. 1857, 1858.

—————————. Invitation. Commencement Party, Baylor University. December 13, 1859. Texas Collection, Baylor University.

Boston Vital Report. Dorchester District, 1892.

Brown University. *Necrology of Brown University,* 1864. Photostatic Copy from the John Carter Brown Library Records.

Bryan, Guy Morrison, Chairman. Report of House of Representatives Committee on Education. Third Legislature, No. 107, December 26-28, 1849.

Burleson, Richard Byrd Papers, 1830-1885. Archives, Texas Collection, Baylor University.

Burleson, Rufus C. Papers, 1830-1900. Correspondence, Portions of Diary. Archives, Texas Collection, Baylor University.

Clark Papers. Circular announcing the 1866 faculty. Texas Collection, Baylor University.

Clark Scrapbook. Texas Collection, Baylor University.

Crabtree, Helen Boyer (Mars. C. F.). Geneological Charts, Baylor Family, Xerox. June 19, 1968.

Crane, Royston Campbell. Papers of Royston C. Crane and William Carey Crane. 1700-1950. Archives, Texas Collection, Baylor University.

—————————. Papers: Letters, Records, Diaries, Journals, etc. Texas Collection, Baylor University.

Drake, Dr. Edwin L. (ed.). *Annals of the Army of Tennessee and Early Western History,* I, April-Dec. 1878. Nashville, Tenn.: A. D. Hanes, 1878.

Freeman, J. D. *Map of Empresario Grants,* 1823-1835. Fort Worth, April 1936.

Freestone County. Deed Records and Miscellaneous, 1858-1860.

—————————. *Civil Minutes of the District Court.*

Galveston. Membership of First Baptist Church of Galveston. Photostatic copies.

Garrett, Hosea. Subscription Book of Baylor University. Texas Collection, Baylor University.

Gloucester Vital Report, II, 1806.

Graves, Henry L. Tombstone Inscription, Brenham Cemetery. Brenham, Texas.

Gwanthmey, John M. *Historical Register of Virginians in the Revolution.* Richmond, Va.: The Diety Press, 1938.

Heitman, Francis Bernard. *Historical Register and Dictionary of the U. S. Army,* from its organization September 29, 1789, to March 2, 1903, 2 vols. Washington: Government Printing Office. 1903.

Houston, Texas. *City Directory,* I. 1865.

—————————. *Minutes of Vestry of Christ Church.* March 24, 1845.

———————. *Records of Christ Church.*

Independence Academy. Charter. Archives of Texas State Library.

Independence Papers, Texas Collection, Baylor University.

Independence Baptist Church Rollbook.

Jones, Betty Graves. *Diary of . . . .* Diary in possession of grand-daughter, Mrs. J. L. Russell.

Journal of Texas Constitutional Convention, 1845.

Land Grant Bill Proposed for Texas Colleges. Archives, Texas Collection, Baylor University.

Markers Placed by the Texas Daughters of the American Revolution. Compiled by Anne Johnston Ford, State Historian. Dallas: C. C. Cockrell, 1936.

Mitchell, Colonel Harvey. *List of Original Settlers of Brazos County,* 1841. Vertical Files, Carnegie Library, Bryan, Texas.

Monuments Erected . . . to Commemorate the Centenary of Texas Independence, 1939.

Mullins, Marion Day (compiler). *The First Census of Texas, 1829-1936.* Reprinted from the Quarterly of the National Geneological Society. Washington, D. C., 1959.

Pier, Sarah. *Album, 1856-57.* Texas Collection, Baylor University.

The Record of Southwest Texas. Chicago: Goodspeed Brothers, 1894.

Smith, Winford Broaddus. *Pioneers of Brazos County, Texas,* 1800-1850. Bryan, Texas: Scribe Shop, 1962.

Spanish Land Grants. Office of the County Clerk. Brenham, Texas.

Taylor, Virginia H. *The Spanish Archives of the General Land Office of Texas.* Austin: The Lone Star Press, 1955.

Texas. *Abstract of Land Claims of State of Texas General Land Office.* Compiled from the Records of the General Land Office of the State of Texas. Published under the superintendency of the comptroller by the authority of an Act of the Legislature, approved February 11, 1852. Galveston: Civilian Book Office, 1852.

———————. *Abstract of all Original Grants and Locations Comprising Texas Land Titles to August 31, 1947.* Austin, Texas: General Land Office.

———————. *Census of 1826; 1832.* Austin, Texas: General Land Office.

———————. *The Texas Declaration of Independence and the Fifty-nine Signers.* Information Circular No. 36. Austin, Texas, October 1947.

———————. General Land Office Records. The Texas State Archives, Austin, Texas.

Texas Constitution. Section 23, Article I.

Texas Legislature, *House Journal,* May 9, 1893.

Trinity River Baptist Association. *Minutes,* 1855-1870.

Tryon Land Grant. Photostatic copy of original.

Tryon. "The Name and Family of Tryon." Washington, D. C.: The Media Research Bureau.

U. S. Seventh Census 1850. Statistics of Texas. Washington: Robert
   Armstrong, 1853. (Detached from the Seventh Census of the
   U. S.)

United States Census Reports for 1860.

Washington County Tax Roll: 1837; 1838; 1840.

Washington County. Grants of Land. Office of the County Clerk,
   Brenham, Texas.

——————. Marriage Records, Book A. Office of the County
   Clerk, Brenham, Texas.

——————. Miscellaneous Records Prior to 1838. Office of the
   County Clerk, Brenham, Texas.

Wetumpa, Alabama. Coosa River Church Minutes.

William and Mary College. A Provisional List of Alumni, Grammar
   School Students, Members of the Faculty, and Members of the
   Board of Visitors of the College of William and Mary in
   Virginia from 1693 to 1888. Richmond: Division of Purchase
   and Printing, 1941.

Williams, Howard D. "Colgate University: 130 Years Young!"
   Northwestern-Colgate Program, November 12, 1949.

Winkler, Ernest W. (ed.). *Check List of Texas Imprints,* 1846-
   1860. Austin: The Texas State Historical Association, 1949.

Minutes and Proceedings

Baptist General Association of Texas. *Minutes of the First Session
   of the General Association of the State of Texas.* Held at
   Laressa in Cherokee Co., November 1853. Tyler: Parsons &
   Bro. Telegraph Office, 1854.

——————. Proceedings of the Fifth Annual Session. Rowlett
   Creek, Collin Co., July 26, 1872. The Baptist Annual, copy
   belonging to Mrs. Georgia J. Burleson. (Cover missing).

——————. Proceedings of the Sixth Meeting. First Baptist
   Church of Jefferson, July 25-28, 1873. Jefferson: J. C. Rogers,
   Printer, 1873.

——————. Minutes of the Eighth Anniversary. Baptist Church,
   Sherman, July 23-27, 1875. Dallas: Office of the Religious
   Messenger, 1875.

Baptist General Convention of Texas. Proceedings of the First
   Annual Session. First Baptist Church, Waco, June 29, July 2,
   1886. Dallas: Texas Baptist Publishing House.

——————. Proceedings of the Second Annual Session. First
   Baptist Church, Dallas, September 29-October 2, 1887. Dallas:
   Texas Baptist Publishing House, 1887.

Baptist State Convention of Texas. *Organization Proceedings.* Held
   at Antioch Church, Anderson, Grimes Co., September 8-12, 1848.
   Huntsville: Texas Banner Printing, 1848.

——————. Proceedings of the First Anniversary. Held in the city
   of Houston, May 11, 1849. Huntsville: Office of the Texas
   Banner.

——————. Minutes of the Fourth Annual Session, Independence,
   June 1851. Washington: The Texas Ranger Office, 1851.

————————. Minutes of the Fifth Annual Session, Marshall, June 1852. Washington: Lone Star Office.

————————. Minutes of the Sixth Annual Session, Huntsville, June 1853. Galveston: The Civilian Office.

————————. Minutes of the Seventh Annual Session, Palestine, Anderson, June 1854. Anderson: The "Central Texian" Office, 1854.

————————. Minutes of the Eighth Annual Session, Independence, Washington Co., November 1855. Anderson: "The Texas Baptist" Office, 1855.

————————. Proceedings. Held with the Church in Anderson, October 1856. Anderson: Office of Texas Baptist, 1856.

————————. Proceedings. Held with the Huntsville Baptist Church, October 24, 1857. Anderson: The Texas Baptist Office, 1857.

————————. Minutes. Held with the Independence Church, Washington Co., October 1858. Anderson: "Texas Baptist" Books and Job Establishment, 1858.

————————. Minutes of the Twelfth Annual Session, Waco, McLennan Co., October 22-26, 1859. Anderson: The Texas Baptist Power Press, 1859.

————————. Minutes of the Thirteenth Session. Held with Independence Church, Washington Co., October 27-November 1, 1860. Anderson: The Texas Baptist Book and Job Power Press, 1860.

————————. Minutes of the Fourteenth Annual Session. Sessions of 1861 and 1862. Held with Huntsville Church, Walker Co., October 26-29, 1861. Houston: E. W. Cave, Texas Printing House, 1863.

————————. Minutes of the Sixteenth Annual Session. Held with Church at Independence, October 24-28, 1863. Houston: Telegraph Book and Job Establishment, 1864.

————————. Minutes of Seventeenth Annual Session. Held with the Church of Huntsville, Walker Co., October 22-25, 1864. Houston: E. H. Cushing and Co., 1865.

————————. Minutes of Eighteenth Annual Session, Anderson, Grimes Co., September 30-October 3, 1865. Navasota: The Texas Ranger Office, 1866.

————————. Minutes of the Nineteenth Annual Session. Independence, October 6-9, 1866. Houston: Office of Texas Baptist Herald, 1866.

————————. Minutes of the Twentieth Annual Session. Held with Gonzales B. C., November 30, 1867. Houston: Office of Texas Baptist Herald, 1868.

————————. Minutes of the Twenty-First Annual Session, Independence, October 3-6, 1868. Houston: Texas Baptist Herald, 1868.

————————. Minutes of Twenty-Second Annual Session, Galveston, October 2-6, 1869. Houston: Texas Baptist Herald, 1869.

————————. Minutes of the Twenty-Second [sic] Annual Session, First Baptist Church of Brenham, October 1-3, 1870. Houston:

Texas Baptist Herald Print., 1870. (In conjunction with Minutes of Sixth Annual Session of Baptist Sunday School and Colportage Convention.)

————————. Minutes of the Twenty-Fourth Annual Session, Bryan Baptist Church, September 29-October 2, 1871. Houston: Texas Baptist Herald, 1871.

————————. Minutes of the Twenty-Fifth Annual Session, Independence, October 6-8, 1872. (Cover missing)

————————. Minutes of the Twenty-Sixth Annual Session, Austin Baptist Church, November 15-17, 1873. Houston: Texas Baptist Herald Printing, 1873.

————————. Minutes of the Twenty-Seventh Session, Galveston, October 3-6, 1874. Houston: Office of the "Baptist Herald," 1874.

————————. Minutes of the Twenty-Eighth Annual Session, First Baptist Church of Calvert, October 2-4, 1875. Houston: Office of the Baptist Herald, 1876.

————————. Minutes of the Twenty-Ninth Annual Session, Independence, September 30-October 3, 1876. Houston: Ed. Smallwood, Book and Job Printer, 1876.

————————. Minutes of the Thirtieth Annual Session, Bryan, October 6-8, 1877. (Cover missing)

————————. Minutes of the Thirty-First Annual Session, La Grange, October 5-7, 1878. Houston: Office of the Texas Baptist Herald, 1878.

————————. Minutes of the Thirty-Second Annual Session, Independence, October 4-7, 1879. Brenham: Stallings and Sayles, Printers, 1879.

————————. Minutes of the Thirty-Third Annual Session, Austin, October 2-4, 1880. Brenham: "Reporter" Book and Job Printing Office, 1880.

————————. Minutes of the Thirty-Fourth Annual Session, Galveston, October 1-3, 1881. Brenham: Frederick R. Carrick, 1881.

————————. Minutes of the Thirty-Fifth Session, Belton Baptist Church, September 30-October 2, 1882. Houston: Office of "Baptist Herald," 1882.

————————. Minutes of the Thirty-Sixth Annual Session, San Antonio, October 6-8, 1883. San Antonio: Times Job Printing House, 1883.

————————. Minutes of the Thirty-Seventh Annual Session, Waxahachie, October 4-6, 1884. Austin: Office of Texas Baptist Herald, 1884.

————————. Minutes of the Thirty-Eighth Annual Session, Baptist Church at Lampasas, Texas, October 3-6, 1885. Austin: Office of Texas Baptist Herald, 1885.

————————. *Report of Baptist State Convention of Texas, 1861.* Houston: Texas Printing House.

Bayland Orphans' Home. *Minutes of the Board of Trustees of Bayland Orphans' Home,* January 15, 1867.

Ruthuen, A. S. *Proceedings of the Grand Lodge of Texas,* 1837-1853, I & II. Galveston, 1858.

Union Baptist Association. Minutes of First Session Begun and Held in the Town of Travis in Western Texas. October 8th 1840. Houston: Telegraph Press, 1840.

——————————. Minutes of the Second Annual Meeting; Held at Clear Creek Meeting House near Rutersville in Western Texas. Commencing on October 7, 1841.

——————————. Minutes of called meeting, Mt. Gilead Church, November 26, 1842.

——————————. Minutes of Fourth Anniversary Meeting, Convened at Providence Church, Washington Co., October 6, 1843 and Days Following. Washington: Printed by Thomas Johnson, 1844.

——————————. Minutes of Fifth Anniversary Meeting Convened at Plum Grove Church, Fayette Co., Texas, August 29, 1844 and Days Following. Washington: The Vindicator Office, 1844.

——————————. Minutes of Sixth Annual Meeting Held with Mount Gillead [sic] Church, Washington Co., Western Texas. October 9, 10, 11, 1845. La Grange: Intelligencer Office, 1845.

——————————. Minutes of Seventh Annual Meeting Held with Dove Church, Caldwell, Burleson Co., October 1, and Days Following, 1846. (n.p., 1846).

——————————. Minutes of Eighth Annual Meeting Held at First Baptist Church of Houston, September 30-October 4, 1847. (n.p., 1847).

——————————. Minutes of 9th [sic]. Annual Meeting. Independence Church, Washington Co., September 28-October 2, 1848. (n.p., 1848).

——————————. Minutes of Ninth Anniversary Held with Huntsville Church, Walker County. October 4-8, 1849. Huntsville: Texas Banner Office, 1849.

——————————. Minutes of Tenth Anniversary Held with Providence Church, Washington Co., October 3-7, 1850. Washington: Texas Ranger Office, 1850.

——————————. Minutes of Twelfth Annual Meeting Held with Washington Church, Washington Co., 2-6th Oct. 1851. Galveston: J. M. Conrad, "News" Job Office, 1851.

——————————. Minutes of Thirteenth Annual Session Held with Montgomery Church, Montgomery Co., September 30-October 4, 1852. Galveston: W. Richardson at the "News" Job Office, 1852.

——————————. Minutes of Fourteenth Annual Meeting Held at Anderson Church, Grimes Co., September 29-October 3, 1953. Austin: J. W. Hampton, "State Gazette" Job Office, 1853.

——————————. Minutes of Fifteenth Annual Meeting Held at Prospect Church, Burleson Co., September 29-October 3, 1854. Austin: "The State Gazette" Job Office, 1854.

——————————. Minutes of Sixteenth Meeting, New Year's Creek Church at Brenham, Washington Co., October 5-8, 1855. Galveston: Civilian Book & Job Office, 1855.

——————————. Minutes of Seventeenth Annual Session, Held with Laurel Hill Church at Cold Spring, Polk Co., October 3-6, 1856. Anderson: Office of Texas Baptist, 1856.

————————. Minutes of Eighteenth Session Held at Bethany Church, Grimes Co., October 2-5, 1857. Anderson: Texas Baptist Office, 1857.

————————. Minutes of Nineteenth Annual Session Held at Mount Zion Church, Washington Co., October 1-4, 1858. Anderson: "Texas Baptist" Book & Job Office, 1858.

————————. Minutes of Twentieth Annual Meeting Held with Post Oak Grove Church, Grimes Co., September 30-October 3, 1859. Anderson: The Texas Baptist Power Press, 1859.

————————. Minutes of Twenty-First Annual Meeting Held at Bellville Baptist Church, Austin Co., August 17-21, 1860. Anderson: "Texas Baptist," 1860.

————————. Minutes of Twenty-Second Annual Meeting, First Baptist Church, Houston, July 12-13, 1861. Anderson: Texas Baptist Office by John H. Wilson, Book and Job Printer.

————————. Minutes of Twenty-Third Meeting Held with the Brenham Church, Washington Co., July 11-13, 1862. Bellville: The Bellville Countryman Office, 1862.

————————. Minutes of the Twenty-Fourth Annual Meeting Held with Plantersville Church, August 14-17, 1863. Galveston: "News" Book & Job Establishment, 1863.

————————. Minutes of the Twenty-Fifth Annual Meeting, Montgomery Church, September 16-19, 1864. Houston: Galveston "News" Book & Job Establishment, 1864.

————————. Minutes of Twenty-Sixth Annual Meeting Held with Washington Church, September 15-18, 1865. Bellville: J. P. Osterhout & J. T. Kimbrough, Printers, "Countryman" Office, 1865.

————————. Minutes of Twenty-Seventh Annual Meeting, Brenham Church, August 17-20, 1866. Houston: Gray Smallwood & Co., Book & Job Printers, Kennedy's Building, 1866.

————————. Minutes of Twenty-Eighth Annual Meeting, Providence Church, Chappell Hill, August 16-19, 1867. Houston: The Texas Baptist Herald, 1867.

————————. Minutes of Twenty-Ninth Annual Meeting, Huntsville Church, Walker Co., September 11-14, 1868. Houston: The Texas Baptist Herald, 1868.

————————. Minutes of Thirtieth Annual Meeting, Navasota Church, Walker Co., September 10-13, 1869. Houston: Office of the Texas Baptist Herald, 1869.

————————. Minutes of Thirty-First Annual Meeting, Independence Church, Washington Co., September 9-12, 1870. Houston: Office of Texas Baptist Herald.

————————. Minutes of Thirty-Second Annual Meeting. Willow Creek Church, Harris Co., August 18-21, 1871. Houston: Office of Texas Baptist Herald, 1871.

————————. Minutes (no number), Held with Oakland Church, Grimes Co., August 16-19, 1872. Houston: Office of Texas Baptist Herald, 1872.

—————————. Minutes of Thirty-Third Annual Meeting, Brenham Church, Washington, Texas, August 15-18, 1873. Houston: Office of the Texas Baptist Herald, 1873.

—————————. Minutes of Thirty-Fourth Annual Meeting, Montgomery Co., August 14-17, 1874. Houston: Office of Texas Baptist Herald, 1874.

—————————. Minutes of Thirty-Fourth [sic], Ebenezer Church, Walker Co., October 22-25, 1875. Houston: Office of the Baptist Herald.

—————————. Minutes of Thirty-Fifth Annual Meeting [sic], Providence Baptist Church, Chappell Hill, Washington Co., August 18-21, 1876. n.p.

—————————. Minutes of Thirty-Seventh Annual Meeting, Willow Creek Church, Harris Co., August 24-27, 1877. Houston: Office of the Texas Baptist Herald.

—————————. Minutes of Thirty-Eighth Annual Meeting, Hempstead Church, Walker Co., August 23-26, 1878. Houston: Office of the Texas Baptist Herald, 1878.

—————————. Minutes of Thirty-Ninth Annual Meeting, Navasota Church, Grimes Co., September 19-22, 1879. Houston: Office of the Texas Baptist Herald, 1879.

—————————. Minutes of Fortieth Annual Meeting, Union Grove Church, Grimes Co., September 17-20, 1880. Brenham: "Reporter" Book & Job Printing Office, 1880.

—————————. Minutes of Forty-First Annual Meeting, Providence Church, Chappell Hill, Washington Co., September 16-19, 1881. Brenham: Sentinel Printing Establishment, 1882.

—————————. Minutes of Forty-Second Annual Meeting, The Prairie Home Church, Walker Co., September 15-18, 1882. Houston: Office of The Texas Baptist Herald, 1882.

—————————. Minutes of Forty-Third Annual Session, Brenham Baptist Church, Washington Co., August 17-18, 1883. Austin: The Baptist Herald Office, 1883.

—————————. Minutes of Forty-Fourth Annual Meeting, Huntsville Baptist Church, Walker Co., August 15-16, 1884. Navasota: The Tablet Job Office, 1884.

—————————. Minutes of Forty-Fifth Annual Meeting, Sealy Baptist Church, Austin Co., August 14-16, 1885. Austin: Texas Baptist Herald, 1885.

—————————. Minutes of Forty-Sixth Annual Session, Independence Baptist Church, Washington Co., June 17-19, 1886. Brenham: Banner Steam Book Printing, 1886.

—————————. Minutes of Forty-Seventh Annual Meeting, First Baptist Church, Houston, Texas, August 19-20. Waco: Advance Book & Job Printing, 1887.

—————————. Minutes of Forty-Eighth Annual Session, Navasota Baptist Church, August 17-20, 1888. Dallas: Kind Words Publishing House.

Masonic Grand Lodge Files, Waco Texas.

——————. Minute Book "E," First Baptist Church (Dec. 24, 1899 to Sept. 15, 1907). Waco, Texas.

Waco Baptist Association. Minutes, 1860-1951.

——————. Minutes of Twentieth Annual Session, 1879.

——————. Minutes of the Twenty-second Annual Session, 1881.

——————. Report, September 1861. Marlin, Texas.

Waco University and Classical School. Minutes of the Board of Trustees, January 21, 1861 to June 7, 1887.

Wake Forest Baptist Church Record Book, October 1, 1837.

Catalogues

Catalogue of the Trustees, Officers, and Students of Baylor University, 1851-1852. Washington "Lone Star" Office.

Catalogue of Trustees, Faculty & Students of Baylor University. Independence, Washington Co., 1852-1853. New Orleans: Office of the New Orleans Baptist Chronicle, 61 Poydras St., 1853.

Laws and Catalogue of the Baylor University, Independence, Washington Co., Texas, 1853-4. Austin: J. W. Hampton, State Gazette Office, 1854.

Catalogue of Trustees, Faculty, and Students of Baylor University, Independence, Washington Co., for 1854 and 1855. Austin: "The State Gazette Job Office," 1855.

Fourth Annual Catalogue of Baylor University. Male Department, 1856-57. Galveston: The Civilian Book and Job Office, 1856. (announced supplement catalogue for Female Department.)

Catalogue of the Trustees, Faculty and Students of Baylor University. Female Department, 1857. Galveston: "News" Book and Job Establishment, 1857.

Fifth Annual Catalogue of Trustees, Professors, and Students of Baylor University, 1857. Galveston: The Civilian Book and Job Office, 1857.

Sixth Catalogue of the Trustees, Professors, and Students of Baylor University for 1856 & 1857. Galveston: "News" Book and Job Establishment.

Seventh Annual Catalogue of the Trustees, Professors, and Students of Baylor University Male Department, Independence, Texas. November 26, 1858. Anderson: "Texas Baptist" Book and Job Office, 1858.

Catalogue of the Trustees, Faculty, and Students of Baylor University. Female Department, 1858-1859. Galveston: "News" Book and Job Establishment, 1859.

Eighth Annual Catalogue of Trustees, Professors, and Students of Baylor University, Male Department, Independence, Texas, November 26, 1859. Galveston: "News" Book and Job Establishment, 1859.

Fifteenth Annual Report of the Female Department of Baylor University, Independence, Texas 1859-60. Galveston: "News" Book and Job Establishment, 1860.

Catalogue of Officers and Students of Baylor University. January 1866-January 1867. Laws and Rules of Discipline Appended. (Twenty-First Year). Houston: Gray, Smallwood and Company, Book and Job Printers.

——————. June 1868-June 1869 (Twenty-third Year). Baltimore: John F. Weishampel, Jr. No. 8. Under the Estaw House.

——————. Twenty-Sixth Year, February 1871-February 1872. Philadelphia: Smith, English and Co., 1872.

——————. Twenty-Seventh Year, May 1872-May 1873. Houston: A. C. Gray, Steam Printer and Book Binder, 1873.

——————. Thirty-Fourth Year, February 1878-February 1879. Cincinnati: Elm St. Printing Company, 1879.

——————. Thirty-Fifth Year, February 1879-February 1880. Moawequa, Illinois: T. M. Hughes, Printer, Illustrated Baptist Office, 1880.

——————. Thirty-Fifth Year, 1880-1881. Brenham: Carrick Printed.

——————. Thirty-Sixth Year, 1882-1883. Brenham: Frederick R. Carrick, 1882.

——————. Thirty-Eighth Year, February 1882-February 1883. Brenham: Banner Steam Book Print, 1883.

——————. Thirty-Ninth Year, February 1883-February 1884. (Mrs. Georgia J. Burleson's personal copy.) Dallas: Texas Baptist Steam Print.

——————. 1884-1885. Brenham: Fred R. Carrick, 1884.

——————. Fortieth Year, Sept. 1884-June 1885. (Mrs. Georgia J. Burleson's copy.) Austin: "Baptist Herald" Print.

Catalogue of the Officers and Students of Baylor University at Waco. 1885-1886, 1886-1887.

Catalogue of Baylor University at Waco, Texas, 1891-1892.

General Catalogue. Hamilton, New York: Colgate University, April 1837.

The First Half Century of Madison University. Colgate University General Catalogue, I, 1872.

Oberlin College *Bulletin.* Oberlin, Ohio, 1966.

Southwestern University Catalogue, 1967. Waco University Catalogues, June 20, 1866-1884.

Letters

Anderson, J. J. to President Crane. January 8, 1865. Crane Correspondence. Texas Collection, Baylor University.

Baines, G. W. to the Board of Trustees of Baylor University. June 24, 1862. Baines Correspondence. Texas Collection, Baylor University.

Barnes, James to President Crane. September 18, 1869. Crane Correspondence. Texas Collection, Baylor University.

——————— to Hosea Garrett, September 17, 1866. Garrett Letters. Texas Collection, Baylor University.

———————— to Hosea Garrett, September 24, 1866. Garrett Letters. Texas Collection, Baylor University.

Barnett, J. F. Palacios, Texas. Letter with No Date. Texas Collection, Baylor University.

Barnett, John F. to Mrs. Lily M. Russell. September 24, 1956. Palacios, Texas.

Baylor, Judge R. E. B. to J. R. Graves. March 25, 1869. Texas Collection, Baylor University.

———————— to unnamed nephew. July 18, 1869. Texas Collection, Baylor University.

————————to unknown addressee. Texas Collection, Baylor University. Also in William B. Sprague. *Annals of the American Pulpit,* VI.

————————to Brother Stribling. Holly Oak: April 13. Texas Collection, Baylor University.

Bowen, John, Waco, to fiancee Miss Emily Grimes of Grimes County. Scroll-bordered invitation. December 1859. Texas Collection, Baylor University.

Breedlove, C. R. and Thomas J. Goree. Letter, *Phi Gamma Delta,* April, 1881.

Broaddus, A. S. to President Crane. January 28, 1865. Crane Correspondence. Texas Collection, Baylor University.

———————— to Rev. H. Garrett. June 4, 1866. Garrett Letters. Texas Collection, Baylor University.

Brockett, Janet to Mrs. Lily M. Russell. February 7, 1945. Mansfield, Texas.

Buckner, H. F. to Dr. Crane. November 10, 1868. Crane Correspondence, Texas Collection, Baylor University.

———————— to Dr. Crane. January 10, 1871. Crane Archives, University of Texas.

Buckner, R. C. to President Crane. August 2, 1871. Texas Collection, Baylor University.

———————— to Dr. Crane. June 1, 1875. Crane Correspondence. Texas Collection, Baylor University.

Burleson, R. C. to Editor G. W. Baines. June 3, 1860. Baines Papers. Texas Collection, Baylor University.

———————— to R. E. B. Baylor. April 7, 1854. Burleson Papers. Texas Collection, Baylor University.

Burleson, Richard to R. C. Burleson. September 15, 1859. Burleson Papers. Texas Collection, Baylor University.

Burleson, Rufus C. to the Board of Trustees. June 26, 1861. Independence Papers. Texas Collection, Baylor University.

———————— to Richard Burleson. September 26, 1847. Burleson Papers. Texas Collection, Baylor University.

———————— to Richard B. Burleson. November 8, 1852. Burleson Papers. Texas Collection, Baylor University.

———————— to Richard Burleson. February 6, 1854. Burleson Papers. Texas Collection, Baylor University.

———————— to Richard Burleson. October 7, 1855. Burleson Papers. Texas Collection, Baylor University.

——————— to Richard Burleson. May 11, 1856. Burleson Papers. Texas Collection, Baylor University.

——————— to Richard Burleson. September 16, 1856. Burleson Papers. Texas Collection, Baylor University.

——————— to Richard Burleson. September 16, 1856. Burleson Papers. Texas Collection, Baylor University.

——————— to Richard Burleson. October 1, 1856. Burleson Papers. Texas Collection, Baylor University.

——————— to Richard Burleson. October 12, 1859. Texas Collection, Baylor University.

——————— to Richard Burleson. October 23, 1859. Waco, Texas. Texas Collection, Baylor University.

——————— to President Crane. May 23, 1869. Crane Correspondence. Texas Collection, Baylor University.

——————— to President Crane. October 27, 1870. Crane Correspondence. Texas Collection, Baylor University.

——————— to Dr. Crane. January 3, 1878. Crane Correspondence. Texas Collection, Baylor University.

——————— to Dr. Crane. February 20, 1878. Crane Correspondence. Texas Collection, Baylor University.

——————— to President of the Board Garrett. April 29, 1861. Independence Papers. Texas Collection, Baylor University.

——————— to Dr. J. H. Starr. November 12, 1859. J. H. Starr Papers. Archives, University of Texas. Austin, Texas.

Carroll, B. H. to Colonel J. C. Barrow. January 7, 1860. Texas Collection, Baylor University.

Cavitt, Mrs. Howard to Mrs. Lily M. Russell. March 28, 1955.

Chancellor, Mrs. Sarah Vickers. Letter April 12, 1955.

Clark, Horace to Brother Baines. June 18, 1860. Baines Papers. Texas Collection, Baylor University.

——————— to G. W. Baines. August 10, 1860. Baines Papers. Texas Collection, Baylor University.

Cochran, W. L. to President Crane. January 16, 1865. Crane Correspondence. Texas Collection, Baylor University.

Coles, John P. to Anthony Butler, U. S. Ambassador to Mexico.

Compere, Thomas H. to Dr. Crane. August 11, 1871.

Confederate Regional Command to President R. C. Crane. February 18, 1865. Crane Papers. Texas Collection, Baylor University.

Conway, Mrs. S. S. to Baylor President S. P. Brooks. November 8, 1929.

Crane, R. C. to Mrs. Lily Russell. May 11, 1951. Crane Papers. Texas Collection, Baylor University.

Crane W. C. to G. W. Baines. December 8, 1873. Baines Papers. Texas Collection, Baylor University.

——————— to Gen. W. R. Boggs. December 18, 1863. Crane Correspondence. Texas Collection, Baylor University.

——————— to President Burleson. June 4, 1869. Crane Correspondence. Texas Collection, Baylor University.

——————— to his wife. August 11, 1863. Crane Correspondence. Texas Collection, Baylor University.

——————— to son William Carey Crane, December 7, 1842. Crane Papers. Texas Collection, Baylor University.

——————— to *Galveston News.* September 22, 1871.

——————— to Garrett. June 6, 1866. Garrett Letters. Texas Collection, Baylor University.

——————— to Rev. Hosea Garrett. September 19, 1866. Crane Correspondence. Texas Collection, Baylor University.

——————— to Albert Haynes. March 29, 1866. Crane Correspondence. Texas Collection, Baylor University.

——————— to John Henderson. April 26, 1867. Crane Correspondence. Texas Collection, Baylor University.

Creath, J. W. D. to President Crane. July 11, 1871. Crane Correspondence. Texas Collection, Baylor University.

Crudup, Josiah. Secretary, Alumni Association. Letter dated December 3, 1941.

Davis, Florence to Alfred B. Davis, April 29, 1859. Texas Collection, Baylor University.

Dilworth, Mrs. Collett B. to Mrs. Lily M. Russell. May 10, 1957.

Dyess, Mrs. of Mexia, (n.d.).

Evan, John E. Pastor, First Baptist Church, Eufaula, Alabama. February 20, 1942.

Farquhar, J. L. to G. W. Baines. April 27, 1861. Baines Papers. Texas Collection, Baylor University.

——————— to President Crane. January 20, 1865. Crane Correspondence. Texas Collection, Baylor University.

——————— to Dr. Crane. September 3, 1869. Crane Correspondence. Texas Collection, Baylor University.

Ferguson, David to Dr. Crane. March 15, 1866. Crane Correspondence. Texas Collection, Baylor University.

Foreman, Lauren. Archivist Sigma Alpha Epsilon, June 10, 1954.

Foscue, F. F. to Dr. Crane. October 8, 1866. Crane Correspondence. Texas Collection, Baylor University.

Furlong, Mrs. I. D. (Velma K.) to Miss Sue Moore. November 13, 1959. Houston Texas.

——————— to Mrs. Lily M. Russell. April 13, 1945.

Garrett, H. to Brother Baines. January 1, 1859. Chappell Hill. Texas Collection, Baylor University.

Gillette, Henry to Ashbel Smith. Archives Collection, University of Texas Library. Letters of: October 17, 1840; July 17, 1841; September 17, 1841; March 21, 1842; January 10, 1842; February 21, 1844; November 3, 1844; August 15, 1846; January 16, 1847; March 11, 1848; September 25, 1849.

Haynes, Coe. Report concerning the American Baptist Home Mission Society.

Harris, W. W. to Dr. Crane. August 22, 1871. Crane Correspondence. Texas Collection, Baylor University.

Harrison, J. E. to Dr. Crane. August 16, 1870. Crane Correspondence. Texas Collection, Baylor University.

Henderson, John N. to Garrett. June 18, 1866. Chappell Hill. Garrett Letters. Texas Collection, Baylor University.

Herndon, William to President Crane. January 6, 1865. Crane Correspondence. Texas Collection, Baylor University.

Hill, Ella to President Crane. February 9, 1865. Crane Correspondence. Texas Collection, Baylor University.

Hill J. I. to President Crane. April 27, 1867. Crane Correpsondence. Texas Collection, Baylor University.

Holbrook, Marcus. July 9, 1956. Director, State of Arkansas Legislative Council. Little Rock, Arkansas.

Holleman, Earleen. Archives Assistant. The Eugene C. Barker Texas History Center. October 8, 1959.

Houston, Sam to G. W. Baines. November 23, 1857. Baines Papers. Texas Collection, Baylor University.

———————— to Margaret Lea Houston. March 1856.

Howard, William to Dr. Crane. November 13, 1869. Crane Correspondence. Texas Collection, Baylor University.

Howell, R. B. C. to *The Tennessee Baptist*. November 20, 1858.

Hoxie, Asa to E. G. Hanrick. May 24, 1834. Hanrick Papers. University of Texas Library.

Huckins, James to Corresponding Secretary of American Baptist Home Mission Society. Galveston: November 10, 1841.

———————— to *The Index*. April 28, 1843.

———————— to his wife. February 14, 1862. Charleston. Texas Collection, Baylor University.

———————— to daughter, Sarah Allen Huckins Davis. February 20, 1862. Texas Collection, Baylor University.

Hurlbus, Dr. to Mr. Huckins. July 5, 1860. Harden, Henry Winthrop. *Huckins Family*. Privately published, 1916.

Ikard, W. to Elder G. W. Baines. November 20 (no year). Baines Papers. Texas Collection, Baylor University.

Kavanaugh, B. T. to Dr. Crane. December 31, 1874. Crane Correspondence. Texas Collection, Baylor University.

Kemp, Mr. L. W. to Mrs. Lily M. Russell. February 16, 1944.

Lakin Letters. Copies in Archives of the University of Texas. Owned by Emma F. Lakin.

Letter. Independence Material. Texas Collection, Baylor University.

Link, J. B. to President Crane. November 27, 1872. Crane Correspondence. Texas Collection, Baylor University.

McGary, Jonathan A., Jr. to his father, J. A. McGary, Sr. October 31, 1859. Texas Collection, Baylor University.

Miller, J. B. to James F. Perry. December 10, 1834.

Morrell, Z. N., A. Buffington, J. R. Jenkins. To the Baptist Board of Foreign Missions in the U. S. November 7, 1837. Archives of the American Baptist Home Mission Board.

Newman, Mr. Gus. Letter supplying material from Mrs. George Armistead. January 1, 1939.

Philips, M. W. to William Carey Crane. November 8, 1857. Crane Papers. Texas Collection, Baylor University.

Ragsdale, Dr. B. D. to Mrs. Lily M. Russell. January 31, 1942.

Rice, Luther. *Journal*. Microfilms by George Washington University Library.

Rolfe, Rollin M. Dean of Students, Austin College, Sherman, Texas, July 24, 1956.

Ross, Michael to William C. Crane. June 1, 1863. Included in the letter is a letter by George W. Graves, representing the Baylor Trustees. Crane Correspondence. Texas Collection, Baylor University.

Rowe, Mrs. Cecile to A. A. Grusendorf. May 15, 1937. Houston.

Shannon, Josephine. August 15, 1945.

Speight, J. W. to Crane. November 12, 1870. Crane Correspondence. Texas Collection, Baylor University.

Taylor, E. W. to Rev. Henry L. Graves. January 20, 1846. Gambrel. "Early Baylor."

Taylor, H. D. to Mrs. Lily M. Russell. February 26, 1944.

Thacker, Mrs. Caroline T. to Mrs. Lily M. Russell. May 17, 1944.

Trask, Frances to Israel Trask. July 6, 1835. Trask Letters. The University of Texas Archives, Austin, Texas.

————— to Col. Hockly. June 20, 1838. Trask Letters. University of Texas Archives.

————— to H. H. Farley. February 18, 1844. Trask Letters. Archives of Texas State Library.

Tryon, J. M. to President Crane. February 19, 1867. Crane Correspondence. Texas Collection, Baylor University.

Wallace, Belle to Georgia Burleson. July 13, 1864. Burleson Correspondence. Texas Collection, Baylor University.

Warton, E. C. to "Dear Uncle." February 1, 1865. Crane Correspondence. Texas Collection, Baylor University.

Wheeler, R. T. to George W. Baines. June 30, 1860. Baines Papers. Texas Collection, Baylor University.

Newspapers

Anonymous Letter. *Democratic Statesman.* August: (n.d.) Crane Scrapbook. Texas Collection, Baylor University.

Atlanta Constitution, November 12, 1903.

Austin. *Southern Intelligencer,* August 18, 1858.

—————. *Texas State Gazette,* August 14, 1852.

—————. *Statesman,* January 18, 1945. "Morrel's body removed from Kyle Cemetery (d. December 19, 1883) and placed beside Rev. Wm. Carey Crane."

—————. *Texas Sentinel* (weekly). June 17, 1841.

Baylor Board of Trustees News Story. "To The Public." Texas Collection, Baylor University (n.d.) unidentified paper.

"Baylor Forerunner: Miss Trask's School For Girls Was First in Texas," *Waco Tribune-Herald,* February 28, 1954.

Baylor Lariat, January 7, 1959.

Baylor Lists Noted Pianos in Collection," *The Dallas Morning News,* January 19, 1941.

Bernard, William C. "Baylor Mannequin," *The Dallas Daily Times-Herald.* March 18, 1950.

Brenham Banner (n.d.) Newsclipping. Texas Collection, Baylor University.

Brazoria. *Texas Republican,* December 13, 1834.

Bryan, Mary E. "Horace Clark," *Houston Post,* February 24, 1908.

Bryan *News Letter,* May 22, 1869.

Brownsville Herald, December 11, 1947.

Burkhalter, Frank E. "Rift, Then Reunion after . . . Baptism of Sam Houston," *Waco Tribune-Herald,* August 4, 1957.

Burleson. Letter to the Editor. *The Houston Tri-Weekly Telegraph,* XXVII, No. 44. Houston: June 27, 1862, July 2, 1862, July 23, 1862.

Carroll, J. M. *Waco Times-Herald,* June 2, 1909.

Corsicana Daily Sun, February 19, 1922.

Clark, Horace. "The Crisis—Secession." Independence: January 17, 1861. Clark Scrapbook. Texas Collection, Baylor University, Circular.

Crane. "Legislative Aid to Existing Colleges and Universities." Crane Scrapbook. Original Bill in Archives, Texas Collection, Baylor University (n.d.).

————. "The Present Free School System," Newsclippings September 21, 23, 1871. Crane Papers. Texas Collection, Baylor University.

————. "Shall Christians Surrender to the State the Secular Education of their Children?" Newsclipping, Crane Scrapbook. Texas Collection, Baylor University.

Cranfill, J. B. "When Baylor University Came to Waco," *The Dallas Morning News,* June 10, 1928.

Crittenden, Pauline. "Texas Tours: Caldwell Area," *The Dallas Morning News,* June 20, 1965.

Dallas Daily Herald, March 26, 1880.

Dallas Herald, October 15, 1859.

Dallas Morning News, July 9, 1935, May 8, 1938, January 19, 1941, November 2, 1944.

Fairfield Recorder, August 30, 1951.

"Female School," *Washington American.* March 19, 1857.

Fort Worth Star-Telegram, March 1, 1936.

"Foundation for Baylor University is Created by Frontier Amazon," *Waco Tribune-Herald,* Sunday, October 20, 1949.

Freytag, Walter P. "Soldier, Statesman, Patriot," *The Fayette County Record,* La Grange, Texas, March 2, 1962.

Galveston Civilian, 1869.

Galveston. *Flake's Bulletin* 18.

————. "Our Third Pastor, March 1849-July 1850," *The Herald* of the First Baptist Church, V, No. 40, March 29, 1936.

————. The *Galveston News,* July 12 (n.d.). Clark Scrapbook. Texas Collection, Baylor University. Also September 22, 1871.

Garrett, C. C. Reminiscences of Sayles, *Brenham Banner,* May 1897.

George, Gerald. "When Honors are Conferred by Degrees," *The National Observer.* June 4, 1967.

Hayes, Robert M. "Father of Texas Had Tough Time with His Rebel Flock," *Dallas Morning News,* November 14, 1937.

Houston Chronicle, Unsigned, undated letter.

Houston Democratic Telegraph and Texas Register, November 18, 1847.

——————— *Daily Telegraph,* September 13, 1866.

——————— *Post,* November 3, 1932, March 6, 1959.

Houston Telegraph, February 6, 1857.

La Grange Journal, Fayette County, March 1, 1962.

Letter in *Lavaca Commercial,* December 1969.

"Patrick Henry's Speech in Defence of the Virginia Baptist Ministers," Richmond, Va.: *Religious Herald,* Old Series XLIV.

Potts, C. S. "The Three Musketeers of the Old Court," *The Dallas Morning News.* Sunday, September 1, 1929.

Ray, Jeff D. "William Carey Crane," *Fort Worth Star Telegram,* September 26, 1937.

"The Life of Rev. James Huckins and His Family," *Charleston Courier,* August 8, 1863.

The Richmond Telescope. June 15, 1839.

Rogers, Mrs. Ernest. "History of First Church, Brenham," *Gulf Coast Baptist,* August 3, 1950.

"Sam Houston Relics Add Aura to Texas Collection," *Houston Chronicle Daily,* September 27, 1945.

Shipe, Mrs. S. L. "Texas in the Sixties," Sunday Magazine Supplement *Galveston News.* Horace Clark Scrapbook. Texas Collection, Baylor University.

——————— . "Old Washington in 1842," *Galveston News* (Magazine Section), July 23, 1905.

"Sketches of the Lives of the Members of the First Supreme Court in Texas," *The Dallas Morning News,* Sunday, September 1, 1920.

Sullivan, Captain W. R. Letter to Six Young Ladies, Baylor University. *The Tri-Weekly Telegraph,* XXVIII, No. 55. Houston: July 23, 1862.

Telegraph and Texas Register. December 26, 1835, March 3, 1838, December 22, 1838, May 15, 1839, May 29, 1839, May 6, 1840, March 9, 1842, November 19, 1845, January 28, 1846, March 4, 1846.

Texas Baptist Herald. Houston, March 18, 1857, December 1, 1859, May 10, 1860.

Texas National Register. Washington-on-the-Brazos, December 7, 1844-October 9, 1845.

"Transplanted Yankee Put Texas Public Schools on Road to Success Before 53rd Legislature in 1954," *Waco Tribune-Herald,* February 28, 1954.

Treytag, Walter P. "Soldier, Statesman, Patriot," *The Fayette County Record.* La Grange, Texas: March 2, 1862.

Wade, Houston. "Fayette County Heroes of San Jacinto," *La Grange Journal,* No. 42.

The Washington Texas Ranger and Lone Star, February 7, 1850.

Wedemeyer, C. H. "William Carey Crane," *The Belton Journal,* December 3, 1909.

Wheeler, R. T. "The Crisis—What is Our Duty?" *The Dallas Herald.* January 16, 1861.

White, Olive Branch. "Margaret Lea Houston," Naylor's *Epic-Century Magazine,* San Jacinto Number, April 1936.

Wilson, Gertrude S. "Trip to Independence," *Waco Tribune-Herald,* Sunday, May 28, 1950.

Addresses

Adams, Joseph T. Lecture on the Subject of Re-Annexing Texas to the U. S. Delivered in New Bedford, February 10, 1845.

Addresses Delivered at the Annual Commencement of the Female Department of Baylor University June 28, 1860. Galveston: Civilian Book & Job Printing, 1860.

Browne, Philip D. "Henry Lee Graves at Fairfield." Presented at the meeting of the Baylor Historical Society, Waco, Texas, May 25, 1956.

Burleson, Rufus C. Address of Dr. Rufus C. Burleson on the one hundredth anniversary of the birth of Gen. Sam Houston, and the fifty-seventh of the independence of Texas. Austin: Ben C. Jones and Company, (n.d.).

—————. Semi-Centennial Address delivered before Union Baptist Association. Houston: 1890.

—————. Baccalaureate Address—President Burleson conferring of Degrees, July 25, 1856. Texas Collection, Baylor University.

Clark, Reverend Horace. An address before the Alumnae of Baylor Female College at the Fiftieth Anniversary of the College. June 10, 1895. Belton, Texas. Also Commencement Address, Baylor College June 3, 1884. Bryan Texas: George Dunlap.

Crane, Royston C. Address Delivered at the Independence Homecoming, August, 1950.

Crane, William C. Address before Baptist State Convention of Texas at Galveston, 1869. Copy in Royston C. Crane Scrapbook and the Minutes of Trustees, Baylor University, November 3, 1869, and the *Biographical Encyclopedia of Texas,* I.

—————. Address on the Life and Character of Jesse Hartwell, D.D. New York: Sheldon and Co., 1860.

—————. "Plan for a State University." To the Members of the Legislature of Texas, February 15, 1875.

—————. "The Scholar." Delivered at Mississippi College, 1852. MS, Crane Papers. Texas Collection, Baylor University.

—————. "Who Ought to Support and Control the Education Needed by the People?" Mexia Education Convention. Reprint of August 6, 1878. Crane Papers. Texas Collection, Baylor University.

Duncan, J. T. "Dr. Crane as a Teacher." Delivered at Baylor University, June 1, 1903. Original in Crane Papers. Texas Collection, Baylor University.

Eby, Frederick. "Texas Education in Transit." Centennial Address, University of Texas, Austin, January 7, 1954.

Morrow, Temple Houston. "Address by Temple Houston Morrow." *Senate Journal,* 49 Texas Legislature, regular session, February 27, 1945.

Reid, Robert L. "S. G. O'Bryan, the Father of Waco University." Address at Annual Meeting of Baylor Historical Society, May 27, 1950.

Sanford, S. V. Address Given at the Centennial Celebration of Mercer University, Macon, Georgia: May 1933.

Semi-Centennial Address Delivered before Union Baptist Association by Rev. J. H. Stribling and Rev. Rufus C. Burleson. August 16, 17, 1890.

Weaver, Rufus W. "The Founders of Baylor University." June 13, 1944.

Appendix

CHARTER OF BAYLOR UNIVERSITY
at
Independence, Texas
ENACTED BY THE CONGRESS OF
THE REPUBLIC OF TEXAS
AS FOLLOWS:

"AN ACT TO INCORPORATE BAYLOR UNIVERSITY"*

Section 1.   Be it enacted by the Senate and House of Representatives of the Republic of Texas in Congress assembled, That an institution of learning be, and is hereby established at such place within the Republic aforesaid, as the Trustees hereinafter named, may designate, to be denominated the Baylor University.

Section 2.   Be it further enacted, That there shall be fifteen Trustees, who are hereby authorized to take charge of said University, and a majority of the whole number shall constitute a quorum to do business.

Section 3.   Be it further enacted, That the following persons have been duly chosen Trustees of said University, and are recognized as such, to wit: R. E. B. Baylor; J. G. Thomas; Albert C. Horton; Edward Taylor; James S. Lester; R. B. Jarmon; James Huckins; Nelson Kavanaugh; O. Drake; Eli Mercer; Aaron Shannon; James Farquhar; Albert Haynes; Robert S. Armstead and W. Tryon.

Section 4.   Be it further enacted, That the trustees aforesaid, be, and they are hereby constituted a body politic and corporate, in deed and in law, by the name of the President and Trustees of the Baylor University, and by that name, they and their successors shall and may have succession, and may be able and capable in law, to have and receive, and enjoy to them and their successors, lands, tenements, hereditaments of any kind, in fee or for life, or for years, and personal property of any kind whatsoever, and also, all sums of money which may be given, granted or bequeathed to them, for the purposes of promoting the interest of said university: Provided the amount of property owned by said corporation shall not at any one time, exceed

*The original copy of the Baylor University Charter is in the State Archives, Austin, Texas.

one hundred thousand dollars, over and above the buildings, library and apparatus necessary to the Institution.

Section 5. Be it further enacted, That there shall be a stated meeting of the Board of Trustees in each year, at the time of conferring degrees, and that the President of said Board, shall have full power to call an occasional meeting of the Board, whenever it shall appear to him necessary.

Section 6. Be it further enacted, That the Trustees shall and may have a common seal, for the business of themselves and their successors, with liberty to change and alter the same from time to time, as they shall think proper, and that in their aforesaid names, they and their successors, shall and may be able to sue and be sued, plead and be impleaded, answer and be answered, defend and be defended in all Courts of law or equity in this Republic, and to grant, bargain and sell or assign, any lands, tenements, goods or chattels that may belong to said University, to construct all necessary buildings for the said Institution, to establish a Preparatory Department, and a Female Department, and such other dependent Institutions as they shall deem necessary—to have the management of the finances, the privileges of electing their own officers, of appointing all necessary committees, and to act and do all things whatsoever for the benefit of said Institution, in as ample a manner as any person or body politic or corporate, can or may do by law.

Section 7. Be it further enacted, That the said Trustees shall have the power of prescribing the course of studies to be pursued by the students, and of framing and enacting all such ordinances and by-laws, as shall appear to them necessary for the good government of said University, and of their own proceedings:

Provided, the same be not repugnant to the Constitution and laws of this Republic.

Section 8. Be it further enacted, That the head of this University shall be styled the President, the male instructors thereof, Professors; and the head of the female department, Principal of said department; and the President and Professors, or a majority of them, the Faculty of the Baylor University; which faculty shall have the power of enforcing the ordinances and by-laws adopted by the Trustees for the government of the students, by rewarding or censuring them, and finally by suspending such of them as after repeated admonitions, shall continue disobedient or refractory, until a determination of a quorum of the Trustees shall be had; but it shall be only in the power of the quorum of the Trustees, as their meeting, to expel any student or students from said University.

Section 9. Be it further enacted, That the Trustees shall have full power, by the President or Professors of said University, to grant or confer such degree or degrees in the arts or sciences, to any of the students of said University, or persons by them thought worthy, as are usually granted or conferred in other Universities, and to give diplomas or certificates thereof, signed by them, and sealed with the common seal of the Trustees of the said University, to authenticate and perpetuate the memory of such graduations.

Section 10. Be it further enacted, That whenever any vacancy shall occur, either by death, resignation or otherwise, in the Board of Trustees, such vacancy shall be filled by the Executive Committee of the Texas Baptist Education Society.

Section 11. Be it further enacted, That all necessary officers of said Institution, shall be appointed by a majority of the Board of Trustees.

Section 12. Be it further enacted, That whenever a vacancy shall occur in the Presidency or any of the Professorships of the University, the Board of Trustees shall have power to fill such vacancy.

Section 13. Be it further enacted, That the Trustees shall have the power of fixing salaries of all the officers connected with the University, and of removing them for neglect or misconduct in office, a majority of the whole number concurring in said removal.

Section 14. Be it further enacted, That the lands, public buildings and other property belonging to the said University, are hereby declared to be free from any kind of public tax.

Section 15. Be it further enacted, That no misnomer of the said University shall defeat or annul, any gift, grant, devise or bequest to the same.

Section 16. Be it further enacted, That the Professors of said University shall not be eligible to act as Trustee or Trustees for the same, and in any case, either or any of the Trustees may hereafter be employed to discharge any of the duties in or about said University, he or they shall resign their station of Trustee or Trustees, before entering upon the discharge assigned him or them.

Section 17. Be it further enacted, That when any law, rule or resolution may be passed by the Board of Trustees at a regular or stated meeting of said Board, it shall not be competent for a called meeting of said Board to repeal or rescind such law, rule or resolution, unless there is a full Board present.

Section 18. Be it further enacted, That this Act shall remain in force fifty years, subject to renewal of Congress.

Section 19. Be it further enacted, That this Act shall be deemed a public one, and judicially taken notice of, without special pleadings.

Section 20. Be it further enacted, That nothing in this Act shall be construed, as to allow banking privileges, or any other privileges not contemplated by this Charter, and a non-compliance with the provisions of this Act, or a breach of the same, shall work a forfeiture of this Act or Charter

Approved, February 1st, 1845.

(From Gammel's *Laws of Texas,* II, pp. 1130-31-32-33.)

The above Act or Charter was amended by the Legislature of the State of Texas January 19th, 1850, in its 10th clause, so as to provide for the naming of the Trustees of the University by Texas Baptist State Convention. (Gammel's *Laws of Texas,* III, pp. 703-4.)

DEED FOR THE FIRST PROPERTY
OF BAYLOR UNIVERSITY

Deed from W. W. Allen to Baylor University
The State of Texas
County of Washington
Know all men by these presents that we William W. Allen & Electra Allen his wife of said State and County in consideration of the useful purposes for which the Baylor University has been Established and the better to enable the President & Trustees of said University to carry out these objects have given granted & donated area foɪ the further consideration of one dollar to us in hand paid by the said President & Trustees the receipt whereof is hereby acknowledged to by these presents bargain and release convey & conform unto the said President & Trustees of the Baylor University & their Successors in office forever a certain tract or parcel of land Situate lying and being in Said County at or near the Town of Independence and having Its. and bounds as follows to wit, Beginning at the South East corner of Henry Kountz's Survey at a Stake marked thence North 74th deg. East at 123 vs Stake marked thence North 15 deg. West at 270 vara, a Stake thence due west at 129th vara, a Stake thence South 15— deg East at 300 vara, the Beginning containing in all an area of 63/10 acres of land more or less and Known as Survey No. 3 otherwise as Wind Mill Hill To have and to hold the above described tract or parcel of land together with an area Singular the rights, members, and appertaining unto them the said President & Trustee of the Baylor University and their Successors in office forever—in fee Simple and we the said William W. Allen do hereby bind ourselves, our kin, Executor, & administrator the above described premises to warrant and forever defend unto the said President & Trustees of Baylor University & their Successors in office, forever, against the claim of ourselves, our kin, Executor and administrators and any and all persons hereafter claiming or to claim the same or any part thereof. In Testimony whereof we have hereunto set our hand and affixed our seals using script by way of seal, this 25 day of Sept. A.D. 1849
Signed sealed & delivered in person of
The State of Texas   Wm. W. ALLEN
 Washington County
Before Mr. Moses Puck   ELECTRA ALLEN
Notary Public in and for the County of Washington personally appeared Wm. W. Allen a citizen of said County who aknowledged

that he signed sealed & delivered the written Instrument for the purposes, therein contained. Also personally appeared Electra Allen wife of Wm. W. Allen being a party to the within instrument bearing date on the 25th day of Sept. 1849 and having been Examined by me privily and apart from her husband and having the same fully Explained to her She the said Electra Allen acknowledged the same to be her act and deed and declared that she had willingly signed sealed & delivered the same and that she wished not to retard it I hereto sign my name and affix my seal of office at the Town of Independence this September 25th 1849.

Sam Puck   clk

Filed for Record 4th March 1850 at 10 o'ck A.M.

BAYLOR'S FIRST BUILDING CONTRACT

The State of Texas
County of Washington

Contract for building made
12th day of July
One thousand Eight Hundred and Fifty-five
by and between the Trustees of Baylor University, located in the town of Independence, State and County above mentioned, of the first part, and John P. Collins, now of the same place of the second part in the following words, to-wit: —The said party of the second part convenants and agrees to and with the said party of the first part, to build and to finish in a good, substantial and workmanlike manner, a two-story, stone school house on the lot of ground, whereon the building now occupied by the Female Department of the above named Institution now stands, agreeable to the draft, plans and specifications, hereto annexed (which draught, plans and specifications are signed by the parties to this contract). And to build and to finish the same of good and substantial materials furnished at his own proper expense, and to deliver over the same completed in all its parts to the party of the first part, by the first day of January, One Thousand Eight Hundred and Fifty Seven. And the said party of the first part, convenants and agrees to pay unto the said party of the second part, for and in consideration of the same the sum of eight thousand Dollars, in payments as follows, —One Thousand Dollars when the rock and lime are on the ground; One Thousand Dollars when the walls are half up; One Thousand and Five Hundred Dollars when the house is covered; and the balance of Four Thousand and Five Hundred Dollars when the work is completed.

And the said party of the first part reserves the privilege, and is conceded by the party of the first part, that they—the Board of Trustees—may furnish contract lumber at the mill at the regular mill prices, and the amount thereof, be it more or less, shall be deducted from the last payment due on this contract.

And the said party of the second part agrees to receive an account of the several payments as they severally fall due, good cash notes, on solvent individuals, and to use all due diligence in collecting the same when due, and to resort to legal measures if in any instance it should be impracticable to collect the same without—provided, that if in any instance the said party of the second part shall then fail to collect the same, the said party of the first part shall be responsible to the said party of the second part for the amount thereof.

In witness thereof, the hereto have here unto set their hands and seals (using scrolls for seals) the day and year above written.

H. Garrett, President   (seal)

John P. Collins   (seal)

Signed and sealed in
presence of us as witnesses:
W. Holmes
H. Clark

Minutes of the Trustees, pp. 124-126.

TRUSTEES OF BAYLOR UNIVERSITY
AT INDEPENDENCE

Name	Term
Adams, F. W.	1870-1871
Armistead, Robert L.	1845-1847
Baines, George W.	1851-1859
Barnes, J. W.	1852-1872
Baylor, R. E. B. (Minister and Judge)	1845-1873
Beall, Thomas J.	1873-1880
Blackburn, J. H.	1871-1877
Breedlove, George W.	1874-1889
Broadus, A. S.	1866-1871
Bryan, L. R.	1885-1889
Bryan, M. Austin	1866-1885
Buckner, H. F. (Minister)	1868-1869
Buffington, T. C.	1883-1885
Campbell, J. D.	Feb. 5, 1889-April 5, 1889
Chandler, P. B. (Minister)	1852-1877
Chaplin, C. C. (Minister)	1878-1884
Crane, R. C.	Feb. 27, 1883
Creath, J. W. D. (Minister)	1848-1881
Dallas, J. W.	1885-1897
Dodge, H. W. (Minister)	1874-1875
Dodson, W. H. (Minister)	1882-1889
Drake, Orin	1845-1851
Dunn, A. W.	1883-1885
Farquahar, James L.	1845-1873
Garrett, Hosea (Minister)	1847-1868, 1870-1886
Graves, George W. (Dr.)	1856-1872
Hairston, J. T.	1872-1897
Hardwicke, J. B. (Minister)	1879-1882
Haueslar, A. (Minister)	1879-1880
Hawthorne, A. T.	1881-1884
Hayden, S. A. (Minister)	1881-1883
Haynes, Albert G. (Esq.)	1845-1870
Haynes, Harry	1881-1889
Haynes, J. R.	June 13, 1850
Hines, J. R.	1848-1851
Hodde, Henry	March 9, 1885-Oct. 22, 1885
Holland, Joseph A. (Dr.)	1866-1870
Holmes, Willet	1873-1882

Horm, W. _____Aug. 21, 1876
Horton, A. C. (Hon.) _____1845-1861
Howard, William, (Minister) _____1874-1885
Huckins, James (Minister) _____1845-1848
Jackson, Terrell J. _____1848-1868
Jarman, R. B. (Colonel) _____1845-1866
Johnston, Jonas (Minister) _____1869-1872
Kavanaugh, Nelson _____1845-1871
Kiefer, F. (Minister) _____1880-1887
King, H. M. _____1877-1878
Law, F. M._____
Lester, James Seaton (Hon.) _____1845-1866
Lipscomb, A. S. (Judge) _____1849-1856
Mays, E. G. _____1859-1868
McIntyre, Hugh C. _____1868-1880
McIver, A. _____1885-1889
McKnight, John _____1886-1887
Mercer, Eli _____1845-1848
Minquitz, C. _____Nov. 9, 1885-Mar. 9, 1885
Montgomery, W. A. _____June 6, 1866-Oct. 10, 1866
Morriss, A. E. _____1870-1873
Pickett, George W. (Minister) _____1873-1889
Rogers, George W. _____1883-1889
Rogers, M. E. _____1883-1889
Shannon, Aaron (Colonel) _____1845-1863
Spaulding, A. T. (Minister) _____
Stewart, William H. _____1874-1878
Taylor, E. W. _____1845-1848
Thomas, J. G. (Esq.) _____1845-1871
Tryon, William M. (Minister) _____1845-1847
Vickers, Reddin _____1868-1876
Weaver, Abram _____ Nov. 15, 1869
Wedemeyer, William _____1879-1883
Williams, Samuel _____1866-1867
Williams, Weston L. _____1870-1873
Wood, William G. _____ 1870-1893

TRUSTEES OF BAYLOR UNIVERSITY
AT INDEPENDENCE
WHO SERVED TWENTY YEARS OR MORE

Baylor, R. E. B.	1845-1873	28 years
Creath, J. W. D.	1848-1880	32 years
Farquahar, James L.	1845-1873	28 years
Garrett, Hosea	1847-1868	37 years
	1870-1886	
Haynes, Albert G.	1845-1872	27 years
Horton, A. C.	1845-1865	21 years
Jarman, Richard B.	1845-1866	21 years
Kavanaugh, Nelson	1845-1866	21 years
Lester, James Seaton	1845-1866	21 years
Shannon, Aaron	1845-1865	20 years
Thomas, J. G.	1845-1871	26 years

PROXIES
BAYLOR UNIVERSITY AT INDEPENDENCE
BOARD OF TRUSTEES

Anderson, M. D.
Beauchamp, S. A.
Blanton, B.
Burleson, Rufus C.
Carroll, James M.
Crane, R. C.
Crumpler, D. D.
Daniels, Ashbury
Ellis, R.
Ewing, E. F.
Fontaine, W. J.
Garrett, C. C.
Graves, Henry L.
Graves, John H.
Hallum, J. L.
Hill, Noah
Hill, O. H. P.
Hillyer, J. F.
Horm, W.
Humphreys, C. J.
Jenkins, J. R.
Law, F. M.
Lipscomb, Abner E.

Massey, R. A.
Matheny, M. P.
McJunkin, S. B.
Nash, W. W.
O'Brien, Solomon Green
Parks, I.
Paxton, J. E.
Pope, O. C.
Powell, W. D.
Robertson, Dr. J. B.
Ross, M.
Roundtree, F. S.
Scalon, William
Shepard, C. E.
Smith, M. V.
Spencer, H. C.
Stribling, James H.
Terrell, J. W.
Thacker, W. H.
Thomas, W. R.
Webb, J. W.
Willingham, C. H.

ADMINISTRATIVE OFFICERS
AND FACULTY OF
BAYLOR AT INDEPENDENCE
1845-1886*

Baylor Female Department became Baylor Female College in September 1866 and thereafter names are listed separately.

Allen, R. L., A.B.,
Assistant in Preparatory Department 1886 (6).

Anderson, John C., A.M.,
Professor of Ancient and Modern Languages 1861-1862 (1, 6).

Andrews, Rev. Reddin, Jr., A.B., A.M., D.D.,
Professor of Natural Science, Vice-President, 1871-1872;
Professor of Greek and English Literature, 1886 (1, 2, 6).

Atkinson, Lucy, A.B.,
Assistant in the Female Department, 1863 (4, 6).

Bailey, W. O., D.D.,
Lecturer, 1881-1882 (2, 6).

Baines, George Washington, A.M.,
President, 1861-1863; Professor of Natural Science, 1861
(1, 4, 6).

Barnes, Eugenia,
Oil Painting, 1859-1860 (2, 6).

Baylor, Hon. R. E. B., LL.D.,
Baylor Law Department, 1848-1849; 1857-1860; 1863; 1866-
1869; 1871-1873 (1, 2, 4, 5, 6).

Berryman, John, J., A.M.,
Professor of Mathematics and Natural Science, 1866-1867
(1, 2, 4, 6, 7, 9).

Bittle, W. J., A.B.,
Tutor in Arithmetic and Primary Science, 1882-1885 (2, 6).

*Sources for information concerning the administrative officers and faculty at Baylor University at Independence are indicated by the following numbers:
1. Minutes of the Board of Trustees
2. Baylor University Catalogue
3. Minutes of Union Association
4. Minutes of the Baptist State Convention of Texas
5. Carroll, *History of Texas Baptists*
6. Wilson, *A Register of Baylor University, 1845-1935*
7. *Texas Baptist Herald*
8. Burleson's Letters
9. Crane's Letters

Boggess, Albert, A.M.,
   Professor of Mathematics and Engineering, 1885; (2) 1870-1873; 1885-1892 (6).

Boyle, John G.,
   Tutor in Preparatory Department, 1866-1867 (2, 6).

Breaker, J. M. C., D.D.,
   Lecturer, 1882-1885 (2, 6).

Buckner, H. F., A.M.,
   Lecturer on Revealed Religion, 1867-1869 (2, 6).

Burleson, Rufus C., LL.D., D.D.,
   President and Professor of Ancient Languages, Intellectual Philosophy and Belles Lettres, 1851-1854; Professor of Latin, Greek, and Spanish Languages and Belles Lettres, President, 1854-1861 (1, 2, 4, 5, 6).
   Spanish; President, Professor of Moral and Mental Philosophy, 1885-1886 (1, 2, 4, 5, 6).

Burleson, Richard B., A.M.,
   Professor of Moral and Mental Philosophy, 1856-1858; Political Economy, and Belles Lettres, 1857; Librarian, Vice-president and Professor of Natural Science, 1859 (2, 6).

Buttlar, Augustus,
   Professor of French and German, 1850-1851 (5).

Buttlar, Louisa, Mrs.,
   First Music Teacher, Baylor Female Department, 1850-1851 (5).

Carroll, W. H.,
   Lecturer, 1878-1879 (4).

Chandler, T. Judson, A.M.,
   Student Assistant, 1872-1874; Professor of Natural Science and English, 1878-1885 (1, 2, 4, 5, 8).

Chaplin, C. C., D.D.,
   Lecturer, 1880-1885 (2, 6).

Chase, Carrie L.,
   Instructor in Drawing, Painting in Oil and Watercolor, and Wax Works, Baylor Female Department, 1858-1860 (2, 3, 6).

Chase, D. W.,
   Director and Principal of Music Department, Professor of Vocal and Instrumental Music, Baylor Female Department, 1858-1860 (2, 4, 6).

Chase, Mary E.,
Instructor in Harp, Piano, and Vocal Music, Baylor Female Department, 1858-1860 (2, 3, 6).

Chase, Oscar A.,
Instructor in Piano and Guitar, Baylor Female Department, 1858-1860 (2, 3, 6).

Clark, Catherine,
Tutor, Female Department, 1859-1869 (2, 6).

Clark, Martha D.,
History and English Literature, Female Department, 1851-1852; Teacher of Preparatory Department, 1856-1857; Governess of Music Department, 1859-1860; Superintendent of Boarding Pupils, 1866 (2, 6, 7).

Clarke, Rev. Horace, A.M.,
Principal and Professor of Ancient Languages, Moral and Intellectual Philosophy, Female Department, 1851-1866 (1, 2, 4, 6, 7, 8).

Clay, Vitula,
Oriental Painting, Grecian Painting, Ornamental Hair Work, Female Department, 1859-1860 (2).

Collins, John P.,
Steward, Female Department, 1857-1858 (2, 6).
Assistant in Preparatory Department 1886 (6).

Constet, F.,
Instructor of French, Spanish, and German, 1870 (1).

Conner, Richard,
Professor of Drawing and Painting, Baylor Female College, 1872-1873 (6).

Cowherd, P. H.,
Literary Department, 1868-1869 (1, 9).

Cowlls, Warren,
Professor of Mathematics or Tutor, 1848-1849 (5).

Crane, Charles Judson, A.B., A.M.,
Instructor in Latin and Greek, 1868-1869; Professor of Mathematics and Natural Science, 1870-1871; Professor of Natural Science and English, 1880-1881 (2, 4, 6, 7).

Crane, Royston C., B.P.,
Tutor, 1882-1884 (2, 4, 6).

Crane, William Carey, A.B., D.D., LL.D.,
   President and Professor of Theology, Ethics, and Belles Lettres, 1864; Professor of Moral and Intellectual Philosophy, and Hebrew, 1866-1885 (1, 2, 4, 5, 6, 7).
Crane, William Carey, Jr., A.B., A.M.,
   Tutor, 1863-1868; Assistant Professor of Ethics, Belles Lettres, and Hebrew, and Professor Pro-tem of Natural Science, 1868-1878 (1, 2, 4, 6, 7).
Creath, J. W. D.,
   Theological School, 1865-1866 (4, 7).
Cross, Rev. S. S.,
   Theological School, 1865-1866 (4, 7).
Dallas, James W.,
   Instructor in Field Surveying, 1876-1879 (4, 6, 7).
Daniel, F. E., M.D.,
   Dean of Medical Department and Professor of Anatomy, Galveston, 1868-1869 (2).
Davis, Florence,
   Preparatory Department, 1863-1866 (4, 6, 7).
Davis, Harriett,
   Assistant in Female Department, Mathematics and Natural Science, 1851-1856; French Language, Drawing, Painting and Embroidery, 1856 (1, 2, 4).
Davis, Marcia,
   Matron, Female Department, 1857 (2, 6).
Davis, Mary R.,
   Instructor in History, Rhetoric ,and English Literature, Female Department, 1856-1859; 1864-1865 (1, 2, 4, 6).
East, W. A., M.D.,
   Professor of Surgery, Galveston, 1868-1869 (2).
Edwards, Thomas George,
   Professor of English Literature and Tutor in Preparatory Department, 1851 (4, 6).
Ellis, Sam
   Student Assistant, 1872-1873 (2, 6).
Etheridge, William T., A.B.,
   Professor of Languages, 1864-1865; Professor of Ancient and Modern Languages, 1866 (4, 6, 7).
Finch, J. H.,
   Tutor, 1848-1849 (5).

Fitzgerald, B. S., A.M.,
    Ancient Languages, Mathematics, Moral and Intellectual Phi-
    losophy, 1851-1854; Assistant Professor of Languages and
    Principal of the Preparatory Department, 1859-1860; 1863-
    1864; Professor of Mathematics and Natural Science, 1865-
    1866 (1, 2, 4, 6, 7, 8, 9).

Fitzgerald, Mrs. B. S.,
    Female Department Boarding House, 1863-1865 (6, 7, 8).

Fleet, A. R., A.B.,
    Instructor, 1870-1871 (4, 6).

Foster, William L., A.M.,
    Professor of French and Spanish and Mathematics, 1851
    (1, 4, 6).

Fox, Mr. Otto,
    Professor of Instrumental Music, Female Department, 1863-
    1865 (4, 6).

Franke, Louis,
    Teacher of Pianoforte, Guitar and Vocal Music, Professor of
    German Language and Literature, Male and Female Depart-
    ments, 1856-1859 (2, 6).

Franklin, W. W., A.M.,
    Professor of Elocution, Penmanship and Commercial Depart-
    ment, 1884-1885 (6).

Gates, Mrs. M.,
    Teacher of Elocution, Female Department, 1865 (4).

Gillette, Henry F.,
    Teacher, 1846-1848 (1, 5).

Goodwin, Mrs. Juilette,
    History, English Language and Literature, Female Department,
    1865-1866 (4, 6, 7).

Graves, Henry Lee,
    President of the University, 1846-1851 (1, 4, 5, 6).

Graves, Mary R.,
    Teacher in Mathematics and Natural Science, Female Depart-
    ment, 1856 (4).

Green, Harris T.,
    Instructor in English, 1871 (2, 6).

Groffe, Engene,
    Instructor, 1872-1873 (6).

Gulich, Mrs.,
Assistant Teacher in English Language and Literature, Female Department, 1865 (4).

Haile, J. T.,
Usher, 1879 (4).

Halbert, H. S.,
Professor of Ancient and Modern Languages 1870-1871 (6).

Hammann, George,
Instructor in German and French, 1882-1885 (2, 4, 6).

Hanks, R. T., A.M.,
Lecturer, 1883-1885 (2, 6).

Hardwicke, J. B., D.D.,
Lecturer, 1878-1881 (2, 4, 6).

Harris, William Asbury, A.M.,
Professor of Latin and Modern Languages, 1886, 1896 (2, 6).

Hatcher, Bennet,
Instructor, 1876-1880 (4, 6, 7).

Heard, T. J., M.D.,
President of College and Professor of Theory and Practice of Medicine, Galveston, 1868-1869 (2).

Heisig, Ferdinand,
Instructor, 1870-1874 (4, 6).

Heisig, Theodore,
Instructor in German, 1879-1881 (2, 4, 6).

Henderson, John,
Principal of English Department, 1864 (1, 8).

Hill, R. A.,
Pennmanship, 1879-1880 (7).

Hillyer, J. F., M.D.,
Professor of Mathematics, 1861-1865 (1, 4, 6).

Hogue, Gertrude,
Wax Work, Female Department, 1859-1860 (2).

Holmes, Willett, Esq.,
Agent, 1865-1869 (1, 2, 7).

Howard, William, D.D.,
Lecturer, Medical Department at Galveston, 1868-1869; 1882-1885 (2, 4, 6).

Hughes, Mrs. M. G.,
Preparatory and Intermediate Department, 1865-1866 (7).

Humphries, C. J.,
Steward Department, Female Department, 1865-1866 (4, 6, 9).
Hunt, Fannie C.,
Preparatory Department, Female Department, 1863-1864
(4, 6, 8).
James, W. W.,
Professor of Ancient Languages, 1863 (1).
Jensen, Charles F.,
Instructor, 1871-1875 (2, 4, 6, 8).
Johnson, James A.,
Professor of Mathematics, 1854 (1, 2, 6).
Kavanaugh, Charles T., A.B.,
Tutor and Assistant Teacher of Ancient Languages, 1857
(1, 2, 6).
Kelley, W. D., M.D.,
Professor of Obstetrics and Diseases of Women and Children,
Medical Department at Galveston, 1868-1869 (2).
Kiefer, Frank,
Professor of the German Language, 1856-1857 (1, 2, 4, 6).
Kimball, J. A.,
Theological School, 1865 (4, 7).
Law, F. M., D.D.,
Theological School, 1865-1885 (2, 6, 7).
Lea, L. G.,
Principal of the English Department, 1864-1865 (1, 4, 6).
Leland, O. H., A.B.,
Professor of Mathematics and Astronomy, 1856-1858; Professor
of Mechanical Philosophy, and Literature, 1859-1861 (1, 2, 6).
Lipscomb, A. S.,
Law Department, 1848-1849 (1, 2, 5, 6).
Lipscomb, J. A., B.P.,
Instructor, 1870-1871 (2, 4, 6).
Long, William H., A.M.,
Tutor, 1858-1859; Professor of Natural Science and Spanish,
1885 (2, 6).
Luther, J. H., D.D.,
Lecturer, Moral and Intelligence Philosophy and Ancient Lang-
uages, 1878-1884; President of the Female College and Profes-
sor of Ethics and Bellets Lettres, Baylor Female College and
Male College, 1885 (2, 4, 6).
Martin, John F., A.B.,
Assistant in the Preparatory Department, 1885-1886 (2, 6).

Martin, W. C., A.B.,
  Principal of the Preparatory Department, 1885-1886 (2, 6).
Massey, R. A., A.M.,
  Lecturer on Elocution, 1883-1884 (2, 6, 8, 9).
May, J. N.,
  Professor, 1867-1868 (6).
McArdle, H. A.,
  School of Arts, Baylor Female College and Male College, Drawing and Painting, Civil Engineering, 1881-1885 (2, 4, 6, 8).
McFarland, S. L.,
  Penmanship, 1875-1876 (4, 6).
McIntire, J. A., Jr.,
  Tutor, 1879-1880 (2, 6).
McKnight, Arthur, B.P.,
  Instructor in Mathematics and English, 1871-1872 (2, 4, 6).
Meyer, Herman,
  Instructor in German and French, 1875-1876 (6).
Montgomery, William A., A.M.,
  Professor of Political Economics and English Literature, 1866-1867 (1, 2, 6).
Morgan, G. L., A.B.,
  Professor of Mathematics, 1855-1856 (1, 4).
Morris, A. E.,
  Assistant, 1870-1871 (4, 6).
Muller, Benjamin F.,
  Instructor in Spanish, 1883 (1, 2, 6).
Newman, Frank W.,
  Tutor and Instructor, 1883-1885 (2, 6, 8, 9).
Nott, Thomas H.,
  Assistant Instructor, 1865-1866 (7).
O'Bryan, S. G., A.B.,
  Professor of Mathematics and Moral Philosophy, 1851-1853 (1, 2, 6).
Pace, E. M., B.S.,
  Professor of Mathematics, 1883-1884 (2, 4, 6).
Pace, Julian K.,
  Usher, 1876 (4).
Palmer, J. C.,
  Penmanship, 1880-1881 (2, 4, 6).
Peete, George W., M.D.,
  Professor of Materia Medica and Therapeutics, Medical Department at Galveston, 1868-1869 (2).

Pickett, George W.,
 Lecturer, 1878-1885 (2, 4, 6).
Polk, Edwin, A.B.,
 Instructor, 1871; 1874 (2, 4, 6, 8).
Polk, Louis, Jr., A.B.
 Instructor, 1874-1875 (4).
Pope, O. C., D.D.,
 Lecturer, 1880-1883 (2, 6).
Pye, E. A., M.D.,
 Professor of Medical Chemistry and Toxicology, Medical Department at Galveston, 1868-1869 (4, 6, 7).
Radford, C. J., A.M.,
 Professor of Ancient and Modern Languages, 1866-1867 (2, 4, 6, 7).
Reid, John, B.P.,
 Professor of Mathematics, 1877-1878 (4, 6).
Reinhardt, Madame R.,
 Vocal and Instrumental Music, Female Department, 1863-1866 (4, 5, 7, 8).
Rogers, William P., (General)
 Law School Instructor, 1856-1859 (1, 2, 4, 6).
Rowe, S. C., A.B.,
 Assistant Professor of Languages, 1855-1856 (4).
Sayles, Hon. John, LL.D.,
 Professor of Law, 1858-1859; 1866-1867; 1871; 1874; 1880; 1882 (1, 2, 6).
Scott, E. B.,
 Instrumental Music, Female Department, 1851-1852 (2, 6).
Scott, Mrs. Sarah J.,
 Preparatory Department, Female Department, 1859-1860 (2, 6).
Shephard, Hon. James E., LL.D.,
 Professor of Law, 1866-1867; Dean of the Law School, 1879-1880; Professor of History and Science of Law International and Constitutional (1, 2, 4, 6, 7).
Simpson, Q. T.,
 Lecturer, 1878-1879 (4).
Sledge, J. J.,
 Theological School, 1865-1866 (7).
Smith, James L.,
 Principal of the Preparatory Department, 1856-1859 (1, 2, 4, 6).

Smith, M. V., A.M.,
> Lecturer, 1883-1885 (2, 6)

Smith, Raiford A.,
> Assistant Teacher of Music, 1855-1856 (1, 2, 6).

Smyth, Hon. R. T.,
> Professor of Law, 1866-1867; Elected to teach, 1860 (1, 2, 4, 6, 7).

Spalding, A. J., D.D.,
> Lecturer, 1882-1885 (2, 6).

Steinhauer, Agnes,
> Instructor in French, German, Drawing and Painting, Female Department, 1856-1857 (4).

Stitler, Mrs. R. M.,
> Natural Science, English Language and Literature, 1867-1868 (7).

Stiteler, J. B., A.M.,
> Professor of Natural Science, German Language, 1852-1857 (1, 2, 4, 6).

Stribbling, J. H., D.D.,
> Lecturer and Tutor, 1880-1885 (1, 2, 4, 6).

Taylor, H. L., M.D.,
> Lecturer on Anatomy and Laws of Health, 1885-1886 (2, 6).

Wallace, David R., A.M., M.D.,
> Professor of Natural Sciences and the French Language and Literature, 1856-1859 (1, 2, 4, 6).

Webb, Charles Shepherd,
> Professor of Mathematics and English Literature, 1858-1869 (1, 2, 6, 7).

Wedemeyer, Charles H., A.M.,
> Professor of Mathematics and German, 1875-1885 (1, 2, 4, 6, 7).

Welch, S. M., M.D.,
> Professor of Physiology and Pathology, Medical Department of Baylor University at Galveston, 1868-1869 (2, 6).

Wheeler, Hon. R. T., LL.D.,
> Law School, 1856-1859 (1, 2, 4, 6).

Willrick, George W.,
> Gymnastics, 1859-1860 (8).

Willrick, Mrs. Liane De L.,
> Modern Languages and Ornamental Needle-work, 1859-1860; Modern Languages, History, Ancient and Modern and Ornamental Needlework, Wax and Hair Work, 1865-1866 (2, 6, 7).

Witt, Daniel,
> Professor of Spanish and Ancient Languages, 1848-1851 (1, 5, 6).

BAYLOR FEMALE COLLEGE FACULTY
1866-1886

Alexander, Laura,
Assistant in Preparatory Department, 1872-1873 (6).

Anderson, T. S.,
Primary Department 1885-1886 (2, 6).

Barton, Lalla,
Teacher of Music, Baylor Female College, 1870-1871 (6).

Beach, Mrs. Katie L.,
Vocal Music, 1885-1886 (2, 6).

Blackburn, Lucille,
Assistant Instructor in Music, 1884-1885 (2, 6).

Brown, J. Alleine,
Vocal and Instrumental Music, 1878-1879; Director of School
of Music, 1884-1885 (2, 6, 7).

Carter, S. G.,
Teacher, 1885-1888 (6).

Conner, Richard,
Professor of Drawing and Painting, 1872-1873 (6).

Dashiell, Dula,
Assistant Instructor in Music, 1884-1885 (2).

Edgar, Mrs. E. S.,
Teacher in Primary Department, 1872-1873 (6).

Fontaine, Mrs. Mary Burrows,
Matron, 1873 (4).

Fontaine, William Spotswood,
Professor of Moral and Natural Sciences and History, 1872-
1873 (4).

Fontaine, Col. W. Winston,
President of Baylor Female College and Professor of Moral and
Natural Science, Ancient and Modern Language, and Matteria,
1872-1875 (4, 6).

Graves, Fannie,
Primary Department, 1878 (7).

Hammann, Anna,
Instructor in German, 1884-1885 (2).

Harris, Julia E.,
Preparatory and Intermediate Department, 1866-1873 (4, 5, 8).

Harrison, Hallie,
  Assistant in Music, 1885-1886 (2, 6).
Jones, S. L.,
  Mathematics, 1884-1885 (2).
Leslie, Virginia,
  Assistant in the Music Department, 1885-1886 (6).
Long, Emma,
  Art Department, 1885-1886 (2, 6).
Long, Fannie,
  Art Department, 1885-1886 (2, 6).
Luther, Anne E.,
  Instructor in English, Literature, and Mathematics, 1878-1879;
  Matron, 1880 (4, 6, 7).
Luther, A. Z.,
  Latin and History, and in charge of Collegiate Department,
  1884-1885 (2).
Luther, J. H., D.D.,
  Lecturer, Moral and Intelligence Philosophy and Ancient Lang-
  uages, 1878-1884; President of the Female College and Profes-
  sor of Ethics and Belles Lettres, Baylor Female College and
  Male College, 1885 (2, 4, 6).
Luther, Mrs. M. A.,
  Home Department, 1884-1885 (2).
McArdle, H. A.,
  School of Arts, Baylor Female College and Male College, Draw-
  ing and Painting, Civil Engineering, 1881-1885 (2, 4, 6, 8).
Moeller, H.,
  Professor of Music, 1876 (4).
Moore, E. C.,
  Instructor in Elocution and Rhetoric, 1884-1885 (2).
Robbins, J. A.,
  Instructor in Vocal Music, 1864-1866; 1873-1874 (4, 6, 8).
Royall, William, D.D.,
  President of Baylor Female College, 1875-1878 (4).
Twells, Mrs. L. M.,
  Principal of Music Department, 1885-1901 (6).

BAYLOR UNIVERSITY LECTURERS

Andrews, R., Jr. _____1880-81, 1884-85

Bailey, W. O. _____1881-82

Breaker, J. M. C. _____1882-85

Buckner, H. F. _____1867-70

Carroll, W. H. _____1878-79

Chaplin, C. C. _____1880-85

Graves, Henry L. _____1879

Hanks, R. T. _____1884-85

Hardwicke, J. B. _____1879-81

Heisig, F. _____1879

Howard, William _____1882-85

Law, F. M. _____1880-85

Luther, J. H. _____1879-85

Pickett, George W. _____1879, 1881-82, 1884-85

Pope, O. C. _____1880-83

Simpson, Q. T. _____1878-79

Smith, M. V. _____1884-85

Spaulding, A. T. _____1882-85

Stribling, J. H. _____1882-85

Taylor, H. L. _____1885-86

BOARDS OF VISITORS FOR EXAMINATIONS
Male Department 1859

Baker, Dr. B. B., Washington

Davis, Ben H., Esq., Brenham

Featherston, Prof. William B.,
Boston, Texas

Harrison, James E., Esq., Waco

Houston, Hon. Sam,
Independence

Huckins, Rev. James, Galveston

Maxcy, Hon. James M.,
Cold Springs

Osborn, Rev. E. H., La Grange

Perry, Rev. James M.,
Anderson

Randle, Dr. Irvin R.,
Independence

Sayles, John, Esq., Brenham

Starr, Dr. J. H., Nacogdoches

Stribling, Rev. James H.,
Wharton

Taliaferro, Rev. R. H.,
Round Rock

Terrill, Rev. J. W., Anderson

Male Department 1867

Bayliss, Rev. Wm. H.,
New Orleans, La.

Bowers, M. H., Esq., Austin

Branch, Hon. A. M., Huntsville

Breedlove, Chas. R., Esq.,
Brenham

Buckner, Rev. H. F., Jefferson

Carpenter, Rev. John C.,
New Orleans, La.

Cross, Rev. S. S., Brenham

Elliott, John D., Esq., Lavaca

Harris, John W., Esq.,
Plantersville

Kimball, Rev. J. A., Bryan City
Montgomery, Ala.

Law, Rev. F. M., Plantersville

Lea, Hon. Pryor, Goliad

Link, Rev. J. B., Houston

McAdoo, Gen. J. D.,
Washington

Sledge, Rev. J. J., Oakland

Smith, Col. Ashbel, Houston

Stribling, Rev. J. H., Anderson

Throckmorton, Gov. J. W.,
Austin

Wail, Gen. Thos. N., Galveston

Male Department 1870

Boom, H. H., Esq., Anderson

Breedlove, Chas. R., Esq.,
Brenham

Carnes, Rev. James E.,
Galveston

Carpenter, Rev. John C.,
New Orleans, La.

Elliott, John D., Esq., Lavaca

Harris, John W., Esq.,
Galveston

Howard, Rev. Wm., Galveston

Kimball, Rev. A. J., Bryan City

Lea, Hon. Pryor, Goliad

Link, Rev. J. B., Houston

Sledge, Rev. J. J., Oakland

Smith, Col. Ashbel, Houston

Smith, Rev. M. V., Brenham

Spaight, A. W., Esq., Liberty

Stribling, Rev. J. H., Anderson

Taliaferro, Rev. R. H., Austin

Waul, Gen. Thos. N., Galveston

Winkler, C. M., Esq., Corsicana

BOARDS OF VISITORS FOR EXAMINATIONS
Female Department 1858-59

Aycock, Hon. Thomas P., Marlin

Dunklin, W. J., M.D., Waco

Greenwood, Rev. T. C., Prairie Lea

Hillyer, Rev. J. F., Grimes Co.

Johnson, Rev. J., Anderson

Montgomery, W. A., Esq., Independence

Robertson, J. B., M.D., Independence

Rogers, W. P., Esq., Houston

Speight, J. W., Esq., Waco

Stuart, E. C., Esq., Marlin

Towns, E. D., Esq., Webberville

Tucker, Rev. George, Houston

Waul, Gen. T. N., Gonzales

Female Department 1859-60

Aycock, Hon. Thomas P., Marlin

Bayless, Rev. W. H., Independence

Dunklin, W. J., M.D., Waco

Hillyer, Rev. J. F., Anderson

Holland, J. A., M.D. Independence

Montgomery, Wm. A., Esq., Independence

Pettus, J. R., M.D., Richmond

Robertson, J. B., M.D., Independence

Rogers, Gen. Wm. P., Houston

Ross, Rev. M., Independence

Smith, J. C., Esq., Independence

Speight, Gen. J. M., Waco

Towns, Hon. E. D., Webberville

Tucker, Rev. Geo., Houston

Waul, Gen. T. N., Gonzales

Female Department 1880-81

Breedlove, Chas. R., Esq.

Chandler, Prof. T. J.

Chaplin, Rev. C. C., D.D.

Davis, Mrs. F. G.

Davis, Mrs. G. B.

Goodwin, Mrs. Mary

Styles, Dr. S. F.

Female Department 1882-83

Breedlove, C. R. Esq.

Chaplin, Rev. C. C.

Davis, Mrs. F. G.

Davis, Mrs. G. B.

Goodwin, Mrs. Mary

Styles, Dr. S. F.

Wedemeyer, Prof. C. H.

Female Department 1884-85

Breedlove, Chas. R., Esq.

Chaplin, Rev. C. C.

Davis, Mrs. F. G.

Davis, Mrs. G. B.

Goodwin, Mrs. Mary

Styles, Dr. S. F.

BAYLOR UNIVERSITY ENROLLMENT
Independence, Texas—1851-1886

Year	Male	Female	Total
1851-52	94*	71	165
1852-53	93*	67	160
1853-54	101*	84	185
1854-55	103*	91	194
1855-56	138*	110	248
1856-57	203*	152*	355
1857-58	175*	100	275
1858-59	156*	150*	306
1859-60	235	166*	401
1860-61**			
1861-62**			
1862-63	40	160	200
1863-64	101	160	261
1864-65	140	180	320
1865-66	97	70	167
1866-67***	114*		114
1867-68	72		72
1868-69	89*		89
1869-70	94		94
1870-71	120		120
1871-72	126*		126
1872-73	78*		78
1873-74	75		75
1874-75	113		113
1875-76	117		117
1876-77	94		94
1877-78	91*		91
1878-79	119*		119
1879-80	117*		117
1880-81	126		126
1881-82	167		167
1882-83	120*		120
1883-84	107*		107
1884-85	64*		64
1885-86	209*		209

*Figures taken from Baylor Bulletin; all others are from the Minutes of the Baptist State Convention of Texas.

**No enrollment figures are available for these war years.

***After 1866, the Female Department was not officially connected to Baylor University.

LAW STUDENTS AT BAYLOR INDEPENDENCE
1857
Blanton, John Saunders, Independence
Breedlove, Charles R., Independence
Brooks, M. A. (A.B., Kentucky Military Institute), San Augustine
Brown, Thomas J., Brenham
Goree, Thomas J. (A.B., Baylor University), Independence
Graves, John L., Independence
Haynes, Thomas B., Independence
Hutchinson, J. Herbert, Washington
Jeffries, James Jr., Cameron
Kavanaugh, C. T. (A.B., Baylor University), Chappell Hill
Parks, W. H. (A.B., Baylor University), Anderson
Waller, Leonard (Baylor Catalogue, 1856-57, p. 16), San Felipe
Watson, P. B., Washington

1858
Alexander, John, Independence
Bailey, Edward, Washington
Bellah, Carroll H., Hempstead
Bookman, Isaiah M., Anderson
Bradshaw, Daniel A., Wharton
Breedlove, Charles A., Independence
Brown, Thomas J., Brenham
Campbell, W. L., Columbus
Davis, G. W., Huntsville
Dodson, J. N., Palestine
Ewing, E. F., Brenham
Goree, Thomas J., Huntsville
Graves, John L., Independence
Gregory, A. S., Fayetteville
Hardin, B. C., Brenham
Haynes, Thomas B., Independence
Horn, William E., Anderson
Hunt, R. B., Gayhill
Hunt, Thomas M., Gayhill
Jeffries, James Jr., Cameron
Jenkins, Cicero, Independence
Kavanaugh, Charles T., Chappell Hill
Liles, Y. I., Amite Co., Miss.
Metcalf, John W., Caldwell

Moore, William L., Crockett
Morris, A. E., Independence
Parks, William H., Anderson
Petty, V. E., Brenham
Read, Stephen D., Hempstead
Thomas, James B., Caldwell
Travis, Charles E., Chappell Hill
Walker, John G., Lynchburg
Waller, Leonard W., San Felipe

1859
Senior Class

Barziza, Decimus U. (A.M. William & Mary College), Galveston
Bookman, Isaiah M. (A.B. Baylor University), Anderson
Bradshaw, Dan A. (A.B. Baylor University), Wharton
Chandler, John W., LaGrange
Davis, George W. (A.M. Austin College), Huntsville
Dodson, Jasper N., Palestine
Edwards, J. M., Eutaw
Gregory, A. Sidney, Fayetteville
Hightower, Levi B. (A.B. Austin College), Huntsville
Jenkins, Cicero (A.B. Baylor University), Independence
Moore, William L., Crockett
Onins, I. M. (Union College), Brenham
Petty, V. E., Brenham
Read, Stephen D. (A.B. Centenary College), Hempstead
Reed, Abner L., Rusk
Travis, Charles E., Chappell Hill

Junior Class

Anderson, O. H. P., Huntsville
Bellah, Carroll H., Independence
Divine, William, Montgomery
Hall, J. W., Springfield
Horn, Wm. E., Anderson
Jenkins, James H., McKinney
Kavanaugh, C. T. (A.B. Baylor University), Chappell Hill
Lewis, Chas. B., Brenham
Lewis, Clinton A., Danville
Murray, Wm. P. A., Huntsville
Perry, James S., Independence
Russell, Daniel L. (A.B. Texas Military Institute), Rutersville
Rogers, Patrick, H., Anderson

Thompson, E. W., Houston
Upshaw, Robert L., Chappell Hill
Webb, Berry M., Marshall
Wheeler, Royal T. (Baylor Catalogue, 1859, p. 33), Independence

1860-1865

No students listed in catalogues

1866

Bledsoe, D. T., Richmond, Va.
Davidson, Thomas, Chappell Hill
Green, E. H., Caldwell
Henderson, John N., Washington
Ledbetter, Jas., Round Top
McGraw, Woodson A., Chappell Hill
Moore, Dyer, Round Top
Newman, Thomas J., Independence
Perry, A. Peter, Independence
Perry, James S., Independence
Roberts, John D., Houston
Robertson, N., Round Top
Robinson, W. S., Waco
Williams, A. (Baylor Catalogue, 1866, p. 10), Round Top

1867-1868

No Catalogue

1871-1872

Dupree, John Smith, Montgomery, Montgomery County, Texas
Garrett, Columbus C. (A.B., B.P.), Brenham
Kittrell, Norman G., Huntsville, Texas
McIntyre, Daniel (A.B.), Brenham
McKinney, E. H. Bowlby, Collins Co., Texas
Wilkes, F. D. (Baylor Catalogue, 1871-1872, p. 7), St. Mary's
    Parish, La.

1879-1880

Axers, Wm., New Orleans
Bryan, Lewis R., Brenham
Chase, Walter D., Brenham
Hall, Jarrett W., Round Top
Johnson, J. W., Prairie Lea
Townsend, M. H., Columbus
Watkins, Albert E., Brenham
Watkins, W. M., Brenham
Willingham, Charles (Catalogue, 1879-1880, p. 7), Brenham

BAYLOR'S FIRST LAW DEGREE
THE CORPORATION
OF
BAYLOR UNIVERSITY
in the
State of Texas, and the Republic of the United States of America.

TO ALL WHO MAY READ THESE LETTERS—GREETING:
Be it Known, That we, the PRESIDENT AND TRUSTEES of said UNIVERSITY, upon the unanimous recommendation of the FACULTY OF LAW, and after diligent examination, have admitted JOHN ALEXANDER to the Degree of BACHELOR OF LAWS, and do hereby invest him with all the rights, honors, dignities and privileges, which to that Degree may appertain; and with this we commend him to all who belong to the REPUBLIC OF LETTERS.

IN TESTIMONY WHEREOF, the PRESIDENT, SECRETARY AND PROFESSORS OF LAW, have set their hands, and the CORPORATE SEAL, to this Diploma.

Universitas Bailor	Given in the Hall of BAYLOR UNIVER-
Pro	SITY on the *twenty-third* day of *Septem-*
Republica	*ber* in the year of our Lord one thousand
et	eight hundred and *fifty-eight*.
Ecclesia	**R. E. B. BAYLOR**
Condita	R. T. WHEELER
MDCCCXLVI	JOHN SAYLES
(ATTEST)	LAW PROFESSORS
N. KAVANAUGH	RUFUS C. BURLESON
Secretary	President

GRADUATES OF BAYLOR UNIVERSITY
AT INDEPENDENCE

Male	Year	Female
	1854	
Stephen D. Rowe, A. B.		
	1855	
		Mary Gentry Kavanaugh (Mrs. Presler)
	1856	
Madison Milton Calloway, A. B.		Zilphia G. Fuller (Mrs. Chew)
Thos. Jefferson Goree, A.B.		Carrie Mooney (Mrs. Willis)
Chas. Thom. Kavanaugh, A.B.		
Oscar Hopestill Leland, A.B.		
Curtis Hudson Oliphant, A.B.		
Wm. Henry Parks, A.B.		
	1857	
George Eaves Davis, A.B.		Ophelia Jenkins (Mrs. Horn)
Wm. Baldwin Denson, A.B.		
Joseph Peter Jackson, A.B.		
Cicero Jenkins, A.B.		
John Franklin Smith, B.P.		
	1858	
Charles Richard Breedlove, A.B.		Emeline Allcorn (Mrs. Gee)
James Thomas Daniel, A.B.		Mary Allcorn (Mrs. Gee)
James L. Smith, A.B.		Rachael Barry (Mrs. Stewart)
James Brook Thomas, B.P.-A.B.		Bettie B. Carter (Mrs. Davis)
		Sarah Chambers (Mrs. Kavanaugh)
		Catherine Clark (Mrs. Ethridge)
		Mary A. Eddins (Mrs. Breedlove)
		Mary A. McKellar (Mrs. Herndon)
		Sallie McNeel
		Eudora Pettus (Mrs. Hobby)
		Julia Ann Robertson (Mrs. Nott)
		Fannie Alabama Rogers (Mrs. Harris)
		Rebecca Skelton
		Mary T. Whiteside
	1859	
James Marshall Arnold, A.B.		Lucy Avery Atkinson (Mrs. Collins)
Daniel Abner Bradshaw, A.B.		
Lucius Henry Brown, A.B.		
George Lewis Chandler, A.B.		
Joseph Emory Deupree, B.P.		
William Henry Long, A.B.		
Wythe Walker Wheeler, A.B.		
	1860	
Thos. Jefferson Cleveland, A.B.		Maria H. Davis (Mrs. Smith)
James Alpheus Dickie, B.P.		Gertrude Hogue (Mrs. Billingsby)
Timothy C. Dunklin, A.B.		Adelia Jarman
Jessie Shivers Eddins, B.P.		Catherine McDowell (Mrs. Garrett)
Pincknie Harris, A.B.		Sarah Posey Traynham (Mrs. Onins)
Benjamin H. Thompson, B.P.		

The young women (1855-1861) received Certificates of Graduation. The male graduates were awarded A.B. degrees.

Male	Year	Female
	1861	

James Lawson Bowers, Ph.B.   Eugenia Barnes (Mrs. Quinney)
Willis Burns Darby, A.B.   Annie Montgomery (Mrs. Metcalf)
Boling Eldridge, Ph.B.
Mark Anthony Kelton, Ph.B.
Harvey Frederick Pahl, A.B.
Michael Moses Vanderhurst, A.B.
A. John Champ Watson, A.B.

The 1861 male class did all its work at Baylor at Independence, but because of the troubles between Drs. Clark and Burleson, declined to receive diplomas from Baylor. On the opening of Waco University in the fall of 1861, under the faculty which had left Baylor, they received their diplomas from that school, though never having attended it.

1862

Mary Ella Chase (Mrs. Parks)
Virginia A. Cleveland (Mrs. Rowe)
Annie Goodwin
Adeline Haynes

1863

Claude Graves

Sally Curry (Mrs. Joynes)
Hattie Grace
Mary Johnson (Mrs. Parker)
Laura Pettus (Mrs. Bass)
Clemantine Smith

1864

Wm. Carey Crane, Jr., A.B.

Adaline Allcorn (Mrs. Gee)
Mary Anderson
Judith Atkinson (Mrs. Taylor)
Emma Blanton (Mrs. Tucker)
Mollie Cushney (Mrs. Burleson)
Sallie Newsome (Mrs. Goodwin)

1865

Fannie Morriss
Annie Muckelroy (Mrs. Campbell)
Lucy Sydnor

1866

Annie D. Crane (Mrs. Bondies)
Mollie A. Crosby (Mrs. D. S. Ross)
Florence Davis (Mrs. Bledsoe)
Mattie Garrett (Mrs. Price)
Winnie S. Goodwin (Mrs. McCraw)
Julia L. Graves (Mrs. Cooper)
Julia Harris (Mrs. McIver)
Ella Holland (Mrs. C. Call)
Annie Humphreys

After the 1866 class the female students were graduated from Baylor Female College.

1868

J. E. Potts, A.B.

1869

Charles Judson Crane, A.B.   Daniel McIntyre, A.B.

1870

Edwin Polk, A.B.

1871

Reddin Andrews, Jr., A.B.   Joel A. Lipscomb, B.P.

1872

Arthur McKnight, B.P.

1873

Daniel Polk, A.B.   Lewis Polk, A.B.

1875

Thomas Judson Chandler, A.B.   Clement S. Robinson, A.B.

1876

James A. Bell, A.B.   James R. Horne, A.B.

1877

Lewis R. Bryan, B.P.   Samuel H. Goodlett, B.P.
James M. Carroll, A.B.   Wm. Howard, Jr., B.P.
Balfour D. Crane, A.B.   John Tyler Randolph, B.P.
Benj. W. Cunningham, A.B.   Joseph F. Randolph, B.P.
John T. Duncan, B.P.   John H. Reed, B.P.

1878

James M. Bean, A.B.   Abner G. Lipscomb, B.P.
James Thomas Crane, B.P.   Felix S. Rountree, A.B.
Samuel Houston Dixon, B.P.   J. W. W. Spencer, B.P.
Tilman J. Dodson, A.B.   T. Wright Styles, B.P.
Temple Houston, B.P.   Charles H. Wedemeyer, A.B.

1879

Earnest D. Cavin, B.P.   Eugene B. Muse, B.P.
Frank C. Cross, A.B.   Zachary C. Taylor, B.P.
Edward P. Curry, B.P.   Charles H. Willingham, B.P.
Lafayette Kirk, B.P.

1880

Wm. C. Breedlove, B.P.   Hosea L. Garrett, A.B.
Gordon S. Crane, B.P.   W. Seymour Rose, B.P.
Wm. P. Ewing, B.P.

1881

Wm. S. Smith, A.B.

1882

J. H. Cobb, A.B.   J. A. McIntyre, A.B.
W. B. Garrett, B.P.   W. C. Voss, B.P.
Theo. Heisig, A.B.

1884

W. Stephen Bittel, A.B.   Frank Keifer, Jr., A.B.
Royston J. Crane, B.P.   J. H. Stribling, Jr., A.B.

1885

Frank M. Newman, B.P.

LAW DEPARTMENT
1858

John Alexander, LL.B.   James Jeffries, Jr., LL.B.
Charles Richard Breedlove, LL.B.   John W. Metcalf, LL.B.
Thomas Jefferson Brown, LL.B.   A. E. Morris, LL.B.
E. F. Ewing, LL.B.   William Henry Parks, LL.B.
Thomas J. Goree, LL.B.   John G. Walker, LL.B.
B. C. Hardin, LL.B.   Leonard W. Walker, LL.B.
Thomas B. Haynes, LL.B.

1859

Decimus U. Barziza, LL.B.   Levi B. Hightower, LL.B.
Isaiah M. Bookman, LL.B.   Cicero Jenkins, LL.B.
Daniel Abner Bradshaw, LL.B.   William L. Moore, LL.B.
John W. Chandler, LL.B.   I. M. Onins, LL.B.
George W. Davis, LL.B.   V. E. Petty, LL.B.
Jasper N. Dodson, LL.B.   Stephen D. Read, LL.B.
J. M. Edwards, LL.B.   Abner L. Reed, LL.B.
A. Sidney Gregory, LL.B.   Charles E. Travis, LL.B.

1866

David F. Bledsoe, LL.B.   John N. Henderson, LL.B.

BAYLOR MEN IN THE CIVIL WAR

Name   *Home*   *Years at Baylor (Independence)*

Arnold, James Marshall, Waco, A.B., 1859; A.M., 1866

*Arnold, Thomas, Independence, 1861

Aycock, Burwell, San Antonio, 1859

Aycock, Thomas, Independence

Baines, Joseph Wilson, Independence, 1851-1852

*Baines, Thomas Nealy, Independence, 1851-1852

Baker, Bouldes B., Montgomery, 1851-1854

Barton, James S., Tennessee, 1849

Barziza, Decimus W., Richmond, LL.B., 1859

Blakey, Josiah, Independence, 1851-1855

Blue, C. D., Independence, 1854-1855

Blue, Willis G. H., Austin, 1859

Breedlove, Charles R., Independence, A.B., 1858; LL.B., 1858

Breedlove, George, Independence, 1851-1853

Brewer, Samuel Buckner, Washington, 1856-1858

Brown, Thomas J., Brenham, LL.B., 1858; LL.D., 1903

*Burleson, Edward, Bastrop, 1856-1858

Burleson, John Anderson, Bastrop, 1859

Callaway, Milton Madison, Wharton, 1856

Carroll, Benjamin Harvey, Caldwell, 1858-1861

Chubb, Thomas, Galveston, 1854

Claiborne, John Marshall, Bastrop, 1857

Clampett, George W., Independence, 1852-1854, 1859

Clampett, Lewis W., Independence, 1856-1857

Clay, Atrius M., Independence, 1851-1859

Clay, Thomas C., Independence, 1851-1855

Cobb, Joe, Independence,

Crane, Willie, Independence, 1864-

Daniel, Algernon C., Independence, 1852-1855

Daniel, James L., Independence, 1851-1855

*Daniel, John Threewits, Fairfield, 1858-1859

Daniel, Robert A., Independence, 1856-1859

Daniel, W. G., Independence, 1851-1852

*Dean, John, Independence, 1851-1855

Dean, Jabez, Independence, 1852-1855

Dean, James, Independence, 1851-1853

Dean, Samuel, Independence, 1852-1855

Denson, William Baldwin, Cold Spring, A.B., 1857

* Killed in action.

Dickie, James, Gatesville
Dodson, Jasper N., Palestine, LL.B., 1859
Dunklin, Timothy Lincoln, Waco, 1859
Dunklin, W. A., Independence
Dunklin, William W., Waco, 1859
Dupree, Joseph E., Brenham
Early, Peter, Independence, 1851-1855
Easton, Moses H., Independence
Evans, Charles Isaac, 1860-1861
Eddins, Jesse S., Independence, 1856-1859
Edney, Fernando, Independence, 1854
Eldridge, Bowling, Independence, 1851-1855, 1857-1858, 1861-1866
Eldridge, Francis, Independence, 1851-1858
Evans, Charles Isaac, Caldwell, 1856-1859
Ewing, Amelius, Brenham, 1851-1854
Farquar, Bud, Washington
Farquahar, Cornelius, Washington, 1856-1859
Farquar, Felix H., Washington, 1856-1858
Fitzgerald, Benjamin S., Independence
Fitzgerald, Robert, Independence, 1859
Fitzpatrick, Joseph T., Port Lavaca, 1856-1859
Fuller, Pulaski, Houston, 1851-1853
Gassoway, B. F., Falls County, 1866
Gassoway, George, Independence
Garrett, Christopher Columbus, Chappell Hill
Gee, Dock, Independence
Gee, James, Independence, 1851-1855
Gee, John, Independence, 1852-1857
Gee, Leonard, Independence, 1852-1857
Goree, Thomas J., Cincinnati, Texas, A.B., 1856; LL.B., 1858
Graves, Charles H., Corsicana, 1866
Hairston, Thomas, Independence, 1851-1858
Halloday, Lon, Washington County
Hallum, Joseph, Independence
Hargrove, W. Joseph, Vernon, La., 1856-1857
Harrison, John Hampton, Hewett, 1861
Harrison, John N., Near Waco
Harrison, Moses, Independence
*Haynes, Richard, Independence, 1851-1854
*Haynes, Thomas J., Independence, 1851-1854

* Killed in action.

Hearn, William, Wheelock, 1858
Henderson, John N., Washington, LL.B., 1866
Hendley, Bud, Washington
Herrington, Jno. A., Galveston, 1857
Hill, William B., Independence, 1858-1859
Holmes, Curran, Independence, 1854-1859
Holmes, James, Independence, 1852-1853, 1856-1857
Holmes, Wm. H., Independence, 1856-1857
Hopkins, T. Thurston, Galveston, 1856-1859
Houston, Sam, Jr., Independence, 1854-1855, 1859
Hoxey, Thomas B., Independence, 1852-1855
Hunt, Richard V., Gay Hill, 1854-1855
Jackson, John A., Chappell Hill, 1856-1859
Jarman, Claibourne C., Fayetteville, 1856-1858
Jarman, Richard A., Fayetteville, 1857-1859
Jenkins, J. Cicero, Independence, A.B., 1857; LL.B., 1859;
    A.M., 1866
Jenkins, James, Independence, 1851-1853
Jenkins, Warwick H., Waco, 1856-1866
Kavanaugh, Charles Thomas, Chappell Hill, A.B., 1856
Leigh, Burleson, Independence
Long, William Henry, Jacksonville, A.B., 1859
Love, Eugene, Independence, 1851-1855
Love, Ogle, Independence, 1851-1855
Maddin, Virgil W., Independence, 1851-1855
McCown, James, Washington, 1857-1858
McDonald, James
McKnight, Edward, Independence, 1852-1859
McKnight, John T., Independence, 1853-1859
Metcalf, John W., Independence, 1852-1853; LL.B., 1858
Montgomery, Thomas J., Independence, 1856-1859
Morgan, Wm., Brenham, 1851-1854
*Norwood, Walter W., Washington, 1856-1858
Oliphant, Wilford, Sabine Town, 1856-1857
Parks, William H., Anderson, A.B., 1856; A.M., 1875; LL.B., 1858
Pettus, William Gibson, Marlin, 1858
Petway, Oliver Cromwell, Enfield, North Carolina, 1859
Randle, David A., Independence, 1858-1859
Randle, Edward, Independence, 1853-1857
Randle, Francis L., Washington, 1851-1855

* Killed in action.

Randle, Irving, Independence, 1858
Randle, John, Caldwell, 1851-1852
Randle, Julius A., Monterey, Mexico, 1853-1854
Randle, Wm. H., Caldwell, 1851-1857
Robertson, D. H., Independence, 1851-1854
Robertson, Felix H., Crawford, 1851-1854
Robertson, Franklin, Independence, 1858
Robertson, Henry O., Independence, 1851-1858
Robertson, James F., Independence, 1859
Robertson, William, Independence, 1851-1854
Rogers, Halbert J., Washington, 1858-1859
Ross, Lawrence Sullivan, Independence, 1855-1856
Ross, P. F.
Royalston, Bart
Rowe, Stephen Decatus, Galveston, A.B., 1854
*Seeley, Darwin, Wheelock, 1856-1858
Shannon, Aaron, Montgomery, 1851-1854, 1856-1858
Sieward, Dietson
*Slaughter, Wm. W., Caldwell, 1852-1853
Stephens, Jerre Wood, Independence, 1858-1859
Sterns, Wallace, Rule, 1852-1855
Thompson, Daniel B., Caldwell, 1855
Thompson, Thos. C., Wharton, 1853-1854
Tucker, John, Houston, 1854-1855
*Vanderhurst, Michael Moses, Waco, A.B., 1861
*Watson, John Champ, Fairfield, A.B., 1861
Whitten, James, Wharton, 1852-1853
Whitten, Isaac, Wharton, 1851-1852
Wheeler, Royal Tyler, Independence, 1856-1859
Wheeler, T. B.,
Williamson, Peter, Independence
Williamson, P. G., Independence, 1852-1857
Williamson, Jack H., Independence, 1854-1857
Williamson, Willie, Independence, 1852-1854
Wood, Bennett, Mullin, 1853-1855

* Killed in action.

THE TRYON CHAPTER OF *PHI GAMMA DELTA*

The following list of members gives the years of admittance to the organization, years at Baylor according to the catalogue listings, and all other facts obtainable.

Aldridge, Owen J.; 1856; Huntsville, Texas; Baylor 1854-58; clergyman; died at Huntsville, 1858.

Alexander, Richard J.; 1884; Caldwell, Texas; Baylor 1881-82; lawyer; died April 20, 1936, at Caldwell.

Arnold, James Marshall; 1859; Waco, Texas; Baylor Grad. 1859; physician; A.M., M.D.,; died 1917 at Houston.

Bittel, William Stephen; 1884; Brazoria, Texas; A.B. 1884; boarded W. C. Crane; deceased.

Bowers, James Lawson; 1861; Brenham, Texas; Baylor 1857-61; Waco Univ. Ph.B.; statesman; died at Turpen, Mexico.

Breedlove, Charles Richard; 1858; Independence, Texas; Baylor 1851-52; 1854-58, with both B.A. and LL.B.; lawyer; died January 9, 1900, at Lamar, Mo.

Brown, Lucius Henry; 1859; Valley P. O.; B. P. 1859; lawyer; died at San Marcos.

Burkett, Jacob C.; 1886; Moulton, Texas; Baylor 1883-84; boarded with W. C. Crane; clergyman; died February 28, 1933, at Abilene, Texas.

Callaway, Madison Milton; 1856; Wharton, Texas; A.B. 1856.

Chandler, Thomas Judson; 1875; Fayetteville, Texas; A.B. 1875; professor; died February 15, 1888, at Gatesville, Texas.

Chandler, Asa John; 1861; Fayetteville, Texas; Baylor sophomore 1859; died at Fayetteville.

Cobb, John; 1881; Decatur, Texas; A.B. 1882; boarded G. W. Breedlove; A.B. Hampden-Sidney 1882, Texas U. 1884; lawyer; died January 2, 1925, at Santa Barbara, California.

Collier, James C.; 1859; Gonzales, Texas; Baylor senior 1858-59; clergyman; died at Gonzales.

Crane, Royston C.; 1884; Independence, Texas; B. P. 1884; LL.B. 1886; son of President W. C. Crane; died January 21, 1956, as last member of the chapter.

Dallas, John C.; 1885; Washington, Texas; Baylor 1881-84; pharmacist; died April 1934.

Daniel, James Thomas; 1858; (Blackstone Davis, Austin, Texas, Baylor 1855) lawyer; died at El Paso, Texas.

Denson, William Baldwin; 1857; Cold Springs, Texas; A.B. 1857; lawyer; died February 21, 1911, at Galveston, Texas.

Eddins, Jesse Shivers; 1860; Independence, Texas; B.P. 1860; physician; M.D.; died at San Marcos, Texas.

Fortune, John Alexander, Jr.; 1856; Marlin, Texas; Baylor sophomore 1857; senior 1859; clergyman; died at Marlin, Texas.

Foster, Thomas C.; 1857; Washington, Texas; Baylor 1856-58; farmer; died at Navasota, Texas.

Garrett, William B.; 1882; Gay Hill, Texas; B.P. 1882; boarded D. R. Ponce; Texas U. LL.B. 1885; lawyer; died January 13, 1931, at Austin, Texas.

Goree, Thomas Jefferson; 1856; Madisonville, Texas; A.B. 1856, B.L. 1858; lawyer; died at Galveston, Texas.

Hammann, George, Jr.; 1887; father instructor in German, Baylor 1882-86; 26 Hafen Strasse, Cassel, Hessen, Germany.

Harris, Pinkney; 1860; Fairfield; A.B. 1860; clergyman; died January 31, 1908, at Harwood, Texas.

Harris, William W.; 1860; Estell's Station, Texas; Baylor Preparatory Department and Theology Department 1859; clergyman; died at Waco, Texas.

Hitchcock, Mathew M.; 1887; Caldwell, Texas; Baylor 1883-84; boarded W. C. Crane; clergyman; died April 28, 1906, at Comanche, Texas.

Hunt, Joseph H.; 1886; (not listed in available Baylor catalogues); died at Waco, Texas.

Jenkins, J. Cicero; 1857; Independence, Texas; Preparatory Department Baylor 1851, A.B. 1857, LL.B. 1859; lawyer; died November 22, 1891, at Waco, Texas.

Kavanaugh, Charles Thomas; 1856; Chappell Hill, Texas; A.B. 1856; lawyer; died 1879 at Brenham, Texas.

Kelton, Mark Anthony; 1861; Belton, Texas; Baylor 1859-61; A.B. Waco U. 1861; lawyer; died November 5, 1898, at Lake View, Oregon.

Kiefer, Frank, Jr.; 1884; Independence, Texas; A.B. 1884; lawyer; died May 3, 1893, at Roby, Texas.

King, W. F.; 1861

Leland, Oscar Hopestill; 1856; Independence, Texas; A.B. 1856; Professor of Mathematics and Astronomy at Baylor 1857-60; died at McGregor, Texas.

Lipscomb, Abner S.; 1884; son of trustee A. S. Lipscomb; died 1930 at Fort Worth, Texas.

Lang, William Henry; 1859; Georgetown, Texas; A.B. 1859; educator; died December 17, 1903, at Jacksonville, Texas.

Maxwell, Charles F.; 1887; Belton, Texas; Baylor 1884-87; deceased.

Morgan, Gilbert L.; 1856; Independence, Texas; Union U. A.B. 1855; Professor of Mathematics at Baylor 1856; died 1866 at Independence, Texas.

Newman, Francis M.; 1885; William Penn, Texas; B.P. 1885; boarded Joel Newman; lawyer; died December 28, 1931, at Brady, Texas.

Oliphant, Hudson Curtis; 1856; Huntsville, Texas; A.B. 1856; physician; died April 5, 1890, at Huntsville, Texas.

Pahl, Henry Frederick; 1861; Anderson, Texas; Baylor 1859 sophomore and Theology Department; Waco U. A.B. 1861; physician; died December 23, 1912, at Brenham, Texas.

Pelham, Charles T.; 1859; Austin, Texas; Baylor 1857-59; killed in 1865, in Battle of Resocca, Georgia.

Renfro, Henry C.; 1856; Hickory Hill, Cass County, Texas; Baylor 1856-57; clergyman; died 1902 at Galveston, Texas.

Smith, John Franklin; 1857; Austin, Texas; B.P. 1857; clergyman; died March 26, 1909, at Austin, Texas.

Stanton, J. Thaddeus; 1886; Comanche, Texas; B.S. 1887; clergyman; died at Austin, Texas.

Thompson, Benjamin Harrison; 1860; Austin, Texas; B.P. 1860; died at Austin, Texas.

Thompson, Daniel E.; 1858; Nashville, Texas; Baylor 1857 scientific course; farmer; deceased.

Vanderhurst, Michael Moses; 1861; Belton, Texas; Baylor sophomore, scientific course and Theology Department 1859; Chaplain, C.S.A.; killed in 1863 in Battle of Corinth, Mississippi.

Voss, Herman C.; 1882; Wesley, Texas; B.P. 1882; boarded W. C. Crane; salesman; died October 31, 1932, at Houston, Texas.

Wedemeyer, Charles H.; 1881; Burton, Texas; A.B. 1878; Professor of Mathematics at Baylor 1879-81; Dean, Burleson College; died February 9, 1938, at Greenville, Texas.

THE THETA CHAPTER OF *SIGMA ALPHA EPSILON*

Aycock, Burwell Lewis; 1862; Marlin, Texas; Baylor freshman 1859; lawyer; 4th Texas Rangers, C.S.A.; 104 River Avenue, San Antonio, Texas, 1859.

Bradshaw, Daniel Abner; 1859; Preston, 1856; Wharton, Texas, 1859; A.B. and LL.B. 1859; lawyer; Pine Oak, Texas.

Chandler, George Lewis; 1860; Fayetteville, Texas; A.B. 1859; planter; Anderson, Texas.

Cortsen, J. C.; (name does not appear in Baylor catalogues).

Deupree, Joseph Emory; 1859; Bonham, Texas; B.P. 1859; deceased.

Dunklin, Timothy Lincoln; 1861; Spring Hill Plantation, Waco, Texas; A.B. 1860; killed in Civil War at Bull Run, buried on battlefield according to fraternity records. (Mrs. Kathryn Harrison Sarrafian, great-niece of Timothy Dunklin, states that he was killed in Battle of Manassas in August 1862, as he advanced the flag upon the breastworks within enemy lines. He was buried on the plantation where he died, and his father erected a monument there at the close of the war.)

Eager, George B.; 1858; Mobile, Alabama; (not in Baylor records).

Fraylor, W. C.; 1858; Barton, Alabama; (not in Baylor records).

Garrett, John T.; 1860; Washington, Texas; Baylor 1856-58.

Garrison, J. S.; 1862; (not in Baylor records).

Henderson, John Nathaniel; 1862; Washington, Texas; Baylor 1856; LL.B. 1866; veteran of Civil War; District Attorney, Bryan, Texas.

Leonard, Robert Hall; 1861; Waco, Texas; Baylor 1858-59; died 1920.

Maxie, Finnie (not in Baylor records).

Perry, James Samuel; 1858; Independence, Texas; Baylor sophomore 1858; Law Department 1866.

Vanderhurst, Michael Moses; 1861; member also of Phi Gamma Delta (see roll of chapter).

Watson, John Champ; 1860; Fairfield, Texas; Waco U.A.B. 1861; killed in Civil War 1861.

Wheeler, Royal Taylor; 1861; Galveston, Texas; Baylor 1857-59; died October 22, 1900.

Wheeler, Walker Wythe; 1860; Galveston, Texas; A.B. 1859.

Wood, Egbert Osvel; 1859; Owensville, Texas, 1856; Sterling, Texas, 1858.

MEDAL WINNERS AT BAYLOR UNIVERSITY

1872—Hiram Wood's Gold Medal, Best Speaker, Albert C. Haynes
1873—Hiram Wood's Gold Medal, Best Speaker, Sam Ellis
1874—Hiram Wood's Gold Medal, Best Speaker, Geo. W. Baines, Jr.
    President's Silver Medal, Second Best Speaker, James M. Carroll
    President's Silver Medal, Best Scholar, Balfour D. Crane and
                                      T. Judson Chandler
1875—Hiram Wood's Gold Medal, Best Speaker, Clement S. Robinson
    President's Silver Medal, Second Best Speaker, Tilman J. Dodson
    President's Silver Medal, Best Scholar, James A. Bell
1876—Hiram Wood's Gold Medal, Best Speaker, James M. Carroll
    President's Silver Medal, Second Best Speaker, Sam H. Goodlett
    President's Silver Medal, Best Scholar, Hosea L. Garrett
1877—Hiram Wood's Gold Medal, Best Speaker, Lewis R. Bryan
    President's Silver Medal, Second Best Speaker, Robert Andrews
    President's Silver Medal, Best Scholar, James M. Carroll
    James M. Williams' Silver Medal, Best Logican, John T. Duncan
1878—Hiram Wood's Gold Medal, Best Speaker, Tilman J. Dodson
    President's Silver Medal, Next Best Speaker, Albert G. Lipscomb
    President's Silver Medal, Best Scholar, J. Thomas Crane
    James M. Williams' Silver Medal, Best Logician, Temple Houston
1879—Hiram Wood's Gold Medal, Best Speaker, Ernest D. Cavin
    President's Silver Medal, Second Best Speaker, Chas. H. Willingham
    President's Silver Medal, Best Scholar, Ernest D. Cavin
    James M. Williams' Silver Medal, Best Logician, Zachery C. Taylor
    Best Junior Speaker, Gold Medal, Ira Gooch
    Second Best Junior Speaker, Silver Medal, J. Clarence Muse
    Best Speller, Gold Medal, Royston C. Crane
    Second Best Speller, Silver Medal, S. David Randolph
    Best Sub-Junior Speaker, Gold Medal, Arthur S. Ujiffy
    Second Best Sub-Junior Speaker, Silver Medal, W. A. Dallas
1880—Hiram Wood's Gold Medal, W. Seymour Rose
    President's Silver Medal, Wm. P. Ewing
    Best Scholar, Silver Medal, W. C. Breedlove
    Best Junior Speaker, Gold Medal, D. A. Wilson
    Second Best Junior Speaker, Silver Medal, ?
    Best Sub-Junior Speaker, Gold Medal, ?
    Second Best Sub-Junior Speaker, Silver Medal, ?
    Best Speller, Gold Medal, Royston C. Crane
    Second Best Speller, Silver Medal, ?
1881—Hiram Wood's Gold Medal, W. J. Smith
    President's Silver Medal, Best Scholar, W. J. Smith
    J. M. Williams' Best Logician, W. J. Smith
    Best Junior Speaker, Gold Medal, W. B. Garrett
    Second Best Junior Speaker, Silver Medal, H. C. Voss
    Best Sub-Junior Speaker, Gold Medal, Frank Ponce
    Second Best Sub-Junior Speaker, Silver Medal, Houston Williams
    Best Speller, Gold Medal (Note—The name of R. C. Crane has been
        erased)
    Second Best Speller, Silver Medal, T. H. Clampitt
1882—Hiram Wood's Gold Medal, T. Heisig
    President's Medal, Silver, W. S. Bittel
    Best Logician, Silver Medal, J. H. Cobb
    Best Junior, Gold Medal, ?
    Best Sub-Junior, Gold Medal, S. F. Styles
    Best Speller, Gold Medal, J. H. Gee
    Second Best Junior, Silver Medal, ?
    Second Best Sub-Junior, Silver Medal, Hoxie Williams
    Second Best Speller, Silver Medal, ?
1883—No medals—
1884—Hiram Wood's Gold Medal, Best Speaker, 4 points: 1 Matter, 2 Logic,
      3 Memory, 4 Delivery, Royston C. Crane
    Best Speller, M. M. Hitchcock

HONORARY DEGREES CONFERRED BY
BAYLOR UNIVERSITY AT INDEPENDENCE*

Bailey, W. O., Rev.—Galveston, Texas—D.D., 1880

Baines, George Washington, Rev.—Independence, Texas—A.M., 1861

Bester, Daniel P.— Columbus, Mississippi—D.D., 1867

Buckner, H. F.—Eufaula, Oklahoma—A.M., 1867

Burleson, R. B.—Waco, Texas—LL.D., 1875

Chambliss, A. W., Rev.—D.D., 1869

Chaplin, C. C., Rev.—Austin, Texas—D.D., 1878

Clark, Horace—Independence, Texas—A.M., 1865; L.L.D., 1873

Clark, T. N., Prof.—Liberty, Missouri—L.L.D., 1880

Cook, J. F., Pres.—La Grange College, Missouri—L.L.D., 1871

Corey, C. H.—Richmond, Virginia—D.D., 1881

Crane, Chas. J., Col.—San Antonio, Texas—A.M., 1872

Crane, Wm. Carey—Independence, Texas—L.L.D., 1873

Crane, W. C., Jr.—Houston, Texas—A.M., 1867

Davis, Noah K., Pres.—Bethel College, Russellville, Kentucky—L.L.D., 1870

Dobbs, C. E. W., Rev.—Bowling Green, Kentucky—D.D., 1878

Fitzgerald, Ben S.—Independence, Texas—A.M., 1865

Fontaine, W. W.—Austin, Texas—A.M., 1878

Hillyer, John F., Rev.—Lockhart, Texas—L.L.D., 1873

Howard, Wm., Rev.—Galveston, Texas—D.D., 1869

Kimball, J. A., Rev.—Larissa, Texas—D.D., 1880

Lannear, James F.—William Jewell College, Liberty, Missouri—A.M., 1870

Law, F. M., Rev.—Mt. Giddings, Texas—D.D., 1882

Leland, O. H.—McGregor, Texas—A.M., 1860

Long, J. C.—Chester, Pennsylvania—D.D., 1880

Maple, J. C.—Mexico, Missouri—D.D., 1881

McIntyre, Daniel—Brenham, Texas—A.M., 1872

Mitchell, W. J.—Marshall, Texas—D.D., 1884

Murphy, J. D., Rev.—Bryan, Texas—D.D., 1878

---

* The precedent for the conferring of honorary degrees was set by Harvard University long before the Revolutionary War. The first recipient was Harvard's own president, Increase Mather, who was awarded a doctorate in sacred theology. The two other members of the Harvard faculty at that time received bachelor-of-sacred-theology degrees. See Gerald George, "When Honors are Conferred by Degrees," *The National Observer,* June 5, 1967, p. 22.

Baylor conferred her first honorary degree in 1860; recipients were staff members.

INDEPENDENCE BAPTIST CHURCH MEMBERS

Mrs. Bertie McCrocklin has identified the pictures on the walls of the Independence Baptist Church.

Next to door, left:

1. Terrell Jackson
2. Mrs. Terrell Jackson
3. Mrs. Wm. Carey Crane
4. Rev. Wm. Carey Crane
5. Rev. Wm. G. Wood
6. Mrs. Wm. H. Cleveland
7. Mrs. Virginia Cleveland
8. J. H. Stribling
9. Hon. John McKnight
10. Rev. Abraham Weaver
11. Mrs. Abraham Weaver
12. Weaver granddaughter
13. Rev. Marion Law
14. Prof. Henry Flavor Gillette
15. Mrs. Charles R. Breedlove
16. Hon. Charles Breedlove
17. Mrs. Fannie Breedlove Davis
18. George B. Davis

On East Side:

19. Hon. Harry Haynes
20. Judge R. J. Alexander
21. Mrs. R. J. Alexander
22. Mrs. Henry L. Graves
23. Mrs. Willie Graves White
24. Mrs. John Hill Luther
25. Mrs. Annie Luther Bagby
26. Mrs. Austin J. Bryan

Second Row:

27. Gen. Sam Houston
28. Mrs. Margaret Lea Houston
29. Mrs. Weston Lafayette
30. Mrs. Margaret Houston Williams
31. James Madison Williams
32. Mrs. Sarah Ann Hoxie Williams
33. Mrs. Sallie Johnson Key

Third Row:

34. Hon. Thomas S. Henderson
35. Hon. Sam R. Henderson
36. Judge John N. Henderson
37. Geo. West Lee and wife, and Mary Young Lee
38. Hon. Wm. Gaston Wilkins
39. Mrs. Eunice Lewis Wilkins
40. Mr. Charlee L. Wilkins

Northend West Side:

41. Dr. John Hill Luther
42. Rev. Michael Ross
43. Horace Clark
44. Wm. Carey Crane
45. Rufus C. Burleson
46. Rev. Geo. W. Baines
47. Dr. Henry L. Graves
48. James Huckins
49. Dr. J. B. Link
50. Oliver Hazard Perry Garrett
51. Hosea Garrett
52. Mrs. Lewis R. Bryan
53. Judge Lewis R. Bryan
54. Major Moses Austin Bryan
55. Mrs. Bryan
56. Mary Jane Newman Holmes
57. Mrs. John Willitt Holmes
58. Mrs. Elizabeth Madden
59. Mrs. James Dallas
60. Mr. James Dallas
61. Mrs. James M. Ross
62. Dr. J. M. Ross
63. Gen. Felix H. Robertson
64. Dr. Jerome B. Robertson
65. Mr. and Mrs. Lee Booker
66. Miss Sarah Willie
67. Mrs. R. J. Alexander
68. Judge W. H. Jenkins

Index

A

Adams, Alice N.: 98
Adams, Arthur: 68
Adams, Col. F. W.: 266
Adams, Wayman: 278
Adair, Garland: 31, 64
Adair, William (uncle of R. C. Burleson): 100
Aiken, Wreathy: 313
Aldrich, Catherine (Mrs. John Clark): 105
Alexander, John: 247, 284
Allcorn, Elijah: 1
Allcorn, Emiline and Mary: 165
Allcorn, Mr. and Mrs. J. D.: 46
Allcorn, John H.: 271
Allen, Rev. Earl: 127
Allen, J. S.: 42
Allen, Newton: 130
Allen, T. S.: 239
Allen, W. W.: 67, 95
American Baptist Home Mission Society: 8, 10-13, 17, 19, 61, 82, 202, 219
Anderson, Miss (Mrs. R. H. Taliaferro): 137
Anderson, J.C.: 195, 197-198
Anderson, J. J.: 228
Anderson, J. W.: 287
Anderson, Kenneth L.: 24, 149
Anderson, M. D.: 34, 197
Anderson, Washington: 137
Andrews, Mrs. Bettie Eddins: 301
Andrews, Martha J.: (Mrs. James E. Shepherd): 183
Andrews, Reddin, Jr.: family of, 22; commencement report, 242-43; "usher," 264; ministerial aid, 268; theological student, 270; agent, 274; Baylor faculty, 277; McArdle portrait of, 279; brother of, 281; resignation, 283; named president, 299-301; salary, 303; Baylor Female College location, 307; leaves Baylor, 308; final work, 314
Andrews, Robert J.: 281, 284
Andrews, S. P.: 21
Ardney, James M.: 149
Armistead, Mrs. Georgia: 26
Armistead, Lou Brown: 26
Armstead, Robert S.: 26
Armstrong, A. J.: 208
Ashmore, Mary Ann (Mrs. Wm. Berry Smith): 129
Austin, Stephen F.: colonization, 1-2; Trask letter, 5; San Felipe meeting, 38; camp, 45; Coles letter, 48; Borden letter, 49; colony, 53; nephew M. A. Bryan, 54; nephew James S. Perry, 174; Bryan portrait, 278; statue, 297

B

Babb, Joseph: 245
Bailey, Mrs. E. W.: 173
Bailey, Lucy: 310
Bailey, Rev. W. D.: 286
Baines, Anne (Mrs. J. P. Reesing): 213
Baines, Annie Melissa (Mrs. Wm. Edwin Rosborough): 201
Baines, Mrs. Cynthia W. Williams: marriage, 211; death, 212
Baines, George: 199
Baines, Rev. George Washington: proxy trustee, 41; Independence pastor, 47; agent, 96; trustee committee, 99; against state aid, 103-104; trustee assignments, 105-106, 109; lecturer, 110; Huckins letter, 112; real estate, 114; examination committee, 115; Houston conversion, 126; graduate of Alabama, 131; Taliaferro, 137; boarding house for Baylor girls, 153; resignation Baylor board, 170; Burleson-Clark, 175-176, 181, 191, 193; elected president, 195; salary, 197; degree award, 198; biography, 199-204; children, 201; buys Negro boy from Houston, 208; resignation, 210; subsequent activities, 211-214; death, 212; Convention committee, 239; portrait, 279; Baylor Female College, 305, 314
Baines, Rev. G. W., Jr.: Washington Church, 62; family, 201; baptized, 202; Baylor student, 212; missionary, 213; ministerial student, 274; honorary degree and professor at S.M.B.A., 281
Baines, G. W. III: 213
Baines, Huffman, Jr.: 213-214
Baines, James W.: 237
Baines, Janet (Mrs. E. D. Brockett): 213
Baines, Johnnie Paxton: 201, 211
Baines, Joseph Wilson: 201, 213, 214, 237
Baines, Mary (Mrs. Arthur Sheeran): 213
Baines, Mary Elizabeth: 201
Baines, Melissa Ann Butler: 201; death, 212